Fourth
Edition
Canadian
Government

Robert J. Jackson
Doreen Jackson

in Transition

PEARSON
Prentice
Hall

Toronto

Library and Archives Canada Cataloguing in Publication

Jackson, Robert J., 1936–
Canadian government in transition / Robert J. Jackson, Doreen
Jackson. - 4th ed.

Includes index.
ISBN 0-13-197529-3

1. Canada-Politics and government. I. Jackson, Doreen, 1939–
II. Title.
JL65.J318 2006   320.971   C2005-905164-7

ISBN 0-13-197529-3

Vice President, Editorial Director: Michael J. Young
Executive Acquisitions Editor: Christine Cozens
Sponsoring Editor: Carolin Sweig
Marketing Manager: Leigh-Anne Graham
Senior Developmental Editor: Joel Gladstone
Production Editor: Kevin Leung
Copy Editor: Joe Zingrone
Proofreader: Bonnie DiMalta
Production Coordinator: Peggy Brown
Permissions and Photo Research: Amanda McCormick
Composition: Christine Velakis
Art Director: Julia Hall
Cover and Interior Design: Anthony Leung
Cover Image: J. David Andrews/Masterfile

Photo Credits: p. 4, CP Photo/Tom Hanson; p. 159, Yousuf Karsh/Library and Archives Canada/
C-021562; p. 202, The Supreme Court of Canada/Philippe Sandreville; p. 225, CP Photo/Tom Hanson; p. 227,
CP Photo/Jonathan Hayward; p. 228, CP Photo/Andrew Vaughan; p. 229, CP Photo/Andrew Vaughan.

Statistics Canada information is used with the permission of the Minister of Industry, as Minister responsible for Statistics Canada. Information on the availability of the wide range of data from Statistics Canada
can be obtained from Statistics Canada's Regional Offices, its World Wide Web site at www.statcan.ca, and
its toll-free number 1-800-263-1136.

   4 5 6   10 09 08 07

Printed and bound in the United States of America.

Contents

CONTENTS

Chapter 10
Parties and Interest Groups 219

Chapter 11
Elections and Political Behaviour 248

Preface

The fourth edition of *Canadian Government in Transition* continues to provide a concise, current analysis of the country's most important political institutions, processes and issues in the twenty-first century. *Canadian Government in Transition* systematically describes and dissects the key elements of federal institutions, providing relevant history to help students place them into context. The text also addresses the major current issues and difficulties affecting Canadian governments today, including:

- the 2004 general election and the impact minority government has had on Parliament, politics and specific hot-button topics that make up the nation's business;
- the security measures put in place since the attacks on the United States on September 11, 2001;
- political issues of particular interest to young people, such as gay and lesbian rights (including an examination of Parliament's same-sex marriage debate in 2005), youth unemployment, child poverty, funding for colleges and universities, and other topics.

This book does not replace or summarize our comprehensive work, *Politics in Canada*. That volume links culture, institutions, behaviour and public policy in a unified theory to depict and explain the dynamics of politics. This shorter, condensed book is intended for courses at the university and college level, for joint Canadian studies courses in the United States and abroad, for the general reader, and possibly for advanced politics and government courses in schools. As such, it is to a large extent about understanding the basic elements of our political institutions and processes.

Underpinned by studies of the economic and social environment as well as the Constitution, federalism and nationalism, the text distinguishes between types of institutions. State institutions include the executive, bureaucracy, legislature, the courts and judicial administration, with its police and prisons; political institutions include political parties, interest groups and elections. The text concludes with a chapter on ethics in Canadian government, a relevant and current issue in politics and government today.

Our method in writing this text has been to provide the maximum amount of information on Canadian institutions in a brief and orderly fashion, summarizing vast amounts of information and data, and then arranging the facts and ideas under multiple headings to facilitate easy access to the material. In doing so, we have attempted to capture the excitement, vitality and importance of Canada's political institutions.

As usual with our books, there is a degree of constructive criticism and balanced argumentation with an overall tone of optimism throughout. There are solid reasons to look optimistically to the future. Unity continues to be a vital issue, but it should not define the country. Canadians must move on to confront the other dangers of the twenty-first century. Vital decisions about economics and public security will be made within the present federal institutions of Canada — organizations that are unlikely to undergo fundamental change for many years.

NEW TO THE FOURTH EDITION

There have been numerous changes to this edition of the text, including:

- Chapter 1, "What Is Politics?", focuses on the foundations of Canadian government and politics, but updates the current issues Canadians argue and negotiate about.
- Chapter 2, "The Context of Government," offers a new section on political ideas in politics as well as increased coverage of the issues concerning Native people and the external context of politics in Canada.
- Chapter 3, "The Constitutional Framework," continues to give a concise overview of the current problems of constitutional developments in Canada.
- Chapter 4, "Contested Federalism," brings up-to-date the often very divisive issues and developments in federalism.
- Chapter 5, "Nationalism and Regionalism," assesses current events and ideas in the area of nationalism and regionalism, providing more discussion about the grievances of Western Canada.
- Chapters 6, "The Executive," and 7, "Parliament," have been reframed in light of the current minority government situation.
- Chapter 8, "Public Administration," brings budgetary issues up to date.
- Chapter 9, "The Administration of Justice," contains new material on security policy and institutions in light of recent terrorist attacks.
- Chapters 10, "Parties and Interest Groups," and 11, "Elections and Political Behaviour," have been completely revised to reflect changes in political parties, political leadership, electoral rules and the 2004 election, with analyses of how well the electoral system works and how it might be changed.
- Chapter 12, "Ethics in Canadian Government and Politics," puts into context the issue of corruption (in particular, the Québec sponsorship scandal) that has plagued Prime Minister Paul Martin's minority government and diminishes the respect Canadians have for politicians in general. It discusses the kinds of issues that have arisen over the years and what is being done to correct them.

Throughout, this new edition brings up-to-date political events and research of recent years. These have been politically exciting times, with dramatic changes and policy evolution. One of the most notable events was the 2004 general election and the formation of the thirty-eighth Parliament. Three of the parties went into the election with new leaders, and the Conservative Party of Canada was formed from the amalgamation of the Progressive Conservatives and Canadian Alliance parties. Regional concerns have become stronger and found more of a voice, thus fragmenting the electorate and making it more likely that Canadians will experience more minority governments.

The issue of Québec separatism continues to simmer with new separatist strategies being formulated and another major crisis awaiting the next economic recession or political change in Québec.

PEDAGOGY

This textbook uses the following pedagogical aids to help in understanding the material more easily and to reinforce concepts.

- Learning Objectives begin each chapter and list what students should accomplish after reading the material.
- Key Terms appear in boldface and are defined when they first appear in a chapter. They also appear in a list at the end of the chapter for reinforcement.
- Discussion Questions follow the Key Terms list at the end of each chapter; these questions will help students to test their knowledge of the material.
- Close-Up boxes provide topical issues and events for interest and discussion.
- The updated Weblinks section gives students a list of useful websites relating to topics discussed in each chapter. The sites have been chosen for quality and relevance.
- Further Reading, found at the end of the book, provides a list of supplementary reading material.
- The Glossary, also at the end, lists key terms with their respective definitions.

SUPPLEMENTS

The following supplements are available for use with the fourth edition of *Canadian Government in Transition*:

Instructor's Resource CD-ROM (0-13-172981-0): This resource CD-ROM includes the following instructor supplements:

- **Instructor's Manual:** This manual outlines the basic structure of each chapter and contains suggestions on how to use the text more effectively. It includes suggested lecture outlines and answers to end-of-chapter questions.
- **Test Item File:** This test bank contains 40 questions/chapter, graded into three levels of difficulty (easy, moderate and difficult); relevant textbook pages are cited along with the correct answer for each question. Questions consist of multiple choice, fill-in-the-blank, short answer, and true/false. The Test Item File is available in both Word and TestGen formats.

TestGen is a testing software that enables instructors to view and edit the existing questions, add questions, generate tests, and distribute the tests in a variety of formats. Powerful search and sort functions make it easy to locate questions and arrange them in any order desired. TestGen also enables instructors to administer tests on a local area network, have the tests graded electronically and have the results prepared in electronic or printed reports. TestGen is compatible with Windows and Macintosh operating systems, and can be downloaded from the TestGen website located at www.pearsoned.com/testgen. Contact your local sales representative for details and access.

These instructor supplements are also available for download from a password-protected section of Pearson Education Canada's online catalogue, **http://vig.pearsoned.ca.** Navigate to your book's catalogue page to view a list of those supplements that are available. See your local sales representative for details and access.

ACKNOWLEDGMENTS

We would like to thank the following reviewers for their insightful and very helpful remarks: Jeff Braun-Jackson, Memorial University of Newfoundland; Tom Chambers, Canadore College; Avigail Eisenberg, University of Victoria; John Fakouri, Algonquin College; Marlene Hancock, Douglas College; Tom Joseph, Confederation College; A. John Lackner, Durham College of Applied Arts and Technology; George MacLean, University of Manitoba; Brenda O'Neill, University of Manitoba; Elizabeth Smythe, Concordia College; and Tracy Summerville, University of Northern British Columbia. For this edition, Sheila Dhillon, Kwantlen College; Howard Doughty, Seneca College; Chaldeans Mensah, Grant MacEwan College; Harold Jansen, University of Lethbridge; Shanti Fernando, York University; Shauna Longmuir, Sir Sandford Fleming College; Norman Ruff, University of Victoria and, again, Elizabeth Smythe, Concordia College, offered incisive commentary. We are also grateful to our friends and colleagues at Pearson Education Canada who, once again, provided exactly the right mix of encouragement, expertise and assistance. They include Carolin Sweig, Cynthia Smith, Joel Gladstone, Kevin Leung and freelance editor Joe Zingrone. It is a pleasure to work with professionals of this high calibre.

We dedicate this book to the many students, past, present and future, whose perceptive questions about, and enthusiasm for, Canadian government and politics make teaching and research a worthwhile and satisfying vocation.

—*Robert J. Jackson and Doreen Jackson*
University of Redlands, California, and Carleton University, Ottawa
October 2005

1 What Is Politics?

Learning Objectives

After reading this chapter, you should be able to

1. Define and distinguish between the concepts of *state* and *nation*, *politics* and *government*, *self-determination* and *nationalism*.

2. Identify and explain key features that distinguish democratic and authoritarian states.

3. Distinguish between *procedural* and *substantive* arguments about democracy.

4. Identify the main features of Canadian democracy.

*I*n June 2004, Canadians voted for a new slate of political representatives and political parties. The event had all the ingredients of an exciting election — a new political party, three new party leaders, at least one issue that concerned most voters on a personal level, and rhetoric spiced with outrage about government scandal. In the final analysis, the election produced a Liberal minority government — the first minority since 1979 — and generated one of the lowest voter turnouts in Canadian history.

Minority governments are notoriously short-lived, and have a difficult time mustering enough votes to pass their legislation. Yet, the continued fragmentation of the party system makes it exceedingly difficult now for any party to achieve majority status. The challenges of governance in the coming years are immense, but the current prospect is for fragile governments that will have difficulty staying in power.

Yet, the country needs strong government. The threat of political separation that followed the Québec referendum in 1995 is less urgent today than a decade ago, but the Bloc Québécois is enjoying a resurgence that could bring the issue to a vote again soon, posing a serious threat to the country. The economy is in significantly better shape than it was at the close of the century. The deficit is gone, and the country is slowly paying off its large debt. However, the value of the Canadian dollar has been rising, and that makes our exports

1

Dolighan, The London Free Press. Reprinted with permission.

and tourist industry less competitive. Meanwhile, social programs that were left in tatters following the years of budget cutting are still competing for funds. Health care, a high-priority budget item, was the main election issue in 2004. Politicians expressed very different ideas about how it should be resolved. Would the government remain responsible, or would private companies be allowed to provide services? If it moved from a relatively centralized, underfunded health system to a more competitive, private one, would that make things better for patients, or lead to an uneven, hodgepodge delivery of services? These and many other social issues that affect who Canadians are as a people need to be resolved in the coming months and years. What will the fall-out be of the government's newly passed same-sex marriage legislation? Will the rapidly aging population undermine old age security for the coming generation? Should the country's immigration rules be changed? These issues and many more require new policies to face the needs and challenges of our diverse and scattered population.

Meanwhile, many other serious obstacles and challenges to unity, peace and prosperity need to be addressed. The unprecedented terrorist attacks on the United States on September 11, 2001, changed the world in many respects. How can states protect their citizens from more of such atrocities? Security moved high on the agenda in Canada, as elsewhere. Major policy decisions, allocations of resources and international co-operation are required. What will Canada's contribution be to world peace?

Canadian Government in Transition will help readers to make informed judgments and critically assess the role of Canada's political institutions and politicians in resolving these and other issues that lie ahead.

THE STAKES OF CANADIAN POLITICS

The stakes of politics are what Canadians fight about. As well as national unity, they include economic prosperity, full employment, good health care and high levels of education. Although most Canadians want these rewards, they disagree about how to achieve them.

Economic prosperity for many Canadians is elusive. During the past decade and a half, the federal government sought to stimulate economic development by signing and implementing a Free Trade Agreement with the United States. It later expanded it into a North American Free Trade Agreement, with Mexico as the third partner. More recently, the government went further and proposed new arrangements with other countries and areas — an expansion of NAFTA into South America and a formal commitment to work toward a Pacific community economic zone.

Economic issues have a direct impact on citizens and require swift government action. The country now has a balanced annual budget, but social policy remains vital. Economic recovery has not reduced inequalities across regions, provinces, classes or genders. The poor, handicapped and old require government assistance to realize their share of the Canadian dream.

These are only a few examples of the stakes in Canadian politics. Are Canada's major institutions powerful enough to find satisfactory answers to these issues and problems? Can our politicians improve the employment rate? Can they rebuild social and health services that were sacrificed to restore fiscal order? Can majority opinion be prevented from becoming tyrannical, so that the minority of weaker and disadvantaged people will not be shunted aside? Can individual rights and freedoms be protected while the government makes majoritarian decisions to successfully confront the challenges of the twenty-first century?

Such questions require decisions that will ultimately determine the wealth and prosperity of Canada as a country and also of individual Canadians. What the government does will determine, for example, the health care and social services we as Canadians will receive, what freedoms they will enjoy in society, and even whether or not the country will remain strong and united. This book will show how such important decisions are reached through politics within the institutions of the country.

THE GAME OF POLITICS

Canadian politics sometimes seems confused and pointless. There are winners and losers in elections: parties and individuals regularly come and go. However, despite all the activity, there may not appear to be any concrete results or changes for ordinary people. In fact, the following comment in Lewis Carroll's *Alice in Wonderland* seems to depict what many people think about politics.

> The players all played at once, without waiting for turns, quarrelling all the while . . . they quarrel so dreadfully that one can't hear oneself

speak — and they don't seem to have any rules in particular: at least,
if there are, nobody attends to them . . .

However, the democratic ideal in Canada is not a frivolous ideal. After all, it embodies the values and hopes of Canadians. Yet, politics in Canada is in many ways analogous to a team sport. The stakes of politics are often seen as equivalent to the trophies and glory of sports and games. The winners in Canadian elections form the government while the losers go to the sidelines. When Prime Minister Jean Chrétien went abroad on trade missions and took the provincial premiers with him, he called the group "Team Canada."

The sports analogy holds in many respects. The players or politicians are in a collective game with winners and losers. The competitors are organized into teams known as parties or interest groups. All of them are required to play according to rules. Some rules are more precise and codified than others, but nevertheless, they all determine to a large extent how the players organize and conduct themselves. As in sports, the rules vary from country to country. For example, Canada's monarchical democracy has little in common with Saudi Arabia's monarchical authoritarian regime.

As a rule, Canadian politics includes none of the body contact typical of hockey, football or lacrosse. Possibly baseball, or a board game such as chess, would be more appropriate to compare with politics. However, sometimes even military or war analogies are needed. American president Richard Nixon, for example, prepared an enemies list, and Canadian party strategists often develop "whisper lists" to spread false rumours during election campaigns, just as propaganda experts do during a war. Usually, however, the media depict politics between the government and opposition as something like a horse race, or as having the skill and finesse of chess. At the same time, despite what occasional viewers watching them may think, the players act in a context and with rules. Sports may be played on fields or courts; politics is played in the context of histories, economies, social structures and especially institutions.

The game analogy should not detract from the seriousness of politics. However, politics and games share some similar characteristics. Politics, like games, has rules or agreed-upon principles to provide limits to behaviour. In democracies these rules are called constitutions. Politicians may have the advantage of being able to change the rules. In both politics and games, players

Canadian athletes at the 2004 Athens Olympics

with their own interests and ideas contest or compete for power. The political players bring to their activities philosophies, strategies and tactics about how to win at the political game. They prepare plans of attack. They contest for a purpose — they wish to obtain political power. In other words, as in games, there are stakes to be achieved.

Competitive games arose partly from the need to practise for war, but even in sports that were close to warfare, rules were devised to control behaviour. In ancient Greece, for example, a contest called *pankration* (which involved wrestling and boxing) outlawed biting, piercing the eyes and other forms of bodily attack. The Romans even had some rules for contests between gladiators, even though in the final result human beings were killed, to the joy of spectators and emperors.[1] Today's Olympics are descendants of such early games. Amateur athletes are subject to a host of rules including stiff penalties for drug use.

In politics, democracies tend to have more, and more highly developed, rules than authoritarian regimes, which generally have only minimal, crude regulations to control the behaviour of citizens who contest for political power. However, all states have rules and institutions that provide opportunities and constraints concerning political action.

Games and Institutions

The behaviour of politicians and public officials, and also the public policies that emerge from governments, are directed and enforced by institutions. Institutions restrict political players in the same manner that rules delimit the actions of players in sports and games.

The most comprehensive rules of any state or country generally are found in a constitution. When the Fathers of Confederation established the rules for Canadian government in 1867, they joined together normative democratic principles with practical ideas about how government should function. In simple terms, they linked British parliamentary democracy with a federal division of authority — dividing powers between the federal government and the provinces. Ever since that time, these basic rules have provided the framework for Canadian debates about what matters in politics. Since Confederation, the Constitution has determined which issues the state should resolve and which ones should be left for individuals or groups in the private sector to decide upon.

Comprehensive rules, such as those found in constitutions, change only gradually over time. Much like the rules of some games, the principles of play may change over time — but managers, coaches and players must play within the rules whether they like them or not.

Rules for some games, such as checkers and chess, change only rarely, while in other games, such as basketball, some regulations change every year. Rules in political games are designed to do both. Constitutions change slowly or rarely while the rules about elections and parliamentary organizations may change yearly or even more often. This does not mean that rules are never broken. They often are — just as they are in games. Penalties are meted out, but to understand politics and governing, we must first discover what the rules of institutions are, how they were intended to guide behaviour, and whether they actually do so.

Institutions help to organize government and politics much like rules organize sports and games. Some people — say, short people — are organized out of professional basketball. If the height of basketball hoops were changed in relation to the height of the players then, theoretically, players of any size could play in the pros. Unfortunately for the height-impaired, the rules are the same for short, medium, tall and very tall players. The same thing is true in politics; rules constrain some players and groups. They also limit which issues can develop, which individuals can play, and at what level.

Of course, where do the rules come from in the first place? In contemporary professional sports, they are usually made by the owners of the teams, or in bargaining sessions between owners and players. In amateur sports, they may be set by university or school sports officials. In government as well, the rules are set in many forums. As in chess, conventions may develop; rules may come from traditions and customs that are many centuries old. Rules also may be conceived and put in place by political players acting on their own assumptions and biases about the task of governing; they may even act according to their own selfish interests. Separating the opinions and philosophies of individual political players from those of their friends and allies is a difficult task. Participants in the political game are bound together by common interests just as other groups of people are united in developing and changing the rules for games and sports.

STATES AND NATIONS

This book is concerned with politics that takes place within Canada. We are all familiar with the concept of Canada as a country, or state, with clearly defined borders, a specific system of government and a legal system. However, when we use the terms state, nation, or ethnic group, the meanings can be obscure. It is important to understand precisely what we mean by each of them.

To do so, think about the various social groups you belong to. Individuals belong to many organizations or institutions. At the most basic level you may be part of a family. You may be a student of a college or university. You may belong to a church, sports or recreation club. You may also belong to a certain town where you might pay municipal taxes. You also belong to a specific province or territory within Canada.

Within Canada, you are also probably a **citizen** — a formal member of the state — and therefore eligible to enjoy specified rights and privileges. States normally consider all persons born on their territory and their children to be citizens. Other individuals may acquire citizenship through a specified process — such as residing in the country for a certain length of time and carrying out a formal duty such as swearing an oath of allegiance (see the "What Should Citizens Know about Their Country?" Close-Up). In Canada, an immigrant may apply for citizenship after a total of three years residence in the country — if they are at least 18 years of age, can communicate in English or French, and have a knowledge of Canada. Many non-citizens also live in Canada: they are residents on an extended or short-term basis.

Most people also consider themselves part of an ethnic group. **Ethnicity** is primarily a subjective characteristic of groups of people who share customs, language, dialect and/or cultural heritage, and sometimes distinct physical or racial characteristics. When combined with religious, territorial or political differences, ethnicity is a strong political force. Canada's earliest founders came from two ethnic groups, French and English, but they settled on lands that had already been occupied by aboriginal peoples.

Nations, like ethnic groups, are *cultural* entities. They are essentially subjective, involving a sense of "we-ness" or belonging. We define a **nation** as a politically conscious and mobilized group of people, often with a sense of territory, who may aspire to greater independence or even statehood. Nations are not the same as ethnic groups, nor do they necessarily correspond to the territory of a country. Some Québec leaders claim to represent a "nation," and so do many aboriginal leaders. English-speaking Canadians, on the other hand, usually proclaim their loyalty to the country as a whole, or perhaps a territorial entity such as a city or province.

CLOSE-UP   What Should Citizens Know about Their Country?

In the fall of 1997, the Angus Reid Group asked a sample of Canadians 200 questions similar to those immigrants must be able to answer before they are allowed to become citizens of Canada. The results were embarrassing. They indicated that nearly half of Canadians would fail the citizenship exam. The questions were about Canadian history, culture, government institutions and laws. Here are some surprising results:

- 95 percent of respondents knew the title of the national anthem, but only 63 percent got the first two lines right.
- Only 8 percent could name the Queen as Canada's head of state; 57 percent believed the prime minister fills the role.

Do you think that Canadians who cannot answer these kinds of questions are able to vote intelligently? Should they lose their citizenship? How can the level of understanding be improved?

What basic questions should Canadians of voting age be able to answer about their country and their form of government?

When we use the word **state**, we are referring to the political unit of an entire territory. A state is made up of a territory, a population and a government. However, a state is also an abstraction that involves many institutions and rules. It is impossible to point at one institution or even a number of them and say, "That is the state."

As a whole, states do not act. Actions may be carried out in the name of the state, as when laws are enforced, or when countries impose taxes or go to war, but even when the government of a state acts in a national emergency or a war, not all state institutions necessarily are united behind them. Some institutions may even actively promote policies that contradict those of the so-called state or government. This has often been the case with the provincial government of Québec, for example, when Parti Québécois ministers promote separation from Canada.

Max Weber, a famous German sociologist, defined the state as a set of institutions that "successfully upholds a claim to the monopoly of the legitimate use of physical force in the enforcement of its order . . . within a given territorial area."[2] This means that the state is able to use coercive force to issue rules that are binding on all those within its territory.

The state is thus defined in terms of its relation to power — both external and internal. A state is normally considered to be **sovereign** when final authority rests in the national government so that it is able internally, for example, to tax its citizens — and also externally to conduct its own relations with the international community, free from outside interference by other states or governments.

Normally, people strongly identify with their state. They proclaim their love for it, sing about it, work to better it, and fight to preserve it. When citizens accept that a government should, or has the right to, make decisions for them, political scientists say the system has **legitimacy**. When the government imposes higher taxes, Canadians pay them even though they don't want to because they elected the government to handle such matters, and therefore, consider the policy to be legitimate. Legitimacy is closely linked to the concept of **authority**, which we may define as the government's "power" to make binding decisions and issue obligatory commands. In the illustration above, the government not only has the legitimacy to impose higher taxes, it also has the authority to do so, because it has the power of the legal system behind it to force individual citizens to pay taxes even though they may not want to.

GOVERNMENTS AND POLITICS

All stable states have governments that exercise authority — they have institutions that the people entrust to make binding decisions. The government resolves disputes and conflicts that arise within society. It issues obligatory commands. It "steers" the country in certain policy directions, makes rules that are legally binding on residents, and obtains resources to carry out its policy goals while attempting to preserve the viability of governmental institutions.[3]

Governments carry out their activities in the context of their societies. Since individuals and groups in society dispute about how resources and other scarce goods should be distributed, leaders must find ways to reconcile these disagreements. Dispute and conflict resolution are often referred to as politics. **Politics** is the activity that entails making binding decisions about who gets what, when and how.[4] **Government** consists of the authoritative structures of the political system.

Governments in democracies are elected by the passengers to steer the ship of state. They are expected to hold it on course, to arrange for a prosperous voyage, and to be prepared to be thrown overboard if they fail in either duty.

Eugene Forsey

LAW AND POLICY

Governments enforce their authority by making laws. **Law** consists of a special body of rules issued by government and backed up by the threat of state force. Not everything governments do is made into law. Governments also spend funds, set up structures and processes for consultation and decision-making, and steer the country in particular policy directions. **Policies** are broadly based patterns of government action. Policies and law both concern values about public goals, and beliefs about the best strategy for a country to take.

Democratic countries set out their laws relatively clearly. They separate courts from politics so that judges can interpret the law in an impartial (non-politicized) manner. Recognized legal authorities such as the police enforce the law by arresting offenders and holding them accountable before the courts. A prison system removes individuals from society when they do not conform to the laws. The prison system is often not included in books about politics, but it should be. It serves several goals of the state such as punishing wrongdoers, safeguarding society, and correcting the behaviour of inmates in preparation for their release.

Laws come in many forms, but all concern how individuals and groups relate to government. Most citizens' contact with political authorities involves dealing with laws concerning such issues as taxes, pensions, business regulations and administrative guidelines.

TYPES OF GOVERNMENT: DEMOCRACY AND AUTHORITARIANISM

States can differ widely in how they are organized and what ideals they hold. Democratic systems normally differ from authoritarian regimes by the amount and quality of participation they allow citizens in making public policy. A **democratic political system** is a system of government that reconciles competing interests through competitive elections. An **authoritarian political system** is a system of government which imposes one dominant interest, that of a political elite, on all others.

Democracy is a very simple idea which is difficult, if not impossible, to replicate in the real world. The word comes from two Greek roots, *demos* meaning the people and *kratos* meaning authority or rule. In ancient Greek culture, therefore, democracy meant that all the people should rule. Today, such an ideal situation is impossible for states and only tends to occur in smaller towns or face-to-face societies.

In the simplest model of democracy, elections provide popular sovereignty. The people elect a few of their fellow citizens to serve for a time as the rulers. After a period, the rulers must be judged by the citizens as to whether they have ruled properly. In the accounting process, known as an election, the people reward or punish the rulers by re-electing or rejecting them. Good government is assured because the elected ruler must satisfy the people in order to get re-elected. Politicians are, therefore, supposed to serve the national interests of a country rather than their own selfish desires.

This simple model is very important. If people *believe* in it, and act accordingly, a country can operate successfully. We have seen that when citizens accept that a government should, or has the right to, make decisions for them, the political system has legitimacy. Nevertheless, this model of democracy is quite simplistic and in some ways misleading.

Six ingredients are generally considered to be necessary for a state to be democratic:

1. *free elections* in which people vote for their political representatives free from intimidation or harassment;

2. *universal voting rights*, so that all adult citizens have the right to vote for their political leaders;

3. *more than one political party* to choose from;

4. *liberty and freedom of expression*, so that individuals and the media can speak freely to praise or criticize governments, politicians and policies. Liberty and freedom of expression assure freedom of assembly and association as well as freedom of the press;

5. policy decisions are made by a majority of the people or elected body — this is known as the **majority principle**;

6. *rule of law* is also a fundamental part of the democratic ideal. Equality is embedded in this democratic notion that all individuals should be treated alike under the law and in rules about "one person one vote" in elections.

In Canada, we say that we are ruled by law and not by people. Laws are made by humans, but under the rule of law, they are to be administered impartially. No individual (regardless of his/her political status) is to be above the law. As we shall see in Chapter 3, the **rule of law** is a guarantee that the state's actions will be governed by law, with fairness and without malice. It means that no citizen is to be deprived of due process or to be punished at the whim of an official. The courts are to ensure that the rule of law is upheld. We shall discuss law and its specific relation with the Canadian Constitution in Chapters 3, 4 and 9, but it is important here to establish the links between democracy and forms of government. States and their governments use laws to regulate and control behaviour.

Democracy: Procedural and Substantive

Before we examine democracy in Canada, we should be aware that there are two distinct ways to think about it. One is known as *substantive*, the other as *procedural*.

Readers will have observed that in the contemporary world, virtually all states — even many that are clearly authoritarian — boast that they are democratic. Democracy has become so linked with "goodness" that they all want to be associated with it. When countries claim to be democratic, they tend to mean that they rule for the common good. They maintain that democracy is the best means of governing because the people to some extent have a say in how they are governed. For them, democracy simply means good government and that is seen as the essential purpose of government. This is known as a *substantive* view of democracy.

For others, however, democracy is *procedural* — it refers to the mechanics or procedures by which a country discusses and organizes political differences and deals with political strife. It also concerns the procedures whereby citizens are able to participate in politics.

We have seen that the simple model of democracy assumes popular participation in law and public policy-making. However, citizens rarely participate directly in decision-making in the modern world. The model of democracy is an ideal that is rarely realized. Most systems today are **representative democracies**, democracies in which elected officials make decisions with the force of law because they have achieved legitimacy through some form of election. Democracy in Canada and elsewhere is not rule by the people themselves. It is representative democracy — rule by elected officials.

Making representative democracy work requires complex structures and a mass public that is fairly knowledgeable about government and politics (consider the "What Should Citizens Know about Their Country?" Close-Up). Those in government, too, must understand the need to reconcile their authority with public influence. They must adapt to operating within a society that holds conflicting beliefs about the role of government.

Let us take one example. For conservatives, individual rights are conceived as immunities — guarantees against government interference in the lives of individuals and groups. A free market economy thus characterizes the type of economic relations desired by conservatives. On the other hand, modern liberals think of rights as the entitlements individuals receive from the state. They do not object to government management of the economy. They applaud it. From this simple conflict in beliefs, we can see that democracy must be about a set of *procedures* that enable the rule of the people to be achieved *despite* differences in judgments about the desirable outcomes of government action.[5]

A further question about democracy concerns what is required for it to be stable and successful. When communism collapsed in the USSR, for example, democracy did not thrive in its place. Having long been deprived of the cultural roots of democracy and a society of groups, associations and participatory institutions such as parties, the new Russia continues to develop in an uncertain direction. On the other hand, democracy in Canada has flourished but sometimes under quite difficult circumstances.

Another question in the analysis of democracy concerns its substantive qualities. At question is whether or not democracy tends to be the cause of, or is caused by, the values of liberty and equality held by its people. The principle of liberty appears to be required in democratic systems because it underlies notions about freedom of thought, assembly and association as well as freedom of the press. The majority principle and the idea of competing parties, rule of law, and free elections also seem to be fundamentally interlocked with democratic ideas. Furthermore, equality is embedded in the democratic notion that all individuals should be treated alike under the law, and in rules about "one person one vote" in elections. Are such values required to establish democracy or are they a by-product of the establishment of democracy?

In this book, we consider democracy to be as a *set of procedures* and *institutions*. While one would be remiss to overlook the values and philosophies that are associated with the democratic process, and while democracies are associated with specific values such as liberty and political equality, it does not mean that democracy can be equated with, or equal to, the "good life."

Canadian Democracy

Canada has very deep democratic roots. When the first British settlers arrived in the early colonies of Canada, they brought with them a long history of experience with democratic ideas and institutions. Canadians established their own unique democratic culture at Confederation in 1867. Their historical background provided them with democratic traditions and institutions and created a firm soil in which Canadian democracy has flourished.

Canada, like other democracies, has both state and political institutions. **State institutions** are related closely to the Constitution and federalism. They include the executive, legislature, bureaucracy, courts, police and prisons. **Political institutions**, on the other hand, structure democratic expression within states and relate more closely to citizen behaviour. Parties, interest groups, elections and the media, for example, link the people to their state and provide ways of influencing state authorities. Both state and political institutions are important elements of Canadian democracy.

As a framework for their state institutions, Canadian leaders rejected the presidential model of government chosen by the United States and instead determined to copy the British model of **parliamentary government** with which they were familiar. This system had already been operating in what is now Central and Eastern Canada for many years. They set up a Parliament with two houses — an elected lower house, the House of Commons, and an appointed upper house, the Senate — and a governor general to represent the Queen. Every province also was given a legislature, with a lieutenant-governor representing the Queen.

Canada's state institutions continue to operate within a framework of **constitutional monarchy**, not a republic as in the United States. In a constitutional monarchy, a monarch is head of state, and a constitution and laws of the state restrict the powers of the monarch and the entire executive branch of government. In Canada, the head of state is Queen Elizabeth II, who is also the Queen of Britain, Australia, New Zealand and many other countries around the world, from the Bahamas to Papua–New Guinea. Canada is a *constitutional* monarchy because the Constitution shapes the arrangements of political power. In a **republic**, on the other hand, there is no monarch. The government of the state is carried out by the people or their elected representatives. The head of state is usually elected by the people.

In Canada, the Constitution outlines a federal system of government — one in which power and authority to govern is shared between the federal (central) government and the governments of the provinces. This means that Canada is a **federation**. A federation has a number of territorially based units, and the activities of government between their regional governments and a central government are in such a way that each kind of government has some kind of activities on which it makes final decisions. The United States, too, has a federal system. Britain, on the other hand, has a **unitary system** in which the power and authority to govern is centralized in one government.

The Canadian Constitution divides formal authority between a monarchical head of state and a governmental leader, the prime minister. Since the Queen resides in Britain, the monarch's titular and symbolic role is carried on in Canada by the governor general. This makes Canada different from the United States and other presidential systems where the president is both the head of state and the political head.

The prime minister heads the *political executive* — known as the ministry and Cabinet — and is the effective head of government. The prime minister derives his or her power from British and Canadian constitutional conventions that give authority to the person who leads the party with a majority or plurality of votes in the House of Commons. We examine the executive in detail in Chapter 6.

The Constitution also provides Canada with a representative assembly, the House of Commons, and an appointed upper house, the Senate. As we have noted, therefore, Canada's democracy is a representative democracy, in which the House of Commons represents the electorate. It is not an idealized system of democracy by the people. The members of the House are chosen by the people on the basis of one person, one vote. As we shall see in Chapter 11, such perfect equality is not always possible in practice, but it is an important goal.

The ministers who make up the government are responsible to the House for the actions of the government, and the House of Commons is answerable to the people. For that reason, we say Canada has **responsible government**. If the ministers cannot keep the support of a majority of the members of the House of Commons, then the government falls. A new general election is called and the people elect a new government.

Canadian democracy, then, is set up as a constitutional monarchy. The Constitution outlines a federal system and a parliamentary system of government with representative, responsible government. It satisfies all six criteria for a functioning democratic state that we noted above. We discuss in detail all of these ingredients of Canadian democracy in the following chapters, but before we begin, it is important to understand some fundamentals about the overall political system and how it operates.

ISSUES CANADIANS ARGUE ABOUT

Since politics is about a struggle for advantage among competitors, it is not surprising that disputes about resources are at the centre of Canadian quarrels. Politics is diffused throughout the whole society and there are many different kinds of contests among individuals and groups. Because of this, it is possible to have a multitude of interpretations of what issues are significant in Canadian politics. The political agenda is created by the interactions between society and the political system and by the decisions of those in power. When government is dominated by a certain group or groups, those groups determine what issues and policies to pursue based on their vision of what is to be done and the priority they give these issues. It is important, therefore, that the composition of parties, legislatures and bureaucracies include significant representation from women and minorities so that their voices can be heard and issues that concern them will not be overlooked or shunted aside.

At the national level, however, a few fundamental and complex issues tend to dominate federal politics. The list is always changing. Today, it would have to include immigration, medical services, the environment, youth unemployment, an aging population, global economics, national security, child poverty and literacy, to name a few.

At the centre of political debate today, however, are two long-term vital issues that tend to overshadow all others. The first is the continuing debate over the future of Québec in the federation; the second concerns the economy.

The issue of Québec nationalism and how to counteract it and accommodate it as much as possible within the Canadian framework is a continuing challenge. It is the most vital issue facing the country. As we shall see in Chapter 5, "Nationalism and Regionalism," the federal government must bear its relationship with Québec in mind virtually every time it acts.

At issue concerning the economy is the massive size of the Canadian government debt and how to reduce it and still inject large sums into programs such as health care that are competing for limited funds. These are highly emotional issues and very important to the economic health of the country. How they are resolved will determine the future of the Canadian political system and affect the lives of all Canadians. It is not possible to understand or evaluate Canada's political institutions without also understanding the key issues our leaders are working to resolve. In fact, it is not even possible to read the front pages of the country's newspapers without understanding them.

Just how healthy is the Canadian economy? To begin to understand the financial situation one must be clear about two terms, debt and deficit. The **deficit** is the amount by which government spending exceeds revenues in one year. For about three decades until 1998, the Canadian federal government spent more than it took in, so that each

CLOSE-UP — Federal Government's Financial Situation for the 2004–2005 Fiscal Year in Billions of Dollars

Deficit — 0
Surplus — 4.0
Net public Debt — 510.6
Interest charges on Debt — 35.4
Debt as a percent of GDP — 40.4%

year it had a deficit. When all the deficits are added together, they represent the debt. The **debt** is the accumulation of deficits over the years since 1867. The federal government's debt peaked in 1998–1999 at $583 billion. As of 2005, it is 510.6 billion dollars.

By the end of the 1999–2000 fiscal year, the deficit had been replaced by a $12.3 billion surplus, although the debt load and high-debt interest payments continued. A **surplus** refers to money that is left over each year after the bills for that year are paid. Since 2000, liberals and conservatives have begun to argue over how to spend the surplus. Is it better to build up new social programs in areas such as child care, youth unemployment, and prenatal assistance, or pay down more of the debt or reduce taxes?

The issue of government finances is covered in detail in Chapter 8, "Public Administration," where we consider how the government's yearly budget is prepared and the options that face the minister of finance and the public service in this task.

ISSUES AND INSTITUTIONS

The debt and Québec's status are just two key issues that must be resolved in Canada through the democratic institutions that have been built up slowly over 138 years. With the country caught in what could be a pattern of successive weak, minority governments, it will be much harder to make progress on these and other pressing issues. Throughout the book, we have addressed the issue of minority government, noting how it affects all aspects of how governmental institutions function.

In the following chapters, we examine Canada's institutions. We turn the kaleidoscope to focus on each of them, showing the different shapes, patterns, meanings and interpretations possible about these vital structures of democracy.

In Chapter 2, we describe the environment in which Canadian politics takes place. In Chapter 3, we examine the mega-rules about the political game in the Constitution, and in Chapter 4, the federal aspect of the Constitution and the financing of the federation are analyzed. These over-arching structures and institutions of Canadian democracy are not without their advocates and their critics. Chapter 5 outlines and assesses the forces of nationalism, separatism and regionalism in the country.

State institutions are examined next. Chapters 6, 7, 8 and 9 combine to make clear how executive, legislative, bureaucratic and judicial institutions function. Coercive structures also play a part in democracy, and organizations such as the police and prison systems are shown to mesh with these central government organizations.

It is necessary to examine political institutions as well as state institutions to have a complete view of how the Canadian democratic system operates. Chapters 10 and 11 therefore provide an overview of four political institutions — political parties, interest groups, the media and elections in Canada. These institutions form links between the mass public and state authorities.

Chapter 12 looks at the issue of ethics in politics. Politicians often struggle against negative images, made worse by scandals like the one that plagues the Liberal government of Paul Martin. Are these perceptions deserved? What rules are in place to keep our politicians honest? Are they adequate?

State and political institutions provide a coherent relationship among the elements of our democracy. Together they work to produce a viable system. All states have stresses and strains caused by divisions within their societies, and Canada is no different. Canada must weather crises such as those concerning secession, the national debt, and global terrorism. Elected representatives in the political system are responsible to find answers to these and other issues for their constituents. It is to a large extent in their hands whether the country will continue in its historic form, change, or disrupt as it moves through the twenty-first century.

KEY TERMS

authoritarian political system, p. 9
authority, p. 8
citizen, p. 8
constitutional monarchy, p. 12
debt, p. 15
deficit, p. 14
democratic political system, p. 9
ethnicity, p. 7
federation, p. 13
government, p. 8
law, p. 9
legitimacy, p. 8
majority principle, p. 10
nation, p. 7

parliamentary government, p. 12
policies, p. 9
political institutions, p. 12
politics, p. 8
representative democracies p. 11
republic, p. 12
responsible government, p. 13
rule of law, p. 10
sovereign, p. 8
state, p. 7
state institutions, p. 12
surplus, p. 15
unitary system, p. 13

DISCUSSION QUESTIONS

1. What do you consider to be the major issues and problems the Canadian government must cope with in the coming years?

2. Is the analogy between politics and games a good one? Why or why not? Is politics as competitive as the games analogy implies?

3. Is Canada a state, a nation, or both? Justify your answer.

4. What are the basic components of democracy? Is democracy in Canada "rule by the people"? Why or why not?

5. Does minority government handicap or improve Canadian democracy?

WEBLINKS

Citizenship and Immigration Canada

www.cic.gc.ca

Keele University (UK) Guide to Canadian Government & Politics on the Internet

www.keele.ac.uk/depts/por/nabase.htm#scourt

Government of Canada home page

www.canada.gc.ca

Canada Online — Resources on Canadian Federal Politics and Government

http://canadaonline.about.com

2 The Context of Government
Internal and External Factors of Cohesion and Division

Learning Objectives

After reading this chapter, you should be able to

1. Describe the main geographic and demographic factors that shape politics in Canada.

2. Identify and discuss at least five factors that unite Canadians.

3. Describe the main political ideas and social and economic cleavages that divide Canadians into different groups.

4. Identify the main ethnic divisions in Canada and compare their relative political and social situations.

5. Understand how Canadian politics is a product of many factors, some of which are internal to the country and some of which are external.

The context in which a game is played creates a network of advantages and disadvantages for individual players and teams. Following this analogy, performance is affected by external factors such as the support of "home fans," or bad publicity, as well as by internal factors such as leadership and adherence to traditions and values of competition and fair play.

Similarly, government and politics occur in the context of a wider society. They are nourished by ideas, people and events and are shaped by various circumstances of geography, history, climate and resources. Experiences of the past and expectations for the future affect both politics and government. In this age of global economics, electronic technology and communications, external environments have an ever greater effect on the government and politics of individual countries. Canada is no exception.

In this chapter, we examine elements in the internal and external environments of government and politics, some that unite Canadians and others that divide them. This overview provides a picture of who Canadians are and what kinds of political issues concern them most. Canadians are divided into overlapping groups based on such factors as gender, class, education, region, language and ethnicity. The categories and groups that an individual belongs to help to determine what he or she wants and expects from the country's political institutions. The global environment, particularly relations with the United States, shapes and sometimes limits the ability of the Canadian government to satisfy these aspirations.

THE INTERNAL CONTEXT OF POLITICS IN CANADA
The Land and the People

Canadian politics cannot be understood without a basic knowledge of the geography that provides both obstacles and opportunities for the country's inhabitants and divides them into distinct provinces and regions. Some basic demographic facts must be known. It is a myth that Canada is a young country. Among the world's states, Canada is not an adolescent but well into middle age. In 2005, at 138 years old, Canada has existed longer, for example, than Italy (unified in 1870) or Germany (1871). Fewer than one-third of the 191 countries now represented in the United Nations even existed in 1945 when Canada was already 78 years old.

Geography

Canada is the largest country in the western hemisphere. At nearly ten million square kilometres, it is the second largest country in the world after Russia. East to west, it stretches over five thousand kilometres. The land is diverse, beautiful, often inhospitable to settlement and for the most part rich in resources. The enormous distances that separate the population sometimes contribute to a regionalist mentality and to an alienation from the federal government in Ottawa.

In addition to distance, physical geography also separates Canadians. The low, discontinuous chain of mountains and valleys of the Appalachian region traverse the eastern edge of the country north to south. Central Canada is dominated by the Canadian Shield, a region of formerly volcanic Precambrian-era mountains that extends from the Great Lakes around the horseshoe of Hudson Bay north into the Arctic. The Shield takes up roughly one-half of Canada's surface area. The most fertile land in Central Canada lies along the shores of the St. Lawrence River and in southwestern Ontario. West of the Shield are the Interior Plains, which once formed the bottom of ancient lakes and seas. They are cut off from the coast by a belt of mountains over eight hundred kilometres wide. This Western Cordillera includes coastal mountain ranges, high plateaus, and the Rockies.

Canada's climate is as diverse as its land mass. The Far North is characterized by low-plateau mountains and long, harsh winters. The climate in the rest of the country is more hospitable but still the coldest on the continent, and extremely varied. Areas near large bodies of water enjoy more moderate climates than the inland areas and, because of prevailing westerly winds, the West Coast boasts lower temperatures than the East Coast.

The southern part of the Interior Plains and the lowlands along the southern Great Lakes and the St. Lawrence River are best suited to commercial agriculture. Major population centres are here. Elsewhere there is a wealth of non-renewable mineral deposits, from vast iron ore deposits in the eastern Shield to gold in the Yukon valleys. There are substantial deposits of zinc, nickel, gold, silver, iron ore, uranium, copper, cobalt and lead. Major reserves of natural gas and petroleum, great hydroelectric-power potential and abundant supplies of clean water also exist throughout the country. In terms of renewable resources, lumber is a major asset. The Interior Plains provide one of the great grain-growing areas of the world. However, the once-plentiful fish stocks of the Atlantic and Pacific coasts are seriously depleted.

Natural resources provide constant sources of conflict that governments must resolve. Who owns them, how and by whom will they be regulated and exploited, and who will benefit from them constitute a major focus of politics in Canada.

Demography

Geography confines most of the population to a narrow band along the Canada–United States border, spread out like beads on a string. As a result, it has always been a challenge to develop transportation and communication links to unite Canadians and resist the seductive attraction of the large border populations of the United States. The Québec City-to-Windsor, Ontario, corridor comprises only about 1 percent of the country's land mass but nearly 60 percent of its population. Canadians are largely urban. Over three-quarters of them live in metropolitan areas. Fifty-one percent live in four urban areas: the Golden Horseshoe in Ontario (6.7 million); the Calgary–Edmonton corridor (2.1 million); Montréal and its adjacent region (3.7 million); and southern Vancouver Island and the lower mainland of British Columbia (2.7 million).

From a meagre 3.5 million people at Confederation, Canada has grown to a population of over 31 million today — larger than Austria, any of the Scandinavian countries, Greece, Hungary or Venezuela, to name only a few of the 197 countries of the world.[1] However, in recent years, the country's population growth has slowed to less than 1 percent a year based on natural increase and immigration. Four basic variables affect demography: fertility, mortality, migration, and immigration.

As in other developed countries, Canadian fertility rates began to decline in 1961, after the baby boom of the late 1940s and 1950s. As of 2001, there were roughly 1.4 births per woman. Yet a rate of 2.1 births is needed to maintain the current population level. Current social patterns and technical advances indicate that low fertility rates will continue into the near future.

Mortality rates are also changing. The average life expectancy at Confederation was approximately 45 years; in 2001, it was closer to 80. Women live about five years longer than men. The lowest life expectancy correlates with unskilled and blue-collar workers, the unmarried and Aboriginals.

Immigration has always played a vital role in Canada's development. Canada has one of the largest proportions of foreign-born residents of any country in the world — double that of the United States. In 2001, at the time of Canada's last census, 18.4 percent of Canadians were foreign born, the highest percent in seventy years.

Canada's population, therefore, is far from uniform. What unites Canadians? What ideas and aspirations do they share? The next section provides some answers to these questions. We then consider some of the most important lines of division that set Canadians apart from each other.

What Unites Canadians?

Canadians possess a common land mass, history and political institutions. In the following chapters, we examine the major political institutions, including Parliament, the Constitution, federalism, courts, political parties and police and consider the extent to which they and the issues around them are unifying or divisive. Canadians also share many common interests, including the creation of a peaceful, prosperous country. Next, we will examine some of the most significant shared political culture, values, attitudes and ideas that help unite Canadians.

Political Culture

Citizens of all countries develop perceptions and expectations about their political system and these provide the value and belief structures within which political decisions are made. Cultural values affect the rhetoric and biases of politics. They delineate the accepted parameters of individual and government political activity and enable organizations and institutions to function coherently.

The broad patterns of values, beliefs and attitudes in a society toward political objects are often referred to as **political culture**. Political culture draws individuals together; supports thought, judgment and action; constitutes the character and personality of a community; differentiates it from other communities; and encourages its members to seek common objectives. What citizens know and feel about their political system affects the number and kinds of demands they make on the system and also their responses to laws and political leadership.

The extent to which values and attitudes are shared greatly affects the sense of political community and therefore the degree of national cohesion and stability in a country. Deep cleavages within a state over issues such as language or economic well-being obstruct the sharing of values and contribute to political instability.

It is difficult to measure the strength of something as elusive as a sense of political community. However, as we shall see, Canadians exhibit similar values, attitudes and behaviours toward the political system and government. The collective heritage of values, beliefs and attitudes shared by Canadians is greater than the rhetoric of provincial autonomy and regional cleavages might lead a casual observer to believe.

Political Values

To understand Canadian politics, we must identify the values and beliefs that support the political institutions of the country. **Values** provide standards of judgment about what is right, important and desirable in society. Though generally taken for granted and not articulated, widely accepted values about what is good and worthwhile set the boundaries of acceptable behaviour and underlie citizens' attitudes toward specific political goals. They provide guidelines to define what is right or wrong, what is, or is not, acceptable.

Many values and beliefs pertain to *all* Canadians, while others are shared by only a few. Overarching values and beliefs that bring Canadians together include traditions of personal freedom and civil liberties, respect for the law and the coexistence of heterogeneous communities. In April 1982, the Canadian *Charter of Rights and Freedoms* became the first comprehensive statement of the fundamental values to be entrenched in the Constitution. The preamble sets out the premise that "Canada is founded upon principles that recognize the supremacy of God and the Rule of Law." The Charter then guarantees the fundamental rights of Canada's "free and democratic society." The implicit values of Canadians, as formalized in the Charter, are basically rooted in the Western political tradition and Judeo-Christian religious thought.

Many values of representative democracy are proclaimed in the Charter. These include the right of individuals to four fundamental individual freedoms: freedom of conscience and religion; freedom of thought, belief, opinion and expression, including freedom of the press; freedom of peaceful assembly; and freedom of association. Another value of representative democracy highlighted by the Charter is equality before and under the law, without discrimination. In the political sphere, equality presumes such related values as universal suffrage and elections contested by competing political parties that give voters alternatives from which to choose.

Another associated value recognized by the Charter is acceptance of the rule of law, with civil rights for all citizens. Still another *implicit* value of representative democracy — but one not recognized in the Charter — is majority rule. In Canada, governments are based on an ability to retain a majority of votes in the House of Commons. Members of Parliament (MPs federally) are elected in a system that gives credence to the majority principle but in fact allows members to be elected by a *plurality* — that is, the winner is the individual who gains the most votes in an election. When there are more than two candidates, the winner often has considerably less than 50 percent of the votes.

Since it is deemed necessary to protect minority rights in Canada, some *collective* rights are also named in the Constitution. These include French and English minority language rights in the federal and Québec legislatures and courts and New Brunswick. Canadians also hold equality to be a high value in questions concerning collective rights. Section 15 of the Charter states that there should be no discrimination based on race, national or ethnic origin, colour, religion, sex, age or mental or physical disability.

There are many other values that affect how Canadians conduct their politics. For example, Canadians demonstrate considerable ethnic tolerance. They also share economic well-being, distributing financial resources to less prosperous provinces and disadvantaged individuals. Canadian public policy ensures that all individuals have basic health care, pensions and a host of other forms of social assistance. Canada has many characteristics of a caring society. Such social services are based on deeply held values that politicians ignore at their peril.

Political Attitudes

Attitudes toward political objects are more differentiated and fleeting than basic values and beliefs, but they may also be more immediate determinants of political behaviour.

Attitudes toward specific political issues of the day are ephemeral. They change according to the state of the times. These changing attitudes are often defined as "public opinion," and although they are important in determining short-term political behaviour, they are somewhat less helpful in depicting the political culture of a country than are fundamental values and beliefs.

Canadians generally have the basic information about political institutions necessary to allow them to operate effectively at both provincial and federal levels of government. They also demonstrate a high degree of affect (emotional attachment) for both their country and their respective provinces.[2] However, studies have shown that Canadians lack faith that politicians and the political system will respond positively to their interests. Such attitudes can fluctuate over a relatively short period and vary across the population; however, negative views about politicians have persisted in recent years.

Cynical attitudes toward politicians do not, of course, prevent widespread support for the government in Canada or hamper political participation at either level of government. They may, however, affect how many Canadians regularly cast their ballots in federal and provincial elections. As we shall see, the number of voters has been declining significantly in recent years. On the whole, individuals comply with basic political laws, and major political groups rarely offer violent resistance to authoritative government decisions. Acts of Parliament are considered legitimate and almost always obeyed.

Political Ideas, Customs, Traditions and Symbols

Shared ideas, customs and traditions unite people and so do symbols. Canada's early settlers brought with them political ideas that form the basis of political thought in this country. Of these, the liberal ideas of British philosopher John Locke are widely accepted today. Ideas about the importance of the individual, free enterprise and the right of the individual to pursue personal interests without government interference are firmly embedded in Canadian political culture. However, unlike the United States, there are also evident strains of conservative thought that can be traced to settlers in New France and also United Empire Loyalists who fled revolutionary America. Socialist ideas — holding that the state is responsible for its citizens and should provide for their collective well-being — can also be found throughout Canadian history.

Many Canadian **political customs** — the conventional and accepted practices that are part of the political system — come from Britain. They may not be written down as rules or laws, but they are nevertheless followed. As Canada matured, it also began to develop its own distinctively Canadian customs and traditions. In 1952, for example, Canadians changed the tradition of selecting a British citizen to be governor general to selecting a Canadian.

The *political values* of a country are symbolized by such objects as flags, anthems, leaders, national holidays and historical heroes. These symbols help enforce respect for, and emotional attachment to, political institutions. They can be a focal point for national unity by recalling the achievements, tragedies and idealism of previous generations.

As Canada graduated from a colony to a full-fledged state, the change was reflected in the country's *political symbols*. In the early stages, they manifested a dual allegiance to

Canada and Britain but were gradually transformed to reflect national pride and unity without reference to Britain.

The evolution of the Canadian flag is perhaps the best illustration. At Confederation in 1867, Canada was granted permission to fly the red ensign, the flag of the British Merchant Navy. Attempts to replace it with a uniquely Canadian flag began as early as 1925, but these attempts did not succeed until four decades later when a flag that features a stylized red maple leaf was selected. The maple leaf is a distinctively Canadian symbol with deep historical roots.

Other minor conflicts and reminders of the British heritage have come to the fore from time to time as new symbols evolved. The first day of July, Canada's national holiday, was known as Dominion Day until November 1982. Although the word *Dominion* had been chosen explicitly by the Fathers of Confederation to mean sovereignty from sea to sea, many Canadians had come to feel that it smacked of colonial dependence, so Parliament changed the title of the holiday to Canada Day.

In many countries, a constitution provides a focus for pride and unity. This is not the case for many Canadians. The *British North America Act*, the basis of Canada's written Constitution, was passed by the British Parliament in 1867. As a national symbol, it was a source of embarrassment to Canadians in the twentieth century for two reasons. First, it could not be amended without British approval, and second, it contained no formal guarantee of rights and freedoms. As we shall see in Chapter 5, in the spring of 1982 a revised Constitution, now known as the *Canada Act, 1982*, was patriated, including the old *BNA Act* and a new *Charter of Rights and Freedoms*. However, this was done without the signature of the Québec government. Not until this matter is resolved will the Constitution provide a common focus of pride for Canadians from all regions.

Another predominant political symbol is the monarch. Canada is a constitutional monarchy, and the role of Her Majesty Queen Elizabeth II as sovereign of Canada and head of state is ceremonial. As queen, she personifies the country and is a symbol of allegiance, unity and authority. The ability of this institution to serve as a unifying symbol for Canada's two founding cultural groups is limited. For many, however, the Crown and monarchy represent the best traditions in Canadian democracy.

Historical heroes, as well as sports and literary figures, also can be symbols of national pride and unity. Unfortunately, Canada's gradual evolution to statehood, as opposed to the dramatic (and bloody) revolution that happened south of the border, did not produce as large a pool of charismatic heroes. As well, French and English Canadians each tend to cultivate their own separate symbols and historical memories. Hockey and Olympic sports heroes tend to be some of the country's most successful symbols of pride and unity.

What Divides Canadians?

While shared political ideas, values, attitudes, customs and traditions, symbols, and heroes provide common bonds that unite Canadians, other factors divide them. Differing ideologies provide the basis for fundamentally different ways of looking at political issues and support different policy solutions for problems. As well, several deep and relatively stable cleavages cut across Canadian society, creating different "layers" of Canadians with unique needs, interests and prejudices. Some of these are based on age, class and gender. Others are based on ethnicity, language and regions. They divide Canadians into separate groups that coexist within the state. Group lines mostly overlap, but sometimes they do not. Each stratum or grouping of Canadians makes its own demands on governments. Some groups are cohesive; others are not. Some are politicized; others are not. Some have considerable power and influence; others have very little. As we shall see, these divisions are not necessarily unduly divisive politically, but they do demarcate special needs and interests and help to form the character and culture of the country.

Canadians do not all have equal chances to succeed in life. They have different personal characteristics, abilities, and health and are born into different social and economic circumstances. Factors such as gender, education and socio-economic class to a large extent determine an individual's ideas and political orientations. They shape the experiences and opportunities of Canadians and influence how and even whether individuals wish to participate in the political process. Different political ideologies underpin their political ideas and orientations.

Some of the main factors that divide Canadians are political ideas, age, gender, economic class, ethnicity and language, and regions.

Political Ideas

While many ideas serve to unite Canadians, others divide them into different groups. **Ideology** is an explicit doctrinal structure that provides a particular diagnosis of the ills of society plus an accompanying "action program" for implementing prescribed solutions for these problems. Ideologies are associated to various degrees with particular political parties, structuring their rhetoric and conditioning their policy programs. Other than nationalism, which underpins the Bloc Québécois (and is discussed in Chapter 5), liberal, conservative, and socialist ideologies are the most significant of these forces in Canadian society.

These three ideologies have deep historical roots, and it is important to trace them briefly to understand their contribution to political thought in Canada. Liberalism and conservatism originated in Europe in the nineteenth century as philosophers and thinkers struggled to create logical and consistent patterns of thought about how to restructure the medieval social and political order that new technological developments were rendering obsolete. Socialism developed later but, again, in response to fundamental changes in economics. By the beginning of the twentieth century, the European political and ideological battlefield was a three-way contest, as the socialist ideology added socialist, labour and communist parties to those espousing liberalism and conservatism.

Liberalism

Historically, liberalism was the ideology of a rising commercial class that resented the restrictions of the old feudal order on European society. The ideas it generated provided moral, political and economic guidance. Morally, liberalism affirmed basic values, including freedom and dignity. Politically, it espoused basic political rights such as the right of representative government. Economically, it was dedicated to the right to private property, free trade and free enterprise capitalism.

The historical root of *liberal* is the Latin *liber* meaning *free* (man). The concept of freedom is at the heart of the liberal ideology. Early proponents of liberalism called for freedom (or absence of coercion) in all areas of life: social, political and economic.

The English political philosopher John Locke (1637–1704) was the most influential of the early thinkers who are generally referred to as classical liberals. Locke argued that all human beings have the right to life, liberty and property and that they create government to protect and preserve these basic rights. If the government fails in this task, Locke said, the people have the right to overthrow it.[3] He wrote, "Freedom is . . . to have a standing rule to live by, common to everyone of that society and made by the legislative power erected in it."[4] Civil liberties, or freedoms such as freedom of expression, freedom of speech and freedom to publish and disseminate one's ideas, have been enshrined in the constitutions of most liberal democracies.

Locke, and other liberals including John Stuart Mill (1806–1873), wanted to organize government to maintain law and order but not to infringe on human rights. The way to accomplish that goal was to force governments to operate under the strict limits of a constitution. Locke believed that legislatures elected by the people (at that time still on a very limited franchise) should make decisions for society. He based his idea of representative government on the notion that political authority derives from the people. The elected majority, he said, can make all decisions, but it must respect the natural rights of all citizens.

Liberalism also had important economic implications for the state. Scottish moral philosopher Adam Smith (1723–1790) expounded the principle of *laissez-faire*, which essentially means there should be minimum intervention by government in economic affairs. Smith maintained that society is governed by natural laws, just like the physical universe. One such law holds that prices in a free market are determined by supply and demand. Ideally, Smith reasoned, the government would leave the economy entirely to adjust itself through the free market.

Classical liberalism was deemed harsh to the poor in society because it opposed redistribution of wealth. At the same time, however, it defended the principle of equality before the law for all individuals. Economic inequality was unavoidable, classical liberals said, but eventually the free market system would create wealth and raise living standards for everyone.

Modern liberalism has moved away from some of the tenets of classical liberalism. The new position is often called *reform* liberalism because it expanded or reformed the classical approach to the concept of freedom. Reform liberals moved away from the classical roots in three essential points:

1. The idea that government should be left to the propertied class was replaced by democratic principles of mass participation.

2. The concept of freedom was changed to recognize that the state might have to curb some liberties in order to provide a higher standard of living for the least well-off in society.

3.   Reform liberals abandoned laissez-faire capitalism to accept the teaching of economist John Maynard Keynes (1883–1946) who argued in the 1930s that reliance on market forces could result in a permanent economic depression.

Reform liberals reconciled state action with their notion of individual freedom by arguing that economic intervention was necessary to enable individuals to fulfil their desires and make the market work effectively. They maintained that the government must play a regulatory role in protecting society. The governments of Canada, Britain and the United States all followed this modern liberal reasoning after the Second World War.

Contemporary liberal values include respect for individual rights and freedoms, political equality, limited government, rule of law, minimum conditions of life guaranteed by the state and modified economic freedom. In other words, modern liberalism favours minimal government intervention in the private lives of citizens but reasonable government intervention in economic affairs.

All four parties in the Canadian House of Commons today espouse a kind of nineteenth century liberalism in their stress on the market's role in the regulation of economic life. None of them, however, has completely departed from all aspects of Keynesianism.

Conservatism

Conservatism as an ideology originally justified the positions of the aristocracy and church in the old order of European society. These elements of society resisted the liberal ideology of progressive social change and defended the *status quo*. They sought to conserve such elements as power, property, status and way of life. As it developed, this ideology took the term *conservative*, which comes from the Latin *conservare*, which means to save or preserve.

Irish scholar Edmund Burke (1729–1797) was the first major figure to define and clarify conservatism. Burke, along with other early conservatives, insisted that society must have a stable order and structure so that individuals will know their place in the community and live and work within those confines for the good of the whole. Change, they said, must be gradual. Burke believed that being a responsible member of society allowed an individual to achieve greater happiness than could be gained otherwise. Conservatives believed that it was not the individual but rather the social group that was more important. They accused liberals of being individualistic and selfish.

Whereas classical liberals were suspicious of state power and wanted to limit it, conservatives believed that state power was necessary in order to achieve social order. Burke therefore, for example, opposed extending the right to vote and defended the hereditary aristocracy and established church. However, he viewed such power as including a responsibility to help the weak and less fortunate. In this way, conservatives were able to argue that their approach was better for the less fortunate of society than that of the liberals who believed that everyone, including the poor, should be free to look after themselves. Burke and the early conservatives shared many views about the functioning of the market and economics with Adam Smith and the classical liberals.

Like liberalism, conservatism adapted and changed. After the Second World War, when the old social order had been destroyed in Europe, conservatives gave qualified acceptance to the notion of the welfare state, but they still sought to preserve traditional moral values and a social structure that would provide leadership for society. European conservatism was never a strong part of American culture because the United States was founded and populated largely by liberals. There was no aristocracy or "old order" to defend. However, in the 1930s, those who opposed the welfare-state philosophy of modern liberalism adopted the conservative label.

American conservatism thus stresses individualism, self-reliance and a dislike for state interference, and it views the improvement of the human condition as the inevitable outcome of unrestricted interaction among self-interested individuals — in other words, they are similar to old-style liberals. European conservatism, on the other hand, ranks order and the common good of the community above individual freedom. The former Progressive Conservative party espoused both the traditional and American ideas about conservatism at various times in its history, while the Reform/Alliance parties essentially adopted the philosophy of US conservatism. The Conservative Party of Canada appears to be following the same trajectory (see Chapter 10, "Parties and Interest Groups").

Socialism

Within the first few decades of the nineteenth century, the technological advances of the Industrial Revolution in Europe created a large urban working class that existed in wretched conditions. Socialists sought to ameliorate the lot of these workers by challenging the liberal idea that governments should not be involved in directing the economy of the country. Socialism championed public ownership, a planned economy, and state intervention in market forces. Workers wanted help from a progressive state, but classical liberalism held that the economy should be as free as possible of government control.

In the early years, socialism offered two versions of its doctrine: the *utopian* version found in Britain and France, and the *scientific* version of Karl Marx in Germany. The scientific socialists, led by Marx (1818–1883), dominated socialist thought by the end of the century. Within this group, however, a doctrinal split emerged. Those who wanted to work within the framework of parliamentary democracy became known as *democratic socialists*. Those who clung to the Marxist revolutionary prescription came under the label of *communist*. Both groups sought public control of the means of production and an end to the exploitation of labour under capitalism. However, communism went much further, to promise equalization of material conditions for everyone.

Even before the breakdown of communism in the Soviet Union in 1991, there were significant changes to socialist thought. In Britain, nationalizing industries was no longer a key component of socialist doctrine.[5] In 1995, Clause 4 of the British Labour party constitution (which called for nationalizing industries) was deleted — marking a major turning point in the development of socialism in political parties. Since then, the Labour party has espoused a completely diluted socialism — or not socialism at all, according to many commentators. In Canada, aspects of the socialist doctrine appear regularly in New

Democratic Party debates. On the whole, however, the party under Ed Broadbent (1975–1989) relaxed its relatively strict adherence to the socialist doctrine and has not returned to these ideological roots under subsequent leaders.

Ideology in Action   Ideas derived from these main ideologies, and others such as nationalism and populism, have been taken up by political parties in Canada over the years with varying degrees of ardour and tenacity. There are two main schools of academic thought concerning ideology in Canadian political parties.

The first school maintains that there have been no fundamental ideological differences between the Liberal and Conservative/Progressive Conservative parties over the years. As brokerage parties, both put vote-getting ahead of ideology and pragmatically and opportunistically followed public opinion polls in setting their agendas — rather like Tweedledum and Tweedledee — and even the NDP aspires to brokerage-type policies and actions.

The second academic school says that the Liberal and Conservative parties both vied for the centre ground on issues but still maintained relatively consistent and distinguishable policy differences. For example, Liberals after 1900 were more sympathetic to Québec and French-Canadian interests; Progressive Conservatives after 1957 were more sympathetic to Western interests. For many years Liberals favoured lower tariffs, Conservatives higher tariffs. Liberals supported free trade, while the PCs objected to it. Liberals supported provincial rights, Conservatives advocated strong central government. Clearly, such patterns did exist for specific periods of time, but it is not possible to trace any of these distinctions consistently. In fact, the two major parties reversed themselves on all of these positions throughout the whole twentieth century, especially on tariffs and free trade with the United States in 1988.

Each of these schools of thought is partially correct. Liberal values, based on a belief in a capitalist society, a market economy and the right to private property, are dominant in Canadian society but not to the absolute exclusion of other perspectives. The main parties from Confederation until 1993 — the Conservative, Liberal and New Democratic parties — reflected the broad ideological differences of conservatism, liberalism and socialism but never strayed very far from the "liberal" opinions of the broader public.

Age Stratification

Age divides Canadians into groups with vastly different political interests and issues. Canada's population is aging rapidly, and this has major social and economic implications. In 1881, the median age was 20; by 2001 it was 37, an all-time high. The population is aging rapidly. Largely because of a low fertility rate, the percentage of Canadians over 65 years of age is projected to reach 16 percent by 2016. If the trend continues, by 2041, just under 23 percent of Canadians will be over 65. At the same time, the proportion under 18 will shrink from 25 percent to 19 percent. "Grey Power" will be prevalent in all walks of life.

Such an age imbalance increases financial pressures on working Canadians and raises questions about how best to support the elderly. The demands that are made on government reflect this shifting age stratification. The federal government has already begun to force an increase in contributions to the Canada Pension Plan and to cut benefits. Will it go even further and push back the age at which people are entitled to public pensions from age 65 to 68 or 70?

With the country's current low birth rate of 1.4 births per female and an aging population, governments will have to decide if they should take in more immigrants to balance the effect of the low birth rate.

Gender Stratification

Gender too divides Canadians into groups with different political interests. Today, females make up slightly more than half the population. Males and females share many political values and goals, but there are also significant differences that separate them. The two groups differ greatly in the extent to which they participate and are represented in the country's politics and also in the political issues that concern them.

Throughout history, women around the world have often been treated as inferior to men. Discrimination was enforced by social customs and laws.

CLOSE-UP — Two Issues Vital to Canada's Young People: Social Security and Education

(1) The government's plan for social security policies will have a great impact on today's young people. As older people retire, a bigger economic burden falls on the remaining workers. Government policy will determine how many people you will have to support when you are in the labour force and what proportion of your taxes will go toward supporting seniors. In the future, will older people be required to work — and pay taxes — for longer before they begin drawing pensions? What social security benefits will today's young people have when they are retirement age?

(2) As one of Canada's young people, are you getting the best start you can in life from a good education? Are tuition fees affordable? Are quality courses being offered? Are standards being kept high enough to make Canadians competitive in the global workforce?

Education is particularly vital because it is the primary means by which people achieve upward mobility and escape from poverty. A university education does not guarantee financial success, but it certainly improves the odds. Adult Canadians who have a post-secondary degree or diploma earn approximately 40–45 percent more income than those who have not achieved this educational standard (see Figure 2.1).

Education, together with occupation and income, is also a principal determinant of social status. It increases political interest and awareness, expands opportunities and develops the political skills necessary for effective participation. Post-secondary education has almost become a necessity for holding high public office.

As well as directing students toward particular roles and class positions in society, educational institutions teach relevant facts, values, predispositions and skills. They are the main community facility in which immigrant children learn one or both official languages and acquire basic citizenship training. Recent research indicates that education establishes a receptivity to acquire further knowledge long after formal education has terminated."[6]

Canadians have more education than ever and are staying in school longer. They are among the most highly educated in the world and perform well on international tests. Forty-one percent of Canadians aged 25–64 had post-secondary education in 2001; over 20 percent had a university degree. Canada ranks highest in post-secondary education attainment among the OECD countries but drops to fifth in the proportion of those with university education. Gender bias in educational institutions has greatly diminished. Women accounted for much of the increase in university graduates from 1971 to 1996, and are now over 50 percent in that category.

Figure 2.1 Employment Growth by Level of Educational Attainment, 1990–2003

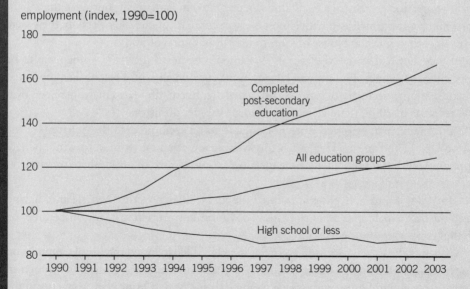

Source: Employment Growth by Level of Educational Attainment, 1990–2003. Adapted from Statistics Canada's Labour Force Survey.

At the beginning of the twentieth century, married women in Canada were still considered to belong to their husbands. Younger women were just beginning to enter universities, medical schools and law schools. Some were fighting for the right to make contracts, own property and work outside the home. Women were assigned, and generally accepted, primary responsibility for children and the family, while men worked outside the home. Initially, they were barred from such societal participation as owning property, holding public office, voting and even higher education.

When women began organizing to press for reforms on issues that concerned them, their impact on policy issues was limited. They were not even allowed to vote for their political representatives. Politics was the prerogative of relatively well-to-do males. Only slowly over time did women of different regions, religions, economic status and backgrounds begin to come together to express what could be identified as women's issues and women's politics. There is still little unanimity among women on many political, social and other issues.

In 1916, Manitoba, Saskatchewan and Alberta were the first provinces to allow women to vote, followed by Ontario and British Columbia. Soon, all the other provinces followed suit except Québec, where women were not enfranchised until 1940. Federally, women in the armed services voted in 1917, as did designated female relatives of soldiers who were abroad. A year later, all Canadian women were given the right to vote, though they did not have the chance to exercise it until 1921.

The 1921 election also brought the first woman, Agnes Macphail, to the House of Commons. Politics was still very much a male profession, however. It was difficult for women to participate in an occupation that required them to be far from home much of the time. They worked in parties but generally in affiliated auxiliaries rather than in the mainstream. Today, women are still under-represented in Parliament, but since the 1970s, their numbers have increased with almost every election. As of the 2004 election, there were sixty-five women in the House of Commons out of a total of 308.

Once they had achieved places in Parliament, the next hurdle for women was to be appointed to Cabinet. This did not happen until 1957 when John Diefenbaker appointed Ellen Fairclough secretary of state. Again, female representation has slowly increased over the years. As of 2005, there were twelve female cabinet ministers.

For many years, women were not eligible to be appointed to the Senate (see the Close-Up, "The Famous Five"). Carine Wilson was the first woman to win a Senate appointment, but it took a long time for more to join her. As of 2005, there were thirty-six senators out of a total of 105.

In 1984, Jeanne Sauvé was appointed the first woman governor general after having been the first female speaker of the House of Commons. Adrienne Clarkson became the second female governor general in 1999.

Much of the impetus for women's gains in political life followed the Royal Commission on the Status of Women. Its report in 1970 was a landmark for Canadian women in providing facts and figures with which to argue their case and bring their concerns to the political arena. Special institutions followed: in 1972, the Office of Employment Opportunity and the National Action Committee on the Status of Women (NAC); in

The Famous Five

In December 1997, MPs voted to erect statues on Parliament Hill in Ottawa honouring the Famous Five — a group of women led by Emily Murphy. The group consisted of Alberta women who, in the late 1920s, challenged the legal definition of the word *persons*, which at the time included only men. Ms. Murphy's associates were Nellie McClung, Henrietta Muir Edwards, Louise McKinney and Irene Parlby.

In 1929, the Supreme Court ruled that women were not "persons," and were therefore ineligible to be appointed to the Senate. The women appealed this ruling to Britain's Privy Council, then the highest court for Canada. The women won, and *persons* was redefined to include both women and men. Women were finally allowed to participate in the political process by such means as running for office or accepting a Senate appointment.

The statues ensure that the women are recognized for their contribution, along with monarchs, dead prime ministers and the Fathers of Confederation — the only individuals so far to have been awarded statues on the Hill.

1973, the Canadian Advisory Council on the Status of Women (CACSW) — government appointees who advise the minister responsible for women's concerns; and in 1982, the first federal–provincial conference on women's issues. During the 1970s, the term *feminist* began to be commonly used to describe those who sought gender equality and an end to the subordination of women. Similar ideas were gaining ground in other countries, and the women's movement became an active and widespread expression of women's interests reaching across state borders.

Today, women are better educated, work more outside the home, enjoy a wider variety of job possibilities, and have greater social and political equality and legal rights than ever before. With their increased participation in the workforce, women have brought new issues to the government's policy agenda; these include affirmative action, legal equality rights, equal access to opportunities, pay equity, sexual harassment, pornography, abortion rights and child care.

In Canada today, many groups advance women's causes. NAC is an umbrella lobbying group for about 580 local and national member groups representing roughly three million women. It is active, especially in rights-related questions. It has fought to ensure that (1) equality rights are inviolable; (2) equality rights are clearly articulated in terms relevant to the needs of women; and (3) that affirmative action should be more clearly and positively entrenched in the *Charter of Rights and Freedoms*.

Canadian women do not speak with one voice. However, the women's movement in Canada has raised the awareness of the position of women in various aspects of society, changed attitudes and introduced many issues into the policy agendas of political parties.

It has not tried to create a party itself but has improved legislation concerning women and promoted attitudinal changes concerning participation.

Women's Key Issues Today *Poverty and Child Care:* One-parent families (more than 80 percent of which are headed by women) are among the worst-off in Canada. They desperately require government help, and so do single persons over 65, who have the lowest incomes of any group over 24 years of age. Policies that could help single-parent families headed by women include higher minimum wages, improved job training, literacy programs, employment equity and available, affordable daycare.

Employment: In 1901, only 13 percent of Canadian women worked outside the home. By 1996, nearly 83 percent did so.[7] Women now account for over 45 percent of the Canadian labour force, yet many of those women earn less money than men. Job opportunities for women are improving. There are dramatically more women in several professional occupations such as doctors, dentists, pharmacists, university professors and lawyers. Policies that would help women in the employment sector include job security, benefits and more convenient hours of work. Governments have not yet been able to place a value on unpaid labour such as housework, care-giving and volunteer work that preoccupies women much more than men. This work makes a major contribution to the economy but never shows up in official statistics or in tax or other credits for women.

Equality Rights: Women lobbied hard to have gender equality protected in the 1982 *Charter of Rights and Freedoms.* Without this clause, legislatures would have been able to override new rights for women by using the notwithstanding clause. After the Charter, feminists continued to challenge laws that they considered discriminatory against them. Women's groups are also vigilant to address how any new constitutional and policy proposals will affect women's rights. They were quick, for example, to support Native women in their quest to ensure that aboriginal and treaty rights were guaranteed equally in the Constitution to male and female persons.

Abortion, Sexuality and Assault Issues: There is an ongoing assortment of issues that concern women but on which there is no clear consensus. For three decades, feminists have sought to ensure that women be able to control what happens to their own bodies. Others reject abortion rights. Pornography and prostitution issues are other concerns, but again, there is no agreement over whether governments should limit freedom of expression and the right to work as one chooses. Sexual assault, sexual harassment and family violence are other ongoing issues.

Class Stratification

Defining *class* is controversial and problematic. **Class** refers to socio-economic status and/or a rank or order in society determined by such characteristics as education, occupation and income. These characteristics provide "objective" indicators, which are sometimes different from "subjective" or self-assigned rankings.

Class divisions based on wealth and income remain significant in Canada. A tiny elite, or *upper class*, of about three percent of the population holds the top positions in business, industry, the professional ranks and the bureaucracy. The extensive wealth of these very few individuals and families in real estate, natural resources, communications and various commercial enterprises, especially large corporations, set them far apart from other Canadians.

The vast majority of Canadians today are part of the huge *middle class* — over 80 percent of the population — sandwiched between the tiny economic elite and roughly 16 percent of the population who are economically deprived. The shape of the economic hierarchy, therefore, is not a pyramid; it is shaped more like a bulging onion.

The Canadian middle class is extremely heterogeneous in terms of income, occupation and lifestyle. It can be subdivided into upper-middle and lower-middle class. The upper-middle tier is extremely varied — generally well educated and financially secure. It does not function as a single unit but has different economic interests and political demands. It includes groups such as lawyers, doctors and business people.

The lower-middle class, or working class, is generally considered to consist of those who do manual as opposed to intellectual work. As a whole, this group is less educated and generally earns less money than others in the middle class. Despite the fact that some of them are unionized, changes in the Canadian economy in the 1980s and 1990s dramatically increased unemployment in this group. The proportion of blue-collar jobs in the workforce increased only marginally, while unskilled and primary labour jobs in fishing, mining and agricultural jobs declined sharply. These job losses, combined with inflation and increased taxation, made individuals in this stratum particularly vulnerable to dropping into the lowest grouping of economically deprived Canadians.[8]

The poor in Canada are considered to be those who exist below the *poverty line*, a theoretical line set by Statistics Canada. Depending on the definition of the poverty line, about four to five million Canadians are poor. In 1999, nearly five million people — over 16 percent of the population — were living on or below the poverty line.[9] It included those who spent more than 70 percent of their income on food, shelter and clothing.[10]

Among those worst-off in Canadian society are one-parent families; the young, of whom more than a million are children under 16 years of age (an astounding 20 percent of all Canadian children); the single elderly (who are mostly widows); and Native people. Women are disproportionately represented among the poorest in Canadian society, particularly elderly women and single mothers. In 2001, there were 1.3 million single-parent families (see Table 2.1 on page 36). Women headed 81 percent of these families, and the majority were impoverished. Roughly one-third of all visible-minority women and Native women were also in the low-income category. Poverty brings fewer educational opportunities, higher mortality rates, more physical and mental illness, poorer, more hazardous working conditions, higher crime rates, and higher suicide and divorce rates.[11]

Unequal opportunity and poor distribution of wealth have significant implications for politics in Canada. There is no doubt that the economic elite exercises considerable influence in the development of the country. On the other hand, it is far from a ruling class.

CLOSE-UP   Child Poverty

Canada is one of the worst of the world's wealthiest nations when it comes to treating children well. A UNICEF report in 2005 ranked Canada nineteenth among twenty-six well-to-do countries. It showed that Canada had not improved in this regard from the first study in 2000. In the 1990s, governments cut social spending in order to balance budgets, and spending on children was seriously affected for the worse. However, when budgets moved into surplus situations, money was directed more to health care and pensions.

Children are one of the most vulnerable groups in society because they cannot speak out for themselves and make demands on governments. Who is responsible for this situation, and what can be done about it?

Political power in Canada is diffused downward at least to the middle class.[12] The political decision-making process is extremely complex and virtually precludes control by one small group. Governments must maintain popular support, and this puts considerable power in the hands of the majority of Canadian voters.

Unfortunately, members of the lowest socio-economic stratum participate the least in the political system, preoccupied as they are with questions of basic survival. A wide range of federal, provincial and municipal welfare programs exists to help them. However, they tend to be scaled back or cut when governments are having trouble balancing their budgets or when governments are ideologically inclined to do so. In the late 1990s in particular, cuts in areas such as home care affected many of the most vulnerable Canadians — seniors living in poverty (mostly women) and people with disabilities.

Table 2.1 Numbers of Canadians by Age and Sex Living in Poverty, 1990 and 1999

	Number of persons in low income/poverty	
	1990	1999
All persons	4,181,000	4,886,000
Children under 18 years	1,195,000	1,298,000
18 to 64	2,357,000	2,942,000
65 and over	629,000	646,000
Males	1,799,000	2,187,000
65 and over	173,000	159,000
Females	2,382,000	2,699,000
65 and over	456,000	487,000

Source: The Canadian Council on Social Development. Available online at www.ccsd.ca/factsheets/fs_pov9099.htm. Accessed September 8, 2004.

Welfare programs are particularly important when unemployment is high. Since 2000, unemployment has hovered around 6–7 percent and has been even higher among youth (see the "Youth Unemployment" Close-Up). The unemployment rate may actually be much higher because many get discouraged and give up looking for employment (and therefore they do not show up in the statistics), or they work at part-time jobs because that is all they can find. Unemployment insurance was introduced in 1941. Renamed "employment insurance" in 1996, it has been made steadily more restrictive since 1989.

CLOSE-UP   Youth Unemployment

Youth unemployment for those 15–24 years of age is approximately double that for Canadians as a whole. In 2003, it was 13.8 percent. As usual, it was particularly high in the Maritime provinces — in Newfoundland and Labrador, it was 24 percent; Prince Edward Island 14.9; New Brunswick 17; Nova Scotia 16.2. Recessions tend to worsen the unemployment rate among youths relative to adults for non-student males while improving it for students.[13]

What can and should governments do about this situation? What can youth do to protect themselves given these circumstances?

Ethnicity and Language

Behind the veneer of Canada's national political culture, there are many political subcultures. Cultural pluralism is encouraged by a number of factors, including the size of the country, different ethnic groups, a sparse and dispersed population and the federal system of government. Among the most significant subcultures are ethnic groups. Ethnicity is primarily a subjective phenomenon, although it is often reinforced by different customs, language, dialect and cultural heritage and sometimes distinct racial or physical characteristics. **Ethnic origin** refers to the ethnic or cultural group(s) to which an individual's ancestors belonged; it pertains to the ancestral roots or origins of the population and not to place of birth, citizenship or nationality.

There are three major ethno-linguistic groupings in Canada: the two founding European nations, French and English, and Native people. The English-speaking majority today is culturally very diverse and becoming more so every year. The French live mostly in Québec but are found in smaller numbers dispersed throughout the country, particularly in New Brunswick, Ontario and Manitoba. The third group includes various groupings of Native people. We consider each group in turn as well as a fourth group, visible minorities, that is growing rapidly.

French-Speaking Canadians

As of 2001, 22.9 percent of Canadians claimed French as their mother tongue. Of these, 81 percent were concentrated in Québec. Their relations with English-speaking Canadians have been characterized by long periods of relative tranquility punctuated by harsh conflicts.

A brief history of the development of the province of Québec is necessary to understand French-Canadian beliefs and attitudes today. From 1663 on, the political development of the colony of New France was dominated by French-style absolutism, modified somewhat by circumstances in the New World. Following the British conquest and the Treaty of Paris, which formally gave up the French colony to Britain in 1763, most merchants and officials returned to France, and the forces for modernization were cut off. Isolated from the turmoil of the French Revolution, the culture of New France was enveloped and preserved by the few remaining institutions: the Roman Catholic church, French language, civil law and the feudal landholding system.

From this inheritance emerged a distinctive political subculture, the most visible characteristics of which are the French language, a civil law code unique in Canada, and traditions, myths and heroes based on early Québec history. The fear of assimilation that permeates politics in Québec, because of the minority status of francophones in Canada as a whole, is also the result of this early history.

Je me souviens.

(Québec's official motto since 1883)

One fundamental difference between the French and English in Canada lies in the understanding of the term *nation*. To French Canadians, the word means *people* or *society*. To many English Canadians, it means *nation-state*, the combined people of a country. Francophones tend to see Canada as two distinct nations or societies, one French-speaking and the other English-speaking. For them, these two societies are qualitatively equal in every way, and the Canadian Constitution should grant special status to francophones both within federal political institutions and also in the province of Québec.[14] Thus, while many anglophone Canadians view Canada as one nation, with an enclave of French Canadians in Québec, francophones have a dualistic conception of a political system composed of Québec and "the rest of the country."

This conception of Québec as a separate nation can be traced through the history of the province. In 1867, the Fathers of Confederation created a union giving Canada every power a country needed to thrive. Georges-Étienne Cartier, who negotiated for Québec, supported this vision. He saw it as the responsibility of the provinces to preserve what he called "cultural nations" — cultures imported from England, Ireland, Scotland and pre-revolutionary France. After Cartier's death, however, his Québec critics began to claim that Confederation was really a "compact" between French and English nations. This myth flourished and continues to thrive in Québec. The **compact theory of Confederation** nourishes the notion of "two founding nations," and continues to provide French Canadians with a claim to equality rather than simple minority status within Canada. The word *compact* also provides a basis for claims that Québec has a right to withdraw from the original bargain.

Whether Canada is one nation or two is obviously a matter of definition; however, different popular usage of the word *nation* regularly causes friction between French- and English-speaking Canadians.

It is generally accepted today that the Confederation arrangement was an implicit bargain between French and English to create one strong political unit, a country that would protect the rights and assist the advancement of two culturally diverse peoples. Both English- and French-language communities were to be protected. From the outset in Québec, both English and French were legal languages in the legislature and courts. However, in the other provinces, the practice until the 1940s was for English-speaking Canadians, wherever they were in the majority, to deprive French-speaking Canadian minorities of public-school facilities in their native language and to refuse them the use of their language in government institutions.

Several historical crises marked the breakdown of goodwill between the English and French in Canada, causing frustration and eventually separatist movements. French Canadians find in these events the emotional justification to defend themselves as a distinct, culturally equal minority in Canada (discussed in Chapters 3 and 5).[15] The most recent such occurrence was the patriation of the Constitution in 1982 without Québec's agreement. Today, the Parti Québécois and the Bloc Québécois, because of a history of conflicts with the federal government, seek Québec's separation from Canada and the foundation of an independent, sovereign Québec (see Chapter 5).

English-Speaking Canadians

In direct contrast to the feudal traditions in New France, Canadian anglophone society, from the beginning, was open to outside influences. Among the early inhabitants of the northern British colonies were United Empire Loyalists fleeing the American Revolution. Their numbers soon surpassed the fewer than 15 000 English colonists already in Canada. The Loyalists brought with them many attitudes still prevalent in English-Canadian society: some aspects of the liberal American tradition but also anti-American sentiments and a corresponding loyalty to the British Crown.

Over the years, the composition of the "English-speaking" element of Canadian society has changed dramatically from its origins of primarily British immigrants. English- speaking Canadians now encompass individuals from over one hundred different ethnic groups, including four million persons categorized as *visible minorities* (see Table 2.2 on page 40).

Ontario is by far the largest centre for nearly all ethnic groups, followed by British Columbia, Alberta and Manitoba. Almost one-quarter of Ontario's population is comprised of immigrants. At the other extreme is Newfoundland and Labrador, where fewer than 2 percent are immigrants.

Because of ethnic diversity, Canadians have "layered" cultures. When immigrants choose Canada, they learn to speak English or French and the cultural layering begins. The United States is often viewed metaphorically as a "melting pot" because it was built through shared experiences and commitment to similar political values. Canada, on the other hand, can be seen more as a "fruitcake" or a tapestry because separate parts of the whole are so distinct. The Canadian ideal has been to encourage different cultures to exist side by side in harmony and tolerance. As the flow of immigrants to Canada continues, the challenge will be to maintain a balance between national unity and respect for diversity as part of Canadian political culture.

Table 2.2 Origins of 1.8 Million Immigrants to Canada, 1991-2001

Source	Percent
Asia and the Middle East	58
Europe	20
Caribbean and Central America	11
Africa	8
United States	3

Source: Statistics Canada, "Canada's Ethnocultural Portrait"; Catalogue 96F0030X1E2001008. Available at www.statcan.ca.

During a high immigration period in the later 1940s and the 1950s, cultural pluralism, or multiculturalism, gained popularity in the country. **Multiculturalism** means that ethnic customs and cultures should be valued, preserved and shared within the context of Canadian citizenship and economic and political integration. In the early 1970s, the federal government formally adopted a policy of multiculturalism. It defined Canada as being multicultural within a bilingual English–French framework. The *Multiculturalism Act* was passed in 1988 to assist ethnic groups that want to maintain their identity and that encouraged the sharing of these features with all Canadians.

By 1978, the new multicultural policies were reflected in a more liberal *Immigration Act*, which declared that immigration policy would be based on principles of non-discrimination, family reunion, humanitarian concern for refugees and promotion of national goals.[16] An average of roughly 235 000 immigrants were admitted to Canada each year from 1990 to 1995, peaking at 256 000 in 1993. In 2004, some 220 000 immigrants and refugees entered Canada. Almost 75 percent of them came from Asia, Africa, Latin America and the Caribbean. Today, European-born immigrants continue to account for the largest proportion of all immigrants living in Canada, but their percentage is shrinking. They constitute less than half of the total immigrant population, while 31 percent are born in Asia and the Middle East.

In recent years, multiculturalism has come under considerable criticism. French-speaking Canadians tend to resent it because they fear it will undermine their place as one of the two founding nations. Others argue that multicultural policies perpetuate the stratification of Canadian society and decrease social and economic mobility. Still other critics contend that by supporting ethnic differences, the government divides Canadians, encouraging immigrants to separate themselves from mainstream culture.[17]

The existence of significant subcultures within a country can be disruptive to the dominant political culture if group ties are stronger than loyalty to the country. In extreme situations, ethnic crises can raise doubts about the efficacy of governments and even about whether the country should stay united. However, such crises are not the norm in Canada.

Regional societal differences are relatively minor in terms of cultural criteria such as dress, cuisine, dialect and broadly shared values. Many studies show that immigrants to Canada assimilate relatively quickly into mainstream society.[18] Our differences shrink beside our similarities.

Optimism about the multi-ethnic nature of Canadian society is supported by research that shows multiculturalism is a strengthening feature of Canadian unity. David Elkins concluded that ignorance of one's own and other nations is associated with parochial, localist sentiments, while knowledge about and appreciation of other nations is an enriching experience that encourages individuals to feel warmer toward their own country.[19]

The Canadian commitment to cultural diversity unites Canadians by helping to combat two threats: American cultural domination and threats of separation by any province or region. Some social science research indicates that multiculturalism is not to be feared, but encouraged, if it is interpreted as is intended — that is, as encouraging those members of ethnic groups "to maintain a proud sense of the contribution of their own group to Canadian society."[20] In this interpretation, multiculturalism is voluntary, marginal differentiation among peoples who are equal participants in one country. It implies moderation — a middle ground — between melting pot assimilation and limitless ethnic division. The formal adoption of bilingual and multicultural policies by the government enshrines ethnic tolerance among the other important values of Canadian political culture. It means that an individual can have more than one cultural identity and still be Canadian. Canada is not like a blanket — one piece of unbroken cloth, the same size, colour and texture. The tapestry metaphor for the country holds true: a rainbow of interwoven colours, held together by a common thread. Canadians are strengthened, not impoverished, by their plural identities.

Visible Minorities

As of 2001, almost four million Canadians were members of visible minority groups — nearly 14 percent of the total population, up from 9.4 percent in 1991 (see Figure 2.2 on page 42). The *Employment Equity Act* defines **visible minorities** as "persons other than aboriginal peoples, who are non-Caucasian in race or non-white in colour." Their percentage is growing quickly — 25 percent between 1996 and 2001 — while the total population grew by just 4 percent. In 2001, Chinese constituted the largest visible minority group, surpassing one million for the first time. Along with South Asians and blacks, they accounted for two-thirds of the visible minority population.

More than half of Canada's visible minorities live in Ontario and British Columbia. In 2001, they formed 36.9 percent of Vancouver's total population, 36.8 percent of Toronto's and 13.6 percent of Montréal's. Vancouver's visible minority population is almost entirely Asian.[21]

In spite of Canada's integrative and pluralist model, ethnic cleavages persist. Ethnic visible minorities tend to integrate less easily into Canadian society than do white European immigrants. In part, this is because they struggle against racist attitudes in the population. **Racial discrimination** is the imposition of handicaps, barriers and different treatment for individuals because of their race. It is fed by prejudice and negative stereotypes. It creates

Figure 2.2 Percentage of Visible Minorities, Canada, 1981–2001

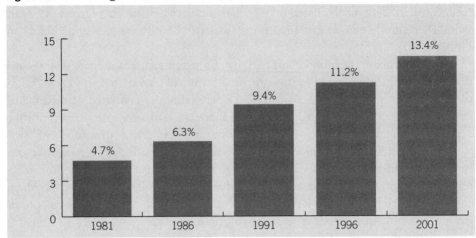

Source: From the Statistics Canada publication "Canada's Ethnocultural Portrait: The Changing Mosaic, 2001 Census"; Catalogue 96F0030, January 21, 2003, available on the Statistics Canada website: http://www12.statcan.ca/english/census01/Products/Analytic/companion/etoimm/charts/canada/vismin.cfm

a vicious cycle in which mainstream society is fearful and suspicious and the minority group is withdrawn and defensive. Often minority groups become concentrated in specific neighbourhoods or geographical areas, and this tends to reinforce their social and ethnic differences.

Institutional discrimination creates an additional hurdle for visible minorities, manifesting itself in high levels of unemployment and exclusion from certain sectors of the economy. Incidents of racial bigotry in Canadian history include the shameful internment of Japanese Canadians during the Second World War and the often-shabby treatment of Native people. Racist ideologies are condemned but still persist.[22]

On the other hand, there is evidence that such incidents are more the exception than the rule. In 2002, a government survey on ethnic diversity asked people whether they had been discriminated against or treated unfairly in Canada in the past five years because of their ethnicity, culture, race, skin colour, language, accent or religion. Amazingly, 93 percent said they had never, or rarely, experienced discrimination or unfair treatment for these reasons. Only 5 percent of visible minorities said they had been discriminated against or treated unfairly sometimes or often.[23]

Since the 1980s, systemic discrimination has been studied and addressed by public policy solutions. The problem has not, however, been eliminated. It is clear that attitudinal changes need to be continually addressed to foster awareness, understanding and tolerance — particularly since Canadians must anticipate an even greater racial mix in the population in the years to come. As noted in a recent Statistics Canada report, "if current trends hold, one in every five faces will be non-white in 12 years when Canadians mark the 150th anniversary of Confederation."[24]

Native People

Another ethno-linguistic division lies between Canada's Native people — including Inuit, status and non-status Indians and Métis — and other Canadians. In 2001, nearly one million Canadians claimed aboriginal ancestry (see Table 2.3). Altogether, they constitute roughly 4 percent of the Canadian population. The aboriginal groups are distinctive, but they are all descendants of Canada's first inhabitants. They share a long history with non-Natives and their governments. For many decades, this relationship was fraught with injustices related to land and a lack of respect for aboriginal values and the traditional ways of Native life. Today, issues emanating from that relationship form the basis of many grievances that include historical maltreatment, lack of respect and understanding of Native cultural heritage and territorial and economic deprivation.

Aboriginal people have many different values than mainstream Canadians because of their unique history in a hunting-and-gathering economy. Their values tend to be collectivist, based on an organic concept of community where individuals are a specialized part of a whole society. Decision-making is generally consensual, not majoritarian. Traditional leadership tends to be diffuse, with different leaders in different areas of specialization.

The Royal Proclamation of 1763, which outlined the territory acquired by Britain from France, clearly defined Indian rights. Unfortunately, they were generally ignored. After Confederation, the federal Parliament was assigned legislative jurisdiction over Indians and the lands reserved for them.[25] Shortly thereafter, Parliament passed legislation designed to assimilate Natives.

The term *Indian* was legally defined in the first *Indian Act* in 1876. This Act aimed to suppress Indian traditions and extend government control over status Indians on reserves and, to a lesser degree, off reserves. Although it was amended many times, the current Act, passed in 1951, remains an essentially nineteenth-century statute that still reflects these early biases and intentions.

The Inuit in Canada, scattered throughout the Arctic in eight distinct communities, were never subject to the *Indian Act* and were largely ignored by government until 1939 when they officially became a federal responsibility. Since then, they have been classified as "Indians" for the purposes of the Constitution.

The *Indian Act* was intended to protect Native peoples within Canadian society by providing a range of social programs. All Indians receive the same benefits as other

Table 2.3 Aboriginal Identity Population, Canada, 2001

*Aboriginal Population	North American Indian	Métis	Inuit
976 305	608 850	292 305	45 070

* 20 percent sample data. Includes multiple Aboriginal responses and Aboriginal responses not included elsewhere.
Source: Statistics Canada 2001 Census data.
Data is presented in two online reports: Canada's Ethnocultural Portrait: The Changing Mosaic, and Aboriginal Peoples of Canada: A Demographic Profile, both available at Statistics Canada's website (www.statcan.ca).

Canadians, such as family allowances and pensions, and status Indians also have a right to a wide variety of benefits in the field of taxation, education, health care and housing. However, such assistance often has left these people in a state of dependency on government.

Most Indians live in abysmal social conditions. In 1994, the rate of tuberculosis was found to be 43 times higher among status Indians than among non-aboriginal Canadians born in this country. [26] One in five Indian reserves has water and sewage problems comparable to the worst of Third World countries. [27] The rate of population growth of Native Indians is well over twice that of the rest of Canadians. Approximately 40 percent are between the ages of 15 and 35, compared to 35 percent for the total Canadian population. Alcoholism and depression plague many Native Canadians as they strive to cope with the loss of their traditional lifestyle. The Inuit, because of their northern location, have been largely bypassed by economic and political modernization — notwithstanding the creation of Nunavut.

In late 1996, the Royal Commission on Aboriginal Peoples delivered a five-volume report with over four hundred recommendations, which, in essence, said that the relationship between Aboriginals and non-Aboriginals in Canada should "be restructured fundamentally." Some of those recommendations proposed radical changes such as setting up a new, third level of government. The Liberal government essentially said that the estimated $30 billion cost of the proposals was too great, and in 1997 adapted the Royal Commission's recommendations to four basic principles: renewing the partnerships; strengthening aboriginal governance; developing a new fiscal relationship; and supporting strong communities, people and economies.

When Paul Martin first became prime minister, he made aboriginal issues a declared priority. He established a Cabinet committee on aboriginal affairs, chaired by himself, and set up a new aboriginal affairs secretariat within the Privy Council Office to assist him as chair of the Cabinet committee. At his first meeting with aboriginal leaders, the prime minister offered them no new money but promised to include them more closely in government decisions affecting their futures. One proposal, for example, is that aboriginal representatives could sit on the aboriginal affairs committee and perhaps be included in First Ministers' Conferences.

Studies of demographic trends, social conditions and economic prospects for Canada's Native peoples for the years 1981 to 2001 indicate that while improvements are being made, the gap between them and their fellow Canadians will remain fairly wide and constant unless there are dramatic policy innovations.

Aboriginal Rights **Aboriginal rights** are based on Native occupancy and use of North American land before Europeans arrived. Traditional aboriginal societies were based primarily on hunting and gathering and, to a minor extent, agriculture. This relationship to the land therefore defines aboriginal culture and economy. They consider that land was put here by the Creator for the use of *all* people and, therefore, in aboriginal culture, belongs to everyone living today and to the unborn to come. It is not "owned."

Politically, Native peoples still occupy a dependent, semi-colonial position in regard to the federal and provincial governments. Proposals to end Indian status and repeal the

Indian Act have been called for by Natives struggling for greater recognition of their traditional rights, settlement of land claims and power to manage their own lands and affairs. Former grand chief of the Assembly of First Nations, Georges Erasmus, put the case this way: "we want to have a relationship with this country that is nation to nation" as expressed in the "two-row wampum" analogy of the Mohawks.

> The two-row wampum is an agreement whereby two nations coexist
> and travel the River of Life in peace and friendship. . . . Legally, it
> means that each of the two nations retains its own respective laws. [28]

The British Proclamation of 1763 recognized the rights of the Indian nations and provided that they could not be taken away without due process, i.e., a negotiated treaty. These obligations were passed on to Canada through the *BNA Act* (the *Constitution Act, 1867*). Section 35 of the *Constitution Act, 1982*, states, "The existing aboriginal and treaty rights of the aboriginal peoples are hereby recognized and affirmed." It gives the federal government exclusive jurisdiction over Indians and lands reserved for Indians (although today many non-status Indians, Métis and Inuit are subject to provincial laws). Clause 35 (3) affirms that "treaty rights" include "land claims agreements" now and in the future.

The Canadian Constitution therefore recognizes aboriginal and treaty rights, and the *Charter of Rights and Freedoms* (section 25) protects them in that aboriginal or treaty rights cannot be abrogated by anything in the Charter. This means that these rights are recognized and even protected without specifying exactly what they are. It is generally agreed, however, that they include rights to hunt and fish, harvest food and have access to and occupancy of land to conduct these activities. Courts have ruled that where previous treaty or land-claims agreements are not in place surrendering such rights, governments are bound by the Constitution to protect or compensate Aboriginals before they can sell the land or grant interest in it to third parties.

There is also a vague, general consensus that aboriginal peoples should be able to enjoy certain rights of self-government (seen, for example, in Native policing on reservations), but it is such a complicated area that courts have not ruled whether Native self-government, like territorial rights, is in fact an aboriginal right.

Land Claims and Other Land Issues Over the years, many treaties were signed giving North American Indians reserves in exchange for land. However, many of them were so blatantly unfair to the Indians that they are now being challenged in courts. In cases where reserves are inadequate for the resource needs of the aboriginal communities, it has been recognized that an expanded land base is required in order for the people to become economically self-sufficient. When no treaties were signed, aboriginal peoples, particularly the Métis, were left without land rights. Eventually, *aboriginal title* — the claim to land on the basis of traditional occupancy even when no treaty had been signed — was tested in the courts. In the 1973 Calder case, the Supreme Court recognized this concept.[29] Soon afterward, the federal government announced that it would negotiate aboriginal title where no treaties existed. This offer later included claims where treaties were signed but unjust.

Section 35 (3) of the *Constitution Act, 1982* clarifies that "treaty rights" include rights that now exist by way of land claims agreements or that may be so acquired. This means that land claims agreements are constitutionalized and cannot be changed at will by governments after they have been completed. There are, therefore, two kinds of land claims currently in process: *comprehensive claims* dealing with cases of aboriginal title not covered by treaty or other legal means and *specific claims* dealing with challenges to existing treaties.

In the North, where the federal government has legal jurisdiction over the land, claims have moved relatively quickly. By 1993, Canada's entire North above the sixtieth parallel was covered by final agreements or agreements in principle about land claims. The territory of Nunavut is inhabited almost solely by Inuit and has full government institutions equal to other territories or provinces. In Yukon, several First Nations have signed self-government and final land claims agreements with the federal and territorial governments.

Further south, where provincial governments are in control of public lands, progress is complicated by provincial jurisdiction, natural resource companies, and non-aboriginal settlements on disputed land. Claims have moved slowly. The main settlements to date have been in Québec and British Columbia.

Progress concerning land claims has been made in the courts. The Supreme Court has clarified aspects of land claim settlements, fishing and Métis rights. In 1997, for example, it ordered that oral history evidence be admissible in certain court cases. It also clarified that a group must establish its exclusive occupation of the land in question at the time the Crown asserted sovereignty. In 2002, the Supreme Court ruled that if Aboriginals can prove that their forebears honestly believed they had reserve lands set aside for them, but in fact did not, they still might have a legal case for their claim.

As of 2005, roughly half of more than six hundred status-Indian bands have not ceded their traditional territories by treaty with the Canadian government. They include the Indians of most of British Columbia, Québec, Northwest Territories and large parts of Yukon. They claim outstanding aboriginal rights over, and title to, their traditional lands, and have asserted historic rights to roughly half the country. In British Columbia, for example, overlapping claims by bands cover 110 percent of the provincial land mass.[30] In 2002, to help speed up the process of specific claims, a new claims commission was set up with the power to grant awards up to $7 million.

Self-Government Indian self-government is another broad, contentious and ongoing issue. Attempts to achieve constitutional recognition for self-government failed with the collapse of the Charlottetown Accord (see Chapter 5, "Nationalism and Regionalism"). According to some Native leaders, such rights should not even be defined in documents such as the Constitution because they are "inherent rights." The courts have never ruled whether there is an aboriginal right to self-government. In fact, there is no agreement about what self-government means. For some, it means a level of government roughly equivalent to a municipality within a province. For others, the First Nations should constitute a third order of government.

Under self-government, as conceived by recent federal governments, First Nations would remain subject to almost all federal and provincial laws and their powers would be only slightly greater than those of Canadian villages, towns or cities. However, some Native leaders maintain they cannot accept any imposition on the *inherent right* of their people to govern themselves.[31] They consider that their right to govern themselves is a pre-existing, continuing, natural right given to them by the Great Creator. It cannot be given or taken away by any government. They reason that they have never given up their right to self-government, and it has never been extinguished by any legislation (because such power could not exist). They are supported by courts and international law, which affirm that aboriginal rights may be extinguished only by treaty or conquest, or by an explicit act of the Parliament of Canada.

The federal *Indian Act* has long provided for limited local government on reserves through band councils. However, their jurisdictions are very narrow, and some communities want them to be much wider. Essentially, groups that desire self-government want control over areas such as the use of their land, community development, economic development, education, policing and so on. They have no interest in broader concerns such as foreign affairs or defence, or banking. However, many policy areas, such as health care and education, are under provincial or territorial jurisdiction, and agreements about funding and sharing of interests have to be reached not only with the federal authorities but also with these governments.

Once they are achieved, the only real way to protect self-government agreements is to conclude them as section 35 treaties, as is done with land claims, so that they have constitutional protection and can be amended only if both or all parties to the agreement give their consent. This procedure does not require constitutional change. In some cases, the federal government and some provincial governments have moved piecemeal to negotiate self-government agreements with aboriginal people who have express such a desire.

First Nations self-government agreements in Yukon were the first to be ratified.[32] Their process has become a model for the negotiation of self-government and comprehensive claims, a precedent for later agreements. The respective Nisga'a and Labrador Inuit Association (LIA) agreements that followed were built on, and added to, the Yukon model.

These model agreements allowed the new governments a wide range of legislative powers that very few aboriginal governments are in a position to finance for themselves from their own revenue sources. Many politicians both federally and provincially are still wary of what the implications of self-government agreements might be.

More progress has been made on the community-based aspects of self-government. Aboriginal people now control 80 percent of their program funding from the Department of Indian and Northern Affairs, and aboriginal authorities increasingly deliver many services such as police, education, child welfare and so on. Some provinces are allowing Aboriginals to police their own reserves, have their own justices of the peace and correction services.

Other Issues There are several other areas where conflicts and controversies have arisen and continue to arise between Native people and other Canadians. Most have to do with special regulations for Natives, such as the right to hunt and fish where and when other Canadians cannot, or the issue of tax exemption for status Indians. Since 1995, status

Indians have been required to pay income tax on employment income earned off reserves.

Historically, when assimilation was the official government policy, Indian babies were frequently removed from their homes and adopted by non-Aboriginals. As well, until the 1970s, Indian children were forced to leave home and attend residential schools, often far from their homes. These homes were often badly run and physically and emotionally abusive. Other issues have been the right to have gambling casinos on reserves and cigarette and other types of smuggling through Indian reserves on the Canada–US border. Occasionally, development has gone ahead on disputed land, causing violent confrontations. An example was Oka, Québec, in 1990 when a dispute over land created an armed confrontation between Mohawks and Québec's provincial police.

Another issue that brings First Nations people into conflict with other Canadians is aboriginal justice. Disproportionate numbers of Aboriginals are incarcerated in Canadian jails. To rectify this, in 1995, the federal government amended the *Criminal Code* to make it more lenient in sentencing Aboriginals who transgress Canadian laws and allow them to be punished in more appropriate ways. As well, more aboriginal police are being recruited.

Regional Divisions Regionalism is discussed in depth in Chapter 5, but it is such an important feature of politics in Canada that it is dealt with in many other chapters as well. In particular, regionalism is a major focus of Chapter 4 on federalism and a major component of Chapters 10 and 11 on parties and elections respectively.

Regional cultures, like political ideas, age, gender, class and ethnicity, can divide Canadians. They develop where economic, ethnic and demographic factors provide a unique identity within a particular geographical setting. Numerous factors promote and sustain regionalism. In Canada, people of varying cultural and linguistic backgrounds settled in specific parts of the country, and the resulting cultural differences, combined with geographic and economic disparities among the regions, fostered distinct viewpoints, loyalties and attitudes toward federal political problems.[33]

In the twenty-first century, Canada continues to face demands from alienated regions, especially the West. Western discontent reflects a unique history and population composition. In Central Canada, a broad perception of national needs has been built around the two founding peoples because of historical relationships between French and English Canadians. This is not, however, the Western vision of Canada. Since the population of the West is ethnically varied and relatively new to the area, the people do not tend to state their political interests in terms of the early history of Central and Eastern Canada.

The main thrust of Western discontent hinges on a feeling of marginalization and alienation from the centres of economic and political power rather than on a desire for separation from it. It reflects "frustration at the lack of national integration as much as it does resistance to integration."[34]

The underlying problem of Western alienation is easily stated but not easily resolved. The population of two provinces, Ontario and Québec, constitutes about 60 percent of the entire country. Because of this maldistribution, the outer regions perceive that the federal parliamentary system often over-represents Central Canada. Many solutions to alienation have been proposed over the years by westerners, but they have agreed on only one goal — a more effective voice in Ottawa. They are not agreed on how to achieve it. The proposals include switching political parties, eliminating parties, electoral reform, Senate reform and abolishing party discipline.

Regional cleavages, like ethnic frictions, divide Canadians, but they are not necessarily a threat to national unity. Analysis of Canada-wide data has shown that although regional loyalty is often high in Canada, it does not necessarily come at the expense of national loyalty.[35] In fact, outside Québec, feelings toward one's province and Canada are strongly correlated: positive feelings toward a province are often accompanied by positive feelings for the country. In addition, the more knowledgeable Canadians are about their country, the more sensitive they are to regionalism and the more they tend to be cosmopolitan people who feel warmly about other countries.

THE EXTERNAL CONTEXT OF POLITICS IN CANADA

Canada's external environment also helps to define who Canadians are and what its government can do. Canada's relationships and role in the world is a large, important topic that unfortunately can only be highlighted here because of space restrictions. We recommend that students who wish to pursue this topic consult Chapter 15, "Canada in the World," in our *Politics in Canada: Culture, Institutions, Behaviour and Public Policy* for a thorough, up-to-date overview and analysis of Canada's place in the global context.[36] Since Canada was founded, there have been significant changes in the power structure of the world and in Canada's position among the world's states. To develop a uniquely Canadian identity after Confederation, Canadians needed to cut the colonial ties that bound them to the United Kingdom. Two major periods of constitutional change secured that independence. The first series of events revolved around the *Statute of Westminster* of 1931, which for the first time gave the Dominion Parliament complete power to make laws concerning foreign affairs. The second involved the patriation of the Constitution in 1982, which finally enabled Canada to determine its legal and political future without formal reference to external authorities.

Canada and the United States

It has been said that, for Canadian foreign policy, geography is destiny. This is because it is so important for the country to maintain good relations and mutual respect with its powerful neighbour to the south. While Canada is a sovereign state in international law, the nature of its relationship with the United States and its relative economic weakness imposes limits upon other government policy-making. Canada's population is only roughly one-tenth that of its southern neighbour. Such disparity has inevitable repercussions: it makes Canada vulnerable to pressures from the United States in the fields of economy, defence, the environment and culture.

Since the Second World War, the United States has been responsible for over 70 percent of foreign investment in Canada. Foreign investment created jobs, and those jobs in turn improved the standard of living and developed Canada as an industrialized country. However, foreign investment also greatly increases the dependence of the Canadian economy on the economic well-being of the United States. Most foreign capital comes in the form of direct investment, which brings a high degree of control and ownership by foreigners, especially in the manufacturing and resource sectors.

Much foreign ownership comes in the form of branch plants that are offshoots of larger foreign companies. They are a mixed blessing. American plants in Canada bring jobs and access to US markets, but they also import values and culture from south of the border. There is also no guarantee that such plants will not withdraw more capital from the country than they bring in. The research and development for branch plants is also generally done in the country of the parent plant, keeping the more skilled and lucrative jobs elsewhere. US laws extend to branch plants in Canada, reducing production and job opportunities here. Yet another problem is that the Canadian economy is based largely on natural resources, and a high degree of US ownership in this sector discourages development of other sectors.

Over the years, Canadian governments have taken various steps to counter the threat of US and other foreign ownership but none has been particularly effective. Many such measures were weakened or withdrawn by the Mulroney governments of 1984 and 1988 in order to increase foreign investment and lay the foundation for the Free Trade Agreement with the United States and later the North American Free Trade Agreement (NAFTA).

Largely because of its location and population size, the United States is Canada's largest trading partner. Canada's exports to the United States surpassed those to Britain for the first time in 1921; they now represent more than 80 percent of total export sales, a growing share of which is manufactured goods. Virtually every region of the country and every major industry, including energy, agriculture, forestry, mining and auto manufacturing depends on the US market for its prosperity. Since 1946, the United States has also provided roughly 70 percent of Canada's imports. Canada enjoys a healthy trade surplus with its giant neighbour.

In recent years, trade arrangements — first with the United States in the form of the Canada–United States Free Trade Agreement, and then NAFTA in 1993 with the US and Mexico — have given Canada extensive regional trading arrangements that govern the flow of goods and services. These are having long-term effects on the domestic economy.

Canadian prosperity is tied to the US economy. This means, for example, that Canada has difficulty maintaining an autonomous interest-rate policy. When interest rates in the United States go up, they tend to go up even higher in Canada, and this can have serious consequences for employment and job security. Canadians must pay higher interest rates to attract investment — otherwise capital would flow elsewhere. Interest rates are also vital in determining whether Canadians can afford to borrow for such purposes as mortgages, cars and job creation.

The gigantic US economy also dwarfs Canada in the area of defence. In essence, Canada shelters under the US military arsenal. This saves money but has costs in terms of reducing Canada's ability to exercise an independent foreign policy. In recent years, the military has been severely cut, but in 2005, the government raised military spending by $9.8 billion over five years, the biggest investment in the military in two decades. This was, at least in part, to assure the US that Canada is doing its share to fight terrorism and secure its borders. Part of the money was designated for a rapid-response brigade of 5000 soldiers that is planned to support humanitarian interventions in failing states. Chapter 9, "The Administration of Justice," outlines some of the steps Canada is taking to counter international terrorism.

Also in 2005, the Canadian government announced that it would not take part in a planned North American ballistic-missile defence (BMD) system despite personal lobbying by President George W. Bush. This was a controversial move, and critics maintained that Canada has, by this rejection, surrendered sovereignty over its airspace to the US. However,

Dolighan. Won't Roll Over. Reprinted with permission.

the prime minister defended the decision on the grounds that since 1958, Canada has been a partner in the North American Aerospace Defence Command (NORAD), which was created to detect and destroy incoming aircraft or cruise missiles, and in 2004, Canada had agreed that NORAD would extend to ballistic missiles. Therefore, the prime minister said, he still expects Canada to be consulted before any US interceptor missile is fired over Canada.

Canada does not slavishly adopt US foreign policy. Even in the wake of the terrorist attacks on Washington and New York on September 11, 2001, Canada did not join the US in its invasion of Iraq in early 2003. It did, however, following the direction of the UN Security Council, join the US in the International Security Assistance Force (ISAF) in Afghanistan. The Canadian contingent will grow to 1250 in 2006. This compromise maintained Canadian independence in foreign policy but was severely criticized by many American officials and media outlets.

Canada also has environmental issues with the United States. The US has generally less restrictive pollution laws than Canada and, with its larger population, creates pollution that impinges on Canada — particularly in areas of shared resources such as the Great Lakes and in air pollution, which causes acid rain.

The United States also represents a major cultural threat. Canadian government policy has been built around guarding a unique space for Canadian cultural and intellectual expression inside Canada and perhaps also abroad. However, the proximity of most Canadians to the border with the United States, a common language, the relative size of the two populations and the penetration of Canadian society by American mass media and other culture-bearers are all potential obstacles to the maintenance of a distinct Canadian identity. Movies, television, magazines, music and books are dominated by US content. Canadian companies in these areas are dwarfed by the subsidiaries of large, mainly US multinationals.

Canada in Global Economics

In a global perspective, Canadians are economically well off with a very high standard of living. The United Nations Human Development Index, which includes factors such as life expectancy, adult literacy, educational attainment and income level, ranked Canada fourth among all countries in the world in 2004.[37]

To help balance the effects of US domination, Canada belongs to many international organizations. Among the world's states, Canada is one of the most powerful both economically and politically. This relative position makes it mandatory that Canada participate fully in international organizations such as the United Nations and its specialized agencies. Through the UN, Canada has made a major contribution to world peacekeeping. Canada is also an active member of the Commonwealth of Nations, made up of former states of the British Empire, and la Francophonie, which is composed of French-speaking countries. Since 1990, Canada has belonged to the Organization of American States (OAS), which links countries in the western hemisphere. In the area of defence, Canada contributes to the security of the West by its membership in the North Atlantic Treaty Organization (NATO) and NORAD. In total, Canada's bilateral and multilateral relations give our political leaders influence in the world but also act as constraints in domestic politics and government.

In terms of trading partners, we have seen that the United States is by far Canada's largest market for both imports and exports. Europe and Asia continue to be Canada's next largest partners, but even combined, these two regions represent only a fraction of exports and imports with the United States. Canada also imports more than it exports with Asia and Europe.

Canada is party to the General Agreement on Tariffs and Trade (GATT), an international agreement, and its institution, the World Trade Organization (WTO), both of which seek to establish a global trading order based on reciprocity, non-discrimination and multilateralism. The main benefit of the WTO for Canada is that it facilitates the expansion of trade relations with other countries. The Free Trade Agreement and NAFTA were signed to boost this trade record and to a large extent this is being accomplished.

In the modern era, increasing interdependence among states has severely constrained the capacity of governments to act independently. This is especially the case for countries that have a high degree of economic integration with a larger, more powerful neighbour. As we have noted, Canada is affected by foreign countries through the flow of capital, in particular through investment. Much of the Canadian national debt is held by foreigners whose purchase or sales of Canadian securities can dramatically change interest rates in the country. The value of the Canadian dollar, too, fluctuates according to external realities and possibilities.

Canada's economy is influenced by foreign investors and creditors. Canadian defence policy is conducted within the context of the NATO alliance, in which the United States is the most important actor. Canada is far from self-sufficient with regard to either economic prosperity or national security. More and more, the well-being and security of Canadians depend on how they collectively respond to the constraints, opportunities and dangers that flow from the international environment and especially from the United States.

The challenge for political leaders in Canada, as in other countries today, is to maintain a strong national economy in a globalized system. To a large extent in free market economies, that entails free trade, budget discipline and minimal regulation by governments. One expert summed up the realities of globalization and the "new economy" this way: "Every world leader is now a carnival barker, seeking to attract investors to that leader's own nation, and every leader is potentially worried that investors will suddenly get up and leave."[38]

KEY TERMS

aboriginal rights, p. 44	multiculturalism, p. 40
attitudes, p. 22	political culture, p. 21
class, p. 34	political customs, p. 23
compact theory of Confederation, p. 38	racial discrimination, p. 41
ethnic origin, p. 37	values, p. 21
ideology, p. 25	visible minorities, p. 41

DISCUSSION QUESTIONS

1. What circumstances serve to unite Canadians? To divide them?

2. Can the French and English concepts of *nation* be reconciled?

3. Is multiculturalism a disruptive or an integrative force in Canadian society?

4. Does gender stratification affect you personally? Explain how and why.

5. Is Canada treating its Native people fairly?

6. In the global context, how does Canada rate as a place to live?

WEBLINKS

Assembly of First Nations

www.afn.ca

Citizenship and Immigration Canada (CIC) — Research and Statistics

www.cic.gc.ca/english/research

Canadian Income Statistics

www.statcan.ca/english/freepub/11-516-XIE/sectione/sectione.htm

Canadian Indian Treaties

www.library.ualberta.ca/subject/nativestudies/treaties/index.cfm

Canadian Population by Age and Sex

www12.statcan.ca/english/census01/Products/Analytic/companion/age/contents.cfm

Ethnic Origins in Canada

www40.statcan.ca/l01/ind01/l3_3867_1712.htm?hili_none

Natural Resources Canada

www.nrcan.gc.ca

3

The Constitutional Framework

Formal Rules of the Political Game

Learning Objectives

After reading this chapter, you should be able to

1. Define *constitution* and *constitutionalism*.

2. Trace the development of Canada's Constitution from Confederation in 1867 to the *Constitution Act of 1982* and on to today.

3. Distinguish between common law and statutory law.

4. Outline the five legal formulas for amending the Constitution.

5. Outline six kinds of basic rights and freedoms protected by the *Charter of Rights and Freedoms*.

A constitution establishes the formal rules for the game of politics. It provides specifically designed state institutions and a set of principles about governing. It outlines the relations between society and the state and establishes the importance of particular institutions. These principles distribute power among citizens, guide deliberations between the rulers and the ruled and grant leaders the legitimacy required to act authoritatively.

In this chapter, we define and explain many of the key ideas used to organize the game of politics. Constitutions, rights and the rule of law are outlined, as well as the key institutional arrangements set out in the Canadian Constitution. Since the rules of the game of politics evolve over time, this chapter analyzes the development of the Constitution from 1867 until today, including its successes and failures.

CONSTITUTIONAL PRINCIPLES

A **constitution** is a body of fundamental rules, written and unwritten, under which governments operate. Modern constitutions outline at least the key institutions of government organization and list rules that restrain political leaders from engaging in arbitrary action. Any law that contravenes constitutional law may be declared invalid, with judges and courts acting as referees.

Constitutions may be written or unwritten. A **written constitution** is the fundamental state law set down in one or more documents. An **unwritten constitution** consists mainly of custom, convention or statutes and is not written down into one comprehensive document. Canada has a written constitution — the *Constitution Act, 1982*. The 1982 constitutional amendment codified all past constitutional laws, including the original 1867 *British North America Act* (*BNA Act*), in one document. It also provided for a *Charter of Rights and Freedoms*, and set up amendment formulas for future revisions.

Constitutional Laws and Conventions

There is also an "unwritten" aspect to Canada's Constitution. Because of Canada's British heritage, many of the most important parts of the constitution are not written down. These include principles such as how the governor general names the prime minister, and all the rules about the relations of the executive with Parliament.

In Canada, as a result, we make a distinction between constitutional laws and conventions. As constitutions develop over time, the norms of a society become incorporated into the rules for governing, but they are not all written down in constitutional documents. In fact, it would not be possible to write down all the rules for conducting state affairs in a constitution. A constitutional **convention** is a custom or practice that, while not necessarily a legal necessity, is nevertheless based on accepted reasons and practices.

Since conventions are not laws, courts cannot make final, legal determinations in conflicts that involve conventions. Conventions can be enforced only in the sense that a government would lose the support of the people if they were not obeyed. If the legislature is dissatisfied with a particular convention, it can simply replace it by statute law. In 1982, for example, the Supreme Court of Canada decided that obtaining provincial agreement for the federal government's request to Britain to pass a constitutional amendment was a convention and not a law.

Individual and Collective Rights

Constitutions may also convey **rights** — that is, entitlements owed to individuals or groups as duties by others or the government. Many constitutions contain statements about such values as natural rights, religious beliefs, life and liberty and political rights such as freedom of speech and assembly. Canada's Constitution contains both individual and collective rights.

Individual rights are defined as individual claims against the state. The *Canadian Charter of Rights and Freedoms* includes the principle of the rights of individuals. Individual rights are based on the principle that the government should draw no distinction among citizens based on their cultural, social, religious or linguistic backgrounds. All individuals should be treated equally before the law.

Collective rights are entitlements or duties owed to certain groups by the state. They call for distinctions to be made among groups in order to ensure equality of condition or bargaining power. The Constitution provides educational rights for specific denominational groups and language rights for others. In short, rights and entitlements have been granted to some groups and not others. For example, the *British North America Act of 1867* accorded rights to the ethno-religious-linguistic francophone group of Québec and to some historical communities on the eastern seaboard. The *Canadian Charter of Rights and Freedoms* lists other collective rights for specific sectors of society.

The Rule of Law

A constitution implies the **rule of law** — a guarantee that the state's actions will be governed by law, with fairness and without malice. No individual should be above the law and no one ought to be exempt from it. As we noted in Chapter 1, adherence to the rule of law and to a constitution are primary distinguishing features of democracies.

In addition to certain general goals, the rule of law provides a guarantee of impartiality and fairness. The authority of the state is to be exercised rationally and without malice, with all citizens protected from the abuse of power. The rule of law means that a citizen, no matter what his or her transgression, cannot be denied the due process of law. No individual or institution is exempt from it, and all are equal before it. No government or administrative official has any power beyond that awarded by law. The rule of law is a fundamental principle without which any constitution, written or unwritten, would be meaningless. The courts are the guardians of the rule of law and as such should be beyond improper influence. The principle of the independence of the judiciary is firmly established, with a British history of over three hundred years.

Common and Statutory Law

Canada incorporated much of its legal tradition from Britain and France. Customary law, or what came to be known as British common law, was imported into Canada along with other traditions. **Common law**, also known as unenacted or case law, consists of a body of established rules based on the principle of *stare decisis*. **Stare decisis** is the principle of following precedents set down in earlier court cases, a principle which binds lower courts to follow decisions made by higher-level courts. Nine provinces (excluding Québec) and the territories use common law as the basis of court judgments.

Another form of law came to Canada via the *Code civil* or *Code Napoléon* of France. A **code** is a body of legislative laws brought together in a single body to provide a relatively complete set of legal rules. To codify laws is to arrange them into a written systematic body, as opposed to unwritten traditions. The *Code civil* is used only in Québec and it performs the same function that common law does in the rest of Canada. Unlike common law, the *Code civil* is a written law. It is stated more in terms of principles and rationality than is common law.

When common law is insufficient or conflicts with contemporary norms, it may be amended by statute law. **Statute law** consists of the authoritative rules set by the Parliament of Canada or the legislative assemblies of the provinces.

As new problems are brought before the courts, judges refer to statute law and previous decisions that are deemed relevant in order to apply them when making their own judgments. If there are no appropriate statute laws or precedents, or there are no laws that precisely fit the case, judges are forced to rely on common sense and reason. They may even appeal to doctrines based on natural law — the recourse to god or nature in establishing legal principles — or their judgments may be based on contemporary norms and values. Existing principles are thereby broadened, and the body of case law is expanded. Judicial interpretation is thus an important source of Canadian law.

The relationship between statutory and common law is defined by the **doctrine of parliamentary supremacy**, a basic premise of British parliamentary democracy. In Canada, it means that all eleven legislatures have the authority, in theory, to repeal or modify any principle set out in common law. However, this power is not absolute. The Supreme Court can declare an act ***ultra vires***. This means that the act in question is beyond a legislature's jurisdiction on the basis of Canada's federal division of powers. The entrenchment of individual and group rights in Canada's *Charter of Rights and Freedoms* also limits parliamentary authority by placing certain rights beyond the reach of any legislature.

Key Institutional Arrangements

Apart from stating fundamental principles, written constitutions also describe the organization of government. Some are remarkably detailed, outlining the entire government structure and the relative powers and limitations of the various institutions in the political process. At a minimum, most written constitutions outline the powers and duties of the executive, the legislature, the judiciary and sometimes other institutions such as the bureaucracy or the military.

The evolution of federalism — the division of power between federal and provincial units — is discussed in considerable detail in Chapter 4, "Contested Federalism." Here, however, it is important to note that federalism normally requires a "federal bargain" in law, an agreement in which the parties agree to give up a degree of autonomy in exchange for becoming part of a more powerful political entity. It is usual, therefore, for federalism to be based on some sort of written document or constitution that enshrines guarantees and concessions to the various levels of governments. The provisions and limitations defined in that document help shape the nature of federalism. As we shall see, this is the case in Canada.

It is important to remember, however, that a constitution is only a legal code about how government *ought* to operate. In practice, a constitution may be set down and then ignored. The institutions it defines may be used, suspended or even demolished. Some constitutions list philosophical platitudes that have little, if any, bearing on how the political system actually works. One must understand how constitutions and institutions operate in the real world, not just on paper.

THE DEVELOPMENT OF THE CANADIAN CONSTITUTION

Constitutions are not static; they evolve and change over time. They are a product of their historical development as well as contemporary values, beliefs and attitudes about how the governments *should* function.

Important aspects of Canada's unwritten constitution evolved in Britain for many centuries before Confederation. British colonists who immigrated to Canada brought with them concepts of basic constitutional principles, such as the rule of law and the right of opposition. The *British North America Act of 1867* was Canada's first constitution. It ensured that Canada was to have a form of government "similar in principle to that of the United Kingdom." This meant that certain institutional arrangements concerning the formal executive were to be reproduced in Canada, and that the British parliamentary system was to be used. Important elements of the Canadian Constitution were therefore already implicitly in place when the Fathers of Confederation met at Charlottetown in 1864.

The *BNA Act* was the product of lengthy, complex negotiations over the terms of union. All the leaders concerned tried to obtain concessions and guarantees that would protect matters of vital local concern. For example, French Canadians sought protection for their culture and language as the price for joining the union, while Nova Scotians argued for economic concessions and subsidies.

The authors of the *British North America Act* had to take into account two dissimilar linguistic groups, a federal system and complex financing regulations. They decided to graft a federal system of government onto the British heritage of representative and responsible Cabinet government. In doing so, they created a hybrid division of jurisdiction between two levels of government, federal and provincial.

The *British North America Act*

The 1867 *BNA Act* was not intended to establish a truly independent state — the formal authority of Canada was to continue to rest with the British monarch, and the Act itself was to be amended only by the British Parliament. Rather, the Act was designed to enable the colonial provinces to join in a political union. Provinces that were already established kept their colonial constitutions, and those that joined after Confederation received their constitutions from the Ottawa government. As we have seen, the English-speaking provinces inherited the common-law tradition from the United Kingdom, while Québec kept its system of civil law based on French traditions such as the *Code Napoléon*. Criminal law, on the other hand, was made a federal responsibility and therefore similar throughout the land. Some general principles, such as liberty and the rule of law, were protected by common law and hence were not included in the *BNA Act*.

The Canadian Constitution is not highly detailed in many areas. Even vital procedural matters concerning the governing of the country go unmentioned; for example, the Cabinet is not mentioned explicitly. Canadian government relies heavily on conventions such as "responsible government," which requires the government to resign when it is defeated in Parliament over a major issue. Of course, many issues that preoccupy governments today were not covered in the 1867 document.

What the Constitution does do is sketch, in rather uninspiring prose, the machinery of government and basic terms of federalism. It is reasonably detailed with respect to the machinery of formal executive power and on matters concerning the division of authority between the federal and provincial governments.[1] The intent of the authors of the document was to create a strong central government. The federal government was given responsibility for the important topics of trade and commerce, defence and foreign affairs. Jurisdiction over education, welfare and other matters perceived to be of lesser and only local interest was left to the provinces. As we shall see in the next chapter, the responsibilities of the provinces became relatively more important over time and, when legal disputes developed between the two levels of government, the British law lords often sided with the provinces. At times, the *BNA Act* has been a very restrictive document and has created an impasse in federal–provincial relations.

An important determinant of the relative power of federal and provincial governments is the financial strength of the two jurisdictions. In a federal state, revenue sources must be divided reasonably between the two levels of government. Otherwise, federalism will wither. A key question, therefore, is always how to distribute funds to the provinces while maintaining federal control of the national economy.

The *BNA Act* gave the federal government the ability to raise money by any system of taxation while, from the beginning, provincial authorities were restricted to collecting revenue through direct taxes or the sale of natural resources. (*Direct taxes*, such as income tax, must be paid directly to a government by the individual or firm assessed, but *indirect taxes*, such as sales tax on commodities, are collected and the money passed along to the government by other persons or institutions.) Thus, it appeared from strict interpretation of the 1867 Act that the provinces could not levy a sales tax that would be passed along to consumers. However, through the ingenious device of making vendors tax collectors for the provincial governments, the rules of the *BNA Act* were evaded, and the provinces were able to employ both types of taxation. This was important because many areas of growing financial responsibility were awarded later to the provinces. Today, both layers of government assess both direct and indirect taxes.

Other Constitutional Documents

Although the *BNA Act* was the centrepiece of Canada's written constitution, there were other relevant documents. Besides the various amendments to the *BNA Act* and the 1931 *Statute of Westminster*, the Canadian Constitution before 1982 could be said to include the Royal Proclamation of 1763; the *Colonial Laws Validity Act of 1865*; the various acts admitting new provinces to the federal union; Letters Patent concerning the office of the governor general[2] and a whole range of common-law precedents and orders-in-council. Together, these made up the essentials of the Constitution from 1867 to 1982.

Interpreting the Constitution

Every federal system requires a court or an arbitration process to interpret clauses of the constitution and resolve disputes over jurisdictional authority. Until 1949, when the Supreme Court of Canada was established, the court of final appeal in Canada was the **Judicial Committee of the Privy Council (JCPC)**, the superior court of the United Kingdom. For the most part, it tended to define federal authority narrowly and provincial authority widely. The emergency powers of the federal government, expressed in the clause, "Peace, Order and good Government," granted extensive residual power to the federal government but were interpreted by the JCPC in a way that virtually obstructed the apparent centralizing intentions of the drafters of the *BNA Act*.[3] The rulings of the JCPC on Canadian federalism were very controversial. Many Canadians complained that the British law lords were too far removed from the political realities of Canada to render appropriate decisions.

The JCPC lost its position as Canada's court of last appeal in 1949 when the Supreme Court became the arbiter of constitutional review. The Supreme Court of Canada, with nine federally appointed judges, is Canada's highest court for civil, criminal and constitutional cases. (See Chapter 9, "The Administration of Justice," for more on the court system.) In recent years, the provinces have shown great reluctance to take jurisdictional matters to the Supreme Court because of its alleged pro-centralist bias. More and more, disputes between the federal and provincial governments tend to be resolved outside the judicial process, through the mechanism of federal–provincial conferences or diplomacy.

This is not to argue that the Supreme Court is irrelevant. On the contrary, there have been many important decisions by the Court on matters such as offshore oil and mineral rights, and resource taxation, not to mention its rulings on the federal government's plan to unilaterally patriate the Constitution (see Chapter 4, "Contested Federalism"). The Supreme Court has also been the arbiter of controversial cases involving civil rights and liberties in interpreting the Charter of Rights and Freedoms (see Chapter 9). Recently the extremely important question about whether or not Québec has the right to unilateral independence was referred to the Supreme Court for judgment (see Chapter 5, "Nationalism and Regionalism").

Constitutional Amendment

Constitutional changes can take place through formal amendment or judicial interpretation. For political scientists, a **"rigid" constitution** is one that is difficult to amend, whereas a **"flexible" constitution** can be amended easily and adapted to changing circumstances. Although there are arguments both for and against the use of either type of amending formula, it is clear that all constitutions must provide *some* means to adapt themselves to new circumstances. Canada's amendment formula was, and remains, quite rigid.

The *BNA Act of 1867* did *not* contain a procedure for constitutional amendment in Canada. Instead, Canada had to appeal to Britain if it wanted to make any constitutional changes and have a bill passed in the British Parliament. Over time, the British role was diminished. In 1931, the *Statute of Westminster* established that the British Parliament could not legislate for Canada except at the request of the Canadian government. At the time, the British government tried to persuade Canada to adopt a specific amending formula and thereby cut the last tie with the United Kingdom. Unfortunately, Canadian politicians could not agree on a formula so the British Parliament remained responsible for constitutional amendment in Canada.

On several occasions after 1931, the Constitution was amended in the United Kingdom after a request from Canada. Among these amendments were the 1940 amendment giving the federal Parliament jurisdiction over unemployment insurance, the 1951 amendment giving Parliament shared power over old-age pensions, and the 1960 amendment changing the retirement age of judges. For all of these, provincial agreement was achieved before asking the UK to amend the Constitution. On the other hand, no provincial agreement had to be reached (nor was it) when representation in the Senate was amended in 1915, or when representation in the House of Commons was altered in 1946, 1952 and 1974.

In other words, a constitutional convention developed with regard to the amendment of the *BNA Act*. On each occasion, the British Parliament accepted the amendments that originated in a Joint Address of both Houses of the Canadian Parliament. On those amendments that affected the federal balance of power, the provinces were always consulted and agreed to the proposals. On the other hand, no substantial amendment was ever made at the request of any province or group of provinces since the British Parliament only accepted communications that arrived by way of the federal Parliament.

Not all constitutional change required the passage of British legislation, however. From the beginning, the provinces were allowed to amend their own constitutions in all spheres except those concerning the powers of the lieutenant-governor. With the passage of the *BNA Act (No. 2)* in 1949, the federal Parliament was empowered to amend the Constitution, except with regard to provincial power, rights and privileges, the rights of minorities with respect to schools and language protection, the extension of the life of Parliament beyond five years, and the necessity to call at least one session of Parliament per year. These were important exceptions, however, as they prevented Ottawa from amending anything that touched on the nature and division of federal and provincial responsibilities.

From 1931 until 1981, strenuous efforts were made to cut the remaining ties to Britain. The difficult question in Canada was never *whether* we should have our own Constitution but *what* it should be. **Patriation**, or bringing the constitutional documents home, involved two seemingly insoluble conundrums for Canadians: how much provincial participation should there be before an agreement to patriate it; and what type of amendment process should ensue.

Though minor efforts to find an acceptable constitutional agreement started as early as the 1930s, it was not until the 1960s that serious discussions took place between the federal government and all of the provinces. Two proposals almost succeeded: the Fulton-Favreau formula of 1964 and the Victoria Charter of 1971.

In each of these cases, the essential stumbling block to finding an amendment formula was Québec's desire to be treated differently than the other provinces. To many Québécois, the idea that federalism refers to a process involving ten equal provinces working under one federal system is unacceptable. Rather, they argue that Canada is a union of two "founding peoples" and each should have a veto over all constitutional amendments. This view is premised on the idea that the Canadian Constitution is a "compact" between two cultural groups, between the English and French provinces. By extension, a large number of Québécois argue that only the Québec state can protect francophone interests.

BRINGING THE CONSTITUTION HOME

The long and at times bitter debate over "bringing the Constitution home" ended in 1982 with the passage of the *Canada Act* by the British Parliament. Patriation of the Canadian Constitution was primarily symbolic, in that it did not involve significant changes in provincial jurisdiction. However, it did include an entrenched *Charter of Rights and Freedoms* and an amending formula that had implications for both federal and provincial authority.

The events leading up to patriation are crucial to understanding Canada's present Constitution and its problems. The catalyst for the final round of constitutional negotiations leading to patriation was the Québec referendum on sovereignty-association. In May 1980, Premier René Lévesque's *indépendantiste* Parti Québécois government sought authority to negotiate sovereign political status for Québec, with continued economic association with Canada. Québec voters ultimately rejected Lévesque's plan by a convincing margin of 60 to 40 percent in a referendum. However, patriation of the Constitution was given new momentum during the referendum campaign when federalists pledged that Canada would begin a process of constitutional "renewal" to address the concerns of Québec citizens.

The concept of "renewed" federalism, while vague, allowed Prime Minister Pierre Elliott Trudeau to resume his efforts for patriation, a goal he had pursued since his first election as prime minister in 1968. He proposed to unilaterally patriate the Constitution with an entrenched *Charter of Rights and Freedoms* as well as equalization and amendment formulas. Of the ten provincial governments, only New Brunswick and Ontario supported the initial federal government proposal.

Six provinces took the issue of patriation to the Supreme Court. Its judgment offered both sides a measure of support. By a vote of seven to two, the judges ruled that the federal government could "legally" and "unilaterally" submit the constitutional resolution to the British Parliament for passage. However, by a six to three vote, the Court also ruled that a constitutional convention requiring provincial consent existed and that Ottawa's process "offended the federal principle."

The patriation package was thus tossed back into the political arena. In November 1981, a federal–provincial conference produced an agreement between the federal government and nine of the provinces (again Québec was the exception). The tenth premier, Lévesque, was enraged — the signators had made a deal without Québec. He commented bitterly that this agreement would have incalculable consequences for Canada.

The major compromise that produced the agreement between the federal government and the nine provinces was the inclusion of a **notwithstanding clause** in the Constitution, a clause, which allowed Parliament or a provincial legislature to override most Charter provisions by a simple declaration to that effect when passing legislation. (The provision also included a "sunset" clause requiring renewal of the exemption every five years.) Supporters of the notwithstanding clause argued that it provided an important political check as it maintained the pre-eminence of legislative power in the event of "awkward" court rulings. Critics of the notwithstanding provision argued that it circumvented the very purpose of an entrenched Charter, which is to give the courts the authority to protect fundamental individual freedoms in the event that legislatures and governments fail to do so.

Another compromise leading to the agreement at the 1981 conference concerned the amending formula. An **amendment formula** is the procedure required to change a constitution. The proposal preferred by the provincial first ministers was accepted. It called for amendments affecting jurisdictions to be made by a joint resolution of both the Senate and the House of Commons, as well as by a resolution of the legislative assemblies of at least two-thirds of the provinces, representing at least 50 percent of the population of Canada. In addition, it granted dissenting provinces the right to opt out of all amendments that affected their status and powers.

There were several other compromises concerning the Charter. The case of Native people is an example. Recognition of their treaty rights was originally excluded from the Charter because several provinces were concerned that Native land claims might impede provincial control over natural resources. However, after intense lobbying by Native groups, recognition of these rights was restored.

Another important lobbying effort ensured the absolute rights of women. Section 28 of the Charter — which simply stated, "notwithstanding anything in this Charter, the rights and freedoms referred to in it are guaranteed equally to male and female persons" — was eliminated in one of the early agreements at the 1981 conference. In response, an *ad hoc* Committee of Canadian Women on the Constitution was formed. In just three weeks, it successfully lobbied all ten provincial premiers to reverse their stand on the issue, and the clause was restored.

The British Parliament was presented with the Canada Bill in mid-February of 1982. The bill was supported by the federal government and nine provinces. Québec still did not agree to the resolution. The bill was eventually passed by the British Parliament at every stage by large majorities. On March 29, the Queen gave royal assent to the *Canada Act*, 115 years to the day after the *BNA Act* had received royal assent. In Ottawa, on April 17, 1982, the Queen proclaimed the *Constitution Act, 1982*, completing the patriation process. At long last, Canada had a comprehensive constitution. However, this success did not come without more problems. The events outlined in the Close-Up feature below ("The Perils of Keeping the Constitution") are perhaps symbolic of the difficulties.

CLOSE-UP The Perils of Keeping the Constitution

Two copies of the Constitution were signed in 1982 by the Queen. One was immediately spotted by rain during the outdoor signing ceremony. The second was damaged in 1983 when a man protesting against US cruise-missile tests poured thick red paint on it. First aid was quickly administered, but a pinkish-orange spot still covered 20 percent of the document. Later, because of an air-conditioning failure at the archives, or perhaps because of the restoration work, the document began to curl up in its frame.

Québec and Constitutional Patriation

As pointed out previously, Québec's political leaders and government rejected the 1982 constitutional reform, which had been adopted without their approval. They claimed to be the sole spokespersons for Québec on this matter, ignoring the facts that Prime Minister Trudeau was a French Canadian, one third of his Cabinet was from Québec and seventy-four of seventy-five MPs from Québec at the time were Liberals, almost all of whom supported patriation. Still, Québec's opposition to patriation prompted some critics to question whether the Supreme Court's call for "a substantial measure of provincial consent" had been achieved.

Premier Lévesque made several arguments against patriation of the Constitution. He argued that Québec's cultural security was threatened by the restriction of the province's exclusive rights in linguistic matters. He said the Charter's guarantee of access to English-speaking schools contradicted Québec's bill 101, which restricted admission to English schools in that province to children who had at least one parent educated in Québec's English system. Lévesque also criticized the new Constitution's failure to recognize "in any tangible way" the character and needs of Québec as a distinct national society. Finally, he disliked the amending formula's removal of what Québec considered its traditional veto over constitutional changes. While the new constitutional proposal did provide financial compensation in the important areas of education and culture, the amending formula did not guarantee financial compensation for provinces that choose to opt out of other programs initiated by constitutional amendments.

The Québec government acted to exempt the province from provisions it disliked in the newly patriated Constitution. It attempted to ensure that Québeckers' fundamental freedoms and legal and equality rights would be subject only to the provincial charter of human rights, not to the *Charter of Rights and Freedoms*. It introduced and passed bill 62 in the National Assembly. According to the provisions of that bill, which came into force in June 1982, a new clause was to be appended to each Québec law, stating that it would operate "notwithstanding" the provision of the Charter.

However, the notwithstanding clause does not apply to language-of-education articles in the Constitution. To bypass this obstacle, therefore, Québec relied on Section 1 of the Constitution, which states that the federal *Charter of Rights and Freedoms* guarantees the liberties it sets out "subject only to such reasonable limits prescribed by law as can be demonstrably justified in a free and democratic society." The Québec government hoped to prove in court that bill 101's provisions could be justified on these grounds. However, in 1984, the Supreme Court rejected its argument that the threat to the survival of the French language in North America justified bill 101's restrictions on English school enrollment. The Court ruled that the section of bill 101 limiting eligibility to English-language schools in Québec was "incompatible" with the constitutional guarantees set out in the Canadian *Charter of Rights and Freedoms*.

In late 1988, the Supreme Court again had to rule on the constitutionality of certain clauses of bill 101. This time it ruled that the law prohibiting business signs in languages other than French was against the Charter's provisions on freedom of expression and speech.

The Québec government invoked the notwithstanding clause to escape from this section of the Charter. It then introduced bill 178, which required French to be used on outdoor signs but allowed English on indoor signs provided that French was "prominently" displayed. Once more, Québec's language law sparked intense criticism.[4] However, these arguments over language were quickly overshadowed by discussions concerning the Constitution as a whole. (Language issues are covered in Chapter 5, "Nationalism and Regionalism.")

THE NEW CANADIAN CONSTITUTION

On April 17, 1982, the *Constitution Act, 1982* subsumed and replaced the *British North America Act* as Canada's Constitution. While none of the changes affected the main structure of central government or federalism, some of them greatly changed how Canadians govern themselves.

Amendment Formulas There are now five legal formulas for amending the *Constitution Act*.

The *first formula* concerns amendments that require unanimous consent. It deals with amendments to the office of the Queen, the governor general, the lieutenant-governors; the right of a province to have at least as many seats in the House of Commons as it has in the Senate; the use of the English and French languages; the composition of the Supreme Court of Canada; and amendments to the amending formulas.

Amendments in these areas must be passed by the Senate and the House of Commons (or by the Commons alone if the Senate has not approved the proposal within 180 days after the Commons has done so), and by the legislature of each and every province.

The *second formula* includes amendments that deal with a) taking away any rights, powers or privileges of provincial governments or legislatures; b) the proportionate representation of the provinces in the House of Commons; c) the powers of the Senate and the method of selecting senators and their residence qualifications; d) the constitutional position of the Supreme Court of Canada (not including its composition, which is covered under the first formula above); e) the extension of existing provinces into the territories; and f) the *Charter of Rights and Freedoms*.

Amendments in these areas must be passed by the Senate and the House of Commons (or by the Commons alone if the Senate delays more than 180 days), and by the legislatures of two-thirds of the provinces with at least half the total population of all the provinces (excluding the territories). In reality, this means that any four less-populous provinces, or Ontario and Québec together, could veto any amendments in this category, and that either Ontario or Québec would have to be one of the seven provinces needed to pass any amendment.

The *third formula* deals with matters that apply to one or more but not all provinces. Amendments in these cases must be passed by the Senate and the House of Commons (or the Commons alone if the Senate delays more than 180 days), and by the legislature or legislatures of the particular province or provinces concerned. These include changes in provincial boundaries or changes relating to the use of the English or French language in any province or provinces.

The *fourth formula* concerns changes in the executive government of Canada or changes in the Senate and House of Commons, which are not covered by the first two formulas. Such amendments can be made by an ordinary act of the Parliament of Canada.

The *fifth formula* concerns amendments that can be made by individual provincial legislatures alone. In the original *BNA Act of 1867* (Section 92), provinces could amend their own constitutions, with the exception of the office of the lieutenant-governor. Section 92 (1) was repealed and this amendment clause moved to Section 45, which places the provinces in a position equivalent to that of the federal government.

The first three amending formulas *entrench* specific parts of the written Constitution. **Entrenchment** means to embody provisions in a constitution so that they are protected and can be changed only by formal amendment procedures. Neither Parliament alone nor any provincial legislature has the power to touch them. All changes must be made according to the particular constitutional formula that applies. Procedural requirements also establish maximum and minimum time periods in which constitutional amendments must be passed.

The constitutional amendment system now in place is quite rigid so that the chances of further major changes to the Constitution by amendment are minimal. The right to amend the Constitution is finally in Canadian hands, but those hands are fairly firmly tied by rules that make major amendments almost impossible. Despite constant efforts and even a national referendum, there have been no amendments made under either the unanimity rule or the two-thirds and 50-percent rule. In 1996, Parliament passed legislation allowing Québec, Ontario, British Columbia and any two Atlantic or Prairie provinces to veto any further constitutional change, and although this was not constitutionalized, it added even more rigidity to the amendment process.

Only eight minor amendments to the Constitution have been completed since 1982. The first occurred in 1984. It created Section 35 and concerned the rights of the Native people of Canada. The second, in 1987, dealt with the entrenchment of the denominational school rights of the Pentecostal Assemblies in Newfoundland. In 1993, the third established the equality of English-speaking and French-speaking communities in New Brunswick. In 1994, the fourth change amended the Constitution so that Canada could be relieved of the obligation to provide steamboat service to PEI upon completion of the bridge joining the island to the mainland. Then, in 1997, the fifth and sixth amendments were passed, both concerning education in Newfoundland. The second of these amendments did away completely with the system of denominational schools in that province. The seventh amendment replaced religious school boards in Québec with linguistic-based boards. The eighth, in 2001, changed the name of Newfoundland to Newfoundland and Labrador.

The *Constitution Act, 1982*, also included the following important changes:

Natural Resources The provinces obtained wider powers over their natural resources. Each province now controls the distribution within Canada of the primary production from its mines, oil wells, gas wells, forests and electric power plants, provided it does not discriminate against other parts of the country in prices or supplies. The federal government can legislate on these matters, however, and in case of conflict, the federal law prevails. The provinces can levy indirect taxes on their mines, oil wells, gas wells, forests and electric power plants and primary production from these sources. Such taxes must be the same whether or not the products are exported to other parts of the country.

Native Peoples Three provisions were included:

1.   The Charter "shall not be construed so as to abrogate or derogate from any Aboriginal, treaty or other rights or freedoms that pertain to the Aboriginal peoples of Canada."

2.   The existing aboriginal and treaty rights of the Native people of Canada are recognized and affirmed (this includes Indian, Inuit and Métis peoples).

3.   The prime minister of Canada was to convene, within one year of patriation, a constitutional conference of first ministers of the provinces, at which constitutional matters affecting Aboriginals would be on the agenda.

Equalization The *Constitution Act* now states that the federal government and Parliament and the provincial governments and legislatures "are committed to promoting equal opportunities for the well-being of Canadians, further economic developments to reduce disparities in opportunities, and providing essential public services of reasonable quality to all Canadians." The federal government and Parliament are also "committed to the principle of making equalization payments to ensure that provincial governments have sufficient revenues to provide reasonably comparable levels of public services and reasonably comparable levels of taxation."

The *Charter of Rights and Freedoms*

Finally, the 1982 Constitution included a *Charter of Rights and Freedoms*. Historically, as we have seen, civil liberties in Britain and the colonies were protected by common law and parliamentary supremacy. It was widely believed that neither the British government nor its master, Parliament, would infringe on individual freedoms because both were held in check by traditions, customs and political culture. Following this tradition Canada, too, relied on the rights provided by British common law and, after 1960, on legislation known as the **Canadian Bill of Rights**, which listed fundamental freedoms but never entrenched them in the Constitution.

Did Canada Need a Charter?

Critics ask why Canada needs an entrenched *Charter of Rights and Freedoms* in light of the fact that Canada existed as a relatively free society for more than a century without such a document. The answer is that, despite the rule of law and British traditions, Canada has not always adequately protected citizens' rights. In 1938, the Alberta legislature enacted a Press Bill, which allowed the government to force newspapers to reveal the sources of unfavourable comment. In 1953, Québec restrained the freedom of religion of Jehovah's Witnesses by restricting their right to hand out pamphlets without permission. Yet another example was the Québec Padlock Law of 1937. By that legislation, the Québec government was allowed to ban the propagation of "Communism and Bolshevism" by padlocking any premises allegedly used for such purposes. The law gave Premier Maurice Duplessis the ability to move arbitrarily against groups opposed to his regime.

Although the courts subsequently overturned these restrictive pieces of legislation, the judges' decisions strengthened the argument for entrenching basic rights in the Constitution. The court rulings were not based on the fact that the legislation represented a violation of fundamental rights, but rather, they were based on the notion that provincial governments did not have the right to restrict civil liberties because of the constitutional division of powers. In all these cases, the courts declared the actions ultra vires — i.e., not within the provincial jurisdiction.

Another notable violation of basic rights in Canada's history was the internment of Japanese Canadians during the Second World War. Under the *War Measures Act*, thousands of people of Japanese descent were uprooted from their communities and placed in camps for the duration of the war for "security" reasons. Decades later, in 1970, Prime Minister Trudeau again invoked the *War Measures Act*, this time in response to Front de Libération du Québec (FLQ) terrorist activities in that province. This action, which suspended civil liberties and allowed the arbitrary detention of hundreds of suspects, is a recent major example of government violation of basic human rights in Canada.

In order to prevent such violations of civil liberties from occurring again, the *Constitution Act, 1982* provides a *Charter of Rights and Freedoms* with both substantive and procedural rights. **Substantive rights** are fundamental rights as defined in a constitution. **Procedural rights** are rights of citizens to access certain processes such as a fair trial. They are devices to protect individuals from arbitrary action by governments.

What Is in the *Charter of Rights and Freedoms*?

The Charter consists of a short introduction or preamble followed by thirty-four sections. The first section defines the limits of Canadians' rights and freedoms, stipulating that they are "subject only to such reasonable limits prescribed by law as can be demonstrably justified in a free and democratic society." This elastic clause allows the courts to determine the validity of laws within very wide parameters.

- The Charter protects *fundamental freedoms*, including those of conscience and religion, of thought, belief, opinion and expression, and of peaceful assembly and association. The basic democratic rights named in the document include the right of every citizen to vote; a five-year limit on the terms of federal and provincial legislatures, except in time of real or apprehended war, invasion or insurrection; and the requirement for legislatures to meet at least once every twelve months.

- The Charter also protects *mobility rights*, the right of Canadian citizens to enter, remain in and leave Canada, and to move to and work in any province. These rights are limited, however, by recognition of provincial residency requirements as a qualification for receiving social services. Affirmative action programs to ameliorate the conditions of an individual who has been socially or economically disadvantaged are also allowed.

- *Legal rights* such as the traditional right to life, liberty and security are listed, along with new legal rights provisions. For example, unreasonable search or seizure and arbitrary detention or imprisonment are prohibited. A detained individual is guaranteed the right to be informed promptly of the reasons for detention, to have counsel without delay and to be instructed of that right, as well as to have the validity of the detention determined and to be released if detention is not justified. Individuals who are charged with an offence have the right to be informed without delay of the specific offence, and to be tried within a reasonable time, have a right against self-incrimination, and are to be considered innocent until proven guilty by an impartial and public hearing. Evidence obtained in a manner that infringes upon an individual's rights and freedoms is to be excluded but only if its admission would "bring the administration of justice into disrepute."

- The Charter further provides *equality rights* guaranteeing that every individual is equal before and under the law without discrimination, particularly without discrimination based on race, national or ethnic origin, colour, religion, sex, age, or mental or physical disability. However, affirmative-action programs aimed at improving the conditions of groups discriminated against are allowed.

- The importance of *linguistic rights* is acknowledged in the Charter. English and French are recognized as Canada's official languages and are awarded equal status in institutions of the federal Parliament and government. Both languages are also recognized in the province of New Brunswick. Thus, in Canada's Parliament and New Brunswick's legislature, both languages may be used in debates and other proceedings. Federal statutes and records, as well as proceedings of the courts, are published in both languages. Individuals have the right to communicate with any head or central office of Parliament or government of Canada in either official language, and the same right is extended to other offices where there is significant demand.

- The Charter also provides *education rights*. All citizens of Canada who received their primary education in Canada in either French or English can exercise the right to have their children educated in the same language in the province in which they reside. This right, however, is applicable only "where numbers warrant," i.e., where the number of children warrants the provision of public funds. Except in Québec, *minority* language education rights are also guaranteed to the children of Canadian citizens whose first language learned and still understood is that of the English or French linguistic minority of the province in which they reside — *even* if the parents received their primary education outside of Canada. This latter guarantee will be applicable to Québec only when it is approved by the Québec National Assembly — and to date it has not been.

- The Charter includes a variety of *other specific rights*. The rights of Native peoples are not to be diminished by the Charter's provisions; for example, the provision that guarantees language education rights in French and English may not be interpreted to deprive the Indian people of James Bay of their right to educate their children in Cree. More broadly, the Charter may not be used to deprive anyone of existing rights and freedoms, and its interpretation must recognize Canada's multicultural heritage. Significantly, in recognition of Canada's federal nature, the Charter states that neither level of government gains power as a result of its provisions.

Despite this impressive list of rights, not all of them are inviolable. Remember that the Constitution was patriated only through political compromises. These included an agreement by the leaders to allow restrictions on citizens' rights in two general ways:

1. In Section 1, the Charter states that the rights and freedoms are guaranteed "subject" to "such reasonable limits presented by law as can be demonstrably justified in a free and democratic society." This means that the courts are allowed to decide that federal or provincial legislation that restricts freedoms is still valid or invalid according to *their* definition of "reasonable limits." The Supreme Court, for example, has allowed the Ontario legislature to impose film censorship as long as the criteria it uses is prescribed by law.[5]

2. Section 33 allows each provincial legislature and the federal Parliament the power to enact laws to override certain Charter provisions. As we have already seen, they may pass legislation counter to the Charter on fundamental freedoms, legal and equality rights by means of attaching a notwithstanding clause. Such bills become inoperative after five years and must be passed again if they are to remain valid. Democratic rights and mobility rights cannot be overridden by this notwithstanding mechanism.

Since the Charter became law, many of its provisions have been challenged in the courts. This has had both positive and negative effects. On the one hand, citizens have been able to ask courts to declare laws unconstitutional when they saw even a potential infringement of their rights. On the other, judges have had to interpret and clarify many provisions and apply them to existing laws that were previously passed by Parliament. Critics of the Charter argue among other things that it confers too much power on lawyers and judges, enabling judges who are not elected to strike down measures enacted by the majority. We examine highlights from these Charter cases in Chapter 9, "The Administration of Justice."

THE MEECH LAKE ACCORD AND LANGEVIN AMENDMENT

Although the Constitution was patriated in 1982, unfinished constitutional business remained. In particular, Québec's objections had still not been dealt with. The new federal Progressive Conservative government, elected in 1984, conducted months of bargaining with the provinces to design amendments that would secure Québec's political assent to the *Constitution Act*. In April 1987, Prime Minister Brian Mulroney and the ten premiers unanimously agreed on what became known as the **Meech Lake Accord**. The final text for this proposed constitutional amendment was agreed to after an all-night bargaining session in June in the Langevin Block on Parliament Hill in April 1987.

Québec premier, Robert Bourassa, demanded five constitutional amendments in the initial bargaining sessions:

- recognition of Québec as a "distinct" society;
- a formal voice for Québec in Supreme Court appointments;
- a Québec policy on immigration;
- limits to federal spending powers in areas of provincial jurisdiction;
- a veto on constitutional amendments affecting the province.

While it was generally agreed that Québec should have these demands met as part of "renewed federalism," the nine other premiers *also* made requests. They wanted changes concerning the Senate, federal spending power and the constitutional amending formula. In the end, the federal government and all ten provincial premiers agreed to all five Québec demands for constitutional reform. A political agreement on Senate reform also was agreed upon, but it was *not* to be part of the constitutional amendment at that time.

When euphoria over the agreement on the proposed constitutional changes subsided, many serious flaws became evident. The Liberals submitted eight amendments and the NDP two, but not one of them was accepted. In spite of this, John Turner, leader of the Liberals, and Ed Broadbent, leader of the NDP, demanded strict party discipline in voting in favour of the resolution. Thus Parliament passed the Meech Lake Accord with little dissent. However, since the Meech Lake amendment called for major constitutional revisions, it required the approval not just of Parliament but of *all ten* provincial legislatures as well. This requirement proved impossible to achieve.

The essential criticism of the secretly negotiated accord was that, in the pressure to win over Québec, important federal powers were given away, which would have weakened Parliament. Critics argued that giving the provinces more control of national institutions represented a radical change in the nature of Canadian federalism. They contended that the Meech Lake Accord was handing over so much power to the provinces that Canada would be transformed from a federation into a weak confederacy. Québec nationalists and some regionalists countered that Meech Lake was a positive affirmation that co-operative federalism could work.

In the final analysis, the Meech Lake Accord was defeated because it required unanimity from the provinces, and two provinces (Manitoba and Newfoundland) failed to pass the necessary resolution before the ratification deadline of June 23, 1990. Symbolically, it was Elijah Harper, standing in the Manitoba legislature with a white feather in his hand, who blocked the accord. Aboriginal demands, he said, would also need to be met before the Constitution was amended.

When the proposals did not obtain provincial unanimity, the whole package was dead. Life went on, but the Québec independence issue, dormant since the 1980 referendum, was revived. Shortly thereafter, the Québec National Assembly, led by Robert

Bourassa and his Liberals, passed bill 150, which required a referendum on "sovereignty" to be put to the people by October 26, 1992.

Post-Meech Efforts at Constitutional Change

Following the death of the Meech Lake Accord, numerous government-sponsored conferences, symposia, federal–provincial meetings and even a Royal Commission were held on the Constitution. On September 24, 1991, Prime Minister Mulroney introduced a new constitutional package in a publication called *Shaping Canada's Future Together*. This time the proposals were not supposed to be engraved in stone; comments and proposed changes were to be encouraged.[6]

Once again, critics argued, the proposals were too decentralizing and too multi-layered to allow effective and efficient government. They found that hundreds of concrete amendments had been hidden in the twenty-seven global suggestions. Not only were the proposals vague, but the overall result of the relations among them was completely unknowable. Again, the proposals created the possibility of a checkerboard Canada in which Canadians living in different provinces would not have the same benefits and opportunities. An example makes this clear. The residual clause — Peace, Order and good Government — which has been used in the past to give necessary powers to the federal government was to be weakened by giving "non-national matters" to the provincial authorities. This suggested, for example, that the environment might be considered as only a provincial matter, so that federal regulations would no longer apply. As well, as part of the compromise, the federal government proposed to withdraw from several specific jurisdictions. Some withdrawals were reasonable; others were more controversial.

Another major area of concern was that the reform proposals would have created a complicated Rubik's cube of federal institutions. The proposed Senate was too powerful as a policy and law-making body compared to the House of Commons. It would have had the right, for example, to ratify major order-in-council positions, a right denied to the House of Commons. Also, under the new proposals, a new layer of appointed government the Council of the Federation, would have been added to the House of Commons. Such a council undoubtedly would have been in constant conflict with the elected Parliament of Canada. Instead of streamlining government and making it more efficient and less expensive, *Shaping Canada's Future Together* threatened to generate even more problems.

The proposals in the document were examined at length by the Joint House and Senate Committee on a Renewed Canada (known as the Dobbie–Beaudoin Committee) in order to produce yet another set of proposals. The joint committee presented a revised set of proposals on February 28, 1992. Québec remained aloof and disdainful. Neither the government's *Shaping Canada's Future Together* nor the Dobbie–Beaudoin proposals were formally presented to Québec and the other provinces, but members of Québec's political elite turned them down in principle. As for the Official Opposition in Ottawa, Liberal leader Jean Chrétien was sufficiently disillusioned to suggest that a moratorium on constitutional reform should be considered.

Despite all these reports and public consultations, then, the federal government still had no acceptable proposals. Public cynicism and criticism was growing and the Progressive Conservative party was falling apart. On June 23, 1990, Lucien Bouchard left the Cabinet and formed the Bloc Québécois, a separatist party that would operate in Ottawa's Parliament. Meanwhile, Québec's Liberal government, led by Premier Bourassa, continued to be bound by bill 150, which called for a provincial referendum on sovereignty by October 27, 1992.

Québec's most divisive input into the constitutional debate came on January 28, 1991, with the provincial Liberal party's Allaire report, *A Québec Free to Choose*, which proposed a drastic decentralization of the country. According to the report, Québec should "exercise exclusive discretionary and total authority in most fields of activity." Twenty-two domains would be in the exclusive power of Québec, including communications, energy, industry and commerce, regional development and income security. Ottawa would be assigned only currency, customs and tariffs, debt management and transfer payments.

Back in Ottawa, the federal government, nine provinces, two territorial governments, and Native leaders came to a new, tentative agreement, called the "Pearson" agreement on July 7, 1992. This deal included a Triple-E Senate for the West; self-government for Native peoples; and a veto and "distinct society" recognition for Québec. Once again, in their totality, the proposals would have weakened federal authority. Québec representatives neither attended the meetings nor agreed to the proposals.

THE CHARLOTTETOWN ACCORD AND THE 1992 CONSTITUTIONAL REFERENDUM

The "Pearson" agreement drew Québec premier, Robert Bourassa, back to the bargaining table. After two years of boycotting constitutional discussions, he returned to the formal discussions on August 4, 1992, along with Prime Minister Mulroney, the other nine premiers and the leaders of the territories and the aboriginal communities. They emerged with a complex and highly controversial constitutional deal, known as the **Charlottetown Accord**, on August 28, 1992. It consisted of an agreement in principle (not a legal text) about what changes should be made to the Constitution and further political accords to be negotiated. All sides wanted to put the tentative principles to the Canadian people in a countrywide referendum two months later on October 26.

The deal called for major innovation in the way Canada is governed. It included a Canada clause, a new division of powers, new Native self-government clauses, a social and economic union and institutional changes in the House of Commons and Senate.[7] The most important proposal was that a definition of **distinct society** be added to the Constitution in a new clause that would ensure that "Québec constitutes within Canada a distinct society, which includes a French-speaking majority, a unique culture and a civil law tradition." As well, the proposals affirmed the role of the legislature and government of Québec "to preserve and promote the distinct society of Québec."

All three federal party leaders approved the package. The opponents of the accord appeared weak and disunited. They included Jacques Parizeau, leader of the Parti Québécois,

CLOSE-UP Canada's Constitutional Highlights

1867: *British North America Act* (now the *Constitution Act, 1867*) is enacted

1931: *Statute of Westminster* is enacted; Britain can no longer legislate for Canada except at the request of the Canadian government

1949: An amendment to the *BNA Act* widens the scope of the Canadian Parliament's authority to undertake further amendments

1949: Supreme Court of Canada becomes final court of appeal

1961: Diefenbaker Bill of Rights is enacted

1964: Fulton–Favreau formula is rejected by Québec

1971: Victoria Charter is rejected by Québec

1980: Québec referendum on sovereignty-association is defeated

1981: Supreme Court rules Trudeau's constitutional resolution is valid but violates political convention

1981: First ministers make three significant changes to resolution; package is rejected by Québec

1981: Constitutional resolution is passed by Parliament

1982: *Canada Act* passed by British House of Commons and patriated; the *Charter of Rights and Freedoms* and an amendment formula become part of the Canadian Constitution; Québec does not sign

1987: The Meech Lake Accord fails

1991: The Spicer Royal Commission reports

1992: The Dobbie–Beaudoin Joint House and Senate Committee report is published followed by constitutional conferences

1992: The Charlottetown Accord is approved by federal and provincial leaders, then massively rejected in a referendum

1995: Québec referendum on independence is held; sovereignty is very narrowly defeated

1996: Parliament passes legislation allowing Québec, Ontario, British Columbia and any two Atlantic or Prairie provinces to veto any further constitutional change

1998: Supreme Court answers three questions about Québec separatism

2000: Federal Parliament passes *Clarity Act* and Québec responds with its own legislation

2003: Election of Liberal and federalist Jean Charest as premier of Québec; temporarily, at least, separatist constitutional challenges from Québec are ended

and Lucien Bouchard, leader of the Bloc Québécois; Preston Manning, leader of the Reform party; and a few provincial Liberals such as Sharon Carstairs in Manitoba. However, the real leader of the No side proved to be former Prime Minister Pierre Elliott Trudeau, who attacked the constitutional deal with fervour and logic.

The third national referendum in Canadian history was a divisive event. In the final analysis, six provinces voted decisively against the deal and only Newfoundland, Prince

Edward Island and New Brunswick voted strongly for it. Ontario very narrowly supported the deal while Yukon voted against and Northwest Territories voted for it. At the national level, 72 percent of the Canadian electorate cast their votes and defeated the proposal by 54.4 percent to 44.6 percent (see Chapter 11, "Elections and Political Behaviour"). The Charlottetown proposal was dead.

The unexpected defeat led politicians to conclude that it was time for a moratorium on constitutional discussions. With a federal election due by the end of 1993 and a Québec provincial election in 1994, the leaders returned to "politics as usual."

The 1992 Charlottetown Accord had been designed to accommodate provincial interests. Its defeat prevented Canada from becoming even more decentralized. However, challenges to the viability of the state continue unabated, as we shall see in the discussions of federalism in Chapter 4 and nationalism in Chapter 5.

Have Canadians patriated the Constitution only to be mired in constitutional deadlock? The amendment procedures may prove too rigid to resolve deficiencies that are glaringly evident in the country. The constitutional dilemma of how to solve regional aspirations and Québec's precise demands while retaining a viable federal government is probably the most vital political challenge now facing Canadians.

The Liberal government relegated constitutional reform to the back burner when it came to power in 1993. Prime Minister Jean Chrétien took the stand that many arrangements between the federal government and the provinces could be dealt with outside the Constitution. This, for example, has been the case to some extent with minor changes in the relationship between the federal government and Native peoples. Some First Nations have achieved much of what they had wanted to be included in the Charlottetown Accord without a constitutional amendment. Others have not. However, major problems in federal–provincial relations continue to dominate Canadian politics; in particular, the future of Québec in Canada (see Chapter 5, "Nationalism and Regionalism").

Despite federal–provincial bickering, the Constitution of Canada clearly is strong and not about to topple. When asked to decide on change, Canadians were skeptical that change was needed. Politicians who attempt to convince Canadians that the country and Constitution do not work will have to do a better job of persuasion and be clear that they are not merely pushing their own agendas for secession, devolution, asymmetry or even themselves.

The next chapter focuses on the federal system and how it works. Decide for yourself whether, and if so how, it needs to be reformed in a major way.

KEY TERMS

amendment formula, p. 64
Canadian Bill of Rights, p. 68
Charlottetown Accord, p. 74
code, p. 57

collective rights, p. 57
common law, p. 57
constitution, p. 56
convention, p. 56

DISCUSSION QUESTIONS

1. What were the two basic obstacles to the 1982 patriation of the Constitution, and what compromises were reached to try to solve them? Why did Québec not agree with the compromises?

2. What were the main additions to the Constitution when it was patriated in 1982? Was it wise to patriate it without Québec's approval?

3. Describe and evaluate the current formula for amending the Constitution.

4. What attempts has the federal government made since 1982 to convince Québec to sign the patriated Constitution? Explain why, in your considered opinion, they have failed so far.

WEBLINKS

The Constitution

www.canoe.ca/Canadiana/constitution.html

Canadian Charter of Rights And Freedoms

canada.justice.gc.ca/en/laws/charter

Charlottetown Accord

www.ola.bc.ca/online/cf/documents/1992CHARLOTTETOWN.html

Virtual Library

www.parl.gc.ca/common/library_prb.asp?Language=E

4 Contested Federalism
The Division of Powers and Financial Resources

Learning Objectives

After reading this chapter, you should be able to

1. Distinguish between unitary, confederal and federal systems of government.

2. Outline the basic distribution of powers between the federal and provincial governments in Canada.

3. Trace the shifting pattern of power in Canadian federalism from 1867 to the present.

4. Explain four key problems at the root of federal–provincial financial arrangements.

5. Describe the two basic funding mechanisms by which money is transferred from the federal government to the provinces.

6. Describe how the federal government currently distributes money to the provinces.

*F*ederalism is a complex, many-sided political game. The basic idea of federalism has been traced back in history to the fusion of ancient Israelite tribes. In North America, its first occurrence is thought to have been among the Five Nations of the Iroquois. The contemporary concept of federalism, however, is best dated to the eighteenth century when the United States' Constitution established the first modern federal system of government. American federalism was based on two main ideas: the distribution of government power on a geographical basis and the philosophy that unity and diversity can coexist. The US federal system has been a model for some other states, including Canada, Australia and Switzerland.

Federalism sets up a multi-dimensional game of politics in which there are powerful political actors at various levels of government. In this chapter, we study the ideas that underpin the federal union and the legal foundations of federalism in Canada: the division of powers between Ottawa and the provincial capitals as well as the funding of the economic union. There is no doubt that controlling taxpayers' money is one of the most, if not the most, important ingredients in federal politics.

THE CONCEPT OF FEDERALISM

We saw in Chapter 1 that a *sovereign state* wields authority and power in that it is capable of maintaining order within its territory. It is able to tax its citizens and run its affairs free from external interference. A sovereign state is recognized as legitimate by its citizens and by other countries.

All sovereign states distribute the power to carry out governmental functions across their territories in some manner. There may be one strong, central government supplemented by insignificant local authorities, or the central government may be weakened by dividing authority and sharing it with regional governments. In some countries, therefore, the constitution gives all final decision-making authority to one level of government. In others, the constitution provides for more than one level of final authority over the same people in the same territory.

Most of the world's states have centralized, one-level political systems called **unitary systems**. In this type of system, the constitution provides for one level of sovereign power in the country. If other levels of government exist — such as cities and regions — they are under the constitutional jurisdiction of the unitary government. The central government may delegate powers to regional or local administrative units, but it alone remains, in constitutional terms, the supreme law-making institution. Examples of unitary governments are Britain, France and Japan.

In a **federal system,** the legal powers are divided between a central government and regional governments in such a way that each level of government has some kind of activities on which it makes final decisions.[1] This means there is more than one level of government over the same geographical territory. In federal systems, the constitution specifically divides jurisdictional powers between the central government and the regional government(s). Neither level of government owes its authority to the other. Both federal and provincial legislatures may make laws that impact directly on the citizens. This is the case in Canada.

There are more than fifteen times more unitary states than there are federal states in the world. However, although there are only some twenty-three federal states, they contain over 40 percent of the world's population.[2]

In a federal system, each level of government has more-or-less complete authority over some specific spheres of activity, while there may be a degree of overlapping jurisdiction on a few others (see Figure 4.1).

The Canadian Constitution outlines a federal system of government with jurisdiction divided or shared between the federal Parliament and the provincial assemblies. Within that broad framework, however, the Constitution leaves much undefined, or loosely defined. Many administrative rules are left for the players of the day to make, based on historical and economic considerations and political judgments.

Since federal and provincial governments govern the same people and the same territory, there is constant rivalry between them. Political conflicts often arise over the authority and jurisdiction of the federal and provincial governments. Most of these disputes concern who should make and who should pay for decisions. However, there are also serious quarrels over whether all of the provinces are, or even should be, equal in

Figure 4.1 Continuum of the Degree of Centralization of Authority

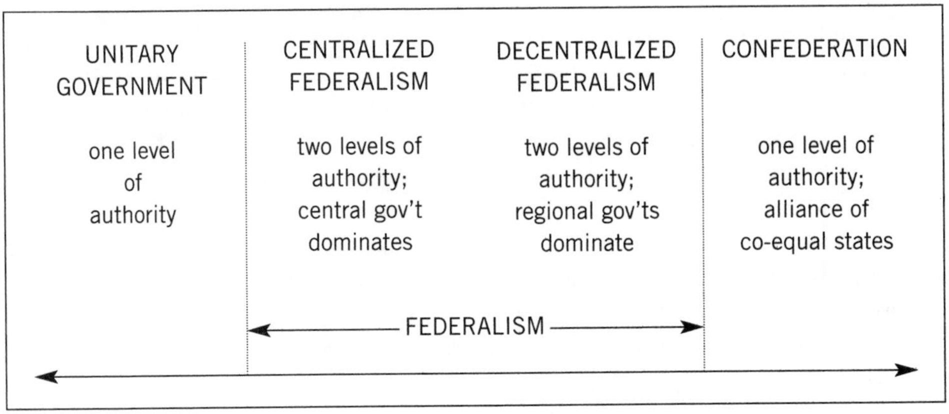

UNITARY GOVERNMENT	CENTRALIZED FEDERALISM	DECENTRALIZED FEDERALISM	CONFEDERATION
one level of authority	two levels of authority; central gov't dominates	two levels of authority; regional gov'ts dominate	one level of authority; alliance of co-equal states

← —————— FEDERALISM —————— →

Source: Adapted from concepts proposed by William H. Riker in *Federalism: Origin, Operation, Significance* (Boston: Little, Brown, 1964).

every respect, or whether some receive, or should receive, special treatment from the federal government.

Federalism, therefore, is constantly changing to meet new needs and circumstances. Developments in federalism reach into the lives of every Canadian. The many social services and programs available to Canadians today are the result of agreements between federal and provincial governments. Some programs are supported by only one level of government, but the majority of them require financial co-operation between the two levels. Just as too many cooks can spoil the broth, the federal system complicates the handling of many vital issues, such as economic planning and control of inflation. On the other hand, it also brings government closer to the people, allowing provinces and regions to retain a degree of control over particular aspects of their development and the day-to-day lives of their residents.

ORIGINS OF CANADIAN FEDERALISM

Throughout the first half of the nineteenth century, Britain's Canadian colonies edged toward political union. The 1841 union of Upper and Lower Canada (now Ontario and Québec) was the first step. As the population of Upper Canada (Ontario) grew in relation to that of Lower Canada (Québec), Upper Canadians demanded more political influence. Meanwhile, Lower Canada steadfastly insisted on non-interference with the French, Catholic way of life. As political deadlock developed, tensions mounted and the experiment of joining the two Canadas failed.

Sir John A. Macdonald played a leading role in resolving the situation by establishing the federal union in 1867. With wisdom and foresight, he placated the smaller Maritime provinces and held forth the prospect of a glorious national destiny.[3]

Each of the British colonies in North America saw advantages for itself in the union. The leaders from Upper Canada looked forward to further economic expansion and development. Those from Lower Canada were willing to consider a federal union if their language and culture could be protected by law. The sparsely populated Maritime colonies of Nova Scotia and New Brunswick were perhaps the most reluctant, but they were attracted by the economic advantages of union, namely a new transcontinental railway and potential subsidies from a future federal government.

Conferences in Québec and Charlottetown and a long process of negotiation culminated in an agreement to form a Dominion of Canada, a *federal* arrangement in which powers would be divided between the federal and provincial legislatures.[4] Confederation was finalized in 1867. As it turned out, *Confederation* was a confusing term. A **confederation** is a form of political organization that very loosely unites strong provincial or state units under a weak government. We still refer to the *Confederation Agreement* and the *Fathers of Confederation*, but the authors intended Canada to be a centralized federation with a strong central government.

THE FEDERAL–PROVINCIAL DIVISION OF POWERS

The need for a "federal bargain" to divide powers between the central and the regional governments was urgent in the 19th century. The colonists were used to rule by local governments, and transportation and communication among the provinces were difficult. Sir Georges-Étienne Cartier and other French Canadian leaders demanded a degree of exemption from central government authority. Therefore, some independence had to be granted to the local entities. While Sir John A. Macdonald would actually have preferred a British-style unitary form of government, the federal principle was accepted as a necessary compromise. It maintained the unity of the political system while protecting the interests of provinces and language groups.[5]

In early Canadian history, provincial constitutional power appeared relatively insignificant. The Constitution provided much more authority to the federal government, giving it three centralizing constitutional powers:

1. In extreme circumstances, the national government could use its power of **disallowance** — the power to disallow provincial legislation, even though the subject matter of the legislation was assigned to the provinces by the *BNA Act*. This power of disallowance was employed 112 times after Confederation, but it has not been used since 1943.

2. The federal government had the power of reservation. **Reservation** refers to the constitutional ability of lieutenant-governors to reserve provincial legislation for federal approval. Reservation has been employed quite often: some seventy bills have been reserved since 1867.[6]

3. The federal government may have had the power of **veto** — the power to block legislation or to block a constitutional amendment by use of the royal prerogative. Since this power was never exercised, however, it is presumed to have atrophied.

These three powers were so centralizing that some experts refer to the early period of Canadian history as one of *quasi-federalism* — a federal appearance (i.e., divided jurisdictions), but a unitary reality (i.e., no divided authority) because there was no significant power in the sub-units. However, it seems unlikely that such extreme federal powers as those of disallowance or reservation will ever be used again in Canada, except perhaps in a circumstance as grave as the secession of a province from the federal union. Today, Canada is certainly not a quasi-federal state.

The Constitution also gave the federal government more powers than the provinces in another way. The Fathers of Confederation regarded the US Civil War as an example of what could happen if a central government did not have strong authority. They therefore included in the Constitution a **residual clause** to allow the federal government to legislate in any matter not specifically assigned to the provinces. **Section 91** of the Constitution specifies the areas belonging to the federal government. It also contains the residual clause. Section 91 states

> It shall be lawful for the Queen, by and with the Advice and Consent
> of the Senate and the House of Commons, to make Laws for the
> Peace, Order, and good Government of Canada, in relation to all
> matters not coming within the Classes of Subjects by this Act
> assigned exclusively to the Legislatures of the Provinces . . .

In addition to granting this sweeping authority, Section 91 specifies 29 items as belonging exclusively to the federal government, including trade, commerce, banking, credit, currency, taxation, navigation, citizenship and defence. **Section 92** of the Constitution, on the other hand, outlines 16 specific areas of provincial jurisdiction, including direct taxation, hospitals, prisons, property, and civil rights. (see the Appendix for constitutional details). These latter, provincial subjects were of only limited and local concern in 1867 but were later to become much more important than the Fathers could have foreseen in their era of more-or-less laissez-faire government.

Problems over the Division of Powers

While the *BNA Act* was a centralist document, it is extremely important to note that certain terms were not defined precisely in the Act, so that they took on new meanings over time. These omissions created a void that both federal and provincial authorities sought to fill to their own advantage after Confederation. The contest continues even now. For example, Section 93 gave power over education to the provinces, but today it is a matter for debate whether education, as a provincial responsibility, encompasses or should encompass cultural matters, broadcasting, occupational training and research.

The conflict over the division of powers is well illustrated in the field of natural resources. The *BNA Act* clearly assigned "ownership" of resources to the provinces. However, it gave the federal government a major voice in the sales of resources by allowing it to control inter-provincial and international trade. Thus, today, the provinces control oil because it is under the ground; but oil wells are in the hands of private or public companies, and the Parliament of Canada also exercises some authority over oil through taxation and jurisdictional powers.

The federal government was also given specific power to interfere in provincial jurisdictions. Through the **declaratory power** (*BNA Act*, Section 92.10(a)), the federal government is allowed to assume jurisdiction over any "work" considered to be for the benefit of Canada as a whole. In the 1920s, for example, Parliament placed every grain elevator under federal control but did not assume ownership. Federal control over uranium exploration is a more recent example. The provinces have often contested the use of the declaratory power, but the courts have backed the federal position.

Clearly, the Constitution has proven inadequate in clarifying many jurisdictions. Today, very few areas of policy are handled exclusively by one level of government.

The only exclusively federal areas appear to be defence, veterans' affairs, the post office and monetary policy. The only exclusively provincial areas appear to be municipal institutions, elementary and secondary education, and some areas of law related to property and other non-criminal matters.[7]

In all other areas, both levels of government engage in activities in the same fields. Sometimes the process is harmonious, as for example when the federal government allows the provinces to regulate inter-provincial highway transportation. In other areas such as external trade, manpower training, communications, language and culture, the two levels are in constant conflict.

Another aspect of the constitutional division of powers that continues to be controversial is the field of **concurrent powers**. Concurrent powers are those shared between the Parliament of Canada and the provincial legislatures. Section 95 of the *BNA Act* called for concurrent powers in agriculture and immigration. However, *de facto* concurrent powers have also arisen in other fields because of the federal government's control of *spending power*. Just because the federal government may have little or no legal jurisdiction over particular matters such as education, health, consumer protection and the environment, this does not prohibit Ottawa from spending money in these areas and therefore influencing policy. The provinces have great difficulty in refusing such "gifts." Although not mentioned in the Constitution as concurrent powers, scientific research, recreational activities, tourism and protection of the environment are handled today as if they were areas of concurrent jurisdiction.

Conflicts over jurisdictional boundaries are to be expected in federal systems. Flexible or woolly clauses are particularly troublesome. In Canada, persistent arguments have arisen because some matters in the provincial sphere, such as "property and civil rights," have become more significant over the years. At the same time, the "Peace, Order and good Government" (or POGG) clause grants the federal government authority in all fields in the case of an emergency. As social and economic policies have evolved, this federal power has increasingly conflicted with the specific provincial powers.

SHIFTING PATTERNS OF CANADIAN FEDERALISM
From 1867 to the Late-1950s

In the new Canadian administration of 1867, the central government was meant to be predominant. The federal government was the beneficiary of the residual peace, order, and good government clause. The limited jurisdiction of the provinces indicated their subordinate position in the federation. Over time, however, this relationship has been interpreted in different ways by the courts, causing different patterns of federalism.

The relative power of the provinces grew during the latter part of the nineteenth century, due to a series of judgments by the Judicial Committee of the Privy Council. A consistent pattern of JCPC decisions favoured provincial over federal rights.[8] Forceful provincial leaders caused the erosion of central government powers to the point that the *BNA Act* came to be interpreted by the JCPC more like an international treaty than the constitution of a new country.[9]

This situation did not last long. Under the *BNA Act*, the provinces had jurisdiction over such matters as education, health and social welfare, which originally required very little expenditure. However, as the demand for social services grew in the twentieth century, the provinces found themselves starved for funds since the other provisions of the Act made it virtually impossible for them to raise the revenues needed. To help the provinces financially, the federal government offered them various grants on the *condition* that the money be spent in a specified manner. The provinces resented this intrusion but had little choice in the matter.

The 1930s Depression deepened the dependency of the provinces on the federal government. The necessity to prepare Canada for war in 1914 and again in 1939 also tended to centralize power in Ottawa. Except perhaps in Québec, where there was considerable opposition to the two World Wars and especially to conscription, the federal government became a focus of patriotism and loyalty for most Canadians, who endowed it with enormous prestige and symbolic influence.

The factors contributing to a centralization of power continued for some time into the second postwar era, but there were early signs that the provinces would eventually seek to regain their lost ground. New ideas about decentralization began to circulate as early as 1937, with the recommendations of the Royal Commission on Dominion–Provincial Relations, perhaps better known as the Rowell–Sirois Commission.[10] This Commission had been set up to investigate the reasons for the near-bankruptcy of the provinces and to recommend ways in which to revitalize the federation. While its suggestions could not be implemented until after the Second World War, the Commission came out strongly against the existing grants procedure. In addition, it recommended that Ottawa take over such expensive responsibilities as unemployment insurance and pensions and generally seek to equalize the financial resources of the provinces.

In the early days of Confederation, then, there was not much need for formal federal–provincial consultations, and the meetings that did occur were of an *ad hoc* nature. However, over time, economic policies that aimed at full employment, growth and trade liberalization and a wide range of social policies necessitated a dramatic increase in intergovernmental relations. New departments or offices were established within the federal and provincial governments to deal with these issues.

Intergovernmental relations immediately after the Second World War had been reasonably harmonious. It was a period of "co-operative federalism," albeit with a decidedly federal predominance. Economic times were good, and federal–provincial relations primarily concerned social programs that did not necessarily involve regional conflict. As a rule, bureaucrats tended to resolve problems before they reached the political agenda.

The 1960s to the Early 2000s

By the 1960s, the provinces needed financial relief. At the same time, important social changes were occurring in Québec and Western Canada.

Throughout the decade, Québec underwent a "Quiet Revolution" in which a new, confident French-Canadian elite led an assault on Ottawa's "paternalism." Ottawa responded by expanding what were referred to as "shared-cost programs" or "conditional grants" (discussed below), which were awarded to the provinces on *condition* that they were spent in a certain way. However, these programs tended to be seen as distorting provincial spending priorities. Québec politicians insisted on the right to "opt out" of certain programs so that they could go their own way. Ottawa was unable to muster a coherent or effective response to meet this challenge.

A simmering sense of grievance against Ottawa also began to emerge in the western provinces during this period. Made confident by enormous resource revenues, Alberta and British Columbia in particular sought greater political clout within the federation to match their recently acquired wealth. While they were not sympathetic to the cultural and linguistic aspirations of the Québécois, the western provinces shared with them a degree of hostility toward what they perceived as paternalism of the federal government and favouritism toward Central Canada.

The 1960s and 1970s were characterized by less co-operation and more confrontation between the two levels of government.

Aislin, The Montreal Gazette. Reprinted with permission.

Economic downturns and an increased concern for the jurisdictional integrity of the provinces changed the nature of federal–provincial relations. The term coined to describe this changed relationship was "executive federalism." Intergovernmental talks shifted from a group of public servants behind closed doors to open discussions among politicians, often in the full glare of publicity. At First Ministers' Conferences, the leaders of the eleven governments met to hammer out deals, often under the scrutiny of television cameras. Some of the most important of these meetings were named Constitutional Conferences.

These public meetings became an opportunity for the provinces to express discontent and resistance to federal authority. They provided political forums in which the premiers appealed to the other heads of government and also directly to their electorates. Soon, the ten provincial premiers began to meet separately from First Ministers' Conferences and approach the final bargaining table as a *unified* group opposed to the federal government. Ottawa was no longer able to dominate its partners in the federation.

There is little question that the era of executive federalism was characterized by decentralization and intergovernmental conflict. Some commentators, for example, argued that the increase in intergovernmental specialists made federal–provincial conflicts more difficult to solve.[11] Jealous representatives at each level of government tended to promote their own government's narrow interests, thereby impeding compromise.

In the 1980s, federal–provincial relations reached a new level of hostility. Discussions about the mechanics and institutional arrangements for consultation between Ottawa and the provincial capitals shifted to major constitutional discord. The 1982 patriation of the Constitution gave rise to continual wrangling between the federal government and the province of Québec. Negotiations and deals — from the Meech Lake Accord to the Charlottetown Accord — dominated federalism. The cozy centralization of the postwar period was over and so were the later pendulum swings between federal and provincial power. In their place was upheaval over the very nature and future of Canadian federalism, especially the role of Québec in it (see Chapters 3 and 5).

MONEY AND FEDERALISM: FOUR KEY PROBLEMS

This short overview of Canadian federalism shows that obtaining and spending money have been, and remain, crucial aspects of federal–provincial relations in Canada. Four general problems have been identified by J.C. Strick as being at the root of federal–provincial financial arguments.[12]

The first and most obvious problem is that there has always been a fundamental incongruence between jurisdictional responsibilities and sources of revenue at the two levels of government. In order to create a highly centralized federal system at Confederation, the federal government was awarded the most significant revenue sources. The Constitution entitled the federal government to raise money "by any mode or system of taxation" while the provinces were limited to direct taxation. As we have noted, however, provincial expenditures mushroomed, and the provinces needed more revenues. This became a constant source of tension and conflict with the federal government.

The second problem stems from the fact that the wealth of the provinces has always differed widely. In the early years, a relatively prosperous province like Ontario or Québec was fortunate in having a strong tax base in the form of a concentration of corporate activities and personal fortunes. Wealthy provinces, therefore, had the ability to raise adequate funds to provide social services. Poorer and relatively depressed provinces like those in the Maritimes, however, were unable to obtain sufficient tax revenue. Increasing provincial taxes would only lower individual incomes and undermine economic growth. Over time, the ability to obtain high tax revenues has shifted from province to province — for example, from Ontario to Alberta during periods of high energy prices.

The third problem resulted from the joint occupancy of tax fields. As we have seen, the Constitution Act gave the provinces control of only direct taxation. **Direct taxation** refers to taxes that are collected directly by the government, such as individual income tax, corporate income tax and succession duties. The federal government, on the other hand, was authorized to tax in any manner. It could institute its own direct taxes in competition with the provinces. It could also levy indirect taxes. **Indirect taxation** refers to taxes that are collected by other persons or institutions and passed along to the government, such as customs, or sales tax. Eventually, however, the provinces obtained the right to collect indirect taxes as well, and then both levels of government began to levy taxes on the same sources. The competition for revenue sources became yet another contentious aspect of federal–provincial fiscal relations.

The fourth problem relates to fiscal policy. It was feared that without close co-operation between federal and provincial taxation and spending policies, the overall economy would not be effectively controlled. If, for example, the federal government sought to cut taxes to stimulate the economy at the same time the provinces decided to increase taxes, the federal initiative would be negated. Without a degree of co-operation, federal and provincial policies would work at cross-purposes.

These four issues have been handled differently since Confederation. Today, Ottawa still collects income taxes for itself and all the provinces except Québec (the provinces set their own rates); Québec takes in its own personal and corporate income taxes. With the exception of Ontario, Québec and Alberta, all provinces have tax collection arrangements with the federal government for corporate income taxes.

Key Concepts

Mechanisms to transfer funds from the federal government to the provinces have evolved over the years from relatively simple grants to complex financial arrangements. To understand these arrangements, it is necessary to understand some basic concepts, including conditional grants, unconditional grants and the federal spending power.

Conditional Grants, Unconditional Grants and Spending Power

Conditional grants are funds given by the federal government to provincial governments on the condition that they be spent in a certain way. In Canada, such grants have been considered essential because of the unequal distribution of resources across the country.

The first conditional grants in Canada were paid out for agricultural instruction in 1912. Larger-scale grants were offered in 1927 to help the provinces finance old-age pensions. These grants also helped to alleviate the financial problems of the 1930s. After the Second World War, increased spending on health and welfare necessitated another major expansion in the field of conditional grants.

The federal government was able to act in these fields, which are under provincial jurisdiction because of its spending power. **Spending power** refers to the federal government's blanket authority to spend money for any purpose in any field even if it has no legal jurisdiction over the area. In most conditional grants programs, Ottawa offered to pay half the costs of a specific program, with the provinces paying the rest. These were **shared-cost programs**, or so-called 50-cent dollar programs in which the federal government paid 50 percent of costs. They were an attractive proposition for some provinces; they encouraged provincial legislatures to spend their resources on programs chosen by the federal government. On some occasions, provincial leaders might have preferred to spend the money on other programs, but there was no way to shift resources unless Ottawa agreed.

In 1964, as a result of criticism of these types of programs, the federal government began to allow any province that did not want to be involved in a joint-cost venture to receive an equivalent sum of money by way of a federal tax withdrawal or in another form. Only Québec took up this offer, highlighting its claim to "special status" within Confederation. Québec's "different" status was also confirmed by the development of its own hospital and old-age pension schemes.

As the financial health of the provinces improved, it was inevitable that they would seek a revision of these fiscal arrangements. In 1977, led by Québec, and to some extent Alberta and Ontario, the provinces won the struggle to end the relatively restrictive conditional grants system. Ottawa increasingly offered **unconditional grants** — money that the provinces could spend in any way they wished. These grants were not designated for any specific policy field. This shift from conditional to unconditional grants can be considered an indication of the decentralization of the federal system during the period.

Key Mechanisms

Over the years, mechanisms have been put in place to implement conditional and unconditional grants. They include equalization grants and established program financing.

Equalization Grants

We have seen how the differing economic prosperity of the provinces has posed a continuing problem in federal–provincial relations since Confederation. In 1867, the financial gap between the provinces was already wide; it has been growing ever since. A primary objective of fiscal policy since the Second World War has been to narrow this gap and to provide a degree of economic stabilization. The main mechanism for accomplishing this has been, and continues to be, the provision of equalization payments to the provinces.

Equalization payments were put in effect in 1957 and enshrined in the Constitution in 1982. They were designed to ensure that the provinces can offer reasonably similar public services in areas such as health care, welfare and education without excessive levels of taxation. These are unconditional transfer payments to the provinces from the federal government, calculated on the fiscal capacity of each province compared to the others. A "standard" tax yield is worked out and provinces that fall below it receive transfers from the federal government to bring them up to the standard yield.

Until September 2004, the pool of funds for equalization rose and fell with the performance of the national economy. Then the prime minister guaranteed $10.8 billion and $10.9 billion for 2004–2005 and 2005–2006 (up from $8.9 and 9.2 billion) and an increase by 3 percent a year after that. Provinces that fall below a given standard are considered "have-not" provinces and are given equalization payments. In 2004, all of the provinces except Alberta and Ontario were in the have-not category and received equalization funds (see Figure 4.2). As of 2005, Saskatchewan joined the "have" provinces.

In terms of per capita provincial government expenditures, equalization payments have proven successful, but they have not brought the have-not provinces up to the level of the have provinces. The provinces may be relatively equal in terms of providing government services, but interprovincial and interregional disparities remain, despite the presence of equalization payments.

Apart from the equalization program, federal transfers to all but the two poorest provinces are paid by taxpayers in the province that receives the money. These

Figure 4.2 The Equalization Formula, 2004–2005

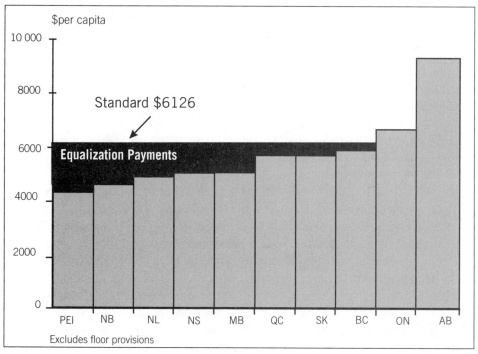

Source: Department of Finance Canada *www.fin.gc.ca/FEDPROV/eqpe.html.* Reproduced with the permission of the Minister of Public Works and Government Services, 2005. Accessed February 21, 2005.

non-equalization transfers do not redistribute income across provincial borders. The equalization program is therefore vital to reduce disparities between provinces and also to reduce inequalities in real income among individuals. It is not surprising, then, that the concept of equalization was enshrined in the Canadian Constitution of 1982, with the unanimous consent of all governments. Even recent budgets, which included proposals to decrease other types of federal transfers to the provinces, continued the commitment to equalization.

The debate over the equalization system reached a new level in the fall of 2004. The federal government promised the provinces that the Equalization and Territorial Financing formula would be increased by over $33 billion over the next ten years. The formula, which is to become effective in April 2006, will include a growth rate of 2.5 percent until 2010. A panel was set up to advise the federal government and the provinces on how these funds should be allocated among the provinces and territories and is to report by the end of 2005. In other words, federal, provincial and territorial leaders have agreed to the necessity of reforming the equalization system, but they have put off for another two years the rancorous debate about *how* equalization funds should be distributed.

CLOSE-UP   Equalization: To Share or Not to Share?

Canada's equalization system distributes federal tax revenue from well-to-do-provinces to have-not provinces so that those less able to afford basic services are brought up to a set standard. The principle is simple, but the system is extremely complex and a source of constant friction.

In 2005, the federal government signed an agreement with two Maritime provinces concerning who would get the revenue from offshore resources. It caused an uproar among the other provinces that will have repercussions into the future.

Previously, in the 1980s, the federal government had signed agreements with Newfoundland and Nova Scotia allowing them to keep 100 percent of their offshore oil and gas revenues. In return, following the rules of equalization, they had to give back about 70 cents of every dollar they took in from their resource industries. The more they "earned," the less they got back in equalization payments.

By 2004, revenue from offshore oil developments at Hibernia and Terra Nova was growing, and a third, White Rose, was scheduled to come online in 2006. The federal government owns the offshore resources under the seabed on behalf of all Canadians. However, the two provinces believed that their equalization payments should no longer be reduced because of any new revenues from the offshore oil. They saw this as their opportunity to become "have" provinces.

In February 2005, the minority Liberal government in Ottawa signed deals allowing Nova Scotia and Newfoundland and Labrador to keep 100 percent of

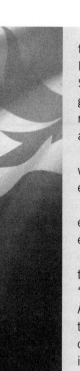

their offshore revenues with no "clawback" of equalization payments until 2012. Newfoundland and Labrador got an advance payment of $2 billion for the estimated $2.6 billion its offshore resources will produce over that period, and Nova Scotia got $830 million, about three-quarters of its estimated revenues. If they do not reach the federal–capacity standard of the "have" provinces by 2012, then the agreement is extended another eight years.

Anger immediately erupted among the other provinces about the impact the deal would have on them. Some provinces resented having to pay so much toward the equalization formula. Others wanted similar breaks for their resource industries.

Saskatchewan, which had recently become a "have-province" and no longer was entitled to payments from the equalization system wanted a similar deal for its energy resources.

Ontario complained loudly of being treated like a cash cow. It calculated that through the equalization formula it was giving more per capita for services in the "have not" provinces than it had for its *own* residents. It said the new Atlantic Accord would make equalization transfers grow by 3.5 percent, a rate greater than the rate at which the province's economy is expected to grow. It therefore demanded at least $5 billion in additional funding from the federal government in compensation.

Was the federal government's decision to unilaterally sidestep the principles of the equalization scheme acceptable? Or was it a poorly thought out decision that breached the spirit of the equalization agreement as it was originally conceived?

Established Program Financing

Both conditional grants and equalization grants have changed over time. The most significant, comprehensive innovation came in 1977, the year the federal government offered the provinces a hybrid **block grant** (a grant of one large sum of money from the federal government to the provinces, to be spent in certain policy fields) earmarked for health and post-secondary education.[13] This block grant program, called the **Established Program Financing (EPF)** was essentially conditional in nature. The federal monies had to be spent in the general fields of health and education as outlined, but within these broad parameters, the provinces were largely free to make their own policy choices.

For the years 1977 to 1982, the EPF provided two types of funding for provincial expenditures on health care and post-secondary education — a tax transfer of personal and corporate income tax points and a cash transfer. While the federal government interpreted the Act as giving autonomy to the provinces, the legislation also placed some of the most expensive areas of social services squarely in the laps of the provincial governments. From the provinces' point of view, the federal government, which got them into these expensive fields in the first place, was simply preparing to disengage itself as costs began to rise.

In spite of the move to block funding, in the EPF, the federal government was able to determine how some of the funds were used. In 1984, for example, the federal *Canada Health Act* declared that the health transfer would be reduced for any province that allowed doctors to extra bill or employ user fees.

After the major changes in 1977, the next negotiations over the renewal of federal–provincial fiscal arrangements came in 1982. The federal government sought to correct what it perceived as two fundamental problems. First, there was a growing fiscal imbalance between the federal and provincial governments; while the federal government's deficit increased there was an overall surplus in provincial revenues. Second, the federal government wanted to maintain what it called a proper "political balance." Ottawa argued that its contributions to provincial government services were not sufficiently visible, and this both hindered proper government accountability for taxes and expenditures and deprived the federal government of recognition for the assistance it did provide. For these reasons, the federal government sought to cut back the level of transfers to the provinces.

The provinces, on the other hand, generally favoured maintaining the status quo. They argued that the federal deficit was not due to federal transfers to the provinces but rather to federal policies of indexation, tax expenditures, the subsidization of oil and gas prices, and interest-rate policies. The provinces also noted that the overall provincial revenue surplus was the result of the resource wealth of a few provinces and did not reflect the overall fiscal capacity of the provinces as a whole. The "have not" provinces were especially concerned with the future of the equalization program. The wealthier provinces, for their part, sought to protect the money they received from the established program's block grants.

FISCAL ARRANGEMENTS IN FLUX

In spite of severe opposition, the federal government remained determined to reduce its transfers to the provinces. In 1982, after months of inconclusive bargaining, it enacted fiscal arrangements that continued in their basic form until the fiscal year 1996–97. In 1982, the EPF formula was amended so that the provincial entitlement was determined for a base year and "escalation indicators" were applied for economic and population growth. From this aggregate number, the federal government subtracted the amount of revenue generated by the tax points given to the provinces and then paid out the remainder as a cash grant.[14] In the succeeding years, the federal government reduced the escalation factor and thus limited the total EPF entitlement of the provinces. This action had the effect of transferring an increasing share of the burden of these programs to the provinces.

In 1982, changes were also made in the method of calculating equalization payments. The federal government proposed Ontario as the standard for determining eligibility for equalization payments, thereby ensuring the province's continued exclusion from receiving such grants. However, the poorer provinces (and Ontario) objected to having the amount of money they received contingent upon Ontario's economic performance, especially in light of that province's economic stagnation during those years. Ottawa therefore dropped the so-called "Ontario standard," replacing it with a formula based on the average revenue of five provinces.

For the 1988–93 period, transfers from the federal to the provincial and territorial governments remained mostly in the Established Program Financing, the equalization program and the **Canada Assistance Program (CAP)**, a program by which the federal government helps to finance welfare and other provincial social services. The CAP is a shared-cost program established in 1966. Under its terms, the federal government pays 50 percent of the costs of provincial and municipal programs in welfare, day care, child welfare services and homemakers' assistance. The basic restriction on federal funding for the CAP is that the provincial social assistance programs must be based on "need." Programs may vary widely across the country.

The New System — Post-1996

In 1995, federal Finance Minister Paul Martin announced that a major shift in the block funding of provincial transfers would take effect in 1996–97. The Established Program Financing and the Canada Assistance Program would be folded into a new block grant system called **Canada Health and Social Transfer (CHST)** (see Tables 4.1 and 4.2).

The federal Liberals defended the new CHST on the grounds that it would simultaneously reduce federal authority over provincial spending and limit overall costs. However, the federal government at the same time maintained that it would continue to

Table 4.1 Basic Federal–Provincial Financing in Canada, 2005

Grants	Unconditional	Conditional	Conditional block	New conditional block (beginning 2004)
Programs	Equalization	Canada Assistance Plan (CAP)	Established Program Funding (EPF)	Canada Health Transfer (CHT) (funding for health)
		(Welfare funding)	(Money given in a lump sum for health and education but with some considerations, plus some specific acts)	Canada Social Transfer (CST) (funding for education, social, etc.)
Funding Mechanisms	Based on revenue sources	Proportion of actual expenditures	Each a combination of cash and tax point room	Each a combination of cash and tax point room

Table 4.2 Basic Federal Financing for "Richer" and "Poorer" Provinces before 1996 and Today

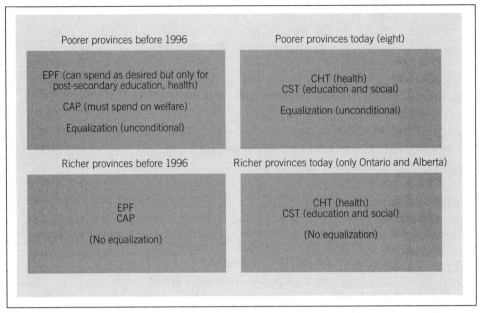

apply both its laws in the *Canada Health Act* and the CAP rules about residency requirements.

This new approach reduced the total federal funds earmarked for social policies by some $7 billion. As could be expected, the move was supported by those who advocate more decentralization and criticized by those who fear it could lead to a reduction in national standards in the fields of health, education and welfare.[15] Finance Minister Martin summarized the government's position: "Provinces will now be able to design more innovative social programs that respond to the needs of people today rather than to inflexible rules. However, flexibility does not mean a free-for-all."[16] There is little doubt, however, that the Liberal government loosened its control over provincial financing in order to reduce the pressure on its own finances and to placate nationalist tendencies in the province of Québec. In light of the massive debt and a continuing separatist challenge in Québec, the Liberals decided to decentralize the country to the greatest degree possible short of amending the Constitution.[17] One major step was to change the method of distributing federal transfers to the provinces.

In 1997, the finance minister announced that CHST payments would not decline further. The federal government was ready to open the purse again for drugs, home care and scholarship programs for universities (see the "Funding for Colleges and Universities" Close-Up). An agreement was signed with all the provinces except Québec in 1999.

In the 1999 agreement, Ottawa agreed to collaborate with the provinces over any future Canada-wide initiatives in fields such as health care, post-secondary education and social assistance. Ottawa further agreed to provide a one-year notice of any future funding changes to the provinces, and a three-month notice and a promise to consult the provinces on any direct payments to individuals. Most important, once Ottawa and any six provinces agree on objectives, new programs in fields such as home care or pharmacare may be introduced by the federal government as long as each province can work out the details of its own program. If a province already has a program in place that meets the objectives of the policy, then it will still receive the federal funds. In other words, the federal government, in effect, allowed provincial constraints on its spending power and in return received provincial acceptance for its willingness to compromise and consult.

In a further agreement in September 2000, Prime Minister Jean Chrétien increased transfers to the provinces by $21.1 billion over the next five years starting in 2001–2002.[18] The federal government's surpluses are being used to fulfill the Liberal promise to enhance provincial funding.

CLOSE-UP   Funding for Colleges and Universities

Because education is a provincial responsibility, the federal role has simply been to provide transfers to the provinces. At first, payments were earmarked directly for post-secondary education, but later the funds came with no strings attached. This meant Ottawa spent billions on post-secondary education but got little credit and no influence on policy, except through the Canada Student Loans Program.

As of 2004, the federal government grants funds to the provinces as part of the Canadian Social Transfer. It continues the Millennium Scholarship Fund of up to $3 billion, with money going to students on the basis of both merit and need. The federal government also has increased funding for university research with such programs as The Canada Foundation for Innovation, the Canada Research Chairs and the Canadian Institutes of Health Research.

Is this use of federal money in post-secondary education justified, or should it be left to the provinces to decide how to allocate funds in this area? What kind of transfer of money to students would you and your fellow students prefer?

HEALTH CARE, THE PRIORITY: 2004

The main issue in the 2004 general election was health care. It is a massive problem. Recent years have witnessed an explosion in health-care costs. An aging population, new technologies and new demands have driven the costs to new heights. In 2003, according to government statistics, funded health-care costs reached $85 billion or 7 percent of Canada's GDP, making Canada the fourth-highest spender among members of the OECD.

With such large sums of money involved and the public's desire for even more health-care money, it is not surprising that, to a very large extent, federal–provincial relations have become heath-care relations. The infectious disease breakouts of severe acute respiratory syndrome (SARS) and avian flu have only compounded the problem.

The issue of health-care costs and rules led to the federal Parliament passing the *Canada Health Act* in 1984, and this Act is still at the heart of provincial complaints today. The Act penalizes provinces that do not meet the five conditions in the Act, including accessibility, comprehensiveness, portability, proper administration and universality.[19]

CLOSE-UP ### Should Canadians Have the Option of Private Health Care?

The *Canada Health Act* has evolved over four and a half decades. It is the cornerstone of Canada's health care system and has become a symbol of Canadian values — "a sacred right". The Act "affirms the federal government's commitment to a universal, accessible, comprehensive, portable and publicly administered health insurance system. It aims to ensure that all residents of Canada have access to necessary hospital and physician services on a prepaid basis."

However, health costs are rising dramatically, and service has been declining. During the general election campaign in 2004, the issue of how to provide better health care to Canadians was widely debated. Alberta premier Ralph Klein argued for a plan to deliver health care using for-profit agencies to supplement public health care. Private diagnostic clinics were already operating in Alberta, British Columbia, Québec and Nova Scotia to allow care for those who could afford the fee (roughly $2500 for a prompt scan on high-tech equipment) and found it unacceptable to have to wait for the public system to admit them. Alberta has allowed private, for-profit clinics to perform surgical procedures and private health clinics have charged "facility fees."

Is it better to allow private health care or to work with the *Canada Health Act* to improve patient services? Those who oppose privatization argue that if money is drained from the public system into a private one, there will be less funds to improve services. The rich will get treated, but the poor will likely have to wait even longer. Canadians who live in wealthy provinces will rely more on private clinics and those in poorer provinces will not have such access. The pressure to improve substandard care will lessen, and the system will deteriorate further. This route would represent a major change in the philosophy of the *Canada Health Act* and the vision behind it.

The federal government will inject $41 billion into the system over the next five years. However, those in favour of privatization are doubtful that the $41 billion will be enough to make a difference in the long term if costs keep escalating.

In 2008, the provinces are required to report to their own electorates on their progress in reducing patient waiting lists. Unfortunately, this means that there will not be a national standard but a different one for every province.

Should Canada opt for private health care, or should we keep trying to fix the system we have so that all Canadians share health-care dollars and resources?

In 2004, the federal government divided the CHST into two parts — the Canada Health Transfer and the Social Transfer, thus separating health-care costs from those of other social programs. As well, the federal government set up a Canada Public Health Agency, reporting to the minister of health, as the focal point for disease control and emergency response.

When the federal and provincial leaders met in the fall of 2004, the primary issues continued to be the amount of funds the federal government should make available to the provinces, privatization, long waiting times, primary and home care and prescription drugs. The federal government and the ten provinces and three territories agreed to a new ten-year plan on how to sustain the health care system. The federal government agreed to provide an extra eighteen billion dollars over the next six years to health care, and it guaranteed a six percent annual increase after that until 2015. The first ministers agreed to a set of principles including such items as universality, accessibility and portability but added the notion of jurisdictional flexibility.

The federal government's demands for national targets on waiting times and an increase in home care were partially met by measures to set benchmarks by December 31, 2005, for waiting times for medical procedures. The first ministers could not agree on a national data collection system, but each jurisdiction agreed to establish comparable indicators and benchmarks for medically acceptable wait times for several stated procedures. The ministers also agreed to increase the amount of funds for certain home care services such as short-term, acute, community, mental health home care, and end-of-life care by 2006. Lastly, the ministers agreed to establish a task force to report on a national pharmaceutical strategy by June 2006.

In order to bring Québec on side for the new health care arrangement, the federal government agreed to exempt Québec from some of the promises made by other provinces.[20] Québec promised to reform its own home care services in its own way. It agreed to set its own benchmarks for waiting times and indicators that would be comparable with the other provinces.

Québec has been allowed to make a special deal with the federal government before. For many years it has had a separate pension plan and been allowed to opt out of some federal/provincial social programs. However, this agreement's explicit assertion of the principle of "asymmetrical federalism" was unique and gave explicit legitimacy to the practice. The federal intergovernmental affairs minister, Lucienne Robillard, declared that other provinces as well can achieve one-on-one agreements with the federal government in the future.

Are we at the beginning of a new era in federalism? Is such an explicit acknowledgment of asymmetrical federalism and its flexibility the sign of a new co-operative federal government, the result of a weak minority government in Ottawa, the recognition of past practice or the caving in of the federal government to provincial demands? All of these assertions have been made by politicians and commentators since the ten-year health agreement was signed.

KEY TERMS

block grant, p. 91
Canada Assistance Program (CAP), p. 93
Canada Health and Social Transfer (CHST), p. 93
concurrent powers, p. 83
conditional grants, p. 87
confederation, p. 81
declaratory power, p. 83
direct taxation, p. 87
disallowance, p. 81
equalization payments, p. 88
Established Program Financing (EPF), p. 91

federal system, p. 79
indirect taxation, p. 87
reservation, p. 81
residual clause, p. 82
Section 91, p. 82
Section 92, p. 82
shared-cost programs, p. 88
spending power, p. 88
unconditional grants, p. 88
unitary systems, p. 79
veto, p. 81

DISCUSSION QUESTIONS

1. What are some of the factors that account for the main shifts in the pattern of federalism in Canada since 1867?

2. Are shared-cost programs an ideal form of government co-operation, or are they an intrusion into areas of provincial jurisdiction?

3. Should Canadians have the option of private health care?

4. Did the new Atlantic Accord signed in 2005 breach the spirit of the equalization agreement as it was originally conceived? Was it fair?

WEBLINKS

Canada Pension Plan

www.sdc.gc.ca/en/isp/cpp/cpptoc.shtml

Canadian Confederation

www.collectionscanada.ca/confederation/index-e.html

Department of Finance

www.fin.gc.ca

Health Canada

www.hc-sc.gc.ca

Intergovernmental Affairs

www.pco-bcp.gc.ca/aia

5 Nationalism and Regionalism
Québec, the West and the Rest

Learning Objectives

After reading this chapter, you should be able to

1. Trace the historical roots of Québec nationalism to present times.

2. Explain the language issue that underlies Québec nationalism.

3. Outline the basic events and issues of the Québec referendums of 1980 and 1995.

4. Discuss the merits and demerits of the federal government's strategy toward Québec separatists.

5. Describe and explain alienation in the West of Canada.

*W*e have seen that questions about the authority and jurisdictions of the federal and provincial governments often give rise to political conflict in Canada. Some of the most divisive of these conflicts have been over separatism in Québec and regional alienation in other provinces. This chapter is concerned with the background and contemporary significance of both nationalism and regionalism. In particular, it addresses the question of nationalism and the separatist movement in the province of Québec, including the 1995 referendum, how the Québec government is proceeding in this regard and what the federal government is doing to address the problem. It also examines regionalism in Western Canada, considering the long history of grievances there.

The Canadian federal structure has proved remarkably resilient in meeting its various challenges since Confederation in 1867. However, during the past three decades, powerful nationalist pressures created the most serious challenge to the federal political system that Canada has ever endured. Separatists in Québec view federalism as obsolete and inadequate to meet the aspirations of their society. Their challenge is not yet resolved. It could yet result in a truncated Canada, a severely weakened federal system or a strengthened one. The ultimate outcome will depend on many factors, including leadership and political circumstances. The lure of regionalism also haunts Canada with possible negative *consequences for the country. Grievances in some of the provinces, particularly in the West, frequently threaten to dominate politics. We consider some of these grievances and threats later in the chapter, but regionalism is such an intrinsic part of politics in Canada that it is also discussed throughout the book, particularly in the chapters on political culture, federalism, the executive, parties and elections.*

NATIONALISM

Nationalism has appeared in many forms in different states over the centuries. Political leaders have used it to justify economic expansionism, protectionism and imperialism. As an ideology, it has been employed to promote the supremacy of particular nations or peoples; it has justified quests for emancipation from colonial rule; and it has been an integrative force in newly independent multiracial or tribal societies in the Third World.[1] It also has been savagely attacked. Albert Einstein called nationalism "an infantile sickness of tribal societies . . . the measles of the human race."[2]

In many cases, nationalism has been used to integrate the members of an existing or future state. However, nationalism can also be a divisive force. Territorially concentrated ethnic minorities that previously have been subjects of a larger state sometimes seek increased autonomy or even total independence. The breakdown of the former Yugoslavia into multiple republics and then the violent fragmentation of one of them, Bosnia, is just one example. Not all organized ethnic activity should be labelled as nationalism, however. Many ethnic demands, such as those for minority-language education, or ethnically oriented television programs, do not challenge the integrity of the existing state and may be quite easily accommodated within its confines.

Disputes about nationalism abound, largely because of disagreements about definitions and explanations. It is used colloquially to mean "love of country" but that is not precise enough to study the phenomena. Some experts see nationalism as anti-colonialism and believe it differs fundamentally in established and developing states. Others contend that it can only appear in modern, developed political systems because it is a product of modernity and came with the Industrial Revolution in Europe. Most authors, however, believe nationalism is closely associated with ethnicity. Some even see it as the political manifestation of ethnicity.[3]

There are a great many theories about the causes of nationalism and its consequences. Several factors are generally thought to give rise to nationalism. Clearly, ethnicity alone is not responsible for nationalism; nor is regionalism — although the two may coincide. Nationalist movements encompass the following features:

- common ethnicity
- a common grievance or threat
- common territory
- leadership
- great emotional intensity
- a common goal (sometimes for a separate state)

In this volume, **nationalism** is defined as the collective action of a politically conscious ethnic group (or nation) in pursuit of increased territorial autonomy or sovereignty. Examples of contemporary nationalist movements may be found in many advanced industrial societies: the Scots and Welsh in the United Kingdom; Bretons and Corsicans in France; Flemings and Walloons in Belgium; the Chechens in Russia; and, of course, the Québécois in Canada. In each case, the ethnic minorities have reduced any previous commitment they may have had to the larger state and have acted collectively to develop political parties, nationalist and cultural organizations and sometimes even terrorist groups in order to pursue fundamental changes in the territorial boundaries and sovereignty of the state.

Ethnic nationalist groups in Québec have sought varying degrees of autonomy, up to proposing independent statehood. Often, they utilized the mechanisms of federalism to challenge the federal status quo. Since federalism institutionalizes territorial divisions through its political structures, provincial power has also been employed to express regional conflicts that lack an ethnic dimension. Throughout Canadian history, provincial government power has been used to press *both* ethnic nationalist and provincial or regionalist demands on Ottawa.

Roots of Nationalism: Early French–English Conflicts

After the British conquest in 1760, the Roman Catholic Church exercised a powerful influence on its French-speaking parishioners. It successfully encouraged them to remain socially separate from the English, maintaining an essentially agrarian society. French Canadians generally remained aloof from political affairs, and even after Confederation in 1867, the English minority within Québec dominated urban and political economic life. By that time, the French were a minority in Canada. Two major conflicts set the tone for French–English relations.

Manitoba School Issue

The ethnic conflicts that periodically erupted after Confederation had their roots in the linguistic and educational rights of the provinces. One of the first and most enduring was in Manitoba. This province, with its large French-speaking community, was created in 1870 on the same basis as Québec, with rights to Roman Catholic schools and bilingual education. By 1885, however, French-speaking Métis in the West were being swamped by English-speaking settlers. To protest land losses, they rallied around Métis leader Louis Riel, who led a rebellion against the government.

English Canadians saw Riel as a traitor or a madman and sent troops to quell the disturbance. Riel was defeated and executed. French Canadians grieved for Riel as a patriot who died to preserve the "Frenchness" of his people. The ethnic groups were thus polarized, and the stage was set for the limitation of French-language rights in Manitoba. Only five years after the rebellion, the government of Manitoba established a non-sectarian educational system in which Roman Catholic schools no longer received provincial aid and French could no longer be used in the secondary schools.

Two decisions of the British Judicial Committee of the Privy Council (JCPC) upheld the Manitoba law but also confirmed that the federal government had the power to restore school privileges. The situation posed a unique problem for French Canadians. Their church and the federal government urged them to support overturning the Manitoba legislation but that required agreeing with the federal disallowance of provincial legislation, and French Québec was against the principle of federal veto power.

The federal Conservative government introduced remedial legislation in 1896, but under pressure it had to be withdrawn. A bizarre election ensued in which Manitoba francophones supported the Roman Catholic Church and the federal Conservative party in demanding federal disallowance of the Manitoba law. Québec francophones, on the other hand, supported the Liberal party, which demanded provincial autonomy and opposed the federal use of the disallowance power. Ironically, the Liberals were also supported by anti-French and anti-Catholic forces. The Liberals won in 1896, and Québec francophones thus, in effect, stopped the legislation that would have protected French Canadian interests in Manitoba.

Conscription Issue

Ethnic division appeared in another guise in the conscription crises of both the First and Second World Wars. The 1917 federal election on the conscription issue divided the country along ethnic and linguistic lines: every riding in which French was the majority language voted against the government and conscription. There were insufficient French votes to prevent conscription, but, fortunately, the war ended before conscription could be enacted, and the issue died.

However, the repercussions for Robert Borden's Conservative party, which had supported conscription, were severe. In the federal election campaign that followed the conscription bill, the Conservatives and English-speaking Liberals united to run Union candidates. They won the election but captured only three seats in Québec. In the first post-war election, in 1921, the Liberals formed the government, this time winning all the Québec seats. Provincially as well as federally, the Conservatives were severely defeated and, except for the Diefenbaker sweep in 1958 and the two Mulroney victories of 1984 and 1988, the party has not regained the confidence of French Canadians.

In 1942, during the Second World War, the conscription issue arose again and the federal government called a plebiscite to settle the issue. The campaign was bitter. French-speaking Québec voted against conscription by a huge majority, while English-speaking Canada was overwhelmingly in favour. The pro-conscription forces narrowly won, but Liberal Prime Minister Mackenzie King postponed the imposition of conscription. The delay minimized the crisis because the war ended before the conscripts were sent into battle. However, the apparent impotence of the French in face of an English majority decision on a topic of life or death helped to fuel Québec nationalism.

Language Issues: Past and Present

Canada's Confederation was essentially a bargain between the French and English in British North America to create one strong political unit that would protect the rights and assist the advancement of two culturally diverse peoples. On this basis, linguistic duality was embedded in the *British North America Act* of 1867. It has had both positive and negative repercussions for Canadians. It has caused divisive social and political tensions, but at the same time, the establishment of two official languages has in many ways enriched the experience of being Canadian.

Although the Confederation arrangement gave constitutional protection to both English and French languages in the federal Parliament and the legislature of Québec, in the other provinces there was no such protection. The practice until the 1940s was for English-speaking Canadians, wherever they were in the majority, to deprive French-speaking minorities of public-school facilities in their native language, and to refuse them the use of their language in government institutions. Even within the federal government, where the *BNA Act* had stated the right of both groups to function in debates, records, journals and courts in their own language, government employees were largely unilingual English. Later reforms have reversed these trends, but they have left a legacy of fear and distrust.

The legal basis for language regulation in Canada is divided across three jurisdictions: a) the Constitution, b) federal law and c) provincial law.

a) The Constitution establishes the framework for rules about language usage and development. In 1867, the *BNA Act* specified that Parliament and the Québec National Assembly were to function in French and English. Much later, in 1982, the *Charter of Rights and Freedoms* enshrined English and French as the two official languages of Canada for matters pertaining to Parliament. Minority language rights were enshrined in Section 23 of the Charter, which stipulates that citizens of Canada whose first language is that of the French or English minority of the province in which they reside, or who have received their instruction in one of these languages in Canada, have the right to have their children educated in that language wherever numbers warrant.[4]

b) Within these parameters, the federal government creates language policies. In 1963, the Liberal government declared Canadian federal institutions to be officially bilingual, and in 1969, it passed the *Official Languages Act*. This Act, updated in 1988, has two parts: it regulates bilingualism in federal governmental organizations and federally regulated institutions like banks and airlines, and it provides a national framework for promoting the two official languages. For example, it gives Canadians the right to be served by federal institutions in the official language of their choice where "significant demand" exists; allows federal employees the right to work in the official language of their choice; and establishes that there should be an equitable distribution of English and French Canadians in the public service.

The passage of the 1982 *Charter of Rights and Freedoms* expanded the basis for legal challenges against government that do not uphold the provisions concerning language. Since it came into effect, many cases have been brought to the Supreme Court to challenge provincial governments and force them to accommodate language minorities in their laws and schools.

c) Provincial assemblies, too, can legislate language policies. However, such language legislation has often been restrictive and controversial. In Québec, the provincial government maintains an Office de la langue française, which enforces the *Charte de la langue française*. This Charter makes French the official language of the province and the normal language of communications, business and the workplace.

In Québec, language policy permeates politics. The fear that French language and culture is in decline in Canada, or may soon be, is widespread and is used by Québec nationalists to rally support. Québec's fertility rate is lower than that for the rest of Canada, which, as we have seen, is not adequate to sustain the current population level. Québec therefore sees a need to attract, hold, and integrate immigrants into the French culture and language. Motivated by these demographic concerns, Québec authorities in the 1960s began to assert and protect the province's distinctive character through legislation concerning language within its jurisdiction.

> *Bilingualism, in spite of widespread belief, is not quite synonymous with hell.*
>
> Keith Spicer, official languages commissioner, 1976

Language policy in Canada has become highly politicized. It is a magnet for intolerance, often based on misinformation and misunderstanding.[5] **Official bilingualism** in Canada as outlined in the *Official Languages Act* does not mean that all Canadians must speak both French and English. It means that Canadians have the right to communicate with their governments in the official language of their choice. It is based on the belief that a highly bilingual public service could be expected to increase sensitivity, tolerance and respect between the two language communities.

Ironically, bilingualism is on the rise, particularly in Québec, but official bilingualism is no longer considered a goal in that province. Rather, many French-speaking Québeckers aspire to be recognized as a "distinct society" with unique rights, to enable them to protect their distinctiveness and make Québec as unilingually French as possible.

CLOSE-UP   Who Is Bilingual in Canada?

As of the 2001 Census, nearly 18 percent of Canadians say they are bilingual in Canada's two official languages:

- 43 percent of all francophones are bilingual;
- 9 percent of all anglophones are bilingual;
- 40.8 percent of Québeckers are bilingual;
- 10.3 percent of Canadians outside Québec are bilingual.

Canada's francophones, both inside and outside of Québec, are learning English in greater numbers, and anglophones inside Québec are also learning French in greater numbers.

The 2001 Census reveals the following facts about Canada's francophones:

- More than 6.4 million Canadians claimed French as their mother tongue in 2001, up from six million in 1986. However, the increase has not kept pace with the overall population growth.

- The proportion of francophones in Québec changed little over the century. In 1900, 83 percent of the population spoke French; in 2001, 81.4 percent declared French as their mother tongue.

- The English-speaking community in Québec dropped from 24 percent at Confederation to 16 percent in 1970, and then down to 8.3 percent in 2001. There are more allophones (people whose first language is neither French nor English) in Québec than anglophones — 10.3 percent of the Québec population.

- The English in Québec are learning French more than previously, and so are new immigrants to the province. Québec's requirements for immigrant children to go to French schools have increased the assimilation rate of these children into the French culture.

- In most other provinces, the proportion of francophones continued to decline because of the high rate of assimilation. Roughly 2.7 percent of Canadians outside Québec speak French at home while 11.7 percent speak a language other than French or English.

Despite federal initiatives, Canada's francophone population is increasingly concentrated in Québec. In 2001, over 81 percent of Canada's French-speaking population lived in Québec. At the present rate of change, that figure could reach 95 percent by the next census.

Since Québec's population is growing more slowly than the national average, its demographic weight within Canada is declining. Given current demographic trends, Canadians should expect Québec francophones to continue their struggle to preserve the pre-eminence of the French language and culture within their province, using whatever tools are available to them.

Table 5.1 Mother Tongue and Bilingualism in Québec, Canada Outside Québec and All of Canada (percentages) 2001 Census

	Mother Tongue			Bilingual
	English	French	Other	English/French
Québec	8.3	81.4	10.3	40.8
Canada Outside Québec	75.2	4.4	20.4	10.3
All of Canada	59.1	22.9	18.0	17.7

Source: Statistics Canada, 2001 Census, cited July 8, 2004. Available at www12.statcan.ca/english/census01/products/analytic/companion/lang/tables/growthrate.cfm and www12.statcan.can/english/census01/products/analytic/companion/lang/tables/bilingual.cfm

Modern Nationalism in Québec

By the late 1950s and 1960s Québec francophones began to demand fundamental change. What began as a "Quiet Revolution" eventually blossomed into an outright challenge to Canadian federalism and the very existence of the Canadian state.

After Confederation, two strains of nationalism developed in *la belle province*.[6] The first, depicted by historian Abbé Lionel Groulx called for a rural vision of Catholic, anti-materialist values and on occasion resulted in proposals for an inward-looking, corporatist and authoritarian solution to the Québec situation. The second, led by Henri Bourassa, politician and editor of *Le Devoir*, called for a pan-Canadian vision and an equal partnership between English and French Canada. For Bourassa, the Canadian dilemma was to be resolved by building a state that was both bicultural and bilingual.

The inward-looking strain of nationalism was characterized by the Union Nationale governments of Maurice Duplessis, 1936–1939 and 1944–1960. The rural-based Union Nationale espoused a philosophy of old-style nationalism buttressed by patronage and intimidation. It was very successful until the 1949 Asbestos Strike. The 1950s were characterized by widespread rejection of both clerical influence and Duplessis's manipulation. Values in the province changed rapidly from rural to urban and from religious to secular. Industrialization and urbanization helped erode the bases of Union Nationale support.

The new, outward-looking strain of nationalism was typified by Québec's Liberal party, which Jean Lesage led to victory in 1960. In the subsequent Quiet Revolution, Lesage's Liberals reversed the philosophy of previous governments in Québec. Instead of preservation of the *patrimoine* (the language, religion and culture of a traditional rural Québec), they defended *la nation* in terms of the economy and social structure of the province. The new government dramatically increased the role of government in society, secularized the school system, nationalized hydroelectricity and reformed the civil service.

Led by a new middle class, French-Canadian nationalism gave way to Québec nationalism. Nationalists were appalled that the French language was on the decline in Canada and that Québec's share of the Canadian population was dropping. The *épanouissement*, or flowering, of Québec-based nationalism was encapsulated in the 1960 political phrase *maîtres chez nous* (masters in our own house). A state-centred nationalism replaced the traditional nationalism.

Québec's new challenges to Canada came in many guises — judicial, social and political. Objections ranged from attacks on specific centralizing mechanisms, such as the constitutional power of disallowance, to general claims that the *BNA Act* did not define a true federal system. Some Québec francophones saw the federal union as lacking the free consent of the contracting parties — in other words, the right to self-determination. Others objected to economic injustices.

Québec increased political pressure on the federal government throughout the 1960s. Some French Canadians took up separatism for Québec as their goal, maintaining that only with their own government could they fulfill the aspirations of their community. Their slogan — *Vive le Québec libre* — drew international credence from a supportive declaration by visiting French president Charles de Gaulle in 1967. Nationalists focused their criticism on the use of English in the private sector, banks and the federal public service as well as on the economic domination of anglophones.

The Front de la Liberation du Québec (FLQ), represented the most extreme separatists. It initiated terrorist activities that culminated in the October Crisis of 1970, in which a British diplomat was kidnapped and the Québec Minister of Labour, Pierre Laporte, was kidnapped and murdered. The federal government invoked the *War Measures Act* for the first and only time during peacetime. The basic freedoms of Canadians, mostly French speaking, were infringed upon. Hundreds of Québeckers were arrested. When the crisis atmosphere faded, it left many Canadians uncertain that the crisis had been of sufficient proportion to necessitate such a large-scale repression.[7]

As Québec nationalism grew in the 1960s and 1970s, Québecois intellectuals became increasingly divided. Pierre Elliott Trudeau and his friends Jean Marchand and Gérard Pelletier entered into federal politics, where they offered the vision of a bicultural and bilingual federal state but with no special status for Québec. As prime minister of Canada, Trudeau later became the major spokesman for Henri Bourassa–style nationalism.

Separatist Parties in Québec

There have been four "successful" nationalist organizations with aspirations for the independence of Québec. The first nationalist party, the Parti Patriote, was elected with a large majority in the early nineteenth century under its very popular leader Louis-Joseph Papineau. The second nationalist party, the Parti Nationale led by Honoré Mercier, was elected in 1886. In 1936, the Union Nationale, led by Maurice Duplessis, came into office as the third successful nationalist party.

In 1968, former provincial cabinet minister René Lévesque left the Québec Liberal Party and formed the fourth nationalist party, the Parti Québecois (PQ). This new party brought nationalists together under a new umbrella organization to fight for separation. Pierre Trudeau, for one, maintained that the Parti Québecois had simply replaced traditional Québec clericalism with the "clericalism of nationalism,"[8] but the party prospered.

In the 1970 Québec election, the Parti Québecois won 24 percent of the popular vote, not enough to prevent Liberal leader Robert Bourassa from forming the government. The October Crisis intervened between this election and the next one in 1973. Playing on the fear of separatism and capitalizing on his success with the James Bay Hydro development project, Bourassa won another landslide victory, despite an increase in PQ votes to 30 percent.

In the face of these defeats, the Parti Québecois softened its stand from outright independence to **sovereignty-association** — political independence but with economic association — to reassure those who were apprehensive about the economic consequences of separatism. The party continued to promote its vision of a Québec in which no taxes would be paid to the federal government and citizens would be subject to no federal law. In the 1976 election, Lévesque offered a referendum on the right to negotiate sovereignty-association and promised a second referendum for Québeckers to ratify the eventual results of the negotiations.[9] Forty-one percent of Québec voters cast their ballots for the

Parti Québécois on November 15, 1976, and the PQ gained control of the government in Québec.

In preparation for the provincial referendum, the Parti Québécois government enacted seductive legislation. While the new government proved moderate in fiscal and monetary policies, it nationalized the Asbestos Corporation to the evident satisfaction of many nationalists. It also introduced Bill 101, the *Charter of the French Language*, in the Québec legislature in April 1977, declaring an intent to make the province unilingually French. It was a highly controversial piece of legislation that created a confrontational atmosphere in Québec, charged with emotion in the period leading up to the referendum.

The Québec Referendum, 1980

The May 1980 referendum on sovereignty-association was a disaster for Premier Lévesque. The vote required Québec residents to choose between *Oui* (for the Québec government to negotiate sovereignty-association) and *Non* (for it not to negotiate). Even this mild resolution was defeated by almost six out of ten votes partially because Prime Minister Trudeau was promising "renewed federalism."

The threat of independence did not die with this vote, however. PQ strategists believed that Québec had both the people and resources necessary to form an independent state. Lévesque knew that his support came overwhelmingly from voters under age 35 and he thought that he could afford to wait. In the 1981 election, the Parti Québécois promised not to call a sovereignty referendum before another election. The PQ won easily with 47 percent of the vote and 80 of 122 seats in the National Assembly. After their defeat, the provincial Liberals replaced leader Claude Ryan with former premier Robert Bourassa. Lévesque continued his attack on the federal government.

Constitutional Patriation (1982) and Its Aftermath

René Lévesque refused to sign the 1982 constitutional amendment package to patriate the Constitution from the United Kingdom, but the federal government and the other nine provinces forged ahead without Québec's approval. Doing so broke a political impasse but handed the separatists an emotional weapon. The country, Lévesque said, had separated from Québec. Although the prime minister and a high proportion of the federal Cabinet were from Québec, the PQ claimed that it alone spoke for the province and declared a boycott of federal–provincial meetings.

When the Progressive Conservatives under Brian Mulroney won power in the 1984 federal election, Lévesque ended the boycott and in January 1985, the PQ declared itself a moderate, nationalist party. Before the next provincial election, however, Lévesque died and the party developed major internal splits. Pierre-Marc Johnson led the party into the 1985 election. They lost. Robert Bourassa's Liberals won 56 percent of the vote and ninety-eight seats, while the PQ was left with 38 percent of the vote and only twenty-four seats.

In 1988, the PQ replaced Johnson with Jacques Parizeau, an arch-nationalist who revived the *indépandantiste* spirit. In 1990, following the advice of Parizeau, the party declared

> . . . we must break the iron collar of a federal system that serves us
> badly, that will always subordinate our national interests to those of
> another majority . . . . If others have become sovereign why not us?[10]

Premier Bourassa continued to espouse policies of federalism with nationalism. In 1985, he successfully demanded that five conditions be included in the Meech Lake Accord (see Chapter 3, "The Constitutional Framework"), and in 1988, he employed the notwithstanding clause of the new Constitution to prevent the use of English signs for business purposes in the province. He easily won the 1989 provincial election.

When the Meech Lake Accord failed in June 1990, several Québec members of the PC and Liberal federal caucuses, led by Lucien Bouchard (former minister of environment in Brian Mulroney's cabinet), left their respective parties to form a separatist group in the House of Commons — the Bloc Québécois (BQ). As we saw in Chapter 3, the federal government continued its efforts to build a constitutional agreement that would bring Québec "on board." This eventually resulted in an omnibus proposal called the Charlottetown Accord, which was put before the Canadian people for approval in a referendum in October 1992. When the proposal was massively rejected, Québec nationalists resumed their call for separation.

In the general election of October 25, 1993, the Bloc won fifty-four seats, just enough to become Her Majesty's Loyal Opposition in the House of Commons. The Bloc's next stated goal was to combine with the Parti Québécois in a campaign to separate Québec from Canada. This became more probable when the PQ, under Jacques Parizeau, won the 1994 provincial election and promised a referendum on sovereignty by the end of 1995.

The Québec Referendum, 1995

Two elections — the general election of 1993, in which fifty-four Bloc Québécois members were elected to the House of Commons, and then the Québec election of September 1994, which brought the Parti Québécois to power — set the stage for a dramatic separatist offensive. The Québec election gave the Parti Québécois of Jacques Parizeau 44.8 percent of the vote and seventy-seven seats. The Liberals, led by Daniel Johnson, won 44.2 percent but only forty-seven seats. The Action Democratique, led by Mario Dumont (the third party with representation in the National Assembly) won 6.5 percent with one seat.

PQ and Bloc Strategy and Tactics

The PQ campaigned for sovereignty in the September 1994 Québec election, contending that Canada could be broken up without creating excessive problems. It formed a temporary alliance with the Bloc Québécois and the Action Democratique. Then on June 12, 1995, the three party leaders joined to ask Québeckers to support independence for Québec, along with political and economic association with Canada, if the Yes side won a referendum. It was a move designed to appeal to nationalist voters who did not want outright secession.

If negotiations succeeded, they said, a treaty would be put in place. It would include a customs union, mobility of people, capital and services, a monetary policy and citizenship. Deals could be struck on topics such as enhanced trade, common transportation, defence, and environmental and fiscal policies. According to the strategy, if negotiations with Canada failed, Québec would become an independent country anyway, while maintaining the use of Canadian currency and Canadian passports.

The thrust of this deal was put into question form for the Québec population to vote on in a referendum on October 30, 1995. It required those who supported the sovereignist option to vote Yes, those who did not support it to vote No. The question, as illustrated below, was highly criticized for being ambiguous and misleading.

The first two weeks of the campaign went badly for the sovereignists. Then Jacques Parizeau announced that Lucien Bouchard would be put in charge of negotiations with Canada after a win in the referendum. "Saint Lucien," took over as head of the campaign, and his personal charisma lifted morale and attracted voter support. Bouchard promoted the emotional attraction of sovereignty. He insisted that market forces would push Canada to negotiate with a sovereign Québec. By the end of the campaign, the Yes and No forces were virtually tied, with indications that the Yes side might win.

Bouchard's high profile in the campaign emphasized perceived historical humiliations of French-speaking Canadians, and defined French-speaking Québeckers as a people who deserved to negotiate equal to equal with Canadians, not just as a province like the others. There was no mention of the fact that Québec had supplied the prime minister of Canada for thirty-five of the fifty years since the end of the Second World War, even though Québeckers comprised only about 35 percent of the population — or that at the time of the referendum, francophones or Québeckers held positions in Ottawa of governor general, prime minister, minister of finance, minister of foreign affairs, chief justice of the Supreme Court, clerk of the Privy Council, and chief of staff of the prime minister. The rhetoric escalated as the campaign neared its conclusion. Prime Minister Jean Chrétien was vilified and derided. The Yes forces carried out a "cherry-picking" operation, choosing those

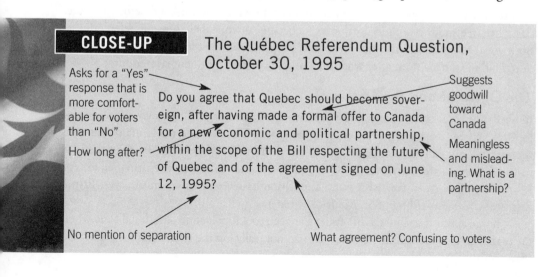

CLOSE-UP The Québec Referendum Question, October 30, 1995

Asks for a "Yes" response that is more comfortable for voters than "No"

How long after?

Suggests goodwill toward Canada

Do you agree that Quebec should become sovereign, after having made a formal offer to Canada for a new economic and political partnership, within the scope of the Bill respecting the future of Quebec and of the agreement signed on June 12, 1995?

Meaningless and misleading. What is a partnership?

No mention of separation

What agreement? Confusing to voters

aspects of Canada that would suit their interests in garnering votes — including maintaining the Canadian dollar and the Canadian passport.

Federal Strategy and Tactics

At the beginning of the referendum campaign, the No strategy was to wait for the separatists to act, but once the question was set, the opposition became more vocal, mainly attacking the question itself. Prime Minister Chrétien put it bluntly the day after the PQ plan was announced: "It's a mirage. It is still a proposition for separation, but they don't have the guts to say they are separatists." Chrétien declared at home and abroad that Québec would never leave Canada. He said separatists have

> a contempt for democracy . . . the way of those who count on tricks and turnarounds. . . . There is now a very cynical and very transparent attempt to confuse Québeckers, to mislead them, to suggest that you can separate from Canada and still be Canadian.[11]

His strategy was to lie low and let the provincial leader of the Québec Liberals, Daniel Johnson, lead the No forces. Johnson waged a cool, unemotional campaign based on the economic consequences of separation.

Initial polls gave the No forces confidence. However, after Bouchard took the lead for the separatists, the polls started to reverse. Johnson tried to counter the Yes forces with something positive, but on October 21, the prime minister dismissed his appeal for the recognition of Québec as a distinct society. The unity of the No forces was temporarily broken. The dollar plunged.

Then, with just over a week to go, Chrétien's strategy changed abruptly. He addressed a federalist rally in Montréal. The next night in a national television broadcast, he pleaded for Canadian unity and suggested the federal government would promote acceptance of Québec as a distinct society and a limited veto for Québec. In an unprecedented outpouring of emotions, citizens outside Québec came by the thousands to a massive rally in downtown Montréal, and rallies and vigils were held in every province the weekend before the vote.

The Cree and the Inuit in northern Québec, meanwhile, held separate referendums. Both voted massively against the sovereignist proposal and their leaders expressed a desire to remain in Canada no matter what the outcome of the imminent referendum.

The Outcome and the Aftermath

In a massive voter turnout of over 93 percent, Québeckers voted narrowly, 50.6 percent to 49.4 percent, to reject the sovereignty proposal. The Yes side made major gains in the vast, mainly francophone regions that stretch from the Madeleine Islands in the East to the Abitibi in the northwest of Québec. All of the regions in the province except Montréal, the eastern townships and the Outaouais voted to separate. Even Prime Minister Chrétien's riding of St. Maurice voted Yes.

The close finish encouraged Premier Parizeau to adopt a confrontational tone when the results were in. He said that Québeckers had not really lost the referendum because more than 60 percent of francophones had voted for independence. "It's true that we were beaten, but by whom? Money and ethnic votes." He also spoke of the "temptation for revenge."[12] In doing so, he isolated and insulted many people in Québec and in the rest of Canada.

Anglophones and allophones make up about 18.5 percent of Québec's population, but more than 80 percent of them live in Montréal and its suburbs. Within metropolitan Montréal, anglophones make up about 15 percent of the population, allophones 17 percent. This numerical strength, therefore, clearly acted as a powerful counterweight to the francophone vote of the area, which was roughly evenly split. Outside Montréal, with the exception of a handful of ridings along the Ontario boundary and the US border, the anglophone population constitutes less than two or three percent of the population.

The polarization of the Yes and No votes, therefore, was clearly related to ethnicity, but other forces also seem to have been at play. The division was typical of urban–rural splits in which recession-ridden rural areas feel isolated from what they perceive as the political power, economic clout and good life of big cities like Montréal.

Leaders for the Yes forces made it clear that the issue of Québec separatism was not resolved, and another referendum would be held in the near future. Within days of the referendum, however, Jacques Parizeau resigned as premier and was replaced by Lucien Bouchard, who gave up his seat in the House of Commons. Given how close the vote was, Prime Minister Chrétien came forward with new and controversial ideas for reforming the Constitution; he also introduced a resolution about the "distinctiveness" of Québec and a bill on regional vetoes over constitutional amendments and held by-elections in Montréal in order to bring new francophones into his Cabinet.

Nationalism and Self-Determination

The issue of Québec independence raises questions about the right of people to self-determination and statehood. International law is instructive but not conclusive on this

Figure 5.1 Support for Separatism in Québec As Expressed in Key Provincial Elections and Referendums

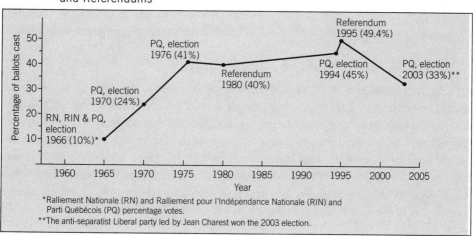

*Ralliement Nationale (RN) and Ralliement pour l'Indépendance Nationale (RIN) and Parti Québécois (PQ) percentage votes.

**The anti-separatist Liberal party led by Jean Charest won the 2003 election.

point. Two principles, in fact, clash as international law seems to recognize both self-determination and the inviolability of borders. Of course, the only thing that actually settles questions of this nature is the political action of other states and the United Nations in recognizing a new country or in defending an old country's territory.

First is the principle of **self-determination**. In international law, the right of self-determination extends only to those circumstances in which people are experiencing foreign or alien domination, or are subject to discriminatory regimes. Neither of these situations applies in Québec. There, citizens have democratic rights as part of Canada. As Prime Minister Chrétien forcefully put it, "In international law, Québec cannot separate from Canada without Canada's consent."

However, recognition of new states has often been accorded even when the parent country did not consent. For example, in December 1991, Canada rushed to recognize the Ukraine before there was any thought of Russian consent. It was a political decision. Canadian leaders did not even wait for other countries in the United Nations to make declarations. On the other hand, the Canadian government did the opposite in the cases of Slovenia and Croatia. It waited to see what decision other countries would take before recognizing these two new states.

Second is the question of borders. If Québec did unilaterally declare independence, then what lands could it claim? Using the same logic as expressed above, it could only claim the territory and people over whom it could maintain effective control. If two rival governments contest a territory, political, not legal, justifications finally resolve the issue. Borders have to be adjusted to conform to the reality of who has the power and legitimacy in the land.

It is extremely unlikely that the federal government would use military power to intervene in a sovereign Québec, but aboriginal peoples would have the legal justification and power to stay within Canada even if there were a Yes victory in the referendum. The Constitution makes it clear in Section 91(24) that "Indians and their lands" come under the federal authority, and Section 35(1) protects aboriginal rights and treaties that were made with Canada, not Québec. Moreover, at a minimum, the federal government would have a moral duty to help those Canadians who did not wish to stay in Québec — including Aboriginals and, for example, Canadians in the western part of the province, near Ottawa.

Is the Constitution Merely a "Red Herring"?

During the referendum, many argued that if Québec voted to separate, the Constitution would be irrelevant. Clearly, since secession would destroy fundamental institutions such as the monarchy, the governor general and lieutenant-governors, a change of such magnitude would require the application of the most rigid constitutional amendment rule — the unanimous consent of all the provinces of Canada plus a majority of members of both houses of Parliament. Provincial politicians have no authority to make a unilateral declaration of independence, as they are elected only to govern over classes of subjects mentioned in the Constitution and secession is not one of them.

It is clear, therefore, that a **unilateral declaration of independence (UDI)** — in which the province declares its independence outside of the law) by Québec would be unconstitutional. The Canadian Constitution provides no rules about the right of a province to secede from Canada. Nowhere in the list of jurisdictional powers does a province have the right to separate from Canada. The courts, therefore, could be called upon by the federal government or by private interests to contest the validity of the referendum — or any decision to declare a UDI. The federal government and the courts have no justification or legal obligation to pay any attention to a UDI. Thus, constitutionally speaking, if a UDI were declared, political legitimacy and power would remain with the federal government and the provinces.

Two arguments are fundamental. Without the guidance of a constitution, there would be chaos. Politicians become dictators and the political system becomes authoritarian when there is no legal framework. If Québec were to vote Yes in a future referendum, the federal government would be required to adhere to the Constitution. Without adherence to the Constitution, there would not be any authoritative body to deal with Québec or any process of law or deliberation about the future of Québec should it decide to separate. Without adherence to the Constitution, whose law would apply to those Québeckers who want to remain Canadians and pay taxes to Ottawa? What courts would determine the status of the Crees and Inuit who do not want to belong to a new Québec?

Those who stress the significance of the Constitution understand that "the will of the people" is important and that a national election or referendum may be required if Québec ever did vote to separate from Canada. However, without the Constitution, how could democracy be actualized? What would constitute a fair and just process? Answers to these questions cannot be determined outside the Constitution. To say that the legal issue is irrelevant is tantamount to saying that a small majority in one province could effectively deprive millions of citizens of their country. Canada would have to be reinvented.

Federal Post-Referendum Strategy

On October 24, six days before the 1995 Québec referendum, a desperate Jean Chrétien promised that he was open to change, including constitutional change, and would fight for the concept of a distinct society for Québec. Clearly, nationalists had tapped into a sense of historical humiliation and that needed to be addressed by the federal government. Chrétien therefore examined new measures to appease Québec.

The government's response was eventually formulated in two plans, called **Plan A** and **Plan B:**

Plan A

Plan A was essentially a reconciliation effort — a plan to sell a majority of Québeckers on the success of Canada and the benefits of staying in the federal union. The steps included:

1. An overhaul of the Cabinet in which two star candidates from Québec, Stéphane Dion and Pierre Pettigrew, were approached, assigned to ridings where they could win by-elections and given positions in Cabinet.

2. Efforts to meet the distinct society and veto promises. Within weeks of the referendum, a resolution was passed in the House of Commons recognizing Québec as a distinct society and another one concerning the veto. Parliament was forced to pass its own motion on the distinct society of Québec because the provinces would not allow any distinct society concessions to be entrenched in the Constitution.

    A statutory (but not constitutional) veto was approved by Parliament in February 1996, affirming that any further constitutional changes approved by Parliament would require consent from Ontario, Québec and British Columbia, as well as two of the four Atlantic provinces and two of the Prairie provinces.

3. Decentralization measures, which were important to show that the government was flexible concerning Québec's desires. The government implemented a series of mini-measures to show Canada is on the side of fundamental change in the federation, devolving powers to the provinces in areas such as forestry, mining, recreation, tourism and social housing. The federal government declared it would not use its spending power to encroach further into areas of provincial jurisdiction, and it supported the adoption of measures to strengthen the country's internal economic ties. In 1996, an agreement on labour-market training was reached in which $2 billion was handed over to the provinces — at least a quarter of which went to Québec. The decentralization of labour-market training was significant, as it had been a symbol of federal intransigence in Québec — proof that federalism could not work.

4. A campaign to extol the virtues of being a Canadian. Other initiatives were undertaken, such as free distribution of flags and the setting up of a Unity Information Office (UIO). These plans were intended to counter the negative image of Canada that the separatists had propagated during the referendum. The UIO claimed that separatist leaders had distorted history and used emotive words such as "conquered," "rejected," and "humiliated" to unfairly describe relations with the rest of Canada. It was in this fourth step that money was seriously misspent, later resulting in damaging scandals for the Liberal party (see the material on AdScam in Chapter 12, "Ethics in Canadian Government and Politics").

Plan B

Plan B, dubbed "tough love" by some, was a plan to clarify rational, logical terms for secession — without using harsh federal threats about the risks of partition.

In Prime Minister Chrétien said Québec would never be able to leave Canada unilaterally — even if a majority of Québeckers voted Yes in the next referendum. The law must be respected. The rest of Canada would have to approve the terms of separation through a constitutional amendment.

In September 1996, the federal government asked for a Supreme Court ruling on the legality of unilateral secession by Québec. The federal government sought a ruling to the effect that a unilateral declaration of independence by Québec would be illegal.

With these measures under way to win over public opinion in Québec and clarify the situation, the Liberal government won the 1997 general election. Its hand was strengthened further in early 1998 when Jean Charest left federal politics and the Progressive Conservative party to replace Daniel Johnson as leader of the Québec Liberal party.

Ottawa's Questions and the Supreme Court's Answers Concerning Unilateral Secession

The Supreme Court's conclusions in 1998 were woolly and controversial. Clearly aiming for a political compromise, the Court concluded as follows:

Question 1: *Under the Constitution of Canada, can the National Assembly, legislature or government of Québec effect the secession of Québec from Canada unilaterally?*

Ruling: "The Constitution vouchsafes order and stability, and accordingly secession of a province 'under the Constitution' could not be achieved without principled negotiation with other participants in Confederation within the existing constitutional framework."

And more directly: "The democratic vote, by however strong a majority, would have no legal effect on its own and could not push aside the principles of federalism and the rule of law, the rights of individuals and minorities, or the operation of democracy in the other provinces or in Canada as a whole. Democratic rights under the Constitution cannot be divorced from constitutional obligations."

Clearly, the Court therefore concluded that a regular constitutional amendment would be required in order for separation from Canada to be constitutionally valid. However, the Court did not stand with this strong statement alone. It added, "Nor, however, can the reverse proposition be accepted: the continued existence and operation of the constitutional order could not be indifferent to a clear expression of a clear majority of Québeckers that they no longer wish to remain in Canada."

The Court judgment then goes on to practically demand that "negotiations" take place if there is a "demonstrated majority support for Québec secession."

Question 2: *Does international law give the National Assembly, legislature or government of Québec the right to effect the secession of Québec from Canada unilaterally?*

In this regard, is there a right to self-determination under international law that would give the National Assembly, legislature or Government of Québec the right to effect the secession of Québec from Canada unilaterally?

Ruling: In the circumstances, the National Assembly, the legislature or the government of Québec do not enjoy a right at international law to effect the secession of Québec from Canada unilaterally.

Question 3: *In the event of a conflict between domestic and international law on the right of the National Assembly, legislature or government of Québec to effect the secession of Québec from Canada unilaterally, which would take precedence in Canada?*

Ruling: In view of the answers to Questions one and two, the Court said this third question did not need to be answered.

The immediate political fallout from the judgment was controversial. Chrétien's minister of federal–provincial affairs, Stéphane Dion, seized on the *clear question* and *clear majority* clause in the Court response to attack the 1995 referendum. He proffered that any referendum question with the word *partnership* in it would be invalid and that a successful referendum for the Yes side would need a greater than fifty-percent-plus-one majority to be acceptable to the federal government.

On the other hand, separatists latched on to the crucial Supreme Court demand that negotiations would of necessity have to follow a positive vote on separation in Québec. The idea that the federal government and the provinces had to negotiate after a positive provincial referendum certainly encouraged separatists that their demands were legitimate and reasonable.

Of course, one might ask by what constitutional rule the Supreme Court judges came to their decision on this topic. The reason for the decision — that is, to dampen emotional ire in Québec — was understandable, but the unfortunate part of this decision is that one day Québec might vote to separate and yet one or all of the provinces or federal government might object to negotiating with the secessionists. In this case, the separatists could claim that the Court backed their demands for negotiations. It would seem that the Court's judgment in this regard was illegitimate and unconstitutional. There is nothing in the Constitution saying that those opposed to the separation of a part of Canada are required to negotiate in the face of a positive vote. The judges' hasty and ill-considered decision may one day do more harm than good for the unity of Canada.

In response to the ongoing charge that the federal government was not proactive enough, the Chrétien government tabled Bill C20 in December 1999. This legislation, the **Clarity Act**, sets out the rules by which the government and Parliament of Canada would analyze any future separatist referendum. It concludes that the government will not enter into any negotiations with a province over separation unless the House of Commons determines both that the referendum question is "clear" and that a "clear" expression of will has been obtained by a "clear" majority of the population.

This is bizarre legislation, as few states make such direct provisions about their own destruction. On the other hand, the Liberal government defended the legislation as necessary to spell out precisely how a future referendum in Québec would be handled by the federal government and Parliament. The Parti Québécois government in Québec immediately tabled a competing bill in the National Assembly, claiming that only the Québec people can decide on the legal status of their province and that a 50-percent-plus-one vote will be considered enough for a referendum victory.

Despite the posturing, neither bill is constitutionalized, and both can be changed by any future legislature. The constitutional amendment process remains intact; the secession of a province from Canada would require resolutions to be passed in the federal Parliament and all ten legislative assemblies. There is no easy way to political change short of this high obstacle.

Following the relatively dismal showing of the Bloc in the November 2000 federal election, Premier Bouchard resigned. Bernard Landry, a political veteran who had helped found the Parti Québécois in 1968 and had served as finance minister, replaced him as party leader and premier. Landry campaigned on the need to move sovereignty high on to the political agenda again. In 2005, he resigned and passed the separatist flag to a new leader.

Federalist forces in Québec continue to be divided on what strategy to take toward nationalist aspirations. The Liberal party has adopted a strong devolutionist and pro–distinct society position, which has solidified support in some French quarters while dividing English and allophone support. The most strident federalists are found in those provincial groups that hold to the position that parts of Québec will have the right to separate from Québec if Québec ever decides to separate from Canada.

Some Unresolved Issues

The referendum raised several issues that need to be clarified in the event of another referendum on separation.

The dollar: Could an independent Québec keep using the Canadian dollar? In the long term, probably not. There are no examples of large countries that have taken such an option; only small, dependent countries use the US dollar. Currency is more than bank notes, it is a system of payments, compensation and settlement. Use of the dollar by Québec would be difficult because of the capital flight that would be set off by a separation. Québec would have to choose between a credit crunch and recession, or the establishment of a new currency. The January 1993 example of the break-up of the former Czechoslovakia is instructive on this point. At the beginning, both sides temporarily tried to share the same currency, but a flight of capital from Slovakia after the split forced them to create their own, devalued currency.[13]

There are other questions about the dollar. Would international bankers recognize Québec's use of the Canadian dollar? On another level, it verges on the absurd to contemplate an independent Québec using as its currency bills and coinage that feature the Queen on them.

Passports: Many contest the idea that a new state of Québec could use Canadian passports. The Canadian government and Parliament decide who can use the passport. Since the document begins with the words "The Secretary of State for External Affairs of Canada requests in the name of Her Majesty the Queen . . . " even trying to use the passports would be an absurd situation for independent-minded Québeckers. The question of possible dual citizenship remains unresolved.

Debt: Since the country's debt is in Canada's name, Canada would remain liable for all of it. If Québec separated, Canada would only collect about three-quarters of its former revenue, however. Negotiations about Québec's share of the national debt would therefore be required.

Majority vote: How big a majority would a province need to achieve in order to separate? Is 50 percent plus one large enough? In this scenario, just under half the population of a province would be required to live in a new country against their wishes. About two and a half million votes would be enough to destroy a country of over thirty million people. In 1999, Prime Minister Chrétien declared that 50 percent plus one would not be enough.

Negotiators: With whom would leaders of a sovereign Québec negotiate? Could a federal leader from Québec negotiate for the rest of Canada in the event of a Québec vote for independence? Prime Minister Chrétien said he would not and could not negotiate the independence of Québec.[14]

Economic repercussions: What exactly would be the economic repercussions of separation? The majority opinion of economists appears to be that uncertainty and the high debt load would lead to flight of capital. Clearly, Canada is extremely vulnerable to foreigners who would sell off Canadian and provincial bonds and treasury bills. A Québec unilateral declaration of independence would provoke an economic and political crisis.

Constitutional status of a UDI: What would come of the fact that Québec separation by a UDI clearly would be unconstitutional? Would other Canadians have the right to contest it? Rather than accept Québec's unilateral declaration, for example, Canadian leaders might contest its validity and attempt to force the Québec government to back down. Until terms with Canada were worked out, the federal government would have no choice but to contest the Québec action.

Use of force: Would Canadians use force to defend the country against a Québec UDI? Not likely. They would not need to. It would not be the federal government but the new self-declared state of Québec that would have to coerce hundreds of thousands of its recalcitrant citizens into following its laws. It would have to enforce its unconstitutional claims by coercing those Québeckers who disagreed with them. The new Québec government would have to pass laws, control its citizenship and monitor immigration. It would need a new court system backed up by an army, police and a prison system. States cannot exist without these structures or they are mere colonies of some other state.

It would be Québec's show. In fact, no federal politicians could respond — unless they did so claiming they stood for the legitimacy of the Canadian Constitution — in which case the constitutional rules for amending the Constitution would have to be adhered to, or changed.

Tension and violence: If a UDI were accepted, this breach of the rule of law could lead to nightmare scenarios socially, with ethnic tension and even aboriginal violence.[15] The state would, in fact, have to be reinvented, and that raises the fundamental question of whether Canadians in the remaining provinces would want to go on sharing citizenship under a common constitution. Some provinces might be open to options of partition or joining the United States.

Québec's Major Grievances

Shared grievances are a vital ingredient of nationalism. According to former Québec premier Bernard Landry, Québeckers are victims of discrimination in Canada based on economic maldistribution. In other words, Québeckers do not get their fair share of federal spending. This argument was clearly responded to by Stéphane Dion, Canada's former minister of intergovernmental affairs in Jean Chrétien's Liberal government in the following checklist. The facts are based on 1998 data, which Dion pointed out are entirely representative of what happens every year:[16]

- Québeckers received 24.2 percent of total federal spending. Since Québec's population is 24.2 percent of the Canadian population, the redistribution is eminently fair.

Obviously, Québec does not get 24.2 percent of every item in the federal budget, but it does get that much overall.

- Québec contributed 20.6 percent of federal revenues. Its contribution to Canada's GDP is 21.8 percent. "This shows that Québec is contributing in accordance with the size of its economy and receiving in accordance with the size of its population."

- Québec is slightly less wealthy than the average Canadian province. On a per capita basis, the four Atlantic provinces, Manitoba, Saskatchewan and the three territories obtain a greater proportion of transfer payments than Québec does, but only Ontario and Alberta are considered "rich" provinces in the equalization formula.

- Québeckers receive 21.2 percent of federal research and development spending. This cannot be considered lower than its population share because this does not include spending undertaken in the National Capital Region (NCR). Québec's share of federal R&D spending outside the National Capital Region is 26.8 percent.

- Québec suppliers receive federal spending on goods and services roughly equivalent to the size of Québec's economy within Canada.

- The portion of federal public servants in Canada who work in Québec is 23.1 percent. The number would be higher, but the Québec government assumes some responsibilities that most other provinces leave to the federal government (like policing).

In summary, Québec leadership was, and remains, divided in its vision for the province. *Separatists* favour outright statehood for Québec; *sovereignists* favour a greater degree of independence for Québec but do not necessarily define sovereignty as an absolute break from Canada; *devolution sovereignists* favour an extreme decentralization of Canada in which very few powers would be left to the central government; and *federalists* favour the continued existence of Québec within Canada. The proportion of the Québec population in each camp varies.

After the 1995 referendum, discussion and overt support for the separatist and sovereignist options faded. A December 2003 poll by *Maclean's* found that 69 percent of Québeckers felt "proud to be Canadian." This was reflected in the election of Jean Charest's Liberals in Québec in 2003. However, the situation is volatile. In the 2004 general election, the Bloc Québécois received considerably more support than the Liberals, encouraging PQ leaders to publicly speculate on the date of the next referendum. The Gomery Inquiry into AdScam in 2005 strengthened the Bloc further. It would be ironic in the extreme if Jean Chrétien's attempt to curb separatism in Québec actually provoked its resurgence.

REGIONALISM

In contrast to nationalist demands, which seek to alter existing political structures, **regionalism** refers to territorial tensions "brought about by certain groups that . . . demand a change in the political, economic and cultural relations between regions and central powers *within* the existing state."[17] Regional discontent is most often articulated in economic terms, especially by representatives of poorer, peripheral regions within a country. Residents of these areas demand a share of the affluence enjoyed by others in their society. However, such discontent can also find expression in political terms, particularly, for example, when nouveau riche regions object to the central government's power to impose constraints that prevent them from "cashing in" on their new-found prosperity.

In the short term, regionalism does not directly challenge territorial sovereignty, so it appears to present less of a threat to the existing state structure than does nationalism. In the long term, however, persistent neglect of regionalist demands may result in a serious loss of legitimacy for the state in specific parts of the country. In extreme circumstances, it could even provide the basis for the development of a distinct ethnic or national identity that might seek separation from the state.

At the very least, regionalist protests add to the flow of demands that must be considered by policy-makers. Because most political parties have regional concentrations of support, regionalism has become an important dimension of political life in many countries, especially Canada.

If the greatest modern challenge to federalism is from Québec separatists, the next in significance is undoubtedly regional alienation. A number of factors combine to ensure the persistence of regionally based attitudes and interests in Canada: the enormous size of the country, historical patterns of ethnic settlement, variations in economic activity and wealth, uneven population distribution and the vested interests of provincial governments. Such differences can deprive Canadians of a strong sense of unity, and allow regional or provincial interests frequently to take precedence over those of the state.

All of the non-central provinces have some grievances against Central Canada, which includes Ottawa, Ontario and Québec. The litany includes complaints about official bilingualism, monetary policy, tariff policy, spending decisions and the treatment of Eastern and Western resource and fishing industries. In the Atlantic provinces, there has always been a fierce pride and independence but it is mitigated by the area's need for federal financial assistance (see the "Equalization: To Share or Not to Share?" Close-Up in Chapter 4). In the West, alienation has combined economic discontent and antipathy toward the French language, and the demands of the province of Québec, with a desire for a stronger role for itself in the federation. Largely because of the "melting-pot" mix of cultures and the relatively few francophones in the West, political vision in the Prairies is based more on economic than cultural issues.

Alienation: Views from the West

As we saw in Chapter 2, regional alienation is a major component of Western Canada's political subculture.[18] Throughout the West's history, there has been a strong belief that the resource-rich Prairie provinces were exploited by federal government policies representing central Canadian interests. This belief is based on the perceived economic and political domination of the rest of the country by Central Canada, especially by Montréal and the tiny but populous Golden Horseshoe area of southern Ontario, led by Toronto.

> *We have always had a sense of economic exploitation.*
> *This notion has marked all political parties in the West.*
> *The cartoon that has captured these sentiments is one of*
> *a large cow standing on a map of Canada munching*
> *grass in Alberta and Saskatchewan, with milk pouring*
> *from a bulging udder into the large bucket in Ontario.*
>
> *Former Alberta premier Harry Strom[19]*

The main thrust of western discontent, however, hinges on a feeling of marginalization and alienation from the centres of economic and political power rather than on a simple desire for separation from those centres, and may "reflect frustration at the lack of national integration as much as it does resistance to integration."[20]

Alienation has been a major component of Western Canada's political culture since the early history of the country.[21] Recall that Canada was created from four existing, already flourishing provinces in Central and Eastern Canada. Manitoba was added in 1870; Saskatchewan and Alberta not until 1905. Until 1930, none of the three new additions was allowed jurisdiction over their own natural resources (unlike the eastern provinces and British Columbia).

From a Western alienation point of view, the Fathers of Confederation developed a National Policy in order to forge an east–west economy for Canada, but in doing so they deindustrialized the east, concentrating industry in an economically diversified centre, and used the western hinterland to supply the centre with grain and natural resources. The central government controlled the tariffs and transportation regulations necessary to facilitate this plan. As the population of the West increased, westerners resented their assigned role in this scenario. They felt that their resource-rich Prairie provinces were being exploited by federal government policies that represented only Central Canadian interests. The Prairie provinces in particular began to focus their discontent on the tariff barriers, transportation policies, and natural resource ownership.

Westerners argued that freight-rate and tariff policies made the West a captive market for higher-priced manufactured goods from Central Canada and increased the cost of exporting products from the West. Their arguments concerning tariffs and trade were eventually redefined, addressed and resolved in the Free Trade Agreement that was signed between Canada and the United States late in 1988. However, Western resentment lingers. Freight rates, along with other inequities and discriminatory rules within the freight rate structure were a direct product of the National Policy. For many years, the federal government subsidized railway freight rates by means of the Crow's Nest Pass Agreement of 1897. After a prolonged feud, the Trudeau government reduced the freight subsidy in the 1970s. The Chrétien government finally abolished the Crow rate entirely in 1995, but again, the issue left a bitter legacy.

Resource ownership has been another source of contention. The three Prairie provinces did not gain control of their natural resources until 1930. All of them remained relatively sparsely populated and economically subordinate to Central Canada until the 1970s. In 1973, the Organization of Petroleum Exporting Countries (OPEC) declared an international oil embargo, causing the price of oil to skyrocket. For Western Canada, most particularly Alberta, this meant an economic boom as oil fields increased revenues. At one time among the weak partners of the federal union, Alberta in particular began to acquire enormous economic power through its sale of natural resources. Migration to the West increased and the region began to challenge what it considered the insufferable domination of Central Canada.

For populous, energy-consuming Central Canada, meanwhile, the OPEC embargo brought economic difficulty and a mounting fiscal crisis. In 1980, the Trudeau government intervened by introducing the National Energy Program (NEP). The policy was designed to control oil prices, ensure Canadian ownership of the oil industry, allow the federal government greater oil tax revenues and encourage offshore oil exploration. The Alberta government maintained, however, that their resources were being plundered by a federal Liberal government that held only two seats in Western Canada — neither of them in Alberta. Westerners felt that the ability of the federal government to take such action was a serious flaw in the country's parliamentary institutions.

Eventually, Brian Mulroney's government abolished the NEP, but once again bitterness remained. However, in October 1986, Mulroney's Tories awarded a valuable maintenance contract for the armed force's CF-18 fighter jets to a Montréal company instead of one in Winnipeg. Westerners were outraged. The Meech Lake initiative also infuriated them. For many, the feeling that the political system was stacked against the West simmered. They felt that the small elite that ruled the Progressive Conservative party excluded them. After having supported Mulroney, they turned on him as a symbol of Québec values, including special status for Québec, government largesse and opposition to capital punishment.

The Political Manifestation of Western Alienation

Modern economic issues dividing Western and Central Canada continue to be interpreted within this context of alienation. Westerners continue to perceive that their regional interests are regularly overwhelmed by the interests of Central Canada in the House of Commons. To this end, they support constitutional changes that promote the principle of the equality of the provinces as opposed to the Québec view of two equal founding peoples.

In the 1980s, the jurisdictional issue of whether the provinces or the federal government should control resource development spilled over into the constitutional arena, and the West's political leaders focused primarily on constitutional reform to entrench provincial equality. As we saw in Chapter 3, in the final analysis, all of the Western premiers supported patriation based on other compromises. When the federal government tried to bring Québec on board through the Meech Lake and the Charlottetown accord debates, the West's premiers again tried to force the federal government to address *their* grievances. Both accords failed. What westerners essentially wanted was Senate reform, to provide a regionally based, elected second legislative chamber (see Chapter 7, "Parliament").

Western interests have often been promoted by political protest parties that originated in the region. The Progressive party sent sixty-five MPs to Ottawa in 1921, basically to protest the National Policy tariff and freight rates. Four elections later, it disappeared and its adherents drifted to other parties. The Social Credit party also originated in the West in the 1930s. Always a regional party and never more than a third party federally, it sought radical monetary reform — especially the right of provinces to issue money. The Co-operative Commonwealth Federation (CCF) too was a Western party. It consisted of an assortment of Fabian socialists, Marxists, farmers and labourers that dissolved in 1961 and began anew as the NDP.

Western alienation was manifested again in the early 1980s in various groups and political parties dedicated to the separation of the Western provinces from Canada. The two leading separatist groups in that period were the Western Canadian Federation (West-Fed) and the Western Canada Concept (WCC). Frustrated by a lack of political power within the federal government, westerners complained of powerlessness against "centralist" policies, including bilingualism, metrication and immigration. Yet, the popularity of Western separatism dissipated as quickly as it had risen. While the movement provided an outlet for the expression of frustration, there was little agreement among the groups, let alone within them, concerning what strategy to follow. Internal dissension assured that minor electoral successes were short-lived.

The acute sentiments of Western alienation that characterized the early 1980s declined when oil prices dropped after Brian Mulroney's PCs won the 1984 general election in a landslide. With Mulroney's victory, the Western regionalists thought they would obtain strong and effective Western representation in government. To some extent, these expectations were justified: Mulroney dismantled the National Energy Program and the Trudeau marketing restrictions on the sale of oil and natural gas.

The feeling that the political system was stacked against the West lingered, however, and was given voice by Preston Manning. In the 1988 general election, Manning headed a new movement called the Reform party and conducted a credible campaign for Western interests under the slogan "The West Wants In." Its demands for free trade and Senate reform found a ready audience among small-c conservative voters. The party did not win any seats but it did obtain 15 percent of the votes in Alberta and affected Progressive Conservative and NDP competitions throughout the West.

In 1993, Reform won fifty-one seats, mainly in Alberta and British Columbia. In 1997, it captured sixty seats and formed Her Majesty's Official Opposition in the House of Commons. In 2000, Reform reinvented itself as the Canadian Alliance Party, and Stockwell Day took over as leader. In the ensuing election, the Alliance became the Official Opposition with sixty-six seats. It continued to play on Western alienation, calling for changes to the Senate in order to reduce the power of Central Canada and for populist devices such as referendums, recall and initiative in order to reduce the power of the House of Commons (see Chapter 7, "Parliament"). However it was still unable to expand beyond its Western base and in 2003, joined with the Progressive Conservatives to form the Conservative Party of Canada.

The merger was a recognition of the failure of Reform/Alliance, that it was too regionally based to appeal outside the West. The new Conservative party represents an attempt to bridge regional divides and allow conservatives a chance to form a federal government. Almost all Alliance members were from the Western provinces of Manitoba, Saskatchewan, Alberta and British Columbia. Nearly all Progressive Conservatives were from Ontario and eastern regions. They will have to find enough in common to maintain their support in these areas and add to it.

In the recent past, when the political right has won power federally, it has been because there was a rather bizarre, pragmatic union of the party on the right of centre with decentralist westerners and left-of-centre nationalist Québeckers (who also support devolution). It happened under John Diefenbaker in 1958 and again under Brian Mulroney in 1984. The union of such disparate groups is unstable and short-lived because of their essentially different goals. It is highly unlikely that such a union could happen again in the near future. The new party has a greater possibility of luring Ontario voters while holding on to Western support.

Yet clearly, many westerners feel that they put more into the federation than they receive in benefits. If Ottawa is not able to accommodate the ambition of Western Canadians, the potential for continued challenges remains — perhaps awaiting only a major confrontation with the federal government over the future of Québec within the federation. Or perhaps the confrontation will be over energy again. Alberta produces most of Canada's oil and natural gas. In 2004, as energy prices hit new highs, royalties climbed from an annual average of $3.2 billion between 1993 and 1999 to $7 billion a year. Alberta is Canada's richest province. It has no provincial sales tax, and its economy is growing well above the national average. After lean years in the 1990s, which saw severe cuts in health, education and social services, in 2004 Ralph Klein's Progressive Conservative government announced it would pay off nearly $23 billion in debt, making Alberta the only debt-free province.[22]

The underlying problem of regional alienation continues to be easy to state but not resolve. The combined population of Ontario and Québec considerably exceeds 50 percent of the entire country. Because of this, the outer regions often perceive that the federal parliamentary system represents only Central Canada and, therefore, to an extent, is itself merely a regional government. Yet, if democracy prevails — that is, the rule that votes should count relatively equally — the most populous provinces and regions will always have a majority.

Many solutions to alienation have been proposed over the years by westerners: switch political parties, abolish parties, create new parties, reform the electoral process, decentralize more powers to the provinces, achieve Senate reform, abolish party discipline and so on. All of these proposals are discussed in coming chapters. The landscape is littered with reform initiatives. Some of the demands are obviously based on genuine grievances. Others are mere posturing as the premiers of provinces unify to present a chorus of complaints to the central government to win financial concessions. Few premiers have anything useful to say about the country beyond their provincial borders. As one commentator put it,

> The premiers ask not what they can do for their country; they ask
> what their country can do for them.[23]

Meanwhile, the federal government continues to be the one government voice that speaks for Canadians as a whole. It continues the principle of redistribution — collecting tax money from Canadians and redistributing it according to established formulas based on need, so that the prosperity of one region or province will be shared with others that are demonstrably less fortunate. This assures that all Canadians will at least have the possibility to receive similar access to education, health care and other benefits. Federal governments also are extremely respectful of regions in the assignment of Cabinet portfolios so that regions do get Cabinet representation even when they have not supported the government. Federal–provincial conferences are held regularly in attempts to make accommodations and reach understandings, although they are often occasions for the provincial premiers to "gang up" on the federal government to demand more money and powers.

Current Western Grievances

There are several issues that will be contentious in the next few years. In 2004, Alberta premier Ralph Klein pledged to issue a provincial government report outlining more than twenty recommendations on "all of the things that seem to irk Western Canadians." Topping the list, he said would be health care and bovine spongiform encephalopathy (BSE — known as mad cow disease).

The health-care issue has been contentious since the 1990s when Alberta's PC government privatized and deregulated services such as car licensing, liquor retailing and electricity distribution, and flirted with doing the same thing with aspects of health care. The idea of privatizing health care dismayed Canadians who hold that the *Canada Health Act* represents core Canadian values. The concern over BSE is that a US ban on live cattle was still in place fourteen months after a single case of BSE was discovered in Alberta. The ban was causing severe economic trauma to Canadian cattle farmers, most of whom are from the West. Estimates were that by July 2004 the industry had lost roughly $2 billion. Feeding the unhappiness was the perception that the federal government was not acting effectively to get the ban lifted.

Klein's list of what irks westerners would undoubtedly include other policy irritants such as the gun registry — a federal program to register guns that was unpopular with Western gun owners in the first place and then ran massively over-budget; the wheat-board — a board to market Western grain that is so resented by some grain farmers that they would prefer to go to jail rather than pay fines for breaking the rules; the Kyoto Accord — westerners claim that the implementation would disrupt the economy and cause serious losses to companies connected to the oil industry (supporters argue that the adjustment would be short and would benefit the economy as a whole). The Atlantic Accord of 2005 giving Newfoundland and Labrador and also Nova Scotia the ability to keep the proceeds of offshore oil wells and not have that amount deducted from their equalization payments (see Chapter 4) is the most current divisive issue.

Then, of course, there are structural irritants that are perceived to impede Western influence: the appointed Senate and public policy being made by unelected judges in the Supreme Court. Since Alberta is a "have" province, Albertans see their money flowing to Québec and "Liberal" Atlantic Canada. Compounding this is distaste for the new electoral finance law of 2004 that financially rewards parties for votes won in elections. From a Western viewpoint, the law provides an unmerited financial bonanza for the separatist Bloc Québécois.

Finally, the 2004 election left westerners frustrated. Their ongoing complaints that prime ministers come mostly from Québec; that Ontario and Québec decide the outcome of elections; that votes cast after the polls close in Québec and Ontario carry little or no weight had given way to high expectations for a Conservative government led by Calgary MP Stephen Harper. However, at the last minute, Ontarians did not vote as strongly for the Conservatives as polls had indicated. Of the ninety-nine seats the Conservatives won, sixty-eight were from BC, Alberta, Saskatchewan and Manitoba. Three quarters of the region's ridings voted Conservative, and the Liberals *still* won a minority government! Within days, the anger resulted in the formation of a new provincial separatist party. The depth of feeling was evident in renewed calls for building a "firewall" around Alberta (a call later rejected by Premier Klein).

> *If we cannot achieve more Western influence within Ottawa (the purpose of Senate reform), lets pursue reasonable policies to reduce Ottawa's influence in the West: Withdraw from the Canada Pension Plan and create our own provincial pension plans; collect our own income taxes; cancel our contracts with the RCMP, and create our own provincial police forces; take control of our health-delivery systems; and use the notwithstanding clause when nine, non-elected judges in Ottawa try to impose their notion of good public policy on our democratically elected governments.*

Ted Morton, professor, Alberta.[24]

Prime Minister Paul Martin promised to address "the reality" of Western alienation but with his tenuous minority government has made little headway in this respect. Given the post-election mood, sporadic calls for Western separation can be expected to continue in the near future. As Roger Gibbins, president of the Canada West Foundation, a non-partisan public policy research institute in Calgary, noted, talk of separation "makes the whole situation worse because it fails to offer any sort of positive alternative or positive vision."[25] On the other hand, "Canada's failure to tackle regional discontent with energy and resolve places the country under continual strain."[26]

It is important to keep in mind that in spite of fringe-group separatists and the posturing of the premiers, regional economic disparities and the manner they are dealt with are distinguishing features of Canadian politics. Since Confederation, the belief that the rich provinces and regions should help the poorer ones has been a fundamental part of the Canadian political culture. Sharing through redistribution is built into the political system and is viewed by Canadians as the "just" way to cope with differences in wealth. We can expect this culture of accommodation to continue.

Many westerners still feel that they put more into the federation than they receive in benefits. If Ottawa is not able to accommodate the ambition of Western Canadians, the potential for continued challenges in the West remains — awaiting only a major confrontation with the federal government over the future of Québec within the federation.

KEY TERMS

Clarity Act, p. 118

nationalism, p. 102

official bilingualism, p. 105

Plan A, p. 115

Plan B, p. 115

regionalism, p. 121

self-determination, p. 114

sovereignty-association, p. 108

unilateral declaration of independence

   (UDI), p. 115

DISCUSSION QUESTIONS

1. "Nationalism is the political manifestation of ethnicity; ethnicity is an enduring social formation, through which interest is pursued." Debate.

2. Is the French language threatened in Québec? What factors would make this situation better or worse if Québec formed an independent country?

3. What are some of the main issues raised and left unresolved by the 1995 referendum campaign and its outcome?

4. Why were the results of the 1995 Québec referendum so close?

5. How serious a problem is regional alienation in Canada?

WEBLINKS

Canadian Unity Council

www.ccu-cuc.ca

Office of the Commissioner of Official Languages

www.ocol-clo.gc.ca

Parti Québécois (French only)

www.pq.org

Québec Liberal Party

www.plq.org

Western Canada Concept

www.westcan.org

Official Languages Act

http://canada.justice.gc.ca/en/laws/O-3.01/index.html

6 The Executive
Ceremony and Leadership

Learning Objectives

After reading this chapter, you should be able to

1. Identify the three main components of the *formal* executive and describe the role of each of them.

2. Identify the three main components of the *political* executive and describe the role of each of them.

3. Compare governmental politics in minority and majority governments.

4. Describe the four central administrative agencies and differentiate between their roles in the political system.

*I*n Canada, there are three separate branches of government institutions: the executive, the legislature and the judiciary. We begin our study of government with the executive, the powerful institution that encompasses the key players in the political system. The members of the political executive have the same status as the first string players on a sports team — they are the stars and team leaders.

In politics, **executive** is a broad term that refers to the institutions, personnel and behaviour of governmental power. In modern times, executives are the organizational centre of political systems. Governments have expanded over the years, taking on new functions. As governmental responsibilities have increased, executives have become more important. The executive branch of government has two main categories of tasks: one is performing ceremonial duties, the other is providing political leadership.

Canada's constitutional heritage from Britain includes an executive with two parts. Each part is assigned one of the two key executive tasks. The formal executive, comprised of the Crown, monarchy and governor general, performs largely ceremonial functions. The political executive, comprised of the prime minister, ministry and Cabinet, is concerned with leadership and the realities of power in contemporary Canadian politics. A large network of committees and agencies supports the political executive in its work.

This chapter examines the respective roles of the formal and political branches of the executive in Canada. Power resides with the political branch but, as we shall see, it is difficult to locate. In fact, what exactly is political power, and who exercises it? Political power is an abstract commodity that changes in response to issues, problems and personalities, which come and go. It is dramatically affected by majority or minority government circumstances. In addition, much important information about how the executive operates is shrouded in mystery. Parliamentary traditions and legal devices such as the Official Secrets Act shield the executive from penetrating scrutiny. Nevertheless, a significant amount is known about the executive in Canada. The chapter concludes with the ongoing debate about the role of the prime minister.

THE FORMAL EXECUTIVE

Recall from Chapter 3 that the Canadian Constitution established a government based on the British model. Canada was to be governed by a parliamentary system with British historical traditions and procedures and by a constitutional monarch represented by an appointed governor general. The main difference from Britain was that there was to be a federal division of legislative powers in recognition of the diversity of the country.

The Crown and Monarch

Government functions in Canada are carried out in the name of the Crown. The term **Crown** refers to the composite symbol of the institutions of the state. The Crown assumes a variety of duties and responsibilities. For example, it may be involved in court proceedings, and government property is held in the name of the Crown.

The reigning **monarch**, currently Queen Elizabeth II, is the personal embodiment of the Crown. **Prerogative authority** — powers of a monarch or his or her representatives that have not been bypassed by constitutional or statute law — can be traced to the period of authoritarian rule in Great Britain when the Crown possessed wide discretionary authority. As we shall see, they have been eroded to a very few reserve powers. Although the monarchy is personified in an individual, we must separate individual peculiarities from institutional strengths. Individuals come and go, but the Crown is permanent. It provides history, tradition and an institutional framework that can promote political stability as long as the institution is regarded as legitimate by a large majority of the people.

Although Parliament and the political executive govern in the name of the Crown, the powers of the monarch are severely limited. Even the ability to stay on the throne is no longer a right but subject to acceptance by British ministers and Parliament. The functions of the monarch are largely ceremonial and strictly non-partisan. The monarch reigns but does not govern. He or she carries out ceremonial responsibilities that generate mass support for government. As monarch, the Queen makes royal tours and acts as the symbolic head of the Commonwealth, of which Canada is a member.

The Governor General and Lieutenant-Governors

Since the monarch was not based permanently in Canada, a representative, the governor general, was appointed by the British government. Section 9 of the Constitution states that the "Executive Government and Authority of and over Canada . . . is vested in the Queen." This principle is fleshed out in the **Letters Patent** — the prerogative instruments defining the office of the governor general — that the sovereign makes applicable to each governor general through a commission of appointment. As Canada matured, the nature of this appointment changed. By the Letters Patent of 1947, the sovereign affirmed that all powers delegated to the governor general were to be exercised "on the advice of his [or her] Canadian ministers" as they affect Canada.

Today, the **governor general** is the representative of the monarch, appointed by Her Majesty on the recommendation of the Canadian prime minister and Cabinet. There have been two significant changes concerning the role of the governor general. The first is that since 1952, the governor general has been Canadian. The second is that the post has become politicized in that a candidate may be chosen by a PM primarily for his or her vote-winning characteristics. In 1952, Vincent Massey became the first Canadian to hold the position. It has since become customary to alternate the position between English- and French-speaking Canadians. In 2005, Prime Minister Martin appointed Michaëlle Jean to be governor general. Jean is a Canadian but was born in Haiti.

The governor general resides in Rideau Hall in Ottawa and has a second residence in Québec City. The tenure of office is usually five years, but the officially recognized term is six years, which has occasionally been extended to seven. The title *right honourable* is assigned for life and *excellency* for the period in office. In the event of death, incapacity, removal or absence of the governor general, the chief justice of the Supreme Court, Canada's leading judge, may carry out all duties of the office. The governor general is ceremonial commander-in-chief of the armed forces and is charged with swearing in cabinet ministers and commissioning high state officials. As chancellor of the Order of Canada and the Order of Military Merit, he or she administers the Canadian system of honours.

In performing the Queen's "dignified" roles in Canada, the governor general makes little practical input into the political process. The official duties include purely ceremonial functions such as conferring the Order of Canada awards or reviewing troops. As well, the governor general is a symbol of the state. As such, a function of the position is to socialize Canadians into acceptance of authority through attachment to an authority figure.

As to political duties, the governor general is bound to act on practically every piece of advice received by his or her ministers, but certain functions are the governor general's alone. The most important of these stem from the prerogative powers left to the monarch. The Letters Patent provides the governor general with all the powers of the Queen "in respect of summoning, proroguing or dissolving the Parliament of Canada."[2]

Only a prime minister can ask for, and obtain, a dissolution of Parliament. However, a governor general did once refuse such a request. This incident was the famous Byng–King case in 1926. Governor General Lord Byng declined Liberal Prime Minister Mackenzie King's request for a dissolution and an election. Instead, he called on Conservative leader Arthur Meighen to form a new administration. It was a controversial move and in an ensuing election, the Liberals won. This event set a precedent that governors general should follow the advice of their prime ministers about the dissolution of Parliament.

Another significant power of the governor general is appointing the prime minister. In cases where a party leader holds a clear majority of the seats in the House of Commons, the governor general merely selects the obvious candidate for that position. If, however, no leader has the support of a majority in the House of Commons, the governor general might be forced to use discretion and select the prime minister.

In twenty-nine of the thirty-eight elections since Confederation, one of the two major parties obtained an absolute majority of the seats in the House, so the governor general was not required to exercise personal discretion. In the nine remaining cases, the governor general chose as prime minister the leader of the party that received the largest number of seats in the House of Commons — even when that party did not constitute a majority. However, in the Byng–King case, the previously appointed prime minister asked for a quick dissolution, which was denied by the governor general. No governor general has ever tried to dismiss a prime minister.

Perhaps more significant than these formal constitutional powers is the governor general's informal opportunity to advise ministers. The governor general usually meets regularly with the prime minister and receives Cabinet minutes and therefore has a degree of access that is denied to most ordinary individuals. As head of state, he or she holds the right to be consulted and the right to encourage or warn political leaders.

The monarch has a representative in each province as well as in Ottawa. A **lieutenant-governor**, appointed by the governor-in-council (see below) on the advice of the prime minister, represents the monarch in each province. The lieutenant-governor acts on the advice and with the assistance of his or her ministry or executive council at the provincial level of government, which is responsible to the legislature and resigns office under circumstances similar to those for the federal government.

Although the Constitution makes it clear, then, that the governor general is the country's formal executive, his or her powers and prerogatives are in fact severely limited. Only in extraordinary situations has a governor general attempted to interfere directly in the political process. Executive power, though carried out in the name of the governor general, resides elsewhere in the political structure.

Table 6.1 Canadian Governors General, 1952–2005

Vincent Massey	1952	Jeanne Sauvé	1984
Georges Vanier	1959	Ramon Hnatyshyn	1990
Roland Michener	1967	Roméo LeBlanc	1994
Jules Léger	1974	Adrienne Clarkson	1999
Edward Schreyer	1979	Michaëlle Jean	2005

THE POLITICAL EXECUTIVE

The Prime Minister

The prime minister is unquestionably the central figure in Canadian politics. The basis of the prime minister's power and authority is leadership of a party that commands at least a plurality, and normally a majority, of the seats in the House of Commons. The prime minister, above all else, is an elected member of Parliament, who has been chosen national leader of the party at a leadership convention. Today, convention demands that the prime minister be a member of the House of Commons either before or shortly after investiture (when the title is assumed).

As leader of the party that has been victorious at the polls, the prime minister is able to claim that the "right" to govern is based on a popular mandate. The link with the people through an election gives the prime minister enormous legitimacy and authorizes the pursuit of his or her programs and policies until the next election. This legitimacy is important in controlling the party and dealing with the bureaucracy and the press. As leader of the party and the holder of a mandate, the prime minister needs, and normally can command, obedience and support from cabinet ministers and backbenchers alike. However, in a minority government, the prime minister's power can be very limited.

Canada's Prime Ministers

Canada has had twenty-one prime ministers since 1867 (see Table 6.2 on page 136) — nine Liberal and twelve Conservative. All but Kim Campbell, who became prime minister for a few months in 1993, have been male. Joe Clark was the youngest in Canadian history at the age of 39. As of Jean Chrétien's election in 1993, the average age of a new prime minister was 56. Paul Martin was nearly a decade older than that when he became PM in late 2003. Every prime minister since the First World War has been a university graduate. There have been three prime ministers from the Maritimes, seven from Québec, six Ontarians and five westerners.[3] Three provinces — Prince Edward Island, Newfoundland and Labrador, and New Brunswick — have never produced a prime minister. All nine Liberal prime ministers have come from Ontario or Québec (John Turner was elected in British Columbia but lived in Ontario).

The tenure of Canadian prime ministers has varied enormously. Unlike US presidents, who may serve only two terms, Canadian prime ministers retain power as long as the public and House of Commons support them. In fact, prime ministers in Canada have averaged longer in office than those of almost all Anglo-American and continental European countries.

Among the twenty-one Canadian prime ministers, the shortest careers were those of Sir Charles Tupper (69 days), John Turner (80 days), and Kim Campbell (133 days). At the other extreme, four individuals held the office of prime minister for well over half of Canada's history since Confederation — 72 out of 134 years, as of 2001: Mackenzie King (22 years), Sir John A. Macdonald (20 years), Pierre Trudeau (15½ years) and Sir Wilfrid Laurier (15 years). Laurier enjoyed the longest continuous term of any prime

Table 6.2 The Prime Ministers of Canada

Name	Party	Tenure		
Sir John A. Macdonald	Lib.-Con.	July 1867	–	Nov. 1873
Alexander Mackenzie	Lib.	Nov. 1873	–	Oct. 1878
Sir John A. Macdonald	Con.	Oct. 1878	–	June 1891
Sir John Abbott	Con.	June 1891	–	Nov. 1892
Sir John Thompson	Con.	Nov. 1892	–	Dec. 1894
Sir Mackenzie Bowell	Con.	Dec. 1894	–	Apr. 1896
Sir Charles Tupper	Con.	Apr. 1896	–	July 1896
Sir Wilfrid Laurier	Lib.	July 1896	–	Oct. 1911
Sir Robert Borden	Con.	Oct. 1911	–	July 1920
Arthur Meighen	Con.	July 1920	–	Dec. 1921
W.L. Mackenzie King	Lib.	Dec. 1921	–	June 1926
Arthur Meighen	Con.	June 1926	–	Sept. 1926
W.L. Mackenzie King	Lib.	Sept. 1926	–	Aug. 1930
R.B. Bennett	Con.	Aug. 1930	–	Oct. 1935
W.L. Mackenzie King	Lib.	Oct. 1935	–	Nov. 1948
Louis St. Laurent	Lib.	Nov. 1948	–	June 1957
John Diefenbaker	Con.	June 1957	–	Apr. 1963
Lester B. Pearson	Lib.	Apr. 1963	–	Apr. 1968
Pierre Elliott Trudeau	Lib.	Apr. 1968	–	June 1979
Joseph Clark	Con.	June 1979	–	March 1980
Pierre Elliott Trudeau	Lib.	March 1980	–	June 1984
John Turner	Lib.	June 1984	–	Sept. 1984
Brian Mulroney	Con.	Sept. 1984	–	June 1993
Kim Campbell	Con.	June 1993	–	Nov. 1993
Jean Chrétien	Lib.	Nov. 1993	–	Dec. 2003
Paul Martin, Jr.	Lib.	Dec. 2003	–	

minister. In 2000, Jean Chrétien won a third consecutive majority government — a feat last accomplished by Mackenzie King in 1945.

How are prime ministers' terms ended? Few retire entirely of their own choice; their careers are usually terminated following defeat in a general election. Only Macdonald, King, Meighen and Trudeau managed to stay on as leader and win another general election after their party had been defeated. Macdonald and Sir John Thompson died in office. Jean Chrétien was forced out by party pressures.

Getting rid of a prime minister, even via the electoral route, is difficult. Prime ministers have been defeated in less than one-third of all elections, whereas in over two-thirds, they were returned to the House of Commons — but more than half the time with a reduced majority.

Powers of the Office

The office of prime minister is powerful and prestigious. Its powers include the following:

- The prime minister and Cabinet together control the making and signing of treaties and the conduct of international relations, including the declaration of war and peace.

- The prime minister has the right to advise the governor general to dissolve Parliament. Therefore, the prime minister alone can determine the timing of an election within the five-year term of Parliament. Normally, Parliament is dissolved only when the prime minister believes that the party has a good chance of victory at the polls. This power of dissolution can be used to impose solidarity on a Cabinet or caucus because campaigns are expensive and risky, and most MPs want security. It is a potent weapon, helping to maintain the stability of the Cabinet system. The prime minister may lose the weapon of dissolution if the government is clearly defeated on a major bill due to breakdown of party discipline or loss of confidence of the House of Commons. At such a time, the prime minister has little choice but to call an election immediately to seek a new mandate. Such a turn of events, however, is rare.

- The prime minister controls the organization of government. On appointment, nearly every prime minister implements a new organizational structure to streamline or modernize the government. Cabinet structure can be modified, portfolios limited or combined, bureaucratic agencies abolished, Crown corporations created and Royal Commissions appointed — all on the initiative of the prime minister. Of course, unwarranted or unnecessary modifications may generate significant opposition.

- The prime minister chairs the Cabinet and is the key figure in the Cabinet committee system. No prime minister, however, can deal personally with all of the matters needing attention and therefore delegates authority and responsibility to Cabinet members.

- The prime minister controls appointments. Among them are the members of the ministry (which, as we shall see, includes all ministers and ministers of state, whether in Cabinet or not) chosen from the parliamentary caucus. A number of criteria may guide the prime minister's choice of ministers, including the desirability of having regional and ethnic representation. As we will see, an effort is generally made to have at least one minister from every province and significant representation from the largest ethnic groups in the country.

The prime minister, in consultation with his or her other ministers, is also responsible for appointing parliamentary secretaries. Parliamentary secretaries aid ministers in their duties but have no statutory authority. Usually, ministers agree beforehand, but on occasion, the prime minister may make an appointment without any consultation.[4]

In addition to choosing the members of the executive, the prime minister also appoints senators, judges and the senior staff of the public service, among others. Through these placements, the prime minister's influence is felt throughout the governmental structure. An appointment may be made as a reward for favours or services rendered to the prime minister or the party. Or positions may be withheld as a punishment for some misdemeanour. Legally, the prime minister's appointments are mere recommendations of appointment, forwarded to the governor general for formal approval. However, a modern prime minister's appointees are never rejected. In fact, as we have seen, the prime minister chooses the governor general. Patronage and government ethics are discussed further in Chapter 12, "Ethics in Canadian Government and Politics."

The Prime Minister and Government

The prime minister and his or her personally selected ministers form the government. Together, they formulate policy and direct administrative operations for as long as they are supported by the House of Commons. Once they no longer receive such support, they are replaced or Parliament is dissolved and elections are called. There is no doubt that executive power belongs to the prime minister and government.

Executive and legislative powers are fused or combined in Canada as they are in the British parliamentary system. Canadians vote for members of the House of Commons, including the prime minister, and almost all members of the government emerge from this elected body. Ministers are, therefore, members of both the legislature and the executive.

Historical Origins

The modern Cabinet originated in Britain in the Middle Ages. It began with the Privy Council, a group chosen by the monarch to give advice on state business. During the eighteenth century, these advisors gradually became more powerful vis-à-vis the monarch.

At Confederation, the Constitution established the **Queen's Privy Council for Canada** to assist and advise the governor general. Today, it is a largely ceremonial body whose members are nominated by the prime minister and appointed for life. The members include current and former ministers of the Crown, as well as a few other politically prominent individuals.[5] The Cabinet, which is composed only of current ministers of the Crown, constitutes the real executive power in Canada but acts in the name of the Privy Council. The authority of the prime minister and ministers rests not in the written Constitution but on convention. As members of the Privy Council, the ministers have the right to the title *Honourable* and *Privy Councillor* for life, while the prime minister is designated as *Right Honourable*.

Cabinet and Ministry

Size is an important factor in setting up political executives — the bigger they are the more unwieldy and expensive they become. During the 1984–1993 Progressive Conservative governments, the number of ministers reached a record. At one point, Brian Mulroney named forty ministers. The next prime minister, Kim Campbell, reduced the number to twenty-four.

When Jean Chrétien became head of government in November 1993, he created two types of ministers — appointing thirty to the ministry but including only twenty-two of them in his Cabinet. Paul Martin continued this new system, appointing thirty-one ministers and eight ministers of state in his first government.

The **ministry** is composed of all ministers who are appointed by the prime minister. It consists of both full ministers of the Crown and secretaries of state. The **Cabinet** is a smaller body of the most powerful ministers and acts in the name of the Privy Council. **Ministers of State**, like full ministers, are sworn to the Privy Council and bound by the rules of collective responsibility. However, they are only allowed to attend meetings of Cabinet on request, and their salary and staff allotments are lower than those of full cabinet ministers. Some MPs are also chosen as **parliamentary secretaries** to help ministers — one for each minister and the prime minister. Their responsibilities are assigned by their ministers and they are sometimes considered to be the government's "B Team," waiting for an opportunity to join the Cabinet.

In 2004, Prime Minister Martin appointed twenty-eight parliamentary secretaries and informed them that they would have special responsibilities in a minority government — they were to form a "two-way link between ministers and parliamentarians from all political parties." Perhaps, more significant in the long run was that, for the first time, parliamentary secretaries were sworn in as privy councillors so they could see Cabinet documents and attend Cabinet meetings.

As we have noted, ministers nearly always are chosen from the Commons. In some historical periods, a few have been appointed from the Senate, particularly when the governing party lacked elected representatives from a particular region — as the PCs did from Québec in 1979 and the Liberals did from the West in 1980–1984. Only rarely and temporarily have Cabinet positions gone to persons outside of Parliament. For example, a diplomat, Lester Pearson, was appointed secretary of state for external affairs in 1948 and subsequently won a seat in a by-election.

Cabinet Composition

There is usually a Cabinet member from each province (with the frequent exception of Prince Edward Island), with the largest urban regions receiving extra members. The relationship between distribution of cabinet ministers and provincial population has been relatively constant since Confederation. As a general rule, Ontario has had slightly more members in Cabinet than any other province, with Québec second. For example, because of his large 2004 victory in Ontario and the Liberals' much smaller representation from the rest of the country, Paul Martin chose sixteen ministers from Ontario, only eight from Québec and eight from the West.

The composition of the ministry and Cabinet also depends on how many seats the government controls in the House of Commons. Most elections have produced a **majority government** based on the support of only one party in the House of Commons. Only rarely has a Canadian **coalition government** been formed from more than one party. On other occasions (six times since 1945), Canadians have elected a **minority government**, i.e., the governing party had less than a majority of the members of Parliament. Prime ministers of minority governments have to select Cabinet members very carefully to ensure that a majority of House members will support the government. Even with such precautions, minority governments have tended to be quite unstable and pass less legislation than governments based on single-party majority control of the House.

Ethnicity is also a significant factor in Cabinet composition in Canada. The two founding ethnic groups are usually represented in approximate proportion to their population size. Of the total number of cabinet ministers serving between 1867 and 1965, for example, 28 percent were French Canadians, a figure that is remarkably close to the French-Canadian percentage of the population.[6] Prime ministers generally appoint a chief lieutenant from the opposite official ethnic group. Jean Chrétien, a francophone, appointed Herb Grey from Ontario as his deputy prime minister in 1997 and again in 2000. Smaller ethnic groups have usually been under-represented in Cabinet.

Certain Cabinet posts are distributed according to tradition. The post of minister of agriculture usually goes to a westerner, but when this is difficult, a minister from the West may receive control of the Wheat Board, as in 2000. A Maritime province usually gets the fisheries portfolio, but on occasion, as in 1997 and 2000, it has gone to someone from British Columbia.

Obviously, the distribution of seats that the government has obtained throughout the country is also an important factor in many Cabinet assignments. In the case of the Liberals, the department of finance traditionally went to an Ontarian. However, in 1980, Pierre Trudeau appointed a French Canadian to that post to bolster Québec strength in Cabinet, and when the Liberals returned to power in 1993, Jean Chrétien nominated a bilingual anglophone from Québec, Paul Martin (who served as finance minister until 2002). Martin chose Ralph Goodale as his finance minister upon becoming PM.

Unrepresented, or under-represented, in Cabinet are practically all of Canada's minority groups, as well as one majority group — women. Little significant room has been made in Cabinet for Native peoples, workers and unskilled labourers, or the poor. Those with higher education and high social-status occupations are always over-represented.

The composition of the 2004 Martin ministry followed these principles closely. Every province received one or more ministers, and the membership was reasonably representative of the provinces on a basis proportional to their population with the evident distortion of Québec. The new government members in 2004 were highly educated and professionally trained; they still did not form a social or economic cross-section of Canadians. Business and law continued to be the leading employment areas of ministers. There were few farmers and, as usual, labourers and the poor were not represented at all. Women were still in a minority position, but their numbers were continuing to grow — nine ministers and secretaries of state out of a ministry of thirty-nine appointed in the 2004 Liberal government were female. The Tories had given Canada its first female prime minister, Kim Campbell, and Jean Chrétien countered in 1993 by appointing Sheila Copps as the first female deputy prime minister. In 1997, Herb Gray replaced Sheila Copps. Paul Martin made Anne McLellan his deputy.[7]

Cabinet Conventions

Cabinet is bound by two important conventions: collective and individual responsibility. **Collective ministerial responsibility** means that, as a group, ministers are supposed to be held accountable to Parliament for their government's actions. Cabinet deliberations are held in secret, individual opinions are not publicly voiced and ministers are not supposed to speak or act except in the name of the entire Cabinet. They may speak about policy only after it has been agreed to in private by their colleagues. This convention allows ministers to be frank in private but support the government in public.

Each minister's personal responsibility is referred to as **individual ministerial responsibility**. As heads of departments, ministers receive confidential advice from public servants, make important decisions and then are held accountable for those decisions in Parliament and by the populace. In other words, public servants forego public praise in order to avoid public blame. Ministers accept credit but also any criticism that may be forthcoming. While ministers may delegate authority to their officials, they remain at the apex for appeals of administrative decisions and must be involved in initiating and defending new policies.

In practice, however, it is nearly impossible to follow these two conventions at all times. Where is the line to be drawn between ministerial and departmental responsibility? Ministers do not even know about most of the detailed decisions that are carried out in their names. The main check on ministerial responsibility is the free and open debate that takes place in Parliament and society about ministers' actions. The minister is judged in the department, in Cabinet, in Parliament, before the media and on the hustings. This issue is discussed further in Chapter 8, "Public Administration."

Cabinet Organization

New prime ministers generally change the organization of Cabinet. As we have seen, Jean Chrétien reduced Cabinet size from earlier governments and created an inner and outer ministry system. Priorities and Planning, a formerly powerful committee under both Pierre Trudeau and Brian Mulroney, was dropped, with Cabinet as a whole assuming its function. As well, he established a new committee system, which in 2000 included five committees — Economic Union, Social Union, Special Committee of Council, Treasury Board and Government Communications.

The 2004 Martin government retained the distinction between ministry and Cabinet begun by Chrétien. He appointed thirty-nine members to the ministry, thirty-one cabinet ministers and eight ministers of state, but the PM set up a brand new system of committees. He did not restore the Priorities and Planning Committee but gave its functions to the whole Cabinet and set up eight cabinet committees, reinstating the role of an *operations committee* used by Mulroney (see Figure 6.1).

Today, the Operations Committee controls the day-to-day coordination of government priorities for the Cabinet. *Domestic Affairs* integrates policy development in social, economic and environmental affairs. *Global Affairs* handles foreign issues, defence and trade and development. A special and new Cabinet committee on *Canada–US relations* has been added for the first time. The threat of terrorism and other issues of *homeland security* have been given to the *Security, Public Health and Emergencies Committee*. *Aboriginal Affairs* is also a new committee.

Lastly, the **Treasury Board** is the only committee of Cabinet named in the Constitution. Chaired by the president of the Treasury Board, it has legal responsibility for the authorization of expenditures and is the committee that allocates resources within the government. It is the only committee that does not position itself into a circle for policy deliberations but sits like a jury, facing any petitioners and acting as a tribunal. A

Figure 6.1 The Ministry and Cabinet in the Second Martin Government, 2005

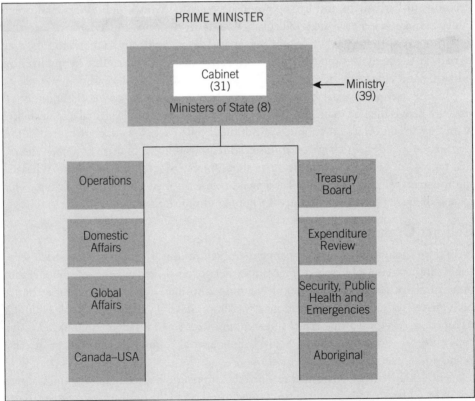

subcommittee called **Expenditure Review** is mandated to see that government expenditures are related to government priorities.

Cabinet Functions

Cabinet performs many functions as part of the political executive:

1. It is the arena in which major decisions are made or ratified. Ministers act collectively in Cabinet to develop policy, approve draft legislation, manage the country's finances and adopt **orders-in-council** — which are decisions that carry legal force rendered by Cabinet under the auspices of the Privy Council. Technically speaking, a Cabinet directive is an agreement arrived at in council with the governor general absent. However, as we have seen, the governor general is obliged by convention to grant formal approval to virtually every Cabinet decision or bill approved by Parliament. The formal executive authority of the governor general, carried out upon the advice and consultation of the Cabinet, is referred to as decisions of the **governor-in-council.**

    Ministers bring policies to their Cabinet colleagues for resolution. The formal process for Cabinet approval of a document is illustrated in Figure 6.2. Every Cabinet document is numbered and awarded a security classification. The minister's memorandum is forwarded to the Privy Council Office, which distributes it to Cabinet members. The memorandum is then discussed by the appropriate Cabinet committee and forwarded to Cabinet for final determination. As Figure 6.2 indicates, the Privy Council Office briefs the prime minister, as does the Prime Minister's Office. Following this series of actions, Cabinet gives final approval or disapproval in a record of decision. Of course, private communications can also increase the complexity of Cabinet decisions.

2. Cabinet, led by the House leader, plans the business of Parliament, making decisions about timetables for legislation and choosing major government speakers.

3. Cabinet members are responsible for the operation of departments of the public service and for bringing departmental initiatives to Cabinet for approval.

Figure 6.2 The Formal Cabinet Policy Process, 2005

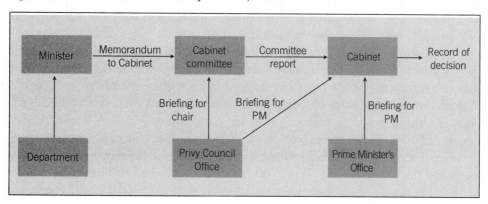

Public policy derives from a multitude of sources, but it is the individual minister who puts the final stamp of approval on departmental initiatives. A minister needs the expertise and the information that comes from his or her department's permanent contact with interest groups. However, only a minister may carry forward departmental requests to the Cabinet.

4. Cabinet provides political leadership for the party in power.

Cabinet Staff

Individual ministers are supported by their departments and political appointees. Each minister's office employs an executive assistant, special assistants, a private secretary and other support personnel. Ministers often second (temporarily transfer) departmental employees to their offices and hire policy and communications advisors under contract. They hire political aides on an individual basis in order to perform largely partisan tasks. Aides are not subject to the regulations of the public service (and hence are called "exempt staff"). Under provisions of the 1967 *Public Service Employment Act*, they are given high priority for permanent positions in the administration after three years of consecutive political service.

MINORITY AND COALITION GOVERNMENTS

If no party has a majority of members of the House of Commons, a Cabinet based on a minority of members will be set up. Such a government is called a minority government. In other words, a minority government is one that emerges from an election that accords it less than a majority of members of the House of Commons. As we have seen, a majority government, by contrast, is one based on a majority of the governing party's MPs in the House.

Constitutionally, the governor general accepts the view of the current prime minister about who to appoint as the incoming prime minister. If the party of the current prime minister has the largest number of seats, or nearly the same as the second placed party, he or she will stay on for a year or so. If soundly beaten, however, the prime minister will ask the governor general to call the leader of the Opposition. Of Canada's thirty-eight general elections, nine resulted in no party winning an absolute majority in the House of Commons and the percentage of minority governments has increased in the post–Second World War period along with the rise of the multi-party system.

In many other democratic countries, particularly in Europe, multi-party legislatures with no single party controlling a majority of members of the legislature usually have coalition governments, with the administration formed by more than one party. States such as Austria, Switzerland and the Netherlands have continual coalition governments and still manage a high degree of government coherence in law-making because of long established norms and practices that enable coalitions to hold together despite party pressures.

Only once in Canadian history has a coalition been constructed from more than one party and this was during the First World War (although the first Prime Minister, Sir John A. Macdonald, did achieve Confederation based on a combination of Liberals and

Conservatives). Ten times since Confederation there have been minority governments (see Table 6.3). There were two different minority governments in the 1926 Parliament. Minority governments have usually (but not always) been short-lived and tended to pass less legislation than majority governments (we do not attempt to assess the quality of the bills). Most minority governments were defeated by a vote of non-confidence in the government, forcing a dissolution and election.

Problems Or Advantages in Minority Governments

The number of seats held usually, but not always, determines which party forms the government. Parties with fewer seats in the House than an opponent have managed to hold on to power — witness Mackenzie King's Liberals in 1925 (they had 99 seats and 40 percent of the vote while the Conservatives had 116 seats and 47 percent of the vote). Minor parties occasionally have had more influence on policy than their support in the country warranted. In order to remain in office, both Pearson and Trudeau had to make major concessions to the NDP.

Parliament is a more exciting and less predictable place during minority governments. Historically, social policy has been dramatically changed in such situations. Minority governments under both Pearson and Trudeau passed important social legislation. With the support of the NDP, they passed the Canada Pension Plan, the Canada Assistance Plan, the Guaranteed Supplement for seniors and medicare. Would the Liberals have passed these measures without the prodding of the NDP?

An early election is almost certain to be called in the case of a minority government. However, minor parties generally find that their number of seats won goes down after minority Parliaments and have to be cautious about trying to provoke an election. As well, the number of bills introduced and passed during minority governments is much lower than in majority governments.

Table 6.3 Canada's Ten Minority Governments

Party	Liberal	Conservatives	Progressive	Labour	Social Credit	CCF/NDP	Crediste	Bloc	Ind.
1921	**117**	50	64	3	—	—	—	—	1
1925*	**101**	116	24	2	—	—	—	—	2
1926	116	91	13	3	11	9	—	—	2
1957	107	**112**	—	—	19	25	—	—	2
1962	100	**116**	—	—	30	19	—	—	—
1963	**129**	95	—	—	24	17	—	—	—
1965	**131**	97	—	—	5	21	9	—	2
1972	**109**	107	—	—	—	31	15	—	—
1979	114	**136**	—	—	—	26	6	—	—
2004	**135**	99	—	—	—	19	—	54	1

* Two minority governments were formed following this election — first Liberal, then Conservative.

A minority situation also affects the type of tactics used by leaders of all parties. Prime ministers need to keep both their own backbenchers and opposition parties contented. The tactics for this include reducing the length of sessions, avoiding controversial legislation to postpone the date of defeat, making deals and compromises with other parties and setting up a liaison system with opposition parties to solicit their views. The government usually attempts to play off one minor party against another, using a "divide and rule" strategy. On occasion, prime ministers have also given out patronage, contracts and employment to members of opposition parties.

WHAT CAN I TELL YOU? JACK SENT IT OVER

Aislin Montreal Gazette, April 28, 2005, Reprinted with permission.

Opposition parties, too, have some new strategic issues during a minority Parliament. They must appear responsible and not be seen to be opposing the government *just* for partisan reasons. On the other hand, they cannot be seen to be pandering to the government. They know that the lack of an overall majority still allows the prime minister some leverage and the ability to claim that the opposition parties are undermining good and strong government.

POLITICAL EXECUTIVES: CANADA AND THE UNITED STATES COMPARED

Because it follows Britain's parliamentary model, Canada's executive differs from that of the United States in a number of ways. First, the US president embodies the formal as well as the political executive — he or she is head of government and head of state. The president is also commander-in-chief of the armed forces, while in Canada, although wars are fought in the name of the Queen, the role of governor general as head of the armed forces is purely ceremonial.

Second, the prime minister of Canada is simultaneously a member of the legislature and the executive. By contrast, the US president is not allowed to serve in Congress but is elected directly by the people. The American presidential form of government, therefore, provides a clear separation of executive and legislative powers.

The US Constitution is based on the premise that a concentration of power is undesirable and that law-making and implementation should be separated by preventing the overlap of key personnel. Thus, the presidential–congressional system of checks and balances creates an atmosphere of public political bargaining not found in Canada. For example, in the United States, the executive must rely on Congress to authorize funds to implement policy, and the Senate must confirm presidential appointments to Cabinet, the diplomatic service, federal courts and other boards and commissions.

Whereas in the United States, an individual may not hold a post in Congress and an executive position at the same time, precisely the opposite of what is true in Canada. All members of Cabinet, including the prime minister, must be either elected to the House of Commons or appointed to the Senate. This fusion of powers creates, at least in theory, a government that is more coherent and responsive to the will of the people. The Canadian executive, assuming a parliamentary majority backs it, can be assured of legislative support on most of the bills and programs it wishes to enact. It will, of course, be held accountable by the people at the next election, but during the interim, it is relatively free to pursue its agenda. The executive in the United States is much more restricted, especially if different parties control the presidency and Congress.

In contrast to the Canadian model, the US executive can also frustrate Congress — for instance, Congress is dependent on the president to implement its policies, and the executive often controls the information needed to formulate effective policies in Congress. On the other hand, the Congress can, and often does, reject executive proposals, an exceedingly rare event in Canada where such behaviour could cause the government to fall and necessitate a new election.

CENTRAL AGENCIES

The Cabinet is assisted in its functions by four central coordinating agencies: the prime minister's Office, the Privy Council Office (now including the Federal–Provincial Relations Office), the Treasury Board and the Department of Finance. The first two report directly to the prime minister; the other two have their own ministers.

The Prime Minister's Office

Of the various executive support agencies, the **Prime Minister's Office (PMO)** is the most overtly political. The upper echelon of the PMO is composed of the personal appointees of the prime minister. It is the largest and most important of the "exempt" staffs and only rarely does it employ public servants.

The PMO performs many roles. It controls the drafting of the Speech from the Throne, the government's program as outlined at the beginning of each session of Parliament. However, perhaps its most crucial task is to act as a monitoring agency tracing political developments and their implications for the prime minister's career. In concert with the Privy Council Office, the PMO provides the prime minister with a range of technical and political advice that may not be available from the non-partisan bureaucratic structures.

It develops policy suggestions to boost the political fortunes of the prime minister and the governing party. In addition, the PMO carries out considerable public relations work. It gathers survey data on the popularity of the prime minister and political initiatives, helps prepare press conferences and deals with the media generally. Other related responsibilities include answering the prime minister's mail, coordinating his or her daily appointment schedule and searching for candidates for nominations and awards.

The organization and structure of the PMO remain the prerogative of the prime minister. Throughout Canada's early history, the PMO was a small, relatively insignificant body. However, under Pierre Trudeau and Brian Mulroney, it achieved unprecedented importance. In 2004, Paul Martin initially appointed long-time Liberal Francis Fox as his senior advisor but later replaced him with Heléne Chalifour. The PMO is likely to continue to be extremely influential in policy-making at the political apex.

The Privy Council Office

The main organization supporting the Cabinet and prime minister is the **Privy Council Office (PCO)**. It is the prime minister's department and Cabinet's secretariat. It supports the prime minister, ministers in the PM's financial portfolio (in 2004, this included the deputy prime minister, minister of intergovernmental relations, leader and deputy leaders in the House of Commons, leader in the Senate and president of the Privy Council) and Cabinet as a whole.

The top position in the PCO is held by the **clerk of the Privy Council**. This post, which has existed since 1867, is mentioned in the Constitution. It was combined with the function of secretary to the Cabinet in 1940. The individual who holds this position (currently Alex Himelfarb) is at the top of Canada's civil service. The clerk is in charge of coordinating Cabinet activities. The clerk's staffers set agendas, take the minutes of Cabinet meetings and convey Cabinet decisions to the bureaucracy. However, the role and stature of the clerk depend to a great extent on his or her rapport with the prime minister.

The PCO performs some of the same functions as the PMO but is staffed by career bureaucrats seconded from various government departments. It has responsibility for the development and coordination of overall government policy. Although the top-ranking staffers of the PCO are appointed by the prime minister on the advice of the clerk, there is normally little emphasis on partisan politics. The PCO must, however, be politically sensitive. Under all recent prime ministers, the PCO, like the PMO, has flourished in size and scope of responsibility, but it has only rarely had political appointees on its staff.

The Privy Council Office possesses an impressive research capability and acts as the "eyes and ears" of the Cabinet in coordinating the numerous governmental departments and agencies. With a staff of about five hundred officers and support personnel, the PCO is divided into several principal units. While the structures and powers of these units "ebb and flow" with the styles of different prime ministers, the most influential tend to include plans, operations, intergovernmental affairs, machinery of government, foreign affairs, senior personnel and security and intelligence. In 2004, Paul Martin added an aboriginal affairs secretariat in the PCO. Each of these divisions has its own staff and is responsible for advising the prime minister, the plenary Cabinet and the various Cabinet committees on matters of national policy.

The relationship between cabinet ministers and officers of the PCO is for the most part cordial and constructive. The staff of the Privy Council may be more expert on specific matters of policy than the ministers, but in the end, it is the elected ministers who make the decisions. In principle, the PCO exists to offer ministers objective advice and suggest policy alternatives since the weight of public responsibility is not on its shoulders.

Issues of concern to both the federal government and the provinces are periodically negotiated and adjusted through federal–provincial conferences. Federal–provincial meetings, especially constitutional revisions, necessitate much intensive planning and preparation on the part of federal officials. A central agency — the Federal–Provincial Relations Office (FPRO) — was established in 1974 within the Privy Council Office to deal with these issues. It became a separate department under the prime minister in 1975. Until 1993, it functioned independently of the PCO while reporting directly to the prime minister. As part of the 1993 government restructuring, it was subsumed once again inside the PCO while reporting to the minister responsible for federal–provincial relations.

The PCO now carries out the traditional FPRO responsibilities for conducting research and analysis to help in coordinating Ottawa's interaction with the provinces and in anticipating provincial reactions. In particular, it has a special mandate to monitor events in Québec and prepare scenarios for action vis-à-vis its government and the issue of independence. It also has ongoing duties in the areas of aboriginal rights, the infrastructure program and constitutional planning.

The Treasury Board

The third central coordinating agency is the Treasury Board, which, as we have noted, is constitutionally a committee of the Privy Council. In 1966, the staff of the Treasury Board was removed from the jurisdiction of the Department of Finance, and the unit was elevated to the legal status of a separate government department. The Treasury Board and its secretariat are headed by a cabinet minister, the president of the Treasury Board. The Treasury Board itself includes five other cabinet ministers, one of whom is always the minister of finance. Aided by its secretariat, the Treasury Board is charged with two broad areas of responsibility: review of government expenditures and personnel management.

Responsibility for the review of expenditures means that the annual budgets of all government departments are screened and approved by the Treasury Board. It monitors all requests for money, evaluates them and provides an overall budget in keeping with the priorities and objectives expressed by the prime minister and Cabinet. There is continuous consultation and negotiation between the Treasury Board and the spokespeople for all of the Cabinet portfolios, as each department attempts to maximize its share of the government's budget. The Treasury Board assesses these requests and makes its recommendations.

Treasury's second major responsibility is the management of civil service personnel. It exerts control over salaries and job classifications across the civil service, expanding the application of the merit principle. Motivating the Treasury Board above all else is the goal of effective utilization of human resources.

To assist the six cabinet members of the Treasury Board, there is a highly qualified staff — the **Treasury Board secretariat (TBS)** headed by a secretary to the Treasury Board. As of 2003, there has also been a district controller general in the department. The staff of the TBS includes some of the brightest and most efficient members of the public service. Its economists, statisticians and efficiency experts analyze departmental budgets.

The Department of Finance

The fourth central coordinating agency is the **Department of Finance**. While it is a regular government department, by virtue of its subject matter it is one of the most politically sensitive. Created in 1967 out of the financial bodies that predated Confederation, its authority is assigned under the *Financial Administration Act*. Finance shares some of the general concerns of the Treasury Board, but its chief preoccupation is analyzing taxation policy and the impact of government activity on the economy. It also engages in long-range economic forecasting and suggests ways to maximize the performance of the economy.

Finance also provides the Cabinet with information on the performance of the economy. On the basis of these facts, Cabinet, led by the minister of finance, establishes priorities. Public servants employed by the Department of Finance analyze four areas: taxation policy, economic development and government finance, fiscal policy and economic analysis, and international trade and finance.

The first major concern, taxation policy, is handled in co-operation with the Department of Revenue. Specialists analyze existing tax measures from the perspective of the business community. A personal income tax unit examines proposals relating to personal taxation, deferred income plans such as retirement savings plans, and trusts and partnerships. Other tax units attempt to determine the effects of taxation on the distribution of income, on the long-term growth of the economy and on the behaviour of individuals and corporations. Finally, the Department of Finance maintains an international tax policy unit, which negotiates tax treaties with foreign countries and examines the effects of foreign taxation on the Canadian economy.

With respect to its second responsibility, economic development, the department seeks to devise policies and strategies to encourage the overall growth of the Canadian economy. Finance is also involved in providing government loans to promote economic development and in negotiating financial guarantees to Crown corporations.

The third responsibility is fiscal policy and economic analysis. The department monitors indicators of the overall economic conditions of the country and prepares forecasts used in the development of the annual government budget. This involves establishing the annual fiscal framework and maintaining a close link with the Treasury Board secretariat.

The fourth concern of the Department of Finance is international trade. It investigates and reports on proposals concerning the Canadian customs tariff and its relation to the General Agreement on Tariffs and Trade (GATT), and various bilateral trade agreements, such as the Free Trade Agreement with the United States and the North American Free Trade Agreement with Mexico and the United States. It also makes recommendations on international trade policy. The department maintains a liaison with international financial organizations and, of course, seeks to promote export development. The international finance section is also concerned with the balance of payments and foreign exchange matters.

Finance maintains a relatively high profile among government departments. The minister of finance presents the government's budget to Parliament and is inevitably the object of criticism or praise by the press and the opposition parties. The present Prime Minister, Paul Martin, spent nearly a decade as finance minister until 2002 before becoming head of the Liberal government in 2003.

DOES THE PRIME MINISTER HAVE TOO MUCH POWER?

Some observers of politics in Canada find that the political executive has overstepped its proper authority, inviting grave consequences for responsible government and the parliamentary system. In a classic article, Denis Smith suggested that Parliament has surrendered its important roles of providing a forum for serious public debate and developing public policy.[8] According to Smith, a great deal ultimately depends on the prime minister, who appoints and dismisses his ministers at will. Although Cabinet may include some unusually powerful and prestigious figures, the decisions Cabinet reaches depend on the prime minister. Cabinet policy becomes government policy, and backbenchers have little choice but to vote in obedience to the party and their prime minister.

There is considerable force to this argument during majority governments. Changes in procedural rules and the expanding jurisdiction of the central coordinating agencies have helped lessen the effectiveness of Parliament in its role of scrutiny and deliberation. House rules permit the government to pass legislation with a minimum of delay or modification. Opposition parties are rarely able to thoroughly scrutinize and effectively criticize the details of government policy.

This exceptional policy-making authority of the prime minister is resented by ministers, middle and upper echelons of the civil service and members of Parliament, and distrusted by the press and opposition. While the descriptions of flagrant abuse of power may be overstated,[9] the potential for abuse has been very real indeed. The power of the prime minister and his or her staff has become enormous and pervasive. A prime minister with a majority government can shape the direction and content of policy, and, except in extraordinary situations, can count on dominating the political process until the next election.

In minority situations, however, prime ministers are considerably weaker. They must bargain not just with opposition members but also their own backbenchers to maintain the confidence of the House. Otherwise, they may be forced to call an election when they do not want to. Their legislative priorities have to be significantly altered to accommodate other parties and get their votes.

Clearly there are powers and advantages in the prime minister's position, but especially in minority situations, there are many limitations on them. The power of the prime minister is not exercised in isolation. The Cabinet and caucus must be guided toward policies that avoid hostile reactions from Parliament and the public. Care must be taken to hold the Cabinet together, to direct a complex government machine and to secure adequate support for government.

Prime ministers obtain much of their strength from holding their team together. This must be done with conciliation, tact and only rarely with force. Pearson was a deft chairman-of-the-board type of leader; Mackenzie King was a master electioneer. Mulroney and Chrétien combined both talents. The skills required are so varied that no prime minister can be said to have had all of them. Paul Martin, with his very weak minority government, was dubbed "Mr. Dithers" because of his shifting priorities as he tried to hold his government together.

Canada does not have prime ministerial government, but it is certainly a powerful position. A minority government, however, creates a weak prime minister, particularly if there is no party or a number of members willing and able to combine their votes with the government to allow it to stop votes of non-confidence.

KEY TERMS

Cabinet, p. 139
clerk of the Privy Council, p. 148
coalition government, p. 140
collective ministerial responsibility, p. 141
Crown, p. 132
Department of Finance, p. 150
executive, p. 131
Expenditure Review, p. 143
governor general, p. 133
governor-in-council, p. 143
individual ministerial responsibility, p. 141
Letters Patent, p. 133
lieutenant-governor, p. 134

majority government, p. 140
Ministers of State, p. 139
ministry, p. 139
minority government, p. 140
monarch, p. 132
orders-in-council, p. 143
parliamentary secretaries, p. 139
prerogative authority, p. 132
Prime Minister's Office (PMO), p. 147
Privy Council Office (PCO), p. 148
Queen's Privy Council for Canada, p. 138
Treasury Board, p. 142
Treasury Board secretariat (TBS), p. 150

DISCUSSION QUESTIONS

1. Where does political power lie in the Canadian system? With the prime minister? With Cabinet? With Parliament? With the people of Canada? Does it matter if there is only a minority government?

2. Who were the two longest-lasting prime ministers in Canadian history? Why do you think they were successful?

3. Does the Privy Council Office have too much control over the prime minister? Explain your response.

4. Does the prime minister have too much power? Why or why not?

WEBLINKS

Governor General of Canada

www.gg.ca

Federal Ministers

www.parl.gc.ca

Prime Minister's Website

www.pm.gc.ca

Queen Elizabeth II

http://canada.gc.ca/howgoc/queen/quind_e.html

Treasury Board of Canada Secretariat

www.tbs-sct.gc.ca

7 Parliament
A Primary Arena of Politics

Learning Objectives

After reading this chapter, you should be able to

1. Name the three major functions of the Canadian legislature in general, and discuss the distinct functions of the House of Commons and the Senate in particular.

2. Describe the major stages in the life cycle of a Parliament and the three major items of business for each session.

3. Name the kinds of committees in the House and describe what they do.

4. Distinguish between non-financial and money bills and trace the path each must follow in order to become law.

5. Describe how politicians interact in Parliament, both within the party and among parties.

The Parliament of Canada is the main arena of politics in the country; when it is in session, the issues, parties, events, personalities and even scandals that are part of political life on Parliament Hill become the focus of national media attention. It is here that the game of power politics is played. With journalists as their guide, Canadians become spectators to a clash of ideas and events that ultimately could affect their lives.

In this chapter, we examine the origin and functions of the Canadian Parliament and explain how Parliament operates. Members of Parliament and senators discuss, debate and argue over the virtues and justice of laws and how they affect ordinary Canadians. They use Parliament as a forum for displaying their ideas about who should get what, when and how in Canada.

THE PARLIAMENT OF CANADA

The Parliament of Canada, established by the *Constitution Act, 1867*, is modelled on the "Westminster Model" of Great Britain. It includes three bodies: the House of

Commons, the Senate and the Crown. As the embodiment of the Crown, the monarch plays a formal role in the Canadian legislative process through the governor general. To become law, legislation must pass through these three bodies. The parliamentary **legislature** — the branch of government that makes or amends laws — is **bicameral**, that is, composed of two houses. It has an elected lower house of representatives (the House of Commons) and an appointed upper house (the Senate). The parliamentary *executive* — the prime minister and Cabinet — is based in the lower house and, as we shall see, is responsible to it. The executive directs parliamentary business, while an institutionalized opposition is charged with criticizing government.

Canada is a parliamentary democracy in that Parliament exercises power on behalf of the public and is therefore the "repository of popular sovereignty." In a parliamentary system, the political executive receives its power to govern from the legislature. The prime minister and Cabinet are accountable to Parliament and may govern only as long as they retain the "confidence" of the majority of the House of Commons. We have seen that this is called *responsible government*. We have also seen that Canada is also a *representative democracy* in which Canadian citizens choose individual members of Parliament (MPs) to represent them in making national policies.

The Origins of Canada's Parliament

All countries have some means of discussing common problems to decide what, if any, action should be taken to resolve them. Canada established Parliament as the main institution for this purpose.

In Britain, the modern parliament can be traced back to the council that the King used to summon regularly for advice. This gathering, over time, was called "parliament" from the Old French, meaning "discussion." As centuries passed, power gradually shifted from the monarch to Parliament. By the eighteenth century, senior ministers sat in the Commons (rather than the upper house); and by the nineteenth century, ministers required the support of the Commons, not just the King, to retain office. In this way, executive power came to be centred in Parliament.

Canadians borrowed the blueprint for their Parliament from Britain and adapted it. From the early stages, Canadians concentrated on making the governor and the executive council responsible to the elected assembly. This was achieved and at Confederation in 1867, Canada joined the world of states as a representative, parliamentary democracy. In doing so, it established an adversarial system of party politics with a clear dichotomy between government and opposition. It also established a code of rules and procedures to govern the behaviour of members and to counteract, to some extent, potential hostility arising from the partisan nature of the House.

While Canada's lower house, the House of Commons, was established as an *elected* assembly, the upper house was *appointed*. The idea of an appointed upper house was considered appropriate for two main reasons. The first was that the founders believed "men of wisdom and good stock" would be among the best qualified to watch out for the public interest. The second was that such a body would protect provincial rights.

Neither of these reasons to have an appointed Senate is considered valid today. Concepts of equality have made obsolete the desire to confine the upper house exclusively to "men of wisdom and good stock". As well, the Senate has not been able to develop a role as a legitimate protector of provincial interests.

The allotment of senators does, however, provide the less populous provinces a degree of regional influence in Parliament. Ontario and Québec receive twenty-four each, and Nova Scotia, New Brunswick and PEI are awarded a combined twenty-four. Québec's francophone population also is assured of a strong voice in the Senate. As other provinces were formed, their rights to representation in the Senate have been established on the same principles.

The Functions of Canada's Parliament

As the vehicle for representative democracy, Parliament provides a forum for members to debate major political issues of the day. The debate is relayed to the public by the mass media, informing and also openly responding to public opinion.

Like many other parliaments, the Canadian legislature has three major functions:

- It has *policy-making functions* including the passage of legislation (a lengthy process which is outlined below).

- It has *representational functions* since it is responsible to express the interests and opinions of an electorate and deal with the problems of constituents.

- It has *system-maintenance functions* that contribute to the working and legitimacy of other parts of the political system and the state itself.

Parliament performs a host of other services as well. It regularly participates in the recruitment and socialization of future members of the government; it aids in the regulation and management of conflict and may serve to integrate and achieve consensus among rival political elites; and it legitimizes public policies. In addition, the two houses of Parliament each have specialized functions, which we shall explore shortly.

The Life Cycle of Parliament

The term *parliament* is used in different ways. Its general usage is, as we have seen, to describe a certain *type* of legislature. However the term *Parliament* is also used to refer to the House of Commons *building* in Ottawa, and it is also used in a very specific way to identify a particular government from the time of its election to the formation of the next government. Parliaments in this latter sense are labelled by consecutive numbers, changing after each general election. For example, the 308 MPs returned in the 2004 general election collectively constituted the thirty-eighth Parliament.

All Parliaments pass through the same life cycle, following the same pattern of events. However, the lifespans of Parliaments may vary and each is unique in other significant ways. In each Parliament, there may be one or a number of **sessions,** or working periods when Parliament is open for business. The number of sessions depends on the wishes of the government of the day and upon the length of the Parliament — that is, upon how much time elapses between general elections. The Constitution requires Parliament to meet at least once a year.

Generally a session of Parliament includes three major events concerning the business of Parliament: the Speech from the Throne, presentation of a budget and presentation of the estimates. Every session begins with the governor general summoning the MPs and senators to Parliament at the request of the prime minister. Members of both Houses come together in the Senate chamber, with great pomp and ceremony, to hear the governor general deliver the **Speech from the Throne**, which outlines the government's proposed legislative program for the forthcoming session. The first Speech from the Throne in a new Parliament tends to be a reiteration of campaign promises. After the speech is read, members return to their respective chambers to commence business. In the Commons, a debate on the Throne Speech usually occupies the first few days of the session; afterward, the normal timetable of the House comes into effect. In total, six days may be used to debate the Speech. A break taken by the House within a session is called an **adjournment**, or a **recess.**

Another feature of parliamentary sessions is the budget. Delivered by the minister of finance, the **budget** is a document primarily concerned with setting out where the revenue will come from to carry out the government's program. It generally includes tax changes to raise revenue and is kept secret until it is unveiled in a dramatic presentation. Tax changes go into effect immediately, although the legislation for them is necessarily drawn up later. A four-day **budget debate** (not necessarily consecutive days) follows the presentation of the budget. The debate can be dramatic because it provides the opposition with an opportunity to try to defeat the government. Such a defeat does not normally happen to governments that have a majority of members in the House of Commons. In 2005, with only a minority, the Martin government survived the vote on the budget — though with considerable difficulty.

Tabling the **estimates** — the government's spending proposals for the next fiscal year — is the third major item of business for each session. Apart from these events, every session is devoted largely to preparing bills to become law and debating the political issues of the day.

When the government wants to end a session of Parliament, it closes it. Closing a session is called **prorogation**. Formally, this is done by the governor general upon the advice of the prime minister. Unless there is prior agreement, any legislation that has not successfully completed all the stages of the process automatically dies when Parliament is prorogued; if the government is still committed to an unpassed bill, it must begin the entire process again in the next session. Sessions used to last a year or less, but in recent years, they have become longer. The first session of the thirty-second Parliament lasted a record three years and eight months. Prorogation of one session is often immediately followed by the summoning of the next.

At least once every five years there is a proclamation by the governor general announcing the dissolution of the House of Commons. **Dissolution**, the end of a particular

Parliament, which occurs at the request of a prime minister who seeks a new mandate or whose government has been defeated in the House[1] brings in its wake a general election.

THE HOUSE OF COMMONS

The House of Commons has 308 members of Parliament, distributed by a formula among the provinces and territories. Rules concerning how many MPs are elected and how the constituency boundaries are determined are discussed in Chapter 11, "Elections and Political Behaviour."

The Functions of the House of Commons

The House of Commons has several distinct functions:

- As a representative institution, it is to reflect the ideas and wishes of Canadians. On the other hand, it is also expected to lead and educate the public.
- It provides the government with authority to govern.
- It supervises work of the Cabinet. Motions of confidence and non-confidence decide who will form the government.
- It passes laws, imposes taxes and authorizes expenditures.
- It adopts resolutions.
- It provides a forum to legitimize decisions that are taken by the government under existing statutes or regulations.
- It allows a forum for backbenchers to initiate ideas and, to a limited extent, even legislation, through Question Period, parliamentary debates and private members' bills.
- It is a forum for extended debates on political questions that expose the advantages and disadvantages of different courses of action.
- It provides a critic or watchdog to keep the government accountable.
- It provides an alternate government in the form of an Official Opposition party.
- It provides a training ground for future cabinet ministers.

Members of Parliament

Each member of Parliament (MP) is elected to the House of Commons (generally on a party "label") in a single-member constituency. Ordinary MPs constitute a visible link between the public and the federal government, but they play only a minor role in determining public policy. Many have short careers in Parliament, and many find the switch back to private life difficult economically and psychologically.

The position of MP has many facets. The work of those who are **backbenchers** — that is, those on the government side who are not ministers, or on the opposition side who are not designated party critics — is of two types: parliamentary and constituency. In Parliament, the job is basically to support their party leadership and attend plenary sessions of the House of Commons to debate and vote on legislation. Apart from this, they also serve on parliamentary committees and are members of parliamentary caucuses, which meet regularly. They also have large caseloads of constituency duties to perform. For many, the constituencies they represent are far from Ottawa, and it takes much time and effort to act as representatives. They hear problems from their constituents and may take up those issues with ministers, public servants or representatives of government agencies in an attempt to resolve them. They also have to inform constituents about legislation and issues that are being discussed in Parliament.

For their efforts MPs, as of January 2004, received a salary of $141 000; benefits and pensions; an office budget averaging $234 819; travel allowances (sixty-four return trips between Ottawa and their respective ridings); and free telephone and mail services.

Theoretically, almost any adult Canadian can run for Parliament and be an MP. In practice, however, it is not so simple. Campaigns are expensive and usually require a significant personal investment in money and time. A good education is necessary to understand the problems of the day and communicate the issues to the public, and it is helpful to have an alternative source of income for security in such a tenuous job. In order to be victorious, one also must be affiliated with, and win a candidacy for, a political party. Independents without a party label are rarely elected.

Members of Parliament do not represent a cross-section of the population. Those with British and French backgrounds predominate, as do those with law degrees. Most MPs come from urban areas because the majority of ridings are clustered around larger city-centres. Most are middle-aged males. No woman was elected to be an MP in Canada until 1921, and the numbers of female MPs did not reach two digits until 1979. In 2004, sixty-five women were elected — a record high.

CLOSE-UP   Agnes Macphail

Agnes Macphail (1890–1954) was the first woman elected to the Canadian House of Commons. She was elected in 1921 (the first year in which all women had the right to vote) and stayed in office until 1940. Three years after leaving Ottawa, Macphail became one of the first two women elected to the Ontario legislature (1943–1945 and 1948–1951).

Macphail began as a member of the United Farmer–Independent Labour party for Grey County in Ontario, but once she was elected, she sat with the Progressive party. Later, she

Agnes Macphail, first woman MP

became an independent and eventually joined the Cooperative Commonwealth Federation (CCF).

Agnes Macphail was concerned with preserving the rural way of life and, particularly in the Ontario legislature, worked to bring issues of concern to women to the attention of the government. She worked to improve civil rights for women, to obtain equal pay for women and to acquire the right to vote for women in Québec.

Rules of the House

The procedures for the daily activities in the Commons are set out in the Standing Orders. The **Standing Orders** contain the rules of the House, which are of a general nature, impartial and more or less permanent. Although the rules of the House prevent any particular party from receiving partisan treatment, they do allow the government to monopolize the time of the House and for the most part to set its agenda. The rules of debate favour the government. Individual members, as we shall see, are guaranteed some time to put forward bills, but this is minimal, and selection is determined by lottery.

Procedural rules have been designed to reduce antagonism in the House of Commons by limiting the direct personal interaction of the members. For example, verbal confrontations during debate are constrained by the requirement that no member may speak officially without recognition by the speaker and that all statements must be addressed to the chair. This means that members do not speak directly to one another or even of one another, inasmuch as individuals are referred to not by name but through more impersonal titles, such as "the prime minister," "the leader of the Opposition" or "the honourable member for constituency X."

There is even a list of terms deemed to constitute "unparliamentary language." It is not permitted, for example, to use expressions that cast doubt on the legitimacy of a member's birth nor to allege that a speech has been inspired by intoxicating substances. On December 8, 1994, the speaker ruled that "mean-spirited" terms constituted unparliamentary language and could not be used in the House. Members have been suspended from the House for suggesting that another member was lying and then refusing to withdraw the accusation.

Other rules that help to reduce antagonism include the principle that, once recognized by the speaker, every MP has the right to speak for a specific length of time without interruption if the speech remains relevant to the motion before the House. Rules also protect certain persons (especially the royal family, the governor general and senators) from explicit attacks in the Commons.

Although this basic code of civility is upheld by the rules, members of both houses enjoy special privileges in regard to freedom of speech that other Canadians do not. This is because of **parliamentary privilege**, a House rule that enables MPs to express themselves freely and without intimidation. This rule, adopted from British tradition, grants individual

MPs freedom of speech in their capacity as members, so that they cannot be prosecuted in court for anything they have said in the House or its committees. As well, an MP cannot be intimidated in the House or in going to or from the House. Nor can an MP be arrested for certain minor offences for a period before, during and after a parliamentary session.

The House of Commons also enjoys collective privileges as a legislative body, which enable the House to conduct its business in an orderly fashion. The House has the power to preserve order and discipline in its proceedings and to punish those who are guilty of making libelous statements concerning it or its members. It has the power to refuse a seat to a person who has been duly elected and can expel any member of the House.

Organization and Officers of the House of Commons

The seating plan of the Canadian House of Commons follows the British model in which the government and opposition face one another with the government to the speaker's right and the opposition to the left. The leaders of the two major parties confront each other surrounded by their lieutenants and backed by their backbenchers. The smaller parties also take their place on the opposition side of the House. This face-to-face positioning physically separates the government from the opposition and reinforces the sense of political identity and party cohesion on both sides of the Commons. (As Figure 7.1 on page 162 shows, when the governing party wins fewer seats than the combined opposition, some opposition members must sit on the "government" side — in this case, the NDP.)

In the central area of the chamber, between the two main rivals, sit the officials of the House. The **speaker of the House of Commons**, who sits at one end, is officially an impartial arbiter elected by the whole House. He or she is not permitted to vote in the House (voting takes place when a "division" is called), except for casting the deciding vote in the event of a tie, when the speaker supports the government of the day.

Since September 1986, the speaker has been elected by secret ballot in a vote of all members of the House. Peter Milliken was elected as speaker in 2001 and re-elected in 2004.

The speaker is in charge of the administration of the House, overseeing the staffing of the House with secretaries, clerks and so on. As well, the speaker is jointly responsible, with the Board of Internal Economy (a body composed of the speaker and deputy speaker of the House, two members of the Privy Council, the leader of the Official Opposition or a designee, and four other members — two from the government caucus and two from the opposition benches), for the economic management of the House, and prepares and steers through the House the annual estimates of the cost of running the Commons. The speaker is aided by a deputy speaker, who is also elected by fellow MPs at the beginning of each Parliament. The speaker is also assisted by two chief permanent employees of the Commons, the clerk of the House and an administrator.

The **clerk of the House** is responsible for ensuring that relevant documents are printed and circulated and for advising the speaker of the House on the parliamentary business of the day. In recent years, the House administrator, a senior bureaucrat, has been added to the House staff to deal with financial and management issues.

The leader of each party in the House designates an MP to manage party conduct in the House — this MP is known as their **House leader**. The government's House leader is a member of Cabinet, responsible for obtaining agreement among the parties in setting the timetable for the House. House leaders have the authority to negotiate the timetable and lists of speakers.

In addition to these individuals, there is a professional staff to manage day-to-day activities of the House. The staff includes translators; transcribers who record verbatim the House of Commons debates in a publication called *Hansard*; secretaries; security personnel; maintenance staff; and staff for the Library of Parliament.

Daily Routine in the House of Commons

The timetable of plenary meetings (meetings of the full House) in the House of Commons varies slightly from day to day. The House has a five-day working week that may be increased by adding evening sittings. Members meet in the House of Commons four mornings and every afternoon during the week while the House is sitting. Wednesday morning is reserved for caucus meetings.

After a brief prayer, the Commons opens its doors to the public[2] and according to the day's timetable proceeds to one of several considerations: routine business; government orders; private members' business; or review of delegated legislation.

Figure 7.1 Who Sits Where in the House of Commons (after the 2004 General Election)

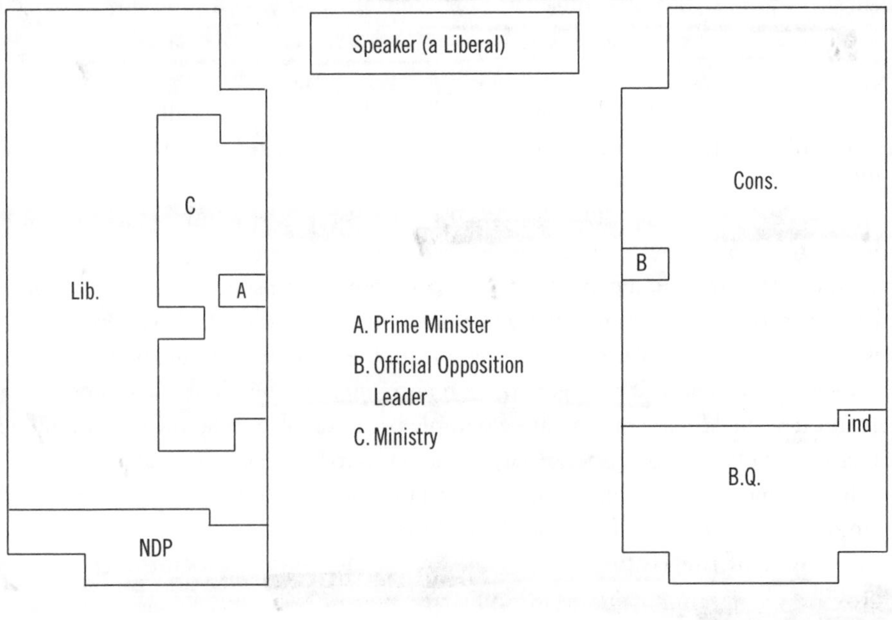

Speaker (a Liberal)

Cons.

C

Lib.   A   B

A. Prime Minister
B. Official Opposition Leader
C. Ministry

ind

B.Q.

NDP

Seats: Liberals–135; Conservatives–99; Bloc Québécois–54; NDP–19; independent–1.

Routine business may encompass a host of items, including announcements and questions of privilege; reports from inter-parliamentary delegations and committees; documents and government papers for the notice of members; statements by ministers regarding government policy; the introduction and first reading of Commons bills and the first reading of public bills that originated in the Senate; government notices of motions to be introduced later; and other motions, particularly those requesting concurrence in committee reports and those pertaining to special arrangements for the sittings and proceedings of the House.

Most time in the plenary session is consumed by the **Orders of the Day**, the procedure under which the House deals with public business placed before it. Orders are the prime means by which the House of Commons formulates instructions in response to motions. They guide the speaker and other members and direct the officers of the House to pursue particular courses of action. The greater part of this period is devoted to government business in the form of the Throne Speech debate, motions dealing with the passage of bills and the referral of legislation, estimates and investigatory tasks to standing and special committees. Resolutions are another way to respond to motions. With the exception of constitutional resolutions, resolutions are not binding on anyone but are simply expressions of *opinion* of the Commons. Orders, on the other hand, express the *will* of the Commons and are binding.

Not all of the House's business is instigated by the government. Private members may put forward bills and motions. These bills and motions are placed in a lottery or draw. The first thirty items chosen are placed in an "order of precedence" for fifteen bills and fifteen motions. The standing committee on procedure and House affairs selects which items will be considered and voted on in the House. The list may contain no more than ten votable items at the same time: five votable bills and five votable motions.[3] The remaining twenty issues are taken up without a vote during private members' hour. This process is a way to manage time, but it also culls out many items and prevents much proposed legislation from being considered at all.

To assure that the opposition voices in the House of Commons are heard, certain sitting days during the year are reserved for *opposition* business when the opposition has a chance to lead major debates on government policy. At the start of the session, the House is permitted six days to debate the address in reply to the Speech from the Throne. A further four days are allocated for the Budget Debate. As well, the opposition parties have twenty **Opposition Days** (or **Supply Days**) on which to debate opposition motions. These are spread unevenly over the three supply periods of the session. Opposition Days provide time for individual opposition parties to mount attacks on government policies, to propose alternative policies and to introduce motions of non-confidence in the government. In practice, these days are more a symbolic recognition of the opposition's right to criticize the government than a forum for policy initiation.

The most entertaining and most publicized aspect of work in the House is the daily **Oral Question Period** — a forty-five-minute period held five days a week, which provides a forum for the opposition parties to embarrass the government, criticize its policies and force discussion on selected issues. The government is subjected each day to relentless questioning by the opposition parties. Ministers are not given prior notice of what issues will be discussed and the speaker allocates questions roughly proportionate to party membership in the House.[4]

There are rules, however, that make it difficult for serious, sustained attacks by the opposition. The speaker calls on members to speak following lists supplied by the party whips. Supplementary questions are permitted in Question Period, but no formal debate is allowed. As a result, ministers can often avoid the main substance of a question. In fact, Reform MPs used to joke that Question Period got its name because only questions are asked — answers are never given. Government backbenchers also use up some of the valuable time Question Period provides by asking their ministers questions about "minor" constituency interests or making "friendly" queries to give their ministers the floor on topics they wish to discuss. The opposition's use of Question Period is thwarted in yet another way. When there is more than one opposition party, the unstructured attack on the government often loses its effect.

In spite of these difficulties, well-directed opposition tactics can still make the daily Question Period an important occasion for calling the executive to account for its actions, for allowing effective participation by backbenchers and for providing an opportunity for the public to see responsible government at work. In 2004–2005, Question Period frequently degenerated into a torrent of verbal abuse.

Considerable effort goes into preparing questions that might provide a favourable "clip" for the evening news. Reporters generally flock around politicians who use the most colourful language or blunt delivery. The media are constantly judging performance and conveying their conclusions to the public.

Question Period, like all plenary sessions, has been televised since 1977, giving MPs a public outlet for their messages. Government MPs know that this daily ritual represents the "public face" of their government. Cabinet ministers prepare diligently. The usual routine is for key people to meet with the House leader at 8:30 a.m. each day to anticipate questions that might arise. Forty-five minutes before Question Period, ministers and parliamentary secretaries meet with the House leader to go through possible questions and responses.

The House is usually not well attended except for Question Period or for important divisions. This is because plenary sessions of the House of Commons are only a part of the total workload of MPs and they are busy elsewhere — such as in committee.

COMMITTEES IN THE HOUSE OF COMMONS

Much of the work carried on by the House of Commons is in committee. There are four basic kinds of committees:

1.   In **committee of the whole,** all of the MPs sit in the chamber in one large committee chaired by the deputy speaker or the deputy chair of committees, using committee rules rather than House procedures. This committee is currently used much less than in previous years; it is reserved mainly for money bills or, on rare

occasions, to expedite passage of other legislation. The **ways and means committee** is a committee of the whole. It considers the resolutions that contain the proposals of the minister of finance. Once they are passed, the resolutions are embodied in one or more bills (such as a bill to amend the *Income Tax Act*) and then proceed through the usual stages necessary to pass a public bill.

2. **Standing committees** are relatively permanent committees that may last for the life of a Parliament. In 2005, there were eighteen standing committees, each with between seven and fifteen members proportional to party standings in the House. They study and report on all matters relating to the mandate, management and operations of the department or departments assigned to them — such as agriculture and agri-food, foreign affairs, international trade, national defence or veterans affairs. Chaired, except in rare circumstances, by a member of the governing party in the House, they focus on program and policy objectives and effectiveness, expenditure plans, and the relative success of the department(s), etc. As of 1994, the finance committee has responsibility to participate in pre-budget discussions. It begins to study the government's financial policies in early September and reports before the end of December — before the annual budget is delivered.

   Standing committees may also handle the committee stage of legislation. When the Liberals came to office in 1993, they began to send all bills to standing committees once again. To assist them, standing committees are empowered to form subcommittees and to "send for persons, papers and records" that might be helpful. All individuals appointed by order-in-council may be scrutinized by these committees:

3. Two **joint standing committees** are composed of members of both the House of Commons and the Senate: the joint standing committee on scrutiny of regulations (which studies all delegated legislation by departments, agencies, boards or other authorities) and the Library of Parliament committee.

4. **Legislative committees** may be set up to examine bills after they have passed second reading. Legislative committees can be numerous or few depending on the amount of legislation before the House.

These four kinds of committees provide MPs with opportunities to make an impact on policy-making. Standing committees are the most important, with three principal areas of operation: detailed consideration of legislation; scrutiny of the financial aspects of government and bureaucracy; and investigation of reports, policy proposals and other items. Under Standing Order 111, these committees are also empowered to judge whether order-in-council appointments have the "competence and qualifications" to do their jobs. If the committees are to perform all these functions well, they obviously need to be well staffed and have the resources to conduct serious investigations. This is not always the case.

Despite various reforms over the years, criticism of the committee system is common.[5] For example, committees do not enjoy an even workload: it is usually very slow at the beginning of a session and very busy in the spring when the major bills usually reach them — right at the same time that they get the spending proposals in the main estimates to scrutinize. Another traditional lament is that after all the work that goes into them, committee reports are ignored; the government is required to respond to all reports in Parliament, but it is not obliged to adopt the recommendations they contain.

PASSING LEGISLATION

We have noted that a key function of the House of Commons is to pass laws. These are presented to the House of Commons as **bills.**

Types of Bills

There are two categories of bills: public and private. **Private bills** are bills that confer special power or rights upon specific individuals, groups or corporations rather than upon society as a whole. They constitute an extremely small proportion of total legislative activity. **Public bills** seek to change the law concerning the public as a whole. There are two kinds of public bills: those sponsored by individual MPs, called **private members' bills** and those introduced by the Cabinet as government policy, called **government bills**. The vast majority of bills passed by the Canadian Parliament are government bills.

Government bills are of two varieties: financial or non-financial. The financial ones are known as **money bills** because they are government bills for raising or spending money. Bills to authorize the spending of money by the government are called **supply (appropriation) bills. Ways and means motions** are motions that introduce bills and legislation to authorize the raising of money by taxation. (For the various kinds of bills, see Figure 7.2.)

Figure 7.2 Types of Bills

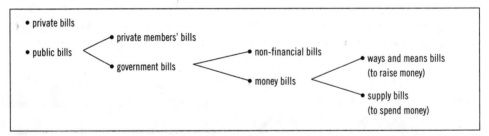

How Laws Are Passed

Preparing, introducing and passing a bill into law is a long process. Besides a lengthy pre-parliamentary process to create a draft bill (discussed in Chapters 6 and 8), there is also a formal parliamentary stage. To become law through an act or statute, a bill must pass three readings in the House, three readings in the Senate, receive royal assent (from the governor general) and (sometimes) be proclaimed by the government.

When a draft bill has been prepared, 48 hours notice is given and the minister responsible presents it to Parliament. All bills that involve raising or spending public money, as well as most other bills, are introduced first in the House of Commons and then go to the Senate. However, there are some bills, as we shall see, that are introduced first in the Senate and then passed through the House of Commons.

The introduction of the bill by the minister is brief; it outlines the purpose of the bill and asks that it be given a *first reading*. The first reading is invariably granted and allows the bill to be printed and numbered (with a *C* prefix if it originates in the House of Commons, *S* if in the Senate) and distributed to MPs. Bills are referred to by a combination of a letter and a number. Numbers C2 to C200 are reserved for government bills, C201 to C1000 for private members' public bills and C1001 on for private members' private bills. The bill now is placed on the **order paper**, the schedule of pending parliamentary business.

Second reading is initiated by a motion, again usually by the sponsoring minister. This is the most important stage in a bill's passage. This time, debate on the principle of the bill is allowed so that the House can decide whether there is need for such a bill and whether what it proposes is sound. No amendments are accepted at this stage. When debate is finished, bills are sent directly to a House of Commons Committee to begin passage through the committee stage. In committee, as we have seen above, the bill concerned is studied in detail by a small group of MPs. The committee may call expert witnesses for advice at this time.

There are a few exceptions to this usual procedure. Since 1994 reforms, bills may be sent directly to a committee *before* second reading. The House can also refer a bill to a special committee set up for the purpose, or to a joint committee (which includes members from the Senate). For supply bills, ways and means motions and certain other legislation upon which the House agrees, the committee stage is undertaken by the committee of the whole. At this stage, the bill receives detailed clause-by-clause consideration and amendments may be moved. The amended bill is then voted on as a whole when it is *reported* back to the House. At the normal report stage, the House has an opportunity to debate and perhaps amend or even block the bill. Unless unanimously agreed otherwise by the House, the third reading then commences. There is often little debate at this time and a final vote is taken on the bill.

If the bill is passed, it must now repeat the whole process in the Senate. Here the passage is normally easier, except when the government party does not control a majority of members in the Senate. First and second readings pass quickly. It is at the committee stage that the major legislative work is done in the Senate. The upper house rarely amends the substance of a bill, but it often improves the details of hastily drafted bills. No Senate changes that cause increased taxation or spending are permitted. As in the House, the final product as revised in committee is then sent back to the Senate for debate, possible further amendment and acceptance. After the final consideration of the bill by the Senate and the third reading vote, the House of Commons is informed whether the Senate has rejected, amended or passed the bill.

Figure 7.3 How a Government Bill Becomes Law

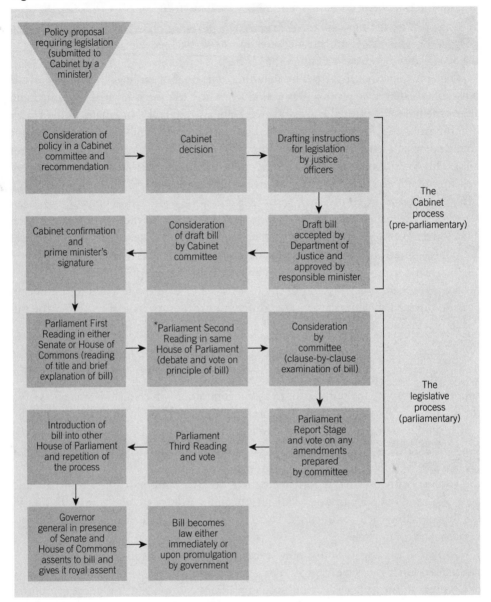

* As of 1994, a bill may be referred to a committee before second reading.

If, as rarely happens, the bill is defeated by the Senate, it must begin the entire process again from the start. If the Senate amends a bill, it must be returned to the lower house for reconsideration. Usually Senate amendments deal with minor details, not the substance of the bill, so they are readily disposed of by the responsible minister. Once this is achieved, the bill is ready for its final stage.

The bill is sent now for **royal assent**. The governor general, sitting in the Senate chambers before the assembled members of both houses, puts the final seal of approval on the bill. The bill thereby becomes an Act of Parliament of Canada, and henceforth is law — unless it contains a requirement for formal government proclamation at a later date. **Proclamation** involves proclaiming, publishing or declaring under the Great Seal a statute that thereby becomes law. The entire process is shown in Figure 7.3.

We have said that there are some unique conditions that apply to money bills (bills to raise or spend money). Ways and means bills originate in the budget speech delivered by the minister of finance. This speech outlines the government's economic policy and summarizes the changes that will subsequently appear in tax legislation. Supply bills are debated by standing committees. Once the estimates are examined, appropriation bills are passed quickly, authorizing the money for the government's spending proposals. Money bills, therefore, follow the same general process as other bills, with five important differences:

1. They must originate in the House of Commons.

2. Ways and means bills are considered by the committee of the whole as "motions" before they go through the normal legislative process as taxation bills.

3. Supply (the process by which Parliament approves the government's projected annual expenditures) has two phases. The estimates (proposals to spend) are tabled along with a royal recommendation (i.e., the Crown agrees) in the House and then referred to standing committees. After the committees report on the estimates, an appropriation bill based on them is prepared. The legislation follows the normal course, except that the committee of the whole replaces the regular committee process for legislation.

4. There are severe limitations upon the Senate's ability to amend such bills.

5. They take longer than other bills because many aspects of them call for extensive partisan debate.

PARTIES IN PARLIAMENT

There are two important aspects to party behaviour in Parliament. One is behaviour within the parties themselves; the other is the relationships among the parties. We consider each of these in turn.

Relations Inside Parties

Almost all MPs belong to a political party. This fact has a profound effect on legislative politics in both houses. The government relies on its backbenchers to remain loyal in order to pass its legislative proposals and even to stay in office. The opposition parties rally their troops in order to present a coherent attack on the government. This often requires individual members to compromise their own short-term interests for the unity of their party.

Party leaders, especially in government, have a number of penalties that they can use to ensure party discipline — i.e., to ensure that the party remains united. Individuals may be coerced in a number of ways. They may lose their positions on parliamentary committees, as several Liberals did when they rebelled against their government's gun control legislation in June 1995. They may be threatened with being suspended from caucus meetings or even expelled from the party. The electorate does not tend to reward rebellious MPs at the polls.[6] As well as these "sticks," party leaders also have a number of "carrots" to keep their backbenchers in line. These include such rewards as promotion to cabinet minister or committee chair; appointment to the Senate; and numerous positions in public corporations and Crown agencies. Obviously, many more of these rewards are available to the government than to opposition parties.

To enforce party discipline, the House leader for each party is assisted by a chief whip and assistant whips. **Whips** are MPs assigned by the party leaders to help maintain party cohesion. They keep in touch with the members, informing them of their duties in the House and on committees. On the whole, unity is maintained more often by party and leader loyalty than by the whips' ability to apply sanctions.

Each party in Parliament forms its own group or **party caucus**. Every Wednesday morning when Parliament is in session, all members of the House of Commons (and any senators who wish to attend) meet in their respective party groups. Caucus meetings are held in private so that backbenchers can speak out without the press reporting division within the parties.

In the governing party, caucus is often consulted only after policies have been decided by Cabinet, and members are expected to support those decisions. However, governments do not tend to act in the face of clear caucus opposition. While a major function of the government caucus is to ensure party unity — and opposition leaders also strive to achieve this — opposition caucuses usually have more latitude because in opposition, there is less of a distinction between leaders and backbenchers. Since opposition MPs do not have as much to lose as their government counterparts, they tend to express their points of view more freely. In any case, a strong degree of party cohesion in the House of Commons is an integral part of representative and responsible government.

It is often argued that MPs should be free to vote according to their conscience, or in accordance with the views of their constituency. Otherwise, the argument goes, they are just "trained seals." The former Alliance Party in particular advocated that MPs should accurately represent their constituents' views when they vote in Parliament. It went so far as to promote public participation devices such as **recall** in which constituents can recall their MPs if they do not vote as instructed.[7]

Just what constitutes the appropriate relations between an MP and his or her constituents has been debated for over two centuries. It is not possible for a member to represent constituents perfectly on every issue because there is no way of determining what constituents want on every topic. Constituents usually do not even know themselves

Figure 7.4 Seats by Province and Party Following the General Election, June 2004

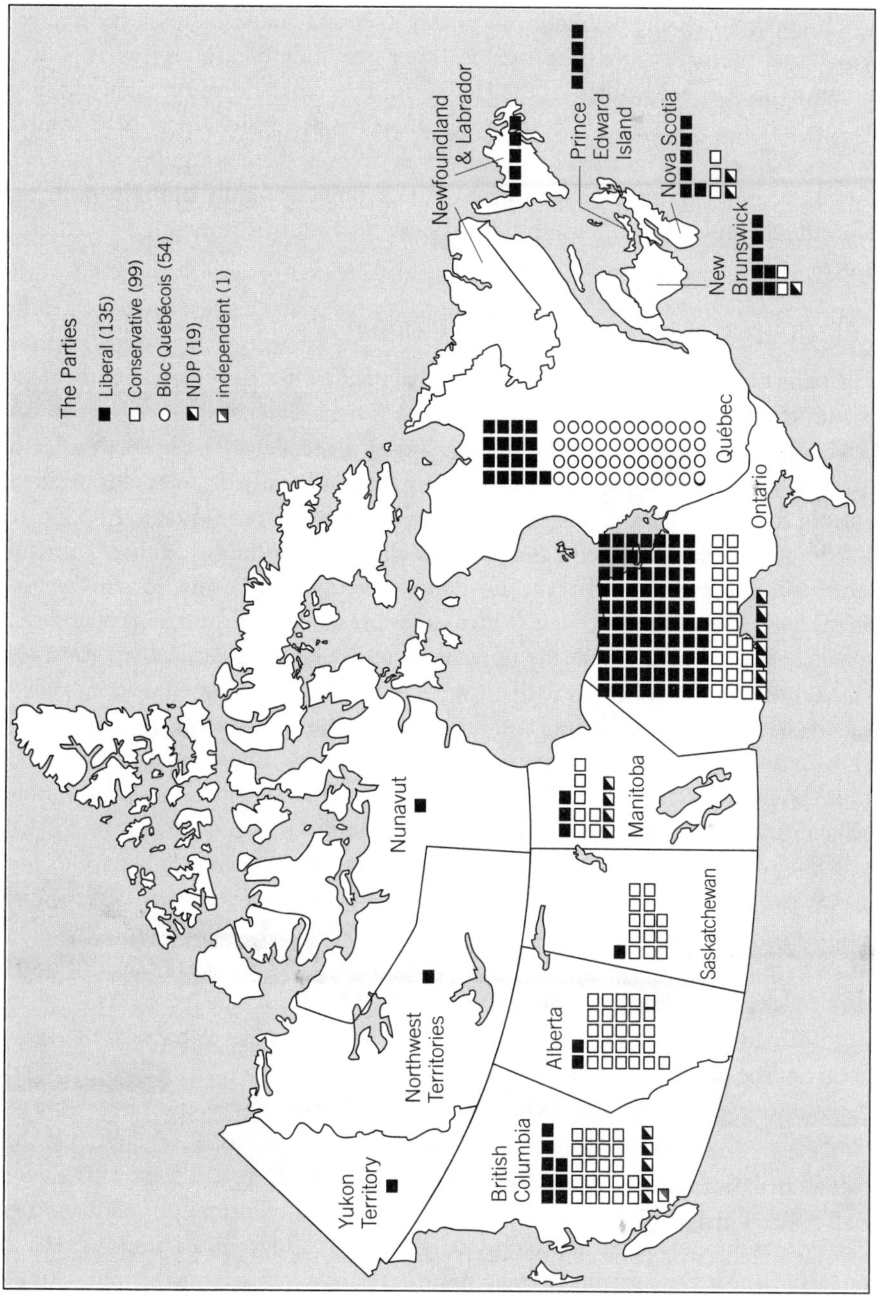

what they want, nor do they often care about issues that do not affect their personal lives. On the other hand, in theory, complete independence for the representative would not be democratic in that the government would not be responsive to its citizens.

It appears that the best solution to this dilemma would be to elect representatives wisely and then allow them to exercise their best judgment about what is needed as circumstances arise. Members of the House will listen to their constituents if they want to be re-elected; and voters will respect that their representatives must have some leeway because of their own values and circumstances. Members are not puppets but neither are they fully independent. Subjecting MPs to following public opinion polls or recall procedures would be cumbersome, expensive and unduly threatening to the democratic process.

Relations among Parties in Parliament

The parliamentary system enhances adversarial politics: it is the function of the opposition parties to criticize. This presents a challenge for the Official Opposition, which seeks to provide effective criticism but does not want to be perceived as mainly negative and without ideas. The Bloc Québécois finds it particularly difficult to appear positive while putting forth its own ideas for the secession of Québec from Canada.

The parliamentary system also creates a challenge for the government in that it is its job to get bills passed, and yet it must allow the opposition time to criticize. To assist them, the parliamentary rules are loaded in favour of the government so that the Cabinet generally gets its way. Before the opening of the thirty-fifth Parliament, it was popular for MPs to claim that the new Parliament would no longer engage in destructive bickering but would be a model of dignity and decorum with no "whimpering and snivelling" from the opposition.[8] Initially, this was true; then, fewer than nine weeks into the session, the atmosphere in the House resumed its usual pattern of insults and accusations. Such behaviour reached a crescendo during the Liberal minority government in 2005.

The adversarial nature of the parliamentary system requires strong party cohesion in the House if there is to be representative and responsible government. The government requires unified support from its backbenchers to retain office and realize its policy goals. At the same time, the Opposition must mobilize all of its resources to criticize the government and portray itself as a viable alternative.

Both government and opposition have developed ways to balance the adversarial nature of the parliamentary system and allow Parliament to work. Opposition members guard their right to criticize government policy, but they also recognize the government's responsibility to carry on the business of governing and sometimes support it to that end. Similarly, the government must recognize the right of the opposition to criticize, without allowing it to obstruct. As we have seen, there are many formal provisions recognizing the right of opposition parties to oppose — through budget and Throne Speech debates and also Supply Days (in which the opposition parties may choose the topics for debate). There is informal co-operation between the two adversaries as well. The government House leader and party whips try to accommodate the needs of their counterparts concerning the disposal of parliamentary time and to foster a spirit of co-operation.

On occasion, however, co-operation breaks down, especially during minority governments when the opposition parties want to bring the government down, or during majority governments when the government is confronted with what it views as "obstruction" by the opposition or when it attempts to ram through a bill with what the opposition regards as "unseemly haste." In a majority situation, the government always has the upper hand. It may resort to **closure** (Standing Order 57), a measure to terminate debate. Closure requires that all outstanding discussion and divisions on a particular stage of a bill must be completed within the next sitting day. A less harsh alternative to closure is **time allocation** in which debate in the House is limited in a pre-arranged allocation of time to a particular bill or its various stages (Standing Order 78, 1, 2 and 3). A balance of power is maintained between government and opposition by rules that become more complex procedurally as they require less inter-party co-operation.[9]

Governments usually resort to closure with the greatest reluctance because of procedural complexity and negative ramifications. The Progressive Conservatives under Brian Mulroney and the Liberals under Jean Chrétien used this device with a reckless lack of concern for parliamentary traditions.

In an adversarial parliamentary situation, the government has the advantage in that it controls the parliamentary timetable and access to departmental information as well as closure and time allocation. Still, the opposition also has ways to combat what it sees as abuse of the parliamentary process. One of the most important avenues is the media. Television broadcasts of Question Period and major debates provide an audience for opposition criticism and also gives opposition leaders and their "teams" countrywide exposure. They can criticize government policy and also present themselves as alternative sources of leadership. Opposition parties also receive public funding for their caucus research groups, and this helps make up to some extent for the government's monopoly of bureaucratic information.

In minority situations, governments lose the upper hand. Government leaders have to be more creative and resourceful to stay in power. During the minority Liberal government elected in 2004, the Conservatives and Bloc Québécois battered the Liberals relentlessly in Question Period and in the media. When it came to the crucial May 2005 budget vote that could have brought down the government, however, Prime Minister Paul Martin managed to scrape up enough votes to keep his Liberals in power. He made a deal with Jack Layton, leader of the NDP, to rewrite the budget in exchange for the NDP's support. The deal provided for an increase of $4.6 billion for the environment, social housing, foreign aid, and post-secondary tuition reduction. The Liberals were also forced to delay their proposed cuts in corporate taxes.

Since the numbers to pass the budget were still lacking, the Liberals wooed Belinda Stronach, co-founder and former leadership candidate of the new Conservative party. She crossed the floor to join Martin and the Liberals just in time for the crucial budget vote, immediately joining the Cabinet and becoming the lead minister on the Gomery Inquiry. Thanks to the fact that the ailing Chuck Cadman — an ex-Reform/Alliance MP turned independent (who died in July of 2005, two months after the suspenseful vote) — also voted with the government, the House was tied at 152 to 152. With the speaker's vote to break the tie, the Liberals won and clung to power. The situation remained tenuous, however, as the government could neither count on control of the House in any future vote nor could it be certain how the committees might act since the opposition parties maintained a majority of members in them.

Minority governments are exciting; the government's tenure is perilous and the Official Opposition's ambition whetted. However, no other occasion in modern Canadian history approaches the shenanigans, procedural bickering and outright horse-trading of the 2005 minority situation.

THE SENATE

The Senate, or upper house of the Parliament of Canada, is housed in the east wing of the centre block of the Parliament buildings. Senators are appointed by the governor general on the advice of the prime minister. Since 1999, the membership of the Senate has been fixed at 105, representing 7 regions of Canada, each according to a set number: Ontario (24); Québec (24); the 3 Maritime provinces, (24 — 10 each from New Brunswick and Nova Scotia, 4 from Prince Edward Island); the four western provinces (24); Newfoundland and Labrador (6); Yukon (1); Northwest Territories (1); and Nunavut (1). There is also a provision (Section 26 of the Constitution) allowing 4 or 8 more members to be appointed when it becomes necessary to break a deadlock between the Senate and the Commons. Prime Minister Mulroney used this provision for the first and only time in Canadian history in 1990, adding 8 additional senators and temporarily increasing their number to 112 in order to pass the Goods and Service Tax legislation.

The prime minister and Cabinet are responsible to the House of Commons because it is the elected representative body. They are not, however, responsible to the Senate. If a government were defeated in a vote in the House, it might have to resign or call an election. If a government bill were defeated in the Senate, the government could remain in power. The fact that it is an appointed rather than an elected body has other repercussions for the Senate. The Constitution awards the Senate almost equal power with the House of Commons, but

Gable, The Globe and Mail. Reprinted with permission.

in reality the upper house is relatively inconsequential. Only very rarely does it try to exercise any kind of control over the Commons. Because it is appointed, the Senate lacks the legitimacy that elections bestow, and over time, it has become a relatively insignificant partner to the House in passing legislation.

The Functions of the Senate

The modern Canadian Senate only imperfectly fulfils many of the formal roles normally assigned to second chambers. It is not a straightforward champion of a particular class nor is it a sanctuary for aging politicians, although it is often criticized along these lines, and is the focus of a continuing array of reform proposals. Still, the Senate performs several important functions:

- As when it was established, the Senate still provides some protection for provincial rights — for example, it assures Québec a set number of senators even if the population of that province were to fall in relation to others. However, the Senate is not manifestly a representative of provincial rights; provinces and regions depend on Cabinet and their provincial governments to stand up for their particular interests.

- It reviews all legislation that is passed in the House of Commons — providing "sober second thought" in order to refine the legislation and prevent errors. Because senators are appointed rather than elected and do not need party or electoral approval, they can criticize freely without the fear of electoral repercussions. Most of the review work occurs in committee deliberations. Committee work is arguably the Senate's most significant contribution.[10]

- Senators can introduce legislation, except for bills dealing with the raising or spending of money.

- On occasions when the government of the day does not have sufficient elected representatives from a region, ministers can be named from the Senate to ensure regional and/or linguistic balance in Cabinet.[11]

- The Senate can delay the passage of constitutional amendments — even those that would abolish the Senate — for up to 180 days.

When legislation has received three readings in the House of Commons, it is referred to the Senate, where it goes through the same process again. Because the legislation has been debated and decided upon by elected representatives in the House of Commons, senators normally approve the bills that reach them, but they scrutinize them carefully, often refining the language and other details. To do more than that would be to raise comments about the propriety of an appointed body, thwarting the will of elected representatives.[12]

On rare occasions, however, the Senate has rejected government legislation. For example, under Prime Minister Mulroney's tenure from 1984 to 1988, when there were far more Liberals than Conservatives in the Senate, there were many clashes between the two chambers. The Senate interfered with or delayed several bills. It tried to amend the Meech Lake Accord, unemployment insurance payments and the Goods and Services Tax. It even succeeded in rejecting an abortion bill after a free vote was called. While, technically, this was the first senatorial veto in three decades, it did not truly represent a rebellion against the government.

In the thirty-fifth Parliament, the Progressive Conservatives held a majority of seats in the Senate for a time even though they had only two MPs in the House. It was enough to delay the passage of Bill C22, the cancellation of the Pearson Airport development legislation. In the thirty-sixth Parliament, the Liberals once more had a majority in the Senate and once more legislation passed smoothly.

The most important incidence of the Senate blocking the elected house was when the Liberal senators, at the request of John Turner, prevented the passage of free trade legislation. When the trade bill reached second reading in the Senate, Liberal senators abstained and allowed it to go to the foreign affairs committee. The Liberal-dominated committee deliberately provoked the PC government by setting up an extensive program of hearings. Because of Senate obstruction, the government was forced to call a general election for November 20, 1988 — an election for which the Senate had helped to set the date and the agenda.

The Senators

The qualifications for senators have changed somewhat since Confederation in 1867. Initially, they were all males who held the position for life. Today they may be male or female and those appointed since 1965 must retire by age 75. Other rules require that senators be Canadian citizens over 30 years of age, with $4000 in property, and residents of the respective provinces they represent. Many are politicians or party workers who have been rewarded with the political appointment for their partisan activities. Others are Canadians who have made an outstanding contribution in other ways.

Senators earn $116 000. Their perks include offices, secretarial help, mailing privileges, free telephone service, and so on. It is rare for a senator to be fired, however it is possible for one of several reasons: if he or she fails to attend two consecutive sessions; loses Canadian citizenship; ceases to meet the residence and property qualifications; is adjudged bankrupt; or is convicted of a criminal offence. In 1997, Senator Andrew Thompson was penalized by his peers in an unprecedented manner when he was suspended because of his poor attendance record even though he had not violated any rules of the Senate or the Constitution. No one can hold a seat in the Senate and the House of Commons at the same time.

Carine Wilson was appointed as the first woman senator in 1930 after the British Judicial Committee of the Privy Council ended a long constitutional wrangle by declaring that women were "persons" under the relevant sections of the *BNA Act*. Since then, appointments of women and leading figures from minority groups have increased slightly. Still, as of January 2005 only 34 of 105 senators were women.

Rules of the Senate

Like the lower house, the Senate is organized into government and opposition ranks, and although senators historically vote across party lines more than members of the

House of Commons,[13] they do vote cohesively on most occasions. Almost all senators have declared loyalties to a political party. The Senate is not, therefore, the independent and non-partisan counterweight to the Commons that its founders may have envisaged. Most senators have highly political career backgrounds.

Many senators hold positions with private companies, are connected to other people who have holdings in corporations or are connected with law firms that represent clients who do business with the government. For this reason, they have been called the "lobby from within" and have reaped considerable public condemnation for informal conflicts of interest. This is an ongoing problem because there are no appropriate guidelines to regulate senators' behaviour (see Chapter 12).

Organization and Officers of the Senate

The Senate has two senior officers: the government House leader and the speaker. The government House leader is appointed by the PM to represent and speak for senators in Cabinet and, conversely, to be the voice of the Cabinet in the Senate. Only rarely are there senators in Cabinet other than the government House leader. The speaker of the Senate, unlike the elected House speaker, is appointed by the governor general on the recommendation of the prime minister for the term of the Parliament. The duties of this position are similar to those of the speaker of the House of Commons.

Senate Reform

Because of perceived problems of legitimacy and the relative failure of the Senate to represent provincial interests in Parliament, there have been many proposals over the years to reform and even abolish it. In the 1990s, a Western initiative for a new **"Triple E" Senate** was a prominent proposal for the Senate to be *elected, effective* and *equal* in its representation of all provinces. The smaller provinces, of course, supported the idea of having an equal number of senators from each province, regardless of size or population base. In the early deliberations, larger provinces tended to support the idea of a "Double E" Senate — one that would be elected and effective in its functioning but whose membership would be based on some principle of representation by population.

Proposals to create a modified "Triple E" Senate were embodied in the Charlottetown Accord in 1992. Since it was rejected, however, the principle of creating such an upper house has been largely abandoned. These days, abolishing the Senate or instituting other far-reaching reforms are almost impossible to achieve; instead, initiatives should be concentrated on creating an institution that is valued for its symbolic contribution to Canadian unity and the federal system and for the minor but important role it plays in the legislative process. Until an accepted constitutional amendment reform can be achieved, the Senate will maintain its role as a usually co-operative but sometimes cantankerous part of the legislative process. The problem for the Senate is simple — if it does little, it is accused of being a "rubber stamp," but if it acts decisively, it is reprimanded for blocking "the will of the people." Calls for Senate reform have been made since at least 1893. It is time to settle for reforming the Senate *within* the existing Constitution.

THE PRESS GALLERY

Print and broadcast media outlets assign journalists to a formal organization in Ottawa called the **parliamentary press gallery**. These accredited correspondents cover the activities of the legislature and government on a daily basis. They are given access to facilities provided by the speaker of the House. Their privileges within Parliament include their own viewing and work areas and access to politicians and bureaucrats.

Press gallery journalists and broadcasters form an important link between the politicians and the public. Informed by their contacts on Parliament Hill and daily Question Period, which supplies news clips well suited to television coverage, they help to set the political agenda for the country by deciding what to print or broadcast and who to discuss or photograph.

Politicians and the media rely on each other. The media need the politicians for information, and the politicians need the media to help them gauge public opinion, to create favourable publicity for themselves and their party and also as a source of information. This relationship is not always as simple as it seems. In principle, reporters should be objective, but they develop friends and "sources," which cannot help but impinge on that neutrality. They are faced with dilemmas about what to make public about personal failings of politicians, or about whether they should release information that they have acquired but are not supposed to have — such as a budget leak.

While it is tempting for journalists to use politicians as a means for career advancement, that temptation also exists on the part of the politicians. It is common for politicians to try to manipulate the news by such means as arranging the time of announcements for maximum effect and stressing certain factors for media consumption while not mentioning others. Information is often passed informally to those journalists who can be expected to offer "friendly" coverage.

This mutually dependent relationship is prevented from becoming too overbalanced on either side in large part by the fundamental democratic right of freedom of the press and other media of communication, as protected by the *Charter of Rights and Freedoms* and by libel and slander laws.

KEY TERMS

DISCUSSION QUESTIONS

1. Is Question Period a noisy, undisciplined waste of time? Simulate a Question Period, formulating questions and answers.

2. Is the procedure of passing a bill into law too time-consuming and cumbersome? Why or why not?

3. Should there be strict party discipline or should MPs be allowed to vote as they wish?

4. Should the Senate be abolished or reformed? Explain your answer. Given what you have learned about how to achieve a constitutional amendment, do you think major changes to the Senate are likely to be achieved?

WEBLINKS

Canadian Senators' Biographies

www.parl.gc.ca/common/senmemb/senate/isenator.asp?Language=E

Contacting Members of the House of Commons

www.parl.gc.ca/common/senmemb/house/members/CurrentMemberList.asp?Language=E&Parl=38&Ses=1&Sect=hoccur&Order=PersonOfficialLastName

Debates of the House of Commons (*Hansard*)

www.parl.gc.ca/cgi-bin/hansard/e_hansard_master.pl

Federal Budget Information

www.fin.gc.ca/access/budinfoe.html

Parliament

www.parl.gc.ca

8 Public Administration
Democracy and Bureaucracy

Learning Objectives

After reading this chapter, you should be able to

1. Name the basic organizational structures found in the Canadian federal bureaucracy (aside from central agencies), describe their basic structures and explain what they do.

2. Describe how the public service has changed over time in terms of size, recruitment and composition.

3. Draw three important distinctions between the political role of the executive and the administrative functions of public servants.

4. Describe the process of drawing up a government budget, including the expenditure and revenue process.

5. Name and evaluate three important ways politicians keep the power of unelected bureaucrats in check.

*A*ll modern states possess an extensive public administration, using civilians, soldiers, police and prison guards to uphold the interests of the state. Public administrators are, if you wish, the groundskeepers and Zamboni drivers for the political players! They collect taxes, inspect agricultural products and provide health care and police services, to name just a few of their contributions.

As the modern state developed, it became extensive in the scope of its activities, complex in its organization and expensive to run. It took on new functions and responsibilities, including economic tasks previously associated with the private sector. The shift in government responsibilities was particularly evident in liberal democracies, including Canada after the two world wars. This chapter examines the structures and employees of the bureaucracy and assesses what it accomplishes.

BUREAUCRACY AND BUREAUCRATS

As the state expanded, it adopted a specific form of government organization often known as *bureaucracy*. The term bureaucracy originated as a satirical combination of the French word *bureau* (desk) with the Greek *kratein* (to rule). In 1745, a French physiocrat first used the term *bureaucracy* to describe the eighteenth-century Prussian system of administration, but in its more technical, modern meaning, **bureaucracy** refers to a specific form of government organization based on the premise that government should be as efficient as possible, and this is best achieved by setting up a hierarchically structured decision-making process that minimizes arbitrary decision-making.

The term *bureaucracy* is often used negatively, associated with inefficiency, red tape and even lazy, overpaid employees. Much of this criticism is explained by the fact that it is easy to blame a large, faceless organization. In the technical sense, bureaucracy has nothing to do with these negative values. Rather, it refers to a hierarchically organized institution that divides work so as to allow the orders of superiors to be communicated effectively to subordinates. Even in this neutral sense, however, a bureaucracy can be criticized, particularly for not being flexible enough to handle all the administrative requirements of a complex, modern society.

In Canada, the Constitution makes the elected executive of the federal government responsible for formulating policies. However, politicians come and go, especially during minority governments, while administrators remain in their jobs to carry out the goals and purposes of their political masters. **Public servants** (or **bureaucrats**) are tenured state officials involved in advising government ministers and implementing policies. Fifty years ago they were a highly respected, elite group who saw public service as a duty and a privilege. Today, there has been a public backlash against bureaucracy and public servants, which goes along with cynicism about politicians and diminished expectations about what governments can do. However, Canadians are generally better served by their public service than they realize.

Bureaucracy and Democracy

The emergence of democratic forms of government forced the development of many specific characteristics of the modern bureaucracy. As the idea of alternation of power between competing parties became accepted as an important component of parliamentary democracy, it became necessary to separate the bureaucracy from the political executive. In this way, the bureaucracy was freed to exercise rational administration without needless political influence, and individual public servants became protected from arbitrary dismissal on political grounds, as long as they maintained partisan neutrality.

Liberal democracy also brought demands for the substitution of *merit* for patronage in the recruitment and promotion of public servants. Appointments to administrative office traditionally had been made on the basis of family and "old school" networks, or as a reward for political services rendered. The democratization of the public service brought a merit system involving open competition.

Thus, a neutral, professional public service based on the organizational principles of modern bureaucracy emerged alongside, and partly as a consequence of, the development of liberal democracy. Yet, a fundamental contradiction exists in the coexistence of bureaucracy and democracy. While easy in theory, it is difficult in practice to separate the political and administrative dimensions of government action. The bureaucracy may not be overtly political, but bureaucrats do influence the formation of public policy in a number of ways, therefore usurping some of the power of their political masters.

For example, cabinet ministers rarely hold their positions long enough to acquire a high degree of expertise in the affairs of their respective ministries. Governments often change hands at general elections, and periodic Cabinet shuffles move ministers from department to department. Each time a minister is put in charge of a new department, it takes a while to come to grips with a new policy field. Since the average departmental tenure of Canadian cabinet ministers has been very short, the average federal minister must spend considerable time in office simply learning the workings of departments.

During this era of minority government, cabinet ministers are required to share policy-making with leaders of opposition parties and thus find it even more difficult than usual to provide coherent advice to the public service about which direction they wish to take the country.

In contrast, the permanence of public servants allows them to develop expertise and practical knowledge on which politicians can draw. Consequently, if, as Max Weber maintained, "knowledge is power,"[1] then the bureaucracy in a complex, technical society may have a great deal of political power. It can screen the data made available to its political masters and influence the direction of government policy.

The relative security and access to information enjoyed by bureaucrats may influence the policy process in a number of other ways as well. Bureaucratic tenure permits public servants to develop a relatively long-term view of policy formulation compared to politicians, who must remain more responsive to short-term shifts in public opinion. Administrative personnel who have close links with interest groups may also be in a better position than politicians to identify specific public demands.

Furthermore, the bureaucracy sometimes acts as an "interest group" in its own right. Policy proposals generated within the bureaucracy may influence the government's choice among competing alternatives. Here again, bureaucrats may be in a better position than politicians to recommend fine-tuning or wholesale changes in existing policies. Finally, even after the government has made a political choice, a degree of discretion has to be left to public servants with regard to policy implementation.

Public servants, then, are linked to politicians through their mutual concern for making public policies. "Policies" are categorized in at least three different ways, as (1) the intentions of politicians; (2) the actions of governments; and (3) the impact of government on individuals and society. In other words, **policy** is defined as the broad framework within which decisions are taken and action (or inaction) is pursued by governments.[2]

The development of public policies involves a complex process of interaction between politicians and public servants. However, in general terms, public policies emerge from the impact of historical, geographical, and socio-economic conditions on mass political behaviour, elite behaviour and governmental institutions.

STRUCTURES OF FEDERAL BUREAUCRACY

Canadians frequently come into contact with two structures within the federal bureaucracy — *government departments* and *Crown corporations*. Few citizens escape encounters — some pleasant, others less so — with institutions such as the Department of National Revenue, which collects taxes and customs duties. Most Canadians have contact with Crown corporations every day — for example, when they watch CBC Television or listen to CBC Radio. However, government departments and Crown corporations that interact directly with the public are merely the most visible tip of the administrative iceberg.

It is possible to classify *central agencies* as a third type of bureaucratic structure. (Recall that we discussed central agencies in Chapter 7, "Parliament," along with the political executive of Canada.) With the exception of the Prime Minister's Office (PMO), these agencies are staffed almost exclusively by career public servants appointed under the aegis of the Public Service Commission. They are all formally headed by a cabinet minister and in all structural and legal respects closely resemble the standard departmental form of organization. For the purposes of this discussion, however, central agencies are viewed as a unique subcategory of government departments.

CLOSE-UP Departmental Names Reflect Values and Biases

The names of federal departments often reflect the values and biases of the government. This is particularly evident in the department dealing with immigration. Since Confederation it has been called:

- Canadian Immigration and Quarantine Services (1867–92)
- Immigration Branch, Department of the Interior (1892–1917)
- Department of Immigration and Colonization (1917–36)
- Immigration Branch, Department of Mines and Resources (1936–50)
- Department of Citizenship and Immigration (1950–66)
- Department of Manpower and Immigration (1966–77)
- Canada Employment and Immigration Commission (1977–93)
- Immigration divided between Department of Public Security and the Department of Human Resources (1993)
- Department of Citizenship and Immigration (1993 to present)

Federal Government Departments

Government departments are administrative units of a government, each of which is headed by a cabinet minister and are largely responsible for the administration of a range of programs serving the public. While the minister is politically responsible for the activities of the department and for formulating general policy, the administrative and managerial head of each department or ministry is the **deputy minister (DM)** — its senior public servant.[3] Departments, on the whole, obtain their staff from the Public Service Commission and their funding through the standard appropriation acts of Parliament.

The deputy minister is at the apex of a pyramidal structure of authority and organizational agencies. Two or more **assistant deputy ministers (ADMs)**, heading branches or bureaus, report directly to the DM. Below the ADMs are directorates or branches, each headed by a director general or director. These directorates are in turn composed of divisions, headed by directors or divisional chiefs; the divisions are further broken down into sections, offices and units. The number of senior officials, and the range of subunits and employees for which they are responsible, differ according to the type of department. The exact titles of departmental subunit and their respective senior officials vary from department to department.

Each new government may change the organization of departments, but such changes require legislation and may be slow in development. After Paul Martin became prime minister, he indicated his preferences for policy direction in reorganizing several departments. A new Department of Public Safety and Emergency Preparedness has been created, enhancing the minister's control over that of the former solicitor general. The department now includes the RCMP, Canadian Security Intelligence Service (CSIS), Parole Board and emergency structures from the Department of National Defence (DND). Two departments, Human Resources and Skills Development and Social Development, were created from the old HRDC. The Department of Foreign Affairs and International Trade (the former DFAIT) was split into two — Foreign Affairs (FAC) and International Trade (ITCan), but the legislation was not passed (see Table 8.1).

Table 8.1 Departmental and Agency Structure of the Public Service, 2005

Departments	National Revenue
Agriculture and Agri-Food	Natural Resources
Canadian Heritage	Public Safety and Emergency Preparedness
Citizenship and Immigration	Public Works and Government Services
Environment	Social Development
Fisheries and Oceans	Transport
Foreign Affairs	Veterans Affair
Health	
Human Resources and Skill Development	**Central Agencies**
Indian and Northern Affairs	Finance
Industry	Privy Council Office
International Trade	Treasury Board Secretariat
Justice	
Labour and Housing	
National Defence	

Crown Agencies

The second organizational form in the federal bureaucracy is the Crown agency. **Crown agencies** include a wide variety of non-departmental organizations including Crown corporations, regulatory agencies, administrative tribunals and some advisory bodies (discussed separately below). Advisory bodies are primarily involved in the process of policy formulation, while Crown agencies are charged directly with attaining government policy objectives — through public ownership, regulation of the private sector and so on.

Depending upon the definition employed, there are approximately four hundred federal Crown agencies. A number of characteristics distinguish Crown agencies from government departments. Agencies are not directly responsible *to* a minister but usually report to Parliament *through* a designated minister. The degree of supervision and accountability of Crown agencies varies but is much less than with departments. Department staff is generally recruited by the Public Service Commission, while employees of agencies are not. Department personnel have deputy ministers as administrative heads, while agencies vary widely in the nature of their management. They usually have boards of directors, led by chairs, commissioners or directors.

Crown Corporations

Crown agencies include Crown corporations. A **Crown corporation** is a semi-autonomous agency of government organized in a corporate form to perform a task or group of related tasks in the national interest.[4]

The variety of Crown corporations is immense. The Bank of Canada regulates the money supply, the Royal Mint prints money and Canada Mortgage and Housing Corporation guarantees housing loans. Transportation Crown corporations include Canadian National Railways, Via Rail, Canada Ports Corporation and the St. Lawrence Seaway Authority. Economic development is fostered by the Canadian Wheat Board, Cape Breton Development Corporation, Export Development Corporation, Farm Credit Corporation and the Federal Development Bank. National integration is aided by the Canada Post Corporation, the Canadian Broadcasting Corporation and the National Film Board.

Public ownership is criticized by neo-conservatives, who view any government intervention as an infringement upon the supremacy of the free-market economy. Thus, while it is improbable that privatization will be carried as far as it has been in some countries, it seems certain that public ownership will be much less common during the twenty-first century and that the present "privatization" trends will continue.

Regulatory Agencies

Crown agencies also include regulatory agencies. **Regulation** is the making of government rules that are intended to change the economic behaviour of individuals in the private sector.[5] A list of the important regulatory agencies would include, for example, the Atomic Energy Control Board, Canadian Labour Relations Board, Canadian Pension Commission, Canadian Radio-television and Telecommunications Commission (CRTC) and many others.

Among other functions, regulatory agencies may be required by government to influence private or corporate behaviour with respect to prices and tariffs, supply, market entry and conditions of service, product content and methods of production. Some agencies have developed quasi-legislative powers, which permit them to set general rules applicable to all cases under consideration, for example, the "Canadian content" regulations applied by the CRTC. Most agencies also enjoy investigative powers allowing them to undertake research and pursue inquiries within their field of competence.

Members of independent regulatory agencies are appointed by the governor-in-council, usually for terms of from five to ten years. On the whole, they are patronage appointments. Most agencies are subject to ministerial directives, but ministers usually are unwilling to infringe upon the traditional arm's-length relationship. Regulatory bodies are required to submit their budgets to the Treasury Board for review (and usually, also, to the auditor general) and to present annual reports to Parliament.

Advisory Bodies

Federal departments and Crown agencies are designed to deal primarily with the implementation and administration of government policies. **Advisory bodies** are Crown agencies, the activities of which are closely related to the formulation of public policies. They include Royal Commissions, government and departmental task forces and advisory councils.[6]

Royal Commissions and task forces are used by the executive as sources of public policy advice. They are generally set up by the government to investigate an area of critical public concern and to recommend a suitable course of action. Typical issues in recent years have included the economy (the Macdonald Royal Commission on the Economic Union and Development Prospects for Canada); cultural policy (the Applebaum-Hébert Federal Cultural Policy Review Committee); Native people (the Royal Commission on Aboriginal Issues); human reproduction (the Royal Commission on Reproductive Technologies); and health care (Commission on the Future of Health Care in Canada).

Such bodies attempt to inform the public about serious national problems and at the same time provide an informed basis for future policy-making by the government. They generally solicit outside views through public hearings at which individuals, groups and organizations are invited to submit briefs. They also initiate programs of directed and commissioned research. Most of the time they have no direct policy impact, although they may contribute to the debate of issues.

PUBLIC SERVANTS AND POLICY-MAKING

Ministers, Deputy Ministers and Public Servants

Although both politicians and public servants are engaged in making policies, three important distinctions can be drawn between the political role of the executive and the administrative functions of public servants in this process.

First, the members of the executive are partisan, while the public service is neutral. Second is the difference of tenure: on the whole, political leaders come and go while public servants enjoy relatively permanent positions. Third, public servants are supposed to administer the policies of government, not make them.

In theory, therefore, public servants make the plans of politicians feasible. In reality, however, the roles of politicians and public servants are considerably blurred. The idea that public servants only *administer* the policies set by politicians is severely disputed. Few scholars today would even agree that executive, legislative and judicial functions can be neatly assigned to a particular structure of government — let alone that civil servants' functions are limited to administering the laws. The public service is involved in many forms of government activity — it is part of the consultation, deliberation, legislative and administrative processes.

What control does Cabinet have over the administrative process to ensure that policies, once made, are actually implemented? The major principle of government organization in Canada — and the primary link between the bureaucracy and Parliament — is the doctrine of **ministerial responsibility** (discussed in Chapter 6, "The Executive").

Civil servants are supposed to be non-partisan, objective and anonymous, shielded from the glare of public attention and from the partisan political arena by their minister, in order to safeguard their neutrality and ensure their ability to serve whichever government is in power. In the event of a serious error in the formulation or administration of policy within a department, therefore, convention dictates that the minister, rather than the officials, be held responsible; and if the minister cannot account to the satisfaction of Parliament, then convention dictates that the minister should resign.

Experience has shown, however, that there are severe limitations to the doctrine of individual ministerial responsibility (as we saw in Chapter 6).[7] The responsibility of ministers for the sole operations of their departments is often sacrificed in favour of another principle, the *collective* responsibility of the Cabinet to Parliament. As long as a minister retains the confidence and support of the prime minister, resignation is extremely unlikely unless political expediency interferes. Another problem stems from the fact that ministers are not held responsible for administrative matters occurring *before* their current appointments. Thus, when questions are raised in the House, a new minister is able to hide behind this convention, saying that the events took place *prior* to his or her appointment.

Perhaps it is reasonable that ministers should not be held responsible to the point of resignation for the administrative errors of public servants. The relative impermanence of cabinet ministers and their multifunctional roles make it impossible for them to be involved extensively in their departments. Ministers are expected to direct their attention primarily to policy matters. For this reason, one observer argues, it is "unrealistic to expect a minister to accept personal responsibility for all the acts of his departmental officials. Why should a minister 'carry the can' when he has little or no knowledge of its contents?"[8]

The role of the deputy minister is crucial to effective administration and the coordination and direction of policy implementation. Certain financial and managerial responsibilities of the deputy minister are laid down by the *Financial Administration Act* and the *Public Service Employment Act*, or are delegated to the DM by the Treasury Board and the Public Service Commission. Otherwise, the DM possesses only whatever power the minister chooses to delegate, and that is a personal decision.

The main function of the deputy minister, apart from the administrative responsibilities of managing the department, is to act as the minister's chief source of non-partisan advice on public policy. The problem for the DM is how to initiate policy proposals and studies without appearing to undermine the ultimate policy-making responsibility of the minister.

Deputy ministers are appointed by the governor-in-council on the recommendation of the prime minister. Their office is held "during pleasure," which means that they can be dismissed or transferred at any time without assigned cause, and they are not protected by the provisions of the *Public Service Employment Act*. This insecurity of tenure naturally creates further ambiguity about the DM's role. Deputies who advise against ministerial decisions risk being dismissed. However, if they become identified with programs that are unpopular with the opposition, they risk losing their jobs when the reins of government change hands.

In spite of these insecurities, the political neutrality and relative permanence of deputy ministers is viewed as both a safeguard against a return to political patronage and partisan bureaucracy and a source of continuity in administration.

THE PUBLIC SERVICE

While the word *bureaucracy* refers to the structures and principles of organization in the administrative arm of government, **public service** is the collective term in Canada for the personnel employed in those structures. Like other political institutions described in this book, the public service of Canada has undergone many profound changes. It has evolved from a loosely organized, patronage-based service, where most people were recruited on the basis of political connections, into a modern, professionalized bureaucracy appointed on the principle of merit; from a predominantly anglophone and almost exclusively male preserve to an equal opportunity employer that consciously attempts to reflect Canada's ethnic and linguistic diversity, that has introduced affirmative-action programs designed to promote the participation of women, Native people, visible minorities and persons with disabilities.

The hierarchical system fosters a definitive chain of responsibility within the bureaucracy. Within each department, a descending order of command is evident. This chain of command, which ultimately begins with a government minister protects against the arbitrary assumption of power by individuals within the bureaucracy. Bureaucratic "red tape" in the guise of standard forms and triplicate copies is, in fact, a necessary part of the process of horizontal and vertical communication among employees and departments. Given the immense number of people involved and the diversity of their duties, it is easy to appreciate why the bureaucracy's primary goal of efficiency is sometimes difficult to achieve.

Who Works in the Public Service?

The federal government is a major employer. Approximately one out of every four Canadian workers is paid in the public sector, including federal, provincial and local governments. In 2004, the federal government employed approximately 400 000 people spread throughout the country in the public service, military, corporations, agencies, enterprises and the Royal Canadian Mounted Police.[9] Of these employees, over half are under the auspices of the Public Service Commission and the remainder work for government enterprises, for National Defence, the RCMP or smaller government agencies.

Entrance into the public service carries no restrictions as to age, race, sex, religion, colour, national or ethnic origin, marital status or disability. Recruitment is carried out across the country on the basis of merit. Qualifications are determined through an entrance exam, the results of which determine the applicant's capabilities and job placement. Recruitment programs are sponsored by the Public Service Commission (PSC). Following the *Public Service Reform Act, 1992*, the PSC is to continue basing its employment practices on merit, but it may initiate employment equity plans to right historical imbalances for designated groups — these include women, Native people, persons with disabilities and visible minorities.

To some extent, the bureaucracy is expected to be representative of the society it serves. Over the past four decades, there has been an increased sensitivity to the under-representation of francophones, women and other historically disadvantaged groups in the bureaucracy. At the same time, accessible university education has helped to enhance opportunities in the civil service for individuals from middle- and lower-class backgrounds.

In 1989, the government set up *Public Service 2000* in an attempt to reorganize the public service to make it more service-oriented and reduce morale problems caused by fiscal restraint. This new set of proposals to streamline public service practices was incorporated into 1992's *Public Service Reform Act*, which constituted the first major amendments to staffing legislation in twenty-five years. It provided for more flexible staffing arrangements and mandated the PSC to initiate employment equity programs while retaining the merit principle.

The reform of human resources management in the public service continued with the *Public Service Modernization Act* (PSMA), which was passed in November 2003. This Act will be fully in place by late 2005. It leaves the PSC as a guardian of the merit principle but allows more delegation of hiring to deputy heads. In theory, the PSMA and others that will need to be passed to put the whole system in place will increase flexibility for departments and agencies to hire the right people but still keep the merit principle in place. The lead agency in Human Resources will be the Public Service Human Resources Management Agency. Training, language education and a new Canada School of Public Service will be under this agency, which will report to the president of the Privy Council.

BUDGETS, DEFICITS AND DEBTS

The Canadian government spends a large amount of taxpayers' money. The main estimates (proposed expenditures) for 2004–2005 totalled $183.3 billion.[10] Of this figure, interest payments on the public debt consumed 19 percent and payments to other levels of government comprised 17 percent. The remainder went to Crown corporations and

Dolighan. Budge Vote. Reprinted with permission.

covered operating costs in such fields as justice and legal affairs and industrial, regional, scientific and technological departments and major transfers to individuals (the latter taking 23 percent of the budget for individuals — including the unemployed, elderly and veterans).

The **budget**, or management of the overall revenue and expenditures of the government on an annual basis, entails two separate processes. The first, the **expenditure process**, brings together the estimated spending requirements of all government departments and agencies for the next fiscal year. It takes place under the watchful eye of the Treasury Board, a Cabinet committee and its secretariat. These estimates are subsequently submitted to Parliament and its committees for scrutiny and approval via supply (appropriations) bills (which grant the government permission to spend public funds).

The second process, the **revenue process**, concerns how funds are to be raised — by taxation and other measures. It is largely the responsibility of the Departments of Finance and National Revenue. Its parliamentary focal point is the Budget Speech delivered by the minister of finance.

The Canadian budget does not contain all of the detailed proposals for spending — these estimates are tabled separately. This runs contrary to the budgetary practices of some political systems (which are not British parliamentary in origin) and to those of private businesses, where budgets present detailed targets for both spending and revenues.

The budget and its proposals are released only after lengthy preparation. Preliminary discussions are held in the Department of Finance to fix an approximate level of expenditures for the fiscal year and an estimate of revenues expected from existing tax rates. From these two estimates — expenditure and revenue — emerges a surplus or a deficit. In recent years, the government had to borrow money by issuing securities in order to finance its deficits. For 2004–2005, the government proposed to raise $187.2 billion, budget $35.4 billion for debt-servicing charges and have $147.9 billion in program expenditures (see Table 8.2).

Table 8.2 Federal Government Budget Projections for 2004–2005 in Billions of Dollars

Revenue Outlook (where government money comes from)		
	2004–2005	**2005–2006**
Personal income tax	86.9	92.5
Corporate income tax	26.3	27.8
Other income taxes	3.3	3.6
Goods and Services Tax	28.5	30.3
Customs import duties	3.0	3.1
Other excise taxes/duties	4.5	4.7
Energy	5.3	5.5
Air Travellers Security Charge	0.4	0.4
Total taxes	158.2	167.7
Employment Insurance	17	17.5
Other revenue	12.1	10.7
Total budgeting revenues	187.2	195.8
Total revenues as percent of GDP	14.8	14.7
Expenditure Outlook (where government money goes)		
	2004–2005	**2005–2006**
Program spending	147.9	156.1
Public debt charges	35.4	35.7
Reserves/Surplus	4.0	4.0
Deficit	0.0	0.0
Net public debt	510.6	510.6
Net public debt as percent of GDP	40.4	38.4

Source: Adapted from general tables in *Budget Plan, 2004* (Ottawa, 2004).

Totals differ due to roundings.

The minister of finance receives an analysis of the economic situation and outlook from departmental officials. These are supplemented by information from the governor of the Bank of Canada on general economic conditions, climate in the money markets, monetary policy and the market's capacity to absorb government bonds. Analysis of this information indicates the appropriate budget surplus or deficit and, in the latter event, the size of deficit that can be financed. This helps the government to formulate overall fiscal strategy.

Departmental officials advise the minister of tax loopholes that may be closed, tax reform proposals that have been made from external sources and changes that might be made in the customs tariff. From these discussions, a general pattern of taxation policy emerges. Costs of tax reduction and revenues from tax raises are totalled and compared with the estimates and the desired fiscal stance. The road is then clear to begin drafting the Budget Speech. Historically, finance ministers have presented the budget at the last possible moment before budget day. Recently, however, there has been a tendency to undertake more lengthy consultation both outside and inside Cabinet. Since 1994, the finance minister has held pre-budget conferences across the country, and the Commons finance committee has also toured the country and reported to the minister before he delivered the budget.

The address and the debate are regulated by the Standing Orders of the House of Commons. The Budget Speech is often delivered in the evening, after the markets have closed. The speech reviews the fiscal plan, the state of the national economy and the financial operations of the government over the past fiscal year. It also provides a forecast of spending requirements for the year ahead, taking into account the estimates. At the end of the Budget Speech, the minister tables the "ways and means" motions, which become the taxation or excise legislation.

Budget making is particularly tenuous in minority governments as Prime Minister Martin discovered in 2005 when he had to make compromises to gain NDP support.

In the early 1990s, there was considerable debate about the dire state of the federal government's finances — that Canada might get into a "debt spiral," with the national debt growing faster than the economy. By 1998, however, then Finance Minister Paul Martin was able to forecast a zero deficit and a decrease in the national debt — the first significant decline in the debt-to-GDP ratio in twenty-five years. By 2000, the government's cuts in program spending, a declining interest rate and a growing economy provided the expected budgetary surplus. In the 2004–2005 budget projections, the government announced a small surplus of $4 billion and a debt of $516.6 billion.

Essentially, governments have four strategies for cutting deficits and reducing debts: decreasing expenditures, increasing taxes, reducing interest rates (in order to reduce payments on the public debt) and increasing productivity. Since ministers have little control in the latter two areas due to Canada's dependence on foreign capital and the country's position in the global economy, the choice is normally between cutting expenditures and raising taxes.

Key Financial Terms

- Deficit: The annual amount by which government spending exceeds revenues.
- Debt: The accumulation of annual deficits less surpluses since Confederation.
- Surplus: The annual funds left over after the budgeted expenditures have been paid.

DEMOCRATIC CONTROL OF THE BUREAUCRACY

Bureaucracy, we have said, is an organizational form ideally suited to provide an efficient means of achieving a given objective. In a parliamentary democracy such as Canada, the selection of policy objectives ought to be the task of the political executive, responsible through Parliament to the people. The bureaucracy's role, in theory, should be to implement the goals (chosen by politicians) efficiently and effectively.

However, the distinctions between administration and politics are not clear. Public servants enjoy relative permanence in their jobs and have immense organizational resources. This gives them considerable influence in the policy-making process. Bureaucrats also have discretionary power in many areas of policy implementation, especially where Parliament has delegated decision-making authority to government departments, agencies and tribunals. How, then, do politicians keep unelected bureaucrats in check? There are three important ways: through strengthened parliamentary committees, the reports of the auditor general and freedom of information legislation.

Parliamentary Committees

Several House of Commons reforms over the last two decades have tried to reduce government dependence on the bureaucracy as a source of information and policy advice. Parliamentary committees are more effective, and their reports present a view of government policy that differs from that of the public service. Opposition parties receive research funds to help them make policy input or, at least, develop more informed criticism of existing policy-making and implementation. Increased staff support for individual MPs, while still not sufficient, does provide some research potential that enables MPs to question bureaucratic decisions more effectively.

The Auditor General

The **auditor general** provides a critical appraisal of the effectiveness of both public spending and accounting practices — to Parliament, and in particular to the Public Accounts Committee. He or she is directly responsible to Parliament (not the executive) and the auditor's reports on government spending trigger major debates in the House of Commons and the press about government policy-making.[11]

Since 1977, the Auditor General's Office (AGO) has had the power to carry out "value for money" audits — to assess policy and the substance of spending decisions. It "has become concerned not only with whether federal funds are properly accounted for, but how they are being managed, at what cost, to what end and with what effectiveness."[12] The increasing size and costs of the Auditor General's Office prompted one expert to conclude that the AGO itself should be subjected to a value-for-money, comprehensive audit. It was the report of Auditor General Sheila Fraser that uncovered the sponsorship scandal that severely weakened the federal Liberals in the 2004 election and beyond.

Parliamentary and administrative reforms in the expenditure budget process have enhanced the potential for democratic control, and the development of multi-year fiscal plans provides a broader, longer-range context for the evaluation of both spending plans and individual estimates. Both of these reforms have foregrounded the importance of the role of the auditor general.

Freedom of Information

In 1983, the federal government took an important step toward providing more open government when it formally promulgated the *Access to Information Act*. With a number of controversial exceptions, Canadian citizens and permanent residents now have the right to obtain or examine records that were previously kept secret by federal government institutions. At stake, in many cases, is the individual's right to know why certain government decisions were taken, or to determine whether these decisions were fairly arrived at or mistakes were made. If the government refuses to disclose information on request, an appeal can be made first to an information commissioner. Ultimate recourse, however, is via the Federal Court — an expensive procedure, which raises the undesirable prospect of having the judicial process replace Parliament as the primary mechanism for ensuring bureaucratic accountability.

The *Access to Information Act* is intended to make government more accountable and to reverse whatever public image exists of public servants scheming to hide blunders or alleged corruption from unsuspecting citizens. Still, some observers are sceptical of the value of the Act in its present form. Donald Rowat has argued that some of the exceptions to access "go against the whole spirit of a freedom of information act by absolutely prohibiting certain types of records from being released, thus turning these exemptions into an extension of the Official Secrets Act."[13] He also notes the long list of subjects on which discretionary exemptions can be made by bureaucrats, which may well "limit the accountability of the government to Parliament."

In the final analysis, public confidence in the Act will depend on how well the mechanics of releasing information work and on whether information that should be released is actually made public. This, in turn, will depend upon the extent to which the Cabinet and the bureaucracy comply with the spirit as well as the letter of the new law.

CLOSE-UP   The Right to Privacy

In his 2000 annual report, Canada's privacy commissioner, Bruce Phillips, revealed that as many as two thousand pieces of information on almost every citizen are stored by the Department of Human Resources.* The huge database is compiled from information such as income-tax returns, child-tax benefit statements, welfare files, disabilities and job records among others. The privacy commissioner and others maintain that the *Privacy Act* is inadequate in preventing the misuse of this information.

Should the laws be reformed to provide penalties for unauthorized access, careless storing or misuse of this data?

The Globe and Mail, May 18, 2000.

The Ombudsman and Other Proposals

For many years, there has been a debate about whether to create the position of federal **ombudsman**, an independent officer who would be responsible to Parliament for the investigation of citizens' complaints against the bureaucracy.[14] Although an ombudsman might provide an additional mechanism of overall surveillance of the bureaucracy, it should be noted that Canada already has a number of specialized ombudsman-like officers, including the commissioner of Official Languages, a privacy commissioner and a correctional investigator for penitentiary services, all of whom act as watchdogs over specific aspects of bureaucratic activity.

Other non-parliamentary means of controlling the bureaucracy's role in policy-making have also been proposed. The judicial process, for example, could play a greater role in protecting citizens against arbitrary bureaucratic decisions. However, although there has been an increase in court challenges to bureaucratic decisions since the *Charter of Rights and Freedoms* was implemented, we agree with the conclusion drawn by one opponent of judicial review of the bureaucracy:

> It would be wrong to abandon democratic processes working through Parliament to check bureaucratic power in favour of a more elitist approach based upon courts, lawyers and tribunals as the primary mechanisms for safeguarding the rights of individuals.[15]

Are More Reforms Needed?

The perceived lack of accountability of Crown corporations to Parliament is one problem that remains in controlling the bureaucracy. Reports of public enterprises and regulatory agencies are automatically referred to standing committees but inadequate auditing provisions and difficulties in imposing ministerial responsibility for these semi-autonomous agencies hinder effective parliamentary control. With this exception, however, the mechanisms for parliamentary control of the bureaucracy are largely in place. The key question is whether MPs have the inclination or time to ensure bureaucratic accountability.

KEY TERMS

advisory bodies, p.187

assistant deputy ministers (ADMs), p. 185

auditor general, p. 194

budget, p. 191

bureaucracy, p. 182

Crown agencies, p. 186

Crown corporation, p. 186

deputy minister (DM), p. 185

expenditure process, p. 191

government departments, p. 184

ministerial responsibility, p. 188

ombudsman, p. 196

policy, p. 183

public servants (bureaucrats), p. 182

public service, p. 189

regulation, p. 186

revenue process, p. 191

Royal Commissions, p. 187

DISCUSSION QUESTIONS

1. Should public servants be chosen for their professional qualifications? Why or why not?

2. Are politicians the masters of public servants? Should ministers have to take responsibility for mistakes made by public servants?

3. What are the four major strategies that can be used for cutting a deficit or reducing debt? Why is it such a difficult task for governments?

4. How might a minority government situation affect the functioning (effectiveness and efficiency) of the bureaucracy?

WEBLINKS

Access to Information Act

http://canada.justice.gc.ca/en/laws/A-1/index.html

Bank of Canada

www.bank-banque-canada.ca

Canadian Broadcasting Corporation

www.cbc.ca

Public Service Employment Act

http://canada.justice.gc.ca/en/laws/P-33/index.html

Public Works and Government Services Canada

www.pwgsc.gc.ca

9 The Administration of Justice

Courts, Police, Prisons and Security

Learning Objectives

After reading this chapter, you should be able to

1. Differentiate between civil and criminal law in the Canadian legal system.

2. Describe the basic organization of the court system in Canada.

3. Trace the changing role of the Supreme Court since Confederation, and describe the respective roles of the Supreme Court and the Federal Court today.

4. Describe how the *Charter of Rights and Freedoms* has influenced judges, politicians, Canadian citizens and police.

5. Describe the organizational arrangements for policing and prisons in Canada.

6. Describe the Canadian government's response to the terrorist attacks on the US on September 11, 2001, in terms of strengthening Canada's security arrangements.

Sports matches require referees to ensure that rules are followed and that appropriate penalties are dispensed when they are broken. This is also true in everyday life. Canada, like all modern states, maintains an extensive system of law, courts, police and prisons. The institutions of law and order allow the government to exercise authority in all disputes between and among individuals and institutions such as corporations. As we have seen, general rules for politics in Canada are established in the Constitution. More specific laws to manage societal conflict are made by legislatures and governments or are delegated by governments to other bodies. Judges and juries act, under the laws of the country, as referees or umpires to settle disputes with authoritative, impartial decisions.

Almost without exception, governments maintain a military organization — for external security, for suppressing internal disorder and for managing large-scale natural disasters. While the military is outside the scope of this book, the courts that interpret the law and count on the administrators of justice to enforce it, as well as the police and the administrative justice officials who enforce law and order, are part of our study of government and politics. The prison or corrections system is also an important part of the authoritative structure of government. It is used against those individuals who do not comply with the law as interpreted by the courts. This chapter, therefore, examines the role and organization of courts in Canada's legal system, the impact of the Charter of Rights and Freedoms, the role and organization of policing and the prison system—the ultimate sanction of the state. Security has taken on increased importance since the terrorist attacks on the United States on September 11, 2001. The last section discusses arrangements for security that the Canadian government has put in place to counter terrorism since that date.

THE LEGAL SYSTEM

The Canadian legal system is derived from British and, to a lesser extent, French models. This complex system is underpinned by the Constitution and constitutional precedents, as well as the laws and regulations emanating from the federal Parliament and the ten provincial legislatures. The courts rely on the Constitution, federal and provincial laws, the Canadian equivalent of English Common Law and the Québec Civil Code to guide their decision-making.

In Chapter 3, we discussed the constitutional rules affecting the Canadian legal system. We saw that the rule of law means that citizens, no matter what their transgressions, cannot be denied the due process of law and that this regularizes the relationship between citizens and their governments. No individual or institution is above the law, no one is exempted from it and all are equal before it. No government or administrative official has any power beyond that awarded by law.

The courts are the guardians of the rule of law and as such should be beyond partisan influence. In Canada today, judges are protected from arbitrary whims of politicians. Judges of the highest courts (the Supreme Court of Canada and the Federal Court) and also the most important provincial courts (the Superior Court of Québec, the highest courts of the other provinces and the provincial courts of appeal) are removable only by an address to the governor general by both Houses of Parliament. No higher-court judge has ever been removed in this fashion. This tradition of the independence of the judiciary is particularly significant in constitutional development because the Supreme Court interprets the written Constitution and therefore defines the limits of federal and provincial power as well as the applicability of the *Charter of Rights and Freedoms.* As a further precaution against undue influence on judges, the Canadian Constitution provides that almost all courts are established by the provincial legislatures but that all judges from the county courts up (except courts of probate in Nova Scotia and New Brunswick) are appointed by the federal government.

The Constitution is an important part of the legal system. It is a body of fundamental rules, written and unwritten, which condition the making of all other law. As we discussed in Chapter 3, this part of dispute resolution normally concerns the basic rules of the political game as set out in the Constitution. It includes rules about federal and provincial jurisdictions and the relationships between individuals or groups and governments. Cases that involve these aspects of law may end up at the Supreme Court for resolution. As we will see, the 1982 *Charter of Rights and Freedoms* has greatly enhanced the judiciary's role in settling the political disputes of the country.

Courts As Arenas for Solving Disputes

Laws and regulations that concern politics and social life are, of necessity, extremely general and abstract because they must apply to a multitude of differing situations. Their meaning and relevance must be interpreted in each specific case. Judges and juries are constantly interpreting and reinterpreting the law and shaping its direction. They not only apply the law but also, in a real sense, make new law with their judgments.

In Canada, when disputes cannot be solved among individuals or between individuals and the state, the courts regulate the conflict. An adversarial system pits lawyers against one another, or against the state's prosecutors, in courts. Judges and juries determine the outcome of cases. The judgments themselves may then add to the development of case law and the common-law tradition of the country.

Canadian law is divided into two categories: civil law and criminal law. The federal structure basically gives jurisdiction over civil law to the provinces and criminal matters to the federal Parliament.

Civil law regulates relations between or among private individuals or corporations. It is concerned mainly with disputes over property and commercial contracts. Following laws based on provincial authority in the fields of "property and civil rights," judges and juries render decisions about the amount of damages and payments. Civil law also includes topics such as torts, wills, company law and family law.

Criminal law pits the individual against the state. Unlike civil law, criminal law comes under federal authority in Canada. It is mentioned in Clause 91 of the Constitution and includes crimes such as theft, assault and murder. Since the "administration of justice" comes under the provincial powers in Clause 92, however, it is police and Crown attorneys, working for the provincial attorneys general, who normally lead the prosecution against wrongdoers. The judges, following the conclusions of juries, make decisions about what penalties (if any) to impose. These may take the form of fines or prison sentences (see the section on Corrections Canada on page 214).

The Organization of the Court System

The Canadian judiciary makes rules in disputes over the law. Whether the law is civil or criminal, judges deliberate in courts. The basic, unitary structure of the court system in Canada is that of a pyramid with a very wide base and a narrow tip, with the Supreme Court of Canada at the top.

The Fathers of Confederation did not establish the Supreme Court in the Constitution but left Parliament to propose and establish it through legislation. Section 101 of the Constitution gave the Parliament of Canada the authority to create a Supreme Court and other courts. The **Supreme Court of Canada** is Canada's highest court for civil, criminal and constitutional cases. It was established by the *Dominion Act* in 1875 as a general court of appeal for Canada. At the time, it was not the final court of appeal, however; that power still rested in Britain with the Judicial Committee of the Privy Council (JCPC). It wasn't until 1949 that the Supreme Court became Canada's final court of appeal.

Today, a chief justice and eight *puisne* judges of slightly lesser rank serve on the Supreme Court (see the Close-Up below). Three of the nine must come from the civil-law tradition and, in practice, that means from Québec. All are appointed by the governor-in-council[1] and do not have to retire until age 75. In 1999, the prime minister appointed Beverley McLachlin as chief justice of the Court. Since 1949, only seven of the Supreme Court judges have been women.

CLOSE-UP   Supreme Court Judges, September 2005

Chief Justice: Beverley McLachlin

Judges:

Madam Justice Rosalie Abella	Madam Justice Louise Charron
Mr. Justice John Major	Mr. Justice Louis LeBel
Mr. Justice Michel Bastarache	Madam Justice Marie Deschamps
Mr. Justice Ian Binnie	Mr. Justice Morris J. Fish

Immediately below the Supreme Court of Canada in the judicial pyramid are the provincial superior or supreme courts. Each province has a superior or supreme court of general jurisdiction, which is charged with administering all laws in force in Canada, whether enacted by Parliament, provincial legislatures or municipalities. They are usually divided into trial and appeal divisions; some may also have county or district courts of both civil and criminal jurisdiction. Article 96 of the Constitution stipulates that appointment to these superior district and county courts is made by the governor general — in practice, by the federal Cabinet. In other words, while each province determines how many judges it will need in these federal courts, Ottawa determines who will be appointed and how they will be paid. All provinces also have courts staffed by judges appointed by the province who deal with lesser criminal and other matters. These provincial courts include magistrates' courts, family courts and juvenile courts. The appeal divisions of the provincial supreme or superior courts hear appeals from the lower courts and from certain provincial administrative tribunals (see Figure 9.1 on page 203).

Chief Justice Beverley McLachlin

As the highest court in the land, the Supreme Court's decisions are binding on all the courts below it. The Supreme Court deals primarily with cases that have already been appealed at least once in the lower courts. In these situations, the task of the Supreme Court is to render "an authoritative settlement of a question of law of importance to the whole nation."[2] On rather rare but important occasions, it also deals with questions referred to it directly by the federal government — as with the 1997 questions on Québec independence. These are called "reference" cases.

Canada's Supreme Court is not required to hear all appeals. It is allowed to be highly selective, concentrating on questions that are of fundamental importance to Canadian society. It shapes the direction of the law by applying general rules to the specific circumstances — rules that then get passed down to the courts as principles to specific courts. It should be remembered as well that, as a general court of appeal, the Supreme Court of Canada has a right to the final say in all areas of law for the country. This combination of selectivity and breadth makes the Supreme Court extremely powerful. Since the adoption of the Charter of Rights, the Supreme Court has become the final arbiter "not only of the division of power between governments but also of the line between the powers of both levels of government and the rights and freedoms of citizens."[3]

Below the Supreme Court of Canada but separate from the provincial court structure is the **Federal Court of Canada**. This court was established by Parliament in 1971 to settle claims by or against the federal government on matters relating to maritime law, copyright, patent and trademark law and federal taxation statutes and to undertake a supervisory role related to decisions of tribunals and inferior bodies established by federal law. The Federal Court has both a trial and an appeal division. Decisions of the Federal Court of Appeal can be appealed to the Supreme Court of Canada when the amount of money involved in the matter exceeds a set amount. Otherwise, an appeal to the Supreme Court requires either the intervention of the Supreme Court itself or the agreement of the Federal Court of Appeal. If the dispute is inter-provincial or federal–provincial in nature, the route of appeal to the Supreme Court is automatically open. There are a few other specialized federal courts, such as the Tax Court of Canada, whose decisions are also subject to review by the Federal Court.

Compared to other countries that operate under a federal rather than a unitary system of government, Canada's judicial system is highly integrated. A purely federal judicial

Figure 9.1 Canadian Courts

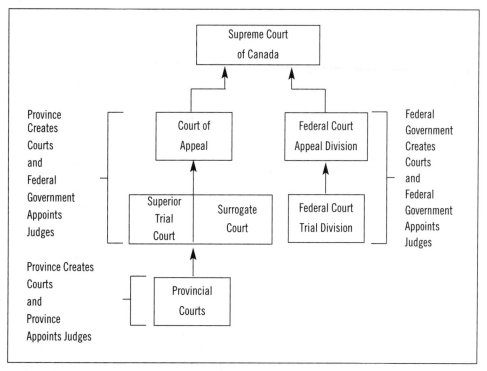

power is not even mentioned in the Canadian Constitution. Instead, the Constitution provides for an integrated system with federally-appointed judges in provincial superior and intermediate courts. Thus, despite the fact that Section 92(14) of the Constitution authorizes the provinces to control the "administration of justice," the federal government appoints the most important judges in each province.[4] Canada is the only federation to have this high level of judicial integration. Parliament established the Supreme Court of Canada as a "general court of appeal" rather than one that is limited to federal law and constitutional law. Another integrating feature of the judicial system is that while Parliament has exclusive jurisdiction in the area of criminal law, the provincial legislatures have powers to establish courts of criminal jurisdiction. This means that federal law is administered in provincially established courts, by federally appointed judges.

However, some constitutional experts note that there has been a tendency, in recent years, to move away from the integrated model to a system of "dual courts." Evidence for this is found in the proliferation of provincial and federal courts, which are established and staffed by their respective levels of government. Because the federal government is increasingly dependent on judges appointed and paid by the provinces to administer federal laws, it is showing a tendency to establish federal trial courts for cases involving federal laws. This combination of events suggests a move in the direction of federalizing Canada's judicial structure. The merits of such a move are highly debatable, in particular because the unitary court system was designed to apply the law equally to all Canadians, regardless of region.

Native justice constitutes a special problem for Canadian law. There is general agreement that the justice system does not work well for Native peoples. Many experts believe that each Native community in Canada should develop its own justice system to conform with its traditions and cultures. This process is already under way in some areas. However, as a general principle, such a policy would create many separate justice systems on small areas of land across Canada. This political issue will grow in significance in the coming years.

The Changing Role of the Supreme Court: Good or Bad?

In its early years, the Supreme Court of Canada was a subordinate, secondary institution. Not until appeal to the Judicial Committee of the Privy Council was abolished in 1949 did the Supreme Court of Canada assume the leadership of the Canadian judicial system. The next major evolutionary change came in 1974 when the Supreme Court of Canada's jurisdiction was changed, allowing it to control its own agenda. Finally, the 1982 patriation of the Constitution, with its *Charter of Rights and Freedoms*, heralded a new and expanded role for all courts in Canada.

In a landmark decision in 1981, the Supreme Court judges ruled in the *Patriation Reference* case that Prime Minister Pierre Trudeau's government could legally patriate and amend the Constitution unilaterally, while warning that to do so would violate an established "constitutional convention." This ruling on a question of "constitutional convention" was unique in that it reached beyond the law, into the realm of politics. It amounted to a legal green light combined with a political red light. Under the circumstances, Trudeau chose to return to the constitutional bargaining table with the provincial premiers and seek an acceptable compromise before proceeding with patriation.

The *Constitution Act, 1982*, greatly increased the political importance of the Supreme Court of Canada, mainly because of the *Charter of Rights and Freedoms*. Under the Charter, the Supreme Court of Canada can overrule legislation and executive acts of government not only on the grounds that they violate the federal division of powers but also on the grounds that they violate the fundamental rights and freedoms of citizens. The consequences of this new development are discussed in the next section on the Charter, but here it is important to note that the Canadian judiciary has gradually become more powerful.

The mandate of judges, however, has remained constant — to respect the laws governing the disputes that they arbitrate and to contribute to the development of those laws. In doing so, they must act, and must also be seen to act, with independence and impartiality. Increasingly, however, judges are perceived by some as "politicians" promoting change in public policy. As Canadians become more conscious of judicial power, they are scrutinizing more closely their judiciary's claims of impartiality.[5]

In particular, the appointment procedure has become the object of public debate. Since the Supreme Court was not established by the Constitution, but by federal legislation, there is no reference in the Constitution either to its composition or the method by which judges are to be appointed. Reform proposals include that potential government appointees be confirmed by parliamentary hearings or that the prime minister choose his or her nominees from a shortlist drawn up by a nominating committee with wide representation.[6] The only mention of the Supreme Court in the *Constitution Act* concerns the amending formula — which requires the agreement of Parliament and all of the provincial legislatures for any change in the composition of the Supreme Court, and the agreement of Parliament and two-thirds of the provinces (representing 50 percent of the population) for any other constitutional change of the court. Another reform proposal is that the Supreme Court be established in the Constitution so that it will not have to depend on federal legislation for its existence and that its composition or method of appointment cannot be changed easily.

The Impact of Charter Politics: Good or Bad?

In Chapter 3, we discussed why Canadians entrenched the *Charter of Rights and Freedoms* in the Constitution and what fundamental rights are protected as a result. Here we are concerned with what impact the Charter has had on the politicians who make laws, the judges who interpret them, the police who enforce them and the Canadians who live under them. The Charter has had a profound influence on all four groups.

On Governments The fact that the Supreme Court now is able to use the *Charter of Rights and Freedoms* to strike down government-made laws, and this has made governments more careful in drafting legislation. On the other hand, the existence of the Charter has often allowed governments to escape from responsibility by making their legislation vague, leaving the tough, unpopular decisions to be made by the courts. Of course, the court must be careful not to be too far ahead of, or behind, public opinion or it may lose the confidence of Canadians. Legislators can override a court decision by using the Charter's Section 33 "notwithstanding" clause but to do so could trigger a public backlash if the public did not agree.

On Judges and Lawyers When the Charter came into effect in 1982, it gave judges significant new powers. Supreme Court judges found their new responsibilities awesome because of the novel abstract principles and the lack of familiar paths. One Supreme Court judge asked:

> What is liberty? What should be the limits to it? We all know what
> we think ourselves. But when it comes to defining liberty, each and
> every state restriction exists in a proper context. There is no way to
> escape these problems . . . [7]

The early court cases indicated that the judges would base their decisions on new considerations. In the *Southam* case, for example, Chief Justice Dickson "traced the right to security from unreasonable searches back to the common law concept of trespass and its application by English judges in the 1700s to make an Englishman's home his castle." Next, he "followed the evolution of this private property interest into a wider concern with personal privacy as a fundamental value of a liberal society."[8]

It was also clear from the beginning that the nine justices of the Supreme Court would play a powerful political role once the Charter came into effect. They quickly began to overturn legislation that they considered conflictual with rights guaranteed in the Charter. In many cases, they have made decisions on social policy matters that used to be in the exclusive domain of politicians. In January 1988, for example, the Supreme Court declared in the *Morgentaler* case that the federal abortion law, which restricted access to therapeutic abortions did not conform to the Charter and struck it down. In that case, a majority of the Supreme Court judges ruled that the law violated the security of the person of the woman and constituted a "profound interference with a woman's body."[9] Despite parliamentary efforts to regain control of abortion policy, the Supreme Court's judgment remains in place with little likelihood of legislation because of the controversial nature of the subject.

Many other highly publicized public policy issues decided by the Supreme Court in recent years involved Charter decisions on fundamental freedoms. These included cases concerning union rights, language legislation, pornography, freedom of the press, street prostitution and the right to die, to cite only a few examples.

The relative importance of the courts rose again in 1985 when the Charter's equality provisions took effect. The provisions immediately established a new, burgeoning area of litigation. In fact, a question soon arose as to whether the courts had the authority to determine what constitutes "equality" without Parliament having an opportunity to respond legislatively. Drawing a line between acceptable and unacceptable forms of discrimination in an attempt to achieve equality is now one of the most difficult tasks under the Charter. In 1988, for example, the Federal Court decided that a section of the *Unemployment Insurance Act* discriminated against natural fathers because it denied them paternity-leave benefits. Eventually, the federal government agreed and extended the benefits to fathers as well as mothers. Clearly, this type of ruling affects the balance of power between Parliament and the courts. As one Supreme Court judge put it, "We are talking about inserting equality into life which is not equal."[10]

Does the Charter confer too much power on lawyers and judges? It does enable judges, who are not elected, to strike down measures enacted by elected politicians. On the surface, this looks unjust; however, one cannot equate democracy with the "raw will of the majority." The Charter assigns the courts the responsibility to ensure that the claims of minorities and those without influence must be heard. Ultimately, elected officials do have the final say because the Charter provides that the equality rights provisions are subject to the legislative override provision (the notwithstanding clause) that can be used if legislatures disagree fundamentally with the courts.

On Police: Another controversial area of Charter politics concerns the police and legal rights. The Charter has made it increasingly difficult for police to build effective cases against criminals. Some applaud that difficulty; others see it as aiding criminals. Section 24(2) of the Charter states that a court shall exclude evidence from the proceedings obtained in a manner that infringed upon or denied any guaranteed right or freedom. Canadian judges have proven willing to dismiss illegally obtained evidence because it might "bring the administration of justice into disrepute." Until 1982, illegally obtained evidence was accepted in Canadian courts. After the Charter came into effect, the courts began to rule that much of this evidence was inadmissible.

On Citizens: As for Canadians in general, the Charter has given them the ability to challenge laws that they perceive to be unjust — i.e., those thought to impinge on basic rights of freedom and equality. However, changes in the law by the Supreme Court also created new problems for Canadians. For example, in 1992, the Supreme Court changed Canada's obscenity law. It tossed out the old test of obscenity, based on the vague and arbitrary notion of "community standards," and replaced it with a "harm-based" test. Material would be judged obscene if it portrayed sexual violence, or degrading and dehumanizing acts, or contained the sexual depiction of children. Within a short time, the new law had become the moral underpinning for prosecutions of the "wrong" people — peaceable gay and lesbian artists and bookstores. Many felt that Canada Customs and the police pushed the interpretation too far, and the new test of obscenity was just as vague and subjective as the old test.[11]

Also on the negative side for many Canadians is a feeling that Charter interpretations are shifting values toward those of the United States. Critics of the Charter believe that traditional Canadian values that emphasized tradition, order and historical continuity are being replaced by American values that stress individual interests above those of the collectivity. This, they say, is a result of the emphasis that the Charter puts on individual versus group interests. Constitutional experts Cheffins and Johnson, for example, have expressed the fear that the Charter "will bring an essentially counter-revolutionary, non-rationalist communitarian society into direct collision with individual-focused legal rights based upon Charter arguments."[12] Doing so, they maintain, will accelerate the Americanization of Canada.

Some Equality Rights Cases Decided by the Supreme Court

Legal equality, including protection from discrimination, is the starting point for any move toward greater equality of opportunity. The equal-rights guarantee in Canada's Constitution took effect in April 1985. In the years since then, women's groups have organized effectively to have the courts examine issues such as child care, harassment and violence. Common-law, gay and lesbian rights activists have also made effective cases. The Supreme Court rulings have indicated that while the Constitution explicitly promises equality to every "individual," it is meant to apply to disadvantaged groups such as women and minorities. Critics, however, ask why Canada prohibits discrimination on the basis of sex, national or ethnic origin, race, age, colour, religion or disability when other characteristics such as character and ability are *also* acquired by chance.

In the first equality case to be heard by the Supreme Court, a white, Oxford-educated male, Mark Andrews, a US citizen, argued that he was discriminated against when British Columbia's law society would not let him become a lawyer because he was not a Canadian citizen. He won his case. The Supreme Court argued that equality rights protections in Section 15 were intended for the disadvantaged. It ruled that Mark Andrews was a member of a disadvantaged group (non-citizens) and as such was the victim of illegal discrimination. It said that equality does not mean sameness. Sometimes groups need to be treated differently. (Based on this same argument, the Court later ruled that female guards can see male prisoners on their toilets, but male guards could not get that close to female prisoners.)[13]

The Mark Andrews decision proved to be a huge victory for women and minorities. All subsequent decisions on equality cases stem from this one. The following decisions reflect how the "equality rights" section of the Charter has been interpreted more than a decade later.

In May 1995, the Supreme Court announced three significant decisions concerning the equality section. In all three cases, the question concerned what constitutes discrimination. The first was followed closely by supporters of women's rights; the others particularly concerned those who supported gay and common-law couples. In essence, the court was asked to lead social change or at least to give official recognition to changes that had already taken place.

In the first case, *The Queen v. Suzanne Thibaudeau*, Suzanne Thibaudeau, a divorced woman in Québec, argued that the fact that she (and not her former husband) had to pay tax on support payments awarded to her for their two children meant that she was discriminated against. The court disagreed by five to two. It found that there was no discrimination; that the government had already taken this kind of situation into account in taxing divorced parents; and "the tax burden of the couple is reduced and this has the result of increasing the available resources that can be used for the benefit of the children."[14]

The decision created a dilemma for the federal government. If it retained a system that taxed the recipients of child support, it would face continued agitation from lobbyists who claimed it was unfair to women. If it changed the rules to shift the tax to the parent making support payments, it would anger others and still not guarantee that more money would go to children.

The second case, *The Queen v. James Egan and Jack Nesbit*, concerned a homosexual couple from British Columbia. Egan, a pensioner, applied for a spousal pension for his partner, Nesbit (the law at the time allowed spouses of some pensioners to receive an allowance). Egan's request was turned down, and he appealed to the Supreme Court on the basis that he had been discriminated against. Again the Court disagreed, even though it unanimously found that homosexuals are covered by the equality provisions of the Charter and cannot be discriminated against on the grounds of sexual orientation. The Court argued that Parliament had set up spousal pensions to benefit aged, needy married couples and that marriage is by nature heterosexual. Marriage is "fundamental to the stability and well-being of the family"[15] — so the government was not discriminating in this case but making political choices. The Constitution stipulates that governments may violate constitutional rights where it is "reasonable" to do so in a free and democratic society.

The judges were badly split in this latter case (five to four). Two of the dissenting judges even wrote, "This distinction amounts to clear denial of equal benefit of the law." One group of judges stressed the traditional family structure and was not willing to extend government policies for traditional families to gay couples. Four other judges took a broader view of the family. They said that legislatures should treat different family structures roughly the same, including gay couples. The "swing vote" was that of John Sopinka, who agreed that discrimination existed but said he was willing to defer to Parliament in this case. He said that "equating same-sex couples with heterosexual couples . . . is still generally regarded as a novel concept."[16]

Lesbian and gay activists saw the court's recognition of sexual orientation as a basis of discrimination as a victory for gay rights even though this specific case had been lost. The decision was only one vote away from a win and there was speculation that in future cases, John Sopinka might be swayed, or a new judge might change the composition and orientation of the Court. The ruling put pressure on the federal government to move faster on gay rights legislation to avoid a spate of lawsuits (see the "Same-Sex Marriage" Close-Up below).

The third case, *John Miron et al. v. Richard Trudel et al.*, was a clear victory for John Miron and Jocelyne Vallière, a common-law Ontario couple with two children. Miron had been injured in a car accident while a passenger with an uninsured driver. Miron would have been covered under provincial law by Vallière's insurance policy but only if they were married. The court decided five to four that the policy constituted unjustifiable discrimination by the Ontario government against common-law couples because it required insurance companies to provide certain benefits to married couples. The ruling went on to declare that common-law couples were a historically disadvantaged group entitled to constitutional protection. This decision means that federal and provincial governments will have to examine a wide array of laws to ensure that they comply with the ruling.

CLOSE-UP   Same-Sex Marriage

The controversial issue of same-sex marriage moved to centre stage in June 2003 with the Ontario Court of Appeal ruling in *Halpern v. Canada* that the opposite-gender requirement for marriage is unconstitutional. It directed that marriage in the province of Ontario be open to same-sex couples, although it said that its decision did interfere with the religious institution of marriage. The high courts of six provinces and one territory, representing more than 85 percent of the population, later ruled that the traditional definition of marriage as a union between a man and a woman is discriminatory and unconstitutional, allowing more than three thousand same-sex couples in various parts of Canada to marry.

These rulings contradicted federal policy because in 1999, the federal Parliament had passed a resolution defining marriage as a strictly heterosexual institution.

On June 17, 2003, Prime Minister Jean Chrétien responded with an announcement that the federal government would not appeal the decisions of the various courts of appeal on the definition of marriage but would draft legislation to legally

recognize the union of same-sex couples, while recognizing the freedom of churches and religious organizations not to perform marriages against their beliefs. In September, the House of Commons rejected 137–132 an opposition motion reaffirming the traditional definition of marriage. Chrétien requested a ruling from the Supreme Court as to whether traditional marriage laws were discriminatory and violated the *Charter of Rights and Freedoms*.

In December of 2004, the Supreme Court gave the go-ahead to the federal government to introduce legislation redefining marriage across the country to include same-sex couples. It stopped short, however, of defining traditional marriage as unconstitutional. It also ruled that the federal government had exclusive authority over the definition of marriage.

In spite of the Liberals' tenuous minority government situation, Prime Minister Paul Martin promised to press ahead with legislation in 2005. Opposition lobbies, including the Canadian Conference of Catholic Bishops, vowed to fight any legislation in favour of equal marriage legislation, while gay rights groups expressed their great enthusiasm for legislation that would make Canada the third country after Belgium and the Netherlands to permit gays and lesbians to marry. In June 2005, the House of Commons voted to extend marriage rights to gay and lesbian couples throughout Canada.

In a controversial issue such as this, is the government essentially hiding behind the Supreme Court to shield it from public blame?

The next set of major Charter equality cases occurred in 1997 when the Supreme Court came closer to establishing the importance or effect of equality rights in the Charter. In *Eaton v. Bryant*, the Court ruled that an Ontario school could place a child in a special education class as long as the child did not suffer adverse affects. In *Eldridge v. British Columbia*, the Court showed its skill in drawing the same distinction when it ruled that the BC Medical Services Commission violated the Charter when it failed to provide sign-language interpreters, causing a child to suffer adverse effects. Lastly, in *Benner v. Canada*, the Court ruled that the *Citizenship Act* violated equality rights when it made a distinction between males and females in concluding that before being granted citizenship, a man required a security check if his mother was a Canadian citizen but not if his father was.

The equality case that generated the most publicity and political controversy involved the *Vriend* decision of April 1998. In *Vriend v. Alberta*, the Supreme Court concluded that gays and lesbians had to be granted the same protection as others under the Alberta *Individual Rights Protection Act* (IRPA). The decision was remarkable because it was based on a ruling that "a legislative 'omission' bears judicial disapproval on the same basis as the legislature's positive acts."[17] In other words, the Court ruled not on what was *in* the Act but on what had been *omitted* from it. The Court ruled in effect that sexual orientation had to be "read into" the IRPA.

On the political front, the Progressive Conservative premier of Alberta, Ralph Klein, hinted that he might invoke the notwithstanding clause to overrule the Supreme Court's judgment on this subject, but he backed off when the expected public approval did not emerge. While social conservatives tried to force the premier to nullify the Court ruling on homosexuals, Klein demurred, declaring, "It's like that train. You can't stop it, you have to deal with it."[18] In other words, politicians have to put up with Supreme Court rulings whether they like them or not.

These cases and many others show that the Charter has become an important Canadian symbol and a significant part of the policy process — a balance to legislative power. It has provided a more active, interventionist role for the judiciary, and this is causing a gradual evolution in the power of the Supreme Court.

CLOSE-UP   Social Policy on Autism

Autism is a neurological disorder that requires special treatment with one-on-one behaviour-modification training. Parents of autistic children contend that they have a constitutional right to have their children's therapy entirely paid for by the government in the same way that a cancer or heart patient would have. They claim that since this is not the case, they are being discriminated against in violation of the *Charter of Rights and Freedoms*.

Their case reached the Supreme Court and its ruling had the potential to bring a cascade of lawsuits from Canadians with other disabilities, including dyslexia.

Provincial governments say they cannot afford to add autistic patients to the already over-stretched health-care system, but in response to suits, lower courts have increased funding for autism therapy. Geoff Plant, attorney general of British Columbia, estimated that if all the autistic children in his province received the intensive therapy demanded, it would cost more than $250 million annually out of a total health budget of $9 billion.

In late 2005, the Supreme Court made its ruling. It refused to force British Columbia to fund specialized treatment for autistic children. It said that the decision to fund or not fund specific health services is for Parliament and provincial legislatures to determine. They determine the services provided in the *Canada Health Act*. The implication is that health-care dollars are not unlimited, and governments need to be able to allocate scarce resources as they see fit.

Some called the decision cold-hearted and mean; others found it principled and thoughtful. Was it a good ruling? Should courts have the last word in such decisions?

POLICE FORCES: ENFORCERS OF LAW AND GOVERNMENT

Police enforce the law and maintain order. They also carry out innumerable functions for society such as detecting crime and protecting life and property as well as imposing parking fines, directing traffic and providing emergency health care. Their activities with respect to domestic disputes, gambling, marijuana smoking, prostitution, pornography and protest demonstrations evoke support from most citizens and derision from others.

The manner in which the police carry out their functions is the subject of considerable discussion. There are many laws, regulations and ordinances that the police must handle. Some would like all of these laws enforced equally by the police, but that is not practical. In choosing which issues to pursue, the police exercise a high degree of discretion. In fact, it may not always be possible to enforce unpopular laws, and since the police must count on public support, some specialists argue that it is counterproductive for the police to force unwanted laws on the public. Other citizens contend that it is not up to the police but politicians to make laws, and those laws should all be enforced equally regardless of their popularity. The best-known example of the questionable use of the police to enforce an unpopular law occurred during the Winnipeg General Strike of 1919. However, the current enforcement of controversial laws about marijuana, cigarette taxes and gun controls may run a close second.

Organization of Policing

Canada's police system is highly complex. It is governed by a maze of laws and regulations, making generalization difficult if not perilous. Federalism, provincial police acts and financing agreements between different governments all complicate the situation. Some things are clear, however. All police forces are responsible to one or all levels of government — municipal, provincial and federal. Policing in Canada costs over $5 billion a year, with municipal policing responsible for about three-fifths of the costs, provincial policing costs running about half that and federal policing about half again.[19]

There are three standard organizational arrangements for policing in Canada: federal (the RCMP); provincial (the Ontario Provincial Police (OPP), Sûreté du Québec (SQ), and Royal Newfoundland Constabulary); and municipal (see Table 9.1). There is roughly one police officer for every 476 persons in Canada.

Table 9.1 Canadian Police Organization*

Level of Government	Police Organization
Federal	RCMP
Provincial	Ontario: Ontario Provincial Police (OPP)
	Québec: Sûreté du Québec
	Newfoundland and Labrador: Royal Newfoundland Constabulary (shared with RCMP)
Municipal	Municipal police force unless there is a contract for RCMP or provincial police to provide this service for municipality

*Other Public Police include CSIS, CN Police, CP Police, Military Police, Ports Canada, and federal and provincial department officials in fields such as income tax, customs and excise, immigration, fisheries and wildlife.

The **Royal Canadian Mounted Police (RCMP)** was created in 1920 out of the North West Mounted Police, which had been established in 1873 to enforce Canadian law in the western prairies. The RCMP is responsible to a commissioner (with the rank of a deputy minister) who reports to the minister of public safety and emergency preparedness (currently Anne McLellan, the deputy prime minister). The force is responsible for enforcing all federal statutes. As well, it is under contract to every province except Ontario and Québec, and to over one hundred municipalities to enforce criminal and provincial law. It also polices the territories. The RCMP maintains forensic labs, identification services, the Canadian Police Information Centre and the Canadian Police College in Ottawa for the advanced education of all police in Canada.

Two provinces (Ontario and Québec) have their own province-wide forces — the **Ontario Provincial Police (OPP)** and the **Sûreté du Québec (SQ)**. In Newfoundland and Labrador, the **Royal Newfoundland Constabulary** shares responsibilities with the RCMP. Besides these special provincial arrangements, specific policing powers throughout the country are also given to Canadian National Railways, Canadian Pacific Railways and Ports Canada. Each city and sizeable town is also required to have police to maintain law and order. They contract the police from the RCMP or OPP, receive them automatically (as in Québec) or must set up their own forces.

Native policing follows several models. Some communities contract with the RCMP or provincial forces to police their territories. Others have their own police forces with their own codes of conduct, answerable to their own police commissions. Still others are in transition, policed by a mixture of RCMP, provincial police and their own officers until they are ready to police themselves.

In addition to the RCMP and these other forces, the minister for public safety and emergency preparedness is responsible for the **Canadian Security Intelligence Service (CSIS)**, an intelligence-gathering institution. Its operations are governed by the 1984 *Canadian Security Intelligence Act*. This Act removed the security function from the RCMP (where it had been lodged since 1920) and established CSIS as a separate unit. The *Canadian Security Intelligence Act* defined the functions of CSIS and the threats to Canadian security such as espionage, sabotage, terrorism and foreign-inspired activities that it would be responsible for. CSIS also continued to do security screenings for appointments to the federal public service. Other intelligence-gathering agencies exist inside the Departments of Foreign Affairs, National Defence, and Citizenship and Immigration.

Many Canadians do not accept the idea that a government agency should maintain a constant watch on their daily lives because they believe such activities run counter to individual liberties. No democracy finds it easy to handle secretive organizations. The problem with supervising CSIS very closely is that the more public scrutiny there is, the less secret and thus the less effective CSIS may become.[20] To ensure that Canada's "snooping" institutions are democratically controlled, an accountability framework was put in place. The *Canadian Security Intelligence Act* set up an external review committee, the **Security Intelligence Review Committee**, to monitor the activities of CSIS. In 2003, CSIS — along with the RCMP — came under a new organization, the Department of Public Safety and Emergency Preparedness (on page 216).

CSIS continues to have its detractors. Many members of the police community believe it should have been left inside the RCMP and not "civilianized." In fact, the RCMP and CSIS have clashed even over such mundane subjects as data handling. Others contend that with the end of the Cold War, Canada does not need a secret service.

Who does the CSIS spy on? It can investigate anyone who presents a threat to "national security." Since it cannot make arrests or lay charges, it gathers information on threats to security. "About 60 percent of CSIS resources go into countering terrorism: watching potential terrorists or advising corporations on how to secure high tech secrets."[21]

THE PRISON SYSTEM: FINAL RECOURSE

The corrections system represents the ultimate sanction of the state against citizens. It represents a failure to socialize all citizens into peaceful and lawful activity.

The prison system represents the final proof that, even in democratic societies, the state retains the ultimate recourse to the use of coercion against its citizens. It exemplifies what the state is finally all about. Issues about prisons in democracies are hidden from view by political parties and politicians who are reluctant to regard the prison system as an important instrument of public policy. Prisons are often overlooked and even despised, but they form an essential part of institutional democracy.

Organization of Prisons

Canada abolished capital punishment in 1976, but approximately thirty thousand inmates are incarcerated in Canadian federal and provincial prisons. Correctional services are divided along federal lines. For adults, the *Criminal Code of Canada* demands that the federal government be responsible for all offenders sentenced to prison for two or more years and provincial governments be responsible for lesser sentences.[22] For youths, the provinces have authority over offenders of any law, including laws covered by the federal *Youth Criminal Justice Act* (YCJA).

The **minister of public safety and emergency preparedness** is responsible for the Correctional Service of Canada and the National Parole Board (as well as CSIS, the RCMP and other areas). Government estimates tend to provide just over $1 billion for these institutions. **Corrections Canada** consists of government officials responsible for inmates in federal prisons and for parolees. The Parole Board has the authority to grant or revoke paroles for prisoners and advises the minister on pardons. Each province has its own laws and rules governing prisons, and coordination and friction with federal authorities is as routine as in other institutions that cross federal–provincial jurisdictions.

Prisons serve a number of purposes. Since the public cannot agree on the major purpose of penitentiaries, these purposes are often contradictory. A list of penitentiary functions would include the somewhat contradictory purposes of punishing wrongdoers, deterring criminal behaviour, safeguarding society by depriving criminals of their freedom and providing opportunities to prisoners so that they can be successfully reintroduced into society with appropriate skills and behaviour.

Despite the fact that political scientists generally overlook the role of corrections in Canadian society, prisons are highly political institutions. Debates about prisons abound. Many citizens believe that prison expenditures should be reduced. But how? Some want to privatize prisons, others seek to reduce prison sentences by encouraging law-makers to use other forms of punishment, such as heavy fines and home leaves. Others complain that early-release schemes put violent criminals back on the streets. Prisoners complain about brutality by prison guards. Corrections guards counter that prison populations are unstable and difficult to administer.

There is no agreement on how to control violent prisoners without repression and detention. Prison inmates include an extremely high proportion of disadvantaged individuals, especially Native people. How are they to be handled? Are the prisons really set up to correct behaviour that is the result of years of intolerable government handling of Native issues? Should Native people have their own justice system and methods of punishment?

The prison system is an important part of the political system. Law and order is crucial to the functioning of the Canadian democratic system, but its application is always controversial and political.

SECURITY POLICY

After the terrorist events of September 11, 2001, in the United States, the Liberal government took several steps to strengthen national security. It introduced two anti-terrorism bills, reorganized several departments, increased budgets for security for the Department of National Defence and set up new organizations to reinforce anti-terrorism and security efforts. It also announced a National Security Policy.

When the government introduced its anti-terrorism bills, they were vehemently opposed by opposition groups and civil libertarians. However, it was passed as Bill C36 in December 2001, increasing the powers of the police and law enforcement to fight terrorism by amending the *Criminal Code* and other statutes. It gave new powers of investigation and detention to law enforcement officers and made it a criminal offence to knowingly aid a banned organization. The groups that currently are banned in Canada include al Qaeda, Hamas, the Islamic Army of Aden, Lebanon's Hezbollah, Abu Sayyef (viewed as an al Qaeda affiliate and based in the Philippines), the Palestinian radical group Abu Nidal and the Sendero Luminoso (or Shining Path, a Maoist organization from Peru). (See a complete list of all banned groups in Table 9.2 on page 216.)

The second bill (Bill C42) was delayed and not passed before prorogation in September 2002. Many believed that C42 went too far in allowing the government to create new regulations without parliamentary oversight because it gave broad declaratory powers to Cabinet. After considerable controversy, it was eventually passed as C55 in February 2004 and called the *Public Safety Act*. This Act permits ministers and officials to make emergency decisions on aviation security and other emergency issues for up to seventy-two hours after a relevant event takes place.

Table 9.2 Groups Listed as Terrorist Organizations as of July 2005

1. Armed Islamic Group	15. Aum Shinrikyo	27. Babbar Khalsa
2. Salafist Group for Call and Combat	16. Hizballah	28. Babbar Khalsa International
	17. Abu Nidal Organization	29. International Sikh Youth Federation
3. Al-Jihad	18. Abu Sayyaf Group	
4. Vanguards of Conquest	19. Sendero Luminoso	30. Lashkar-e-Tayyiba
5. Al Qaeda	20. Jemaah Islamiyyah	31. Lashkar-e-Jhangvi
6. Al-Gama'a al-Islamiyya	21. Islamic Movement of Uzbekistan	32. Palestine Liberation Front
7. Al-Ittahad Al-Islam		33. Popular Front for the Liberation of Palestine
8. Islamic Army of Aden	22. Euskadi Ta Askatasuna	
9. Harakat ul-Mudjahidin	23. Al-Aqsa Martyrs' Brigade	34. Popular Front for the Liberation of Palestine — General Command
10. Asbat Al-Ansar	24. Fuerzas Armada Revolucionarias de Colombia	
11. Palestinian Islamic Jihad		35. Ansar al-Islam
12. Jaish-e-Mohammed	25. Autodefensas Unidas de Colombia	36. Gulbuddian Hekmatyar
13. Hamas		37. Kahane Chai (Koch)
14. Kurdistan Workers Party	26. Ejercito de Liberacion Nacional	38. Mujahedin-e-Khalq (MEK)

(For details on each proscribed group, see Listed Entities, posted by the Department of Public Safety and Emergency Preparedness Canada.)

Source: www.psepc-sppcc.gc.ca/national_security/counter-terrorism/entities_e.asp, Public Safety and Emergency Preparedness Canada. Accessed July 19, 2005.

In the meantime, in September 2003, the government announced that a new organization — the **Department of Public Safety and Emergency Preparedness** — would be set up to monitor national security, crisis management, emergency preparedness, border functions, corrections, policing and crime prevention. The deputy prime minister was put in charge of this department, which subsumed the old departments of the solicitor general, including the RCMP and CSIS. A new Cabinet committee on security, public health and emergencies also was set up to deal with emergency health situations such as pandemics, and a new position of national security advisor to the prime minister was established in the Privy Council Office. The new advisor also acts as deputy minister for policy for the Communications Security Establishment (CSE) discussed on page 217.

The new National Security Policy was published in *Securing an Open Society* in April 2004. It set out the government's strategy for addressing emergencies and terrorism. Declaring that the safety and security of Canadian citizens is its highest priority, it set up an intergovernmental forum on emergencies, a round table on security for ethno-cultural and religious communities and the National Security Advisory Council. The NSP addressed questions concerning intelligence, emergency management, public health, transportation, border issues and international security.[23]

The Communications Security Establishment

The **Communications Security Establisment (CSE)** was established in 1949 as part of the National Research Council to intercept the communications of clandestine organizations. It was transferred to the Department of National Defence in 1975 and put under the authority of the minister. During the Cold War, the CSE gathered secret information on the Soviet Union. It now provides secret data on security, especially terrorism, to the whole government. It collects foreign intelligence for the day-to-day assessment of foreign intentions and capabilities and shares information with the US, UK, Australia and New Zealand. Since the December 2001 anti-terrorism law came into effect, the CSE also intercepts the communications of "legitimate" governments if those communications enter or depart Canada.

A commissioner of the CSE, currently former justice Antonio Lamer, reviews the legality of CSE actions. He submits an annual report to Parliament via the minister and also provides confidential, classified reviews of the Establishment. This watchdog function is vital as the CSE must act within the law and not infringe human right privacy or the rights included in the *Charter of Rights and Freedoms*.

KEY TERMS

Canadian Security Intelligence Service (CSIS), p. 213

civil law, p. 200

Communications Security Establishment (CSE), p. 217

Corrections Canada, p. 214

criminal law, p. 200

Department of Public Safety and Emergency Preparedness, p. 216

Federal Court of Canada, p. 202

minister of public safety and emergency preparedness, p. 214

Ontario Provincial Police (OPP), p. 213

Royal Canadian Mounted Police (RCMP), p. 213

Royal Newfoundland Constabulary, p. 213

Security Intelligence Review Committee, p. 213

Supreme Court of Canada, p. 200

Sûreté du Québec (SQ), p. 213

DISCUSSION QUESTIONS

1. What are the advantages and disadvantages of an "integrated" court system?

2. In what respects has the impact of the *Charter of Rights and Freedoms* been positive? Negative?

3. If you committed a criminal offence in Ontario, what police force would be involved? In Québec? In British Columbia? Does this mean that individuals who break the law are treated differently across Canada?

4. How closely should CSIS be monitored? Explain your answer.

5. What should be the goals of prisons? Should Aboriginals have their own justice system and methods of punishment?

6. Is the government's security policy since September 11, 2001 an adequate balance of security measures and protection of individual rights given the level of terrorist threats today?

WEBLINKS

The Access to Justice Network

www.acjnet.org

Canadian Security Intelligence Service

www.csis-scrs.gc.ca

Correctional Service of Canada

www.csc-scc.gc.ca

National Parole Board

www.npb-cnlc.gc.ca/index.html

Royal Canadian Mounted Police

www.rcmp-grc.gc.ca

Solicitor General of Canada

www.sgc.gc.ca

Supreme Court of Canada

www.scc-csc.gc.ca

10 Parties and Interest Groups
Teams in the Game

Learning Objectives

After reading this chapter, you should be able to

1. Distinguish between political parties and interest groups and identify several functions each performs in the political process.

2. Describe how the Canadian party system has changed over time.

3. Explain the general structure of Canadian parties and how they are organized and financed.

4. Describe the process of electing party leaders.

5. Identify the three main target areas of interest groups and the kinds of tactics they employ to influence public policy, and explain how this might differ in majority and minority governments.

*D*emocratic politics and government, as we have seen, involve determining who will decide how scarce resources and power will be divided. Since politics is essentially a "team game," parties and interest groups are key participants in the decision process. How they function depends on the nature of the political system in which they operate.

In Canada, parties help to organize both the electorate and the government. They organize the electorate by providing a vehicle for ordinary citizens to participate in political discussions. They recruit candidates for elections, organize campaigns, educate the electorate about issues, help individual voters get their names on polling lists and generally stimulate voter participation. Parties organize the government by providing a degree of policy direction and by supplying party leaders as potential prime ministers and cabinet ministers. The winning party fuses the executive and legislative branches of government, establishing the foundation of Cabinet government.

Parties are valuable in other ways as well. They articulate, or express, interests in our society, providing a non-violent outlet for debate, dissent and pressure for change. They shape the opposition and legitimize the individuals and institutions that control political power. Parties also can be a unifying force in that they appeal to and cut across the many classes, *regions, interests and ethnic groups that make up the country. They thus encourage co-operation and compromise. Parties also provide national symbols, heroes and villains.*

Interest groups, too, influence how scarce resources will be divided. In Canada, they organize to petition and influence the government. Like parties, they operate in and help to mould the federal political system. Interest groups represent a host of interests as varied as business, agriculture, medical doctors, and even public interests such as a clean environment. Examples that students might be familiar with would include the Brewer's Association of Canada, which attempts to prevent the importation of inexpensive foreign beer, and the Canadian Federation of Students, which fights for lower university fees for students, but there are literally thousands more.

In this chapter, we examine the respective roles of parties and interest groups in the Canadian political system. We also trace the developments and changes in the parties and party system.

PARTIES AND PARTY SYSTEMS

Political parties are organizations designed to secure the power of the state for their leaders. Unlike interest groups, political parties seek to form a government in order to realize their policies or programs. In democratic systems, this is achieved through open competition in the electoral process.

The relationship among parties in a political system is called the **party system**. In order to compare the various party systems around the world, a number of classifications have been devised. For example, systems have been distinguished by whether or not they are competitive. **Competitive party systems** allow parties to compete for and have access to legislative power. Some competitive systems are **one-party dominant systems** in that a single party regularly wins almost every election, even though opposition parties function freely. Other competitive systems are **two-party systems** in which two major parties dominate and others have only minor political strength. Still other competitive systems are **multi-party systems** in which popular support is divided among several parties so that the largest party must generally form a coalition with one or more other parties to form a government. There are other ways party systems can be compared. We can also categorize them strictly by the number of active parties, so that a state can be seen as one-party, two-party, or multi-party.

Parties and the Party System in Canada

The Canadian party system is competitive, but in terms of numbers of parties, it has changed radically over time. Until the rise of third parties in 1921, when the Progressives from Western Canada won 23 percent of the federal vote, the Canadian party system was developing along the lines of a classic two-party system. From 1921 to 1993, particularly after the New Democratic Party appeared on the scene in 1961, third parties fairly consistently captured roughly a quarter of the federal vote. Between them, the Liberals, Conservatives and NDP consistently took 90 percent of the vote. Until 1993, therefore, the Canadian system fell somewhere between a two-party and a multi-party system. Because of this, Canada was often facetiously said to have a two-and-a-half-party system.

In 1993, this party system dramatically collapsed, creating what is generally seen as Canada's fourth party system. Many factors contributed to the implosion — high voter cynicism; declining public confidence in representative institutions; desire for more direct participation; rejection of consensus politics; and strong regional political interests.[1] The upshot was that the old parties failed to accommodate these forces in society, and two new parties with strong regional bases filled the vacuum. A five-party "pizza Parliament" was elected, shifting the party system further toward the multi-party end of the spectrum. The new Bloc Québécois won 49 percent of the vote in Québec and enough seats to form the Official Opposition. The Reform party got 38 percent of the vote in the West and won only two seats fewer than the Bloc. In 2004, following the amalgamation of the Canadian Alliance and the Progressive Conservatives, the number of parties in Parliament fell to four. The Bloc has kept a strong presence in Parliament. The Liberals were in power for much of the past century because their opposition was so divided.

Other key features of the Canadian party system are that it is both federal and highly regional. The federal structure means that the oldest parties have both federal and provincial organizations. Only in the Atlantic provinces are federal–provincial ties well integrated. The federal structure encourages the development of new parties at the provincial level. Some remain unique to one or to a few provinces and never move into the federal system, while others do enter the federal contest but never come close to winning power. For example, the Bloc Québécois has no intention of extending its base outside of Québec.

The regional character of the party system is very strong and tends to weaken the ability of parties to create governments that are representative of the entire country. Before 1984, general elections increasingly produced governments with great regional distortions. From 1921 to 1984, the West was mildly or severely under-represented in almost *all* government caucuses. Conversely, Québec was highly over-represented in all Liberal government caucuses during the same period. Since 1993, the West has again been poorly represented in Liberal governments.

Over the twentieth century, the Liberal party increasingly became based in Central Canada. Then, in 1984, it lost its hold on Central Canada and also did poorly in every province. On return to power in 1993, for the first time in many years, the Liberal caucus held the Maritimes and Ontario, but it did poorly in Québec (a new development) and the West (a typical result). The party's main opposition was from two new regionally based parties, the separatist Bloc Québécois and the western-based Reform party. In 1997, the Liberals almost lost their majority in the House of Commons — the Maritimes joined Québec and the West in the opposition camp. In 2000, the Liberals gained a few seats but remained basically locked out of Western Canada.

The Progressive Conservative party, generally strong in the West and excluded from Québec, produced governments with strong national mandates in 1958 under John

Diefenbaker and in 1984 and 1988 under Brian Mulroney. However, after its devastating loss in the 1993 election — in which it was reduced to two seats in the House of Commons — the PCs struggled even to exist. The Reform and Alliance parties were formed in the West and largely restricted to that region. In 2003, the PCs joined with the Canadian Alliance to form the Conservative Party of Canada, but in the 2004 election — despite winning ninety-nine seats — the newly formed party showed poorly outside of the West.

To win an election, Canadian parties must obtain substantial support from at least two and perhaps three of five main regions — the Atlantic provinces, Québec, Ontario, the Prairies and British Columbia. When severe regional imbalances occur in the party system, parties are limited in their ability to integrate interests across the country. When imbalances occur on a regular basis, as they have recently in Canada, it encourages the growth of regional parties as a protest against exclusion from the system. This in turn encourages viewpoints that are parochial rather than national and makes Canada more difficult to govern.

Historically, parties have not been able to win a majority in the House of Commons without substantial support from Québec. This is largely because, with rare exceptions, Québec has voted relatively solidly for one party. In the twentieth century, that party was most often the Liberals, but in 1993, 1997 and again in 2000 and 2004, the Bloc Québécois took most of the votes in the province. Ontario, which has the largest number of seats in the House, has tended historically to divide its votes between the two old parties, but in 1993, 1997 and 2000, it gave the Liberals almost all of the seats. In 2004, the Liberals dropped to seventy-five seats in Ontario and only twenty-one in Québec, resulting in a minority government for the Grits.

Theories about the Party System

Many ideas have been proposed to explain Canada's changing party system. The most traditional of these has been brokerage theory. **Brokerage theory** maintains that the two oldest parties in Canada have few coherent ideological interests but rather act as brokers of ideas, selecting those that have the widest appeal and the best likelihood of attracting electoral support. In brokerage theory, parties are seen as basically pragmatic and opportunistic. They act as conciliators, mediators or brokers among the regions' ethnic and linguistic groups, classes, religions, ages, and genders in Canadian society. They become agents of national integration, reconciling as many interests as possible.

As agents of compromise, parties unite Canadians. However, some political scientists maintain that brokerage activities enable parties to disguise their real ideological interests — protecting the capitalist system by emphasizing ethnic and regional concerns rather than class interests. Both the Liberal and Conservative parties are considered brokerage-type parties.

The **one-party dominant thesis** is another general theory about Canadian parties.[2] It holds that, since Canadian government is normally controlled by one party, the system is best characterized as being one-party dominant. Shortly after the beginning of the twentieth century, the Liberals took on the role of the "natural" governing party. Until 1993, the Conservatives were considered to be the "natural" opposition party because they were elected only occasionally when the public wanted an alternative to the Liberals. The general elections from 1993 to 2004 confirmed the Liberals in their role as natural governing party. The PCs had to try to reinvent themselves in the hopes of breaking their losing image by joining with the Canadian Alliance to create a new Conservative party.

As for the two smallest parties, the NDP has been called the "innovative party" — this is in reference to the fact that it never comes close to power federally but brings innovative ideas to the political game. However, since 1993, the NDP's significance has also been at risk. Possibly one could call the Bloc Québécois the "destructive" party because it seeks the break-up of Canada.

POLITICAL PARTIES IN CANADA

In Chapter 2, we discussed the major ideologies that underlie Canadian political parties — liberalism, conservatism and socialism. We saw that liberal values, based on a belief in a capitalist society, a market economy and the right to private property are dominant in Canadian society but not to the absolute exclusion of other perspectives. The main parties from Confederation until 1993 — the Conservative, Liberal and New Democratic parties — reflected the three broad ideologies but never strayed very far from the liberal opinions of the broader public.

Parties are dynamic institutions that contest for governmental power. They are based on ideologies as well as the interests and opinions of their members. To be successful in elections, party leaders must bring together these ideological foundations with the concerns of their memberships. Leaders must be able to convince party militants and supporters as well as large numbers of the general public to support them. In other words, leaders need to balance philosophical principles and the psychology of their membership while courting large numbers of voters through the techniques of mass communication.

In the next section, we outline the history and contemporary fortunes of the four major parties in order to understand the foundations of the current party system and assess its prospects.

The Liberal Party

The nucleus of the original Liberal party consisted of early reformers: the Parti Rouge (French radicals) in Lower Canada; Clear Grits from Upper Canada; and anti-Confederation Nova Scotians. Alexander Mackenzie was the first leader to bring the party to power, but it had little cohesion and was not re-elected.

The philosophical base of the Liberal party derived from British liberalism. The party was initially denied a foothold in Québec because of the antipathy of the Roman Catholic Church for liberalism in all its aspects. Then Wilfrid Laurier, a French-speaking Roman Catholic, became leader in 1887. He solidified French support behind the Liberals and created a strong national Liberal party. Laurier undermined the objections of the ultramontane (papist) clergy of Québec by demonstrating that his liberalism was neither anti-clerical nor anti-religious. He still holds the record for the longest continuous term in office as prime minister — from 1896 to 1911.

After Laurier, the Liberal party endured a decade of discontent that climaxed in bitter divisions in Québec over the Conscription Crisis. In 1919, the party elected William Lyon Mackenzie King as party leader. The Liberals won the 1921 election and King rebuilt a strong organization that dominated Canadian government for most of the next six decades. King set a record for total years in power; he was prime minister for twenty-one years and five months. During his early years in office, King astutely accommodated agrarian protest in the West by forming an alliance with the Progressives. However, as we have seen, that alliance failed and the Liberals lost their support in the West. Louis St. Laurent, who succeeded King, his successors, Lester Pearson (party leader from 1958–1968, prime minister from 1963–1968) and Pierre Trudeau (PM from 1968–79 and 1980–84), all failed to acquire support from the West; To varying degrees, they were all able to accommodate Québec's interests.

In the spring of 1984, having led his party for over sixteen years with all but nine months of those as prime minister, Pierre Trudeau resigned. John Turner took over the party leadership and called an election within days. The Liberal party won only 28 percent of the popular vote in the 1984 election, its worst showing ever. Turner stayed on as party leader, but his caucus was dispirited and fractious, dividing over important issues such as the Meech Lake Accord and the Free Trade Agreement with the United States. They lost to Mulroney's PCs again in 1988. Turner resigned and Jean Chrétien was elected party leader. Chrétien became Canada's twentieth prime minister in 1993 with massive victories in the Maritimes and Ontario as well as moderate support in the other regions.

Over the years, Canadian Liberal leaders have adopted a distinctively pragmatic approach to issues. After the Second World War, successive Liberal governments introduced important social welfare legislation and assumed more responsibility for directing the Canadian economy. In the late nineteenth century, when the Liberal party was generally in opposition in Ottawa and in government in the provinces, it was a staunch defender of provincial rights. When the Liberals held power in Ottawa, however, they gradually dropped into the position of the major opposition party or worse in the provinces and shifted to espouse strong centralizing policies. Bilingualism and a broad commitment to individual and minority rights, both linguistic and legal, were perhaps the most coherently pursued liberal policies under Trudeau, Turner and Chrétien.

When the Liberal government came to power in 1993, the need for deficit and debt reduction forced them to abandon policy positions they had supported for generations. In economic policy, trade, human rights, social programs and immigration, the party's "conservative" element began to dominate. Despite high standings in the polls, many Liberals began to feel uncomfortable with the general policy direction the party was taking. This was evident in the refusal of party veterans to vote the party line on the 1995 budget and other important legislation. The surge to the right, however, continued until after the Liberals won the 1997 election and began to talk about "opening the federal purses" again. With the deficit reduced to zero, Chrétien's ministers began to act on the

Liberal campaign promise to divide future surpluses among debt reduction, reduced taxation and new social programs. Immediately after their 2000 election victory, they announced tax reductions.

Prime Minister Chrétien called an election for November 2000, only three-and-a-half years into the Liberal government's mandate. By the fall of 2000, the government's cuts in program spending, a decline in interest rates and a growing economy had provided an unexpected budgetary surplus for three years in a row. Chrétien's electoral instincts appeared flawless. Before finishing his mandate, however, he was outmanoeuvred and forced to resign by Paul Martin and his supporters (who wanted time to consolidate their leadership before calling the next election).

Martin became Liberal leader in late 2003, but — due in large part to the presence of the newly minted and amalgamated Conservative party — in the ensuing 2004 election won only enough seats for a minority government (see Chapter 11, "Elections and Political Behaviour").

Political Profile: Paul Martin, leader of the Liberal Party

Born: 1938
Birthplace: Windsor Ontario
Education: B.A.—University of Toronto; LL.B.—University of Toronto
Profession: lawyer; executive, Power Corporation of Canada

The Conservative Party of Canada

The current Conservative Party of Canada evolved from various combinations of parties over many years.

The oldest party in a country is often the party of established interests, and this is the case in Canada. The Conservative party originated when John A. Macdonald formed a coalition of pre-Confederation groups. Its goal was to work for Confederation and then a National Policy — which basically meant encouraging national unity and developing the country by means of a national railway, industry and commerce. At first, the coalition was unstable, but gradually an organized political party was formed. It sought to maintain the British connection and establish relatively high tariffs.

The Conservatives floundered after Macdonald left the scene and the party entered its first long period in opposition. Western farmers were wary of the Tories because of their empathy for big business, and French Canadians resented their strong British affiliations. Negative French attitudes toward the Conservatives were consolidated by two events: the execution of Louis Riel and the Conscription Crisis of 1917. Yet another misfortune for the Conservatives was that they were in power during much of the Depression in the 1930s. They also suffered a lengthy leadership vacuum under Arthur Meighen and R.B. Bennett.

Western Canada exhibited no strong, single-party tradition in the pre-war period. After the First World War, westerners formed the Progressive party, which allied itself uneasily with the Liberals. In the 1940s, the Conservatives made a breakthrough by winning Progressive support in the West. They chose John Bracken from Manitoba as leader and renamed their party the Progressive Conservatives (PCs).

George Drew became leader of the PCs in 1948, but the party did not win an election until John Diefenbaker, another westerner, won a minority government for them in 1957, followed by a landslide victory the next year. Within a short time, however, Diefenbaker alienated his supporters outside the West. The Conservative defeat in 1963 deepened party factions and eventually forced Diefenbaker to retire. Divisions plagued the party as it entered its second-longest continuous period in opposition.

Easterner Robert Stanfield took over the divided party from Diefenbaker. After Stanfield lost his third and final campaign in 1974, Joe Clark assumed the leadership. This consolidated Western support, but by then, PC influence was limited to the Atlantic provinces and rural and small-town Ontario.

Clark's 1979 election victory gave the PCs their first hold on power in sixteen years, but just eight months later, their minority government was defeated on a budget vote. Clark accepted the results of the vote as a lack of confidence in the government and advised the governor general to dissolve Parliament. The party was defeated in the ensuing 1980 election and Clark lost the leadership at a bitter convention in 1983. The new leader, Brian Mulroney, forged alliances in Québec and the West. He won relatively evenly across the entire country in 1984 and again in 1988 and formed large majority governments both times.

The Reform party was founded by Preston Manning in late 1987 at the time of the first Mulroney government. It tapped into feelings of economic and political alienation in Alberta in particular and the West in general. It fielded candidates in the 1988 general election but won no seats.

In the spring of 1993, Mulroney was in such disrepute following constitutional reform failures, scandals and unpopular policies that he resigned rather than risk going to the polls again as PM. In June 1993, Kim Campbell became party leader and prime minister. She led the party into a fall election that left the PCs in ruins. Campbell lost her own seat and the party dropped from 154 MPs to only two. Two months later, she resigned. Jean Charest became leader of the party. The Progressive Conservatives retained their majority in the Senate, however, and during the thirty-fifth Parliament, their fifty-eight senators kept the party alive and functioning on Parliament Hill.

Reform, meanwhile, ran candidates in all provinces except Québec in 1993. It won fifty-two seats — not quite enough to become the Official Opposition but enough to displace the NDP and PCs to become the strongest voice of Western interests. However, apart from one seat in Ontario, it had no representation east of Manitoba. By the end of its first session in Parliament, Reform had not climbed higher than 14 percent in public opinion polls.[3]

In the 1997 election, only twenty PCs won seats in the House. Reform, meanwhile had sixty Western MPs elected. Reform formed the Official Opposition in Parliament and began to assert itself as a national party. Shortly after the election, Charest left federal politics to become leader of the Liberal Party of Québec. Former Prime Minister Joe Clark took over the tattered remnants of the PC party but did not gain a seat in the Commons until late 2000. Manning tried to link the PC and Reform parties together, or at least to run joint candidates for the next election to avoid splitting the anti-Liberal vote. Clark vigorously objected to any such co-operation. His refusal led to the creation of a new right-of-centre party in early 2000. Manning forced the creation of the Canadian Reform Conservative Alliance (the Canadian Alliance party), which linked dissident Tory groups with Reform/Alliance supporters. In the process, however, he lost the leadership of the party to Stockwell Day.

In the 2000 election, the Alliance still failed to make an electoral breakthrough in Ontario (where it garnered two seats) or further east (where it won none). The PCs, meanwhile, went into the election with a wide but scattered following that made it difficult to win many ridings. They split the vote with the Alliance party in several Ontario ridings and won only twelve seats in the House of Commons. Clark consistently refused to compromise his Progressive Conservative ideals to form a so-called united right. In 2003, Peter MacKay assumed the PC leadership. He negotiated with Stephen Harper and the Alliance to form a new party, the Conservative Party of Canada, in time to fight the 2004 general election. The union was accomplished at a quasi-national convention held at twenty-seven locations across the country. Ninety percent of Tory delegates and 96 percent of Alliance members voted for the union.

Harper was selected as leader of the new party. The merger was widely depicted as a victory for the Canadian Alliance, but it is not yet clear whether the new party platform will stabilize closer to the stand of the former Alliance or the PCs. What is clear is that the new party is better positioned to compete for government if it can put on a united face, keep national interests ahead of regional ones and become less a movement and more a political party.

Political Profile: Stephen Harper, leader of the Conservative Party of Canada

Born: 1959
Birthplace: Toronto
Education B.A.—University of Calgary; M.A. University of Calgary
Profession: economist; past president, National Citizens Coalition

The amalgamation marked the end of a forty-year struggle over who would control Canada's conservative voice in Parliament. In the 2004 election, the party held the Liberals to a minority government and came in a strong second, winning ninety-nine seats in the House. Throughout much of their long history, the Progressive Conservatives were divided over what the party stood for and MPs bitterly attacked their own leaders when they failed to win elections. It remains to be seen whether the new Conservative party can resolve these failings.

The New Democratic Party

In 1961, the New Democratic Party (NDP) was born with the same social-democratic philosophy as its precursor, the Co-operative Commonwealth Federation (CCF). Tommy Douglas, David Lewis, Ed Broadbent, Audrey McLaughlin, Alexa McDonough and Jack Layton led the party in turn, but the NDP was never able to expand its territorial base into Québec. In 1993, the party was reduced to nine seats and lost its party status in the House. Its traditional protest role in the West was usurped to a large extent by the Reform party. In October 1995, the NDP elected Alexa McDonough, formerly of the Nova Scotia legislature, and in the 1997 election, her party won twenty-one seats, mostly on the East Coast.

Political Profile: Jack Layton, leader of the New Democratic Party

Born: 1950
Birthplace: Hudson, Québec
Education: B.A.—McGill University; M.A. and Ph.D. York University
Profession: professor; founder, Green Catalyst Group Inc.

The party remained in fourth place after the 2000 election but fell from twenty-one seats to thirteen. In January 2003, Jack Layton was elected party leader. The party won nineteen seats in 2004, not quite enough to hold the balance of power but enough to give it some bargaining power with the Liberal minority government.

The NDP has played a larger role in Canadian politics than its success at the polls would indicate. Particularly in minority situations, tacit support from the NDP has often been vital for Liberal governments. The party is also considerably stronger at the provincial level than it is federally and has had a handful of premiers elected.

In general, the NDP platform has been based on diluted democratic socialist goals, advocating policies such as government regulation of the economy, including more government control of private enterprise, higher taxes for big business and industry, increased social welfare and protection from US influence.

The Bloc Québécois

Party leader Lucien Bouchard was a powerful minister in Brian Mulroney's Progressive Conservative government in May 1990 when he quit Cabinet and the party that had brought him to Ottawa. When the Meech Lake Accord died shortly thereafter, he set up a faction in the House of Commons to work for the secession of Québec from Canada. A handful of MPs joined him to create a new faction, the Bloc Québécois, which became the first separatist party to sit in Parliament. Most MPs comprising the Bloc had defected from the PC party, but two were Liberals. The Bloc went into the 1993 election with eight seats and came out with fifty-four, enough to become Her Majesty's Loyal Opposition in Parliament — by tradition, the government-in-waiting. The Bloc Québécois, however, does not want to succeed to power but to dismantle the Canadian federation and make Québec a country. It won 14 percent of the popular vote in Canada but 49 percent in Québec, where it ran all of its candidates.

Political Profile: Gilles Duceppe, leader of the Bloc Québécois

Born: 1947
Birthplace: Montréal, Québec
Education: B.A.—College Mont-St. Louis
Profession: Union Negotiator

Following the Québec referendum in October 1995, Bouchard left the Bloc to become leader of the Parti Québécois and premier of Québec. For a brief while in 1996, the reins of the party went to Michel Gauthier. By 1997, the Bloc had a new leader, Gilles Duceppe, who lacked the charismatic appeal of Bouchard but who grew into the job. In the 1997 election, his party won only 11 percent of the votes and forty-four seats in the House of Commons. In 2000, the Bloc dropped to thirty-eight seats. In 2004, after a good campaign, the Bloc won fifty-four of Québec's seventy-five seats and once again began to stress nationalist goals.

The Bloc plays only one tune — Québec interests. Its *raison d'être* is to bring the issue of Québec separation to the House of Commons and thereby assist a separatist Québec government in achieving a Yes vote in a referendum on sovereignty. The volatile situation and the role of the Bloc in Québec politics are discussed in Chapter 5, "Nationalism and Regionalism."

PARTY ORGANIZATION

Canadian parties vary in the details of their organization, but they tend to follow the same basic structure.

Party Structure

Political parties compete at both federal and provincial levels of government. However, as we have seen, parties at the two levels often act independently even though they may share the same name. The provincial Liberal party in Québec has no official affiliation with the federal Liberal party. On the other hand, a federal party may be closely allied to a provincial party even though it has a different name, like the Bloc Québécois and the Parti Québécois. A party may restrict itself to either the federal or provincial level.

At the federal level, the traditional parties consist of two wings: the **parliamentary wing**, comprised of the party leader and caucus; and a very large, three-tier **extra-parliamentary wing** comprised of the national executive, standing committees, a permanent national office, provincial associations and local constituency associations. The two wings are linked at the upper levels. Both wings are dominated by the party leader.

In the extra-parliamentary party, the **constituency** or riding is the locus of the grassroots organization of political parties. Here a locally elected executive leads the party. At this level, convention delegates are elected, candidates for federal elections are chosen and preparations are made for imminent elections. The dedication of members to this basic unit is vital to party fortunes, but at this level, there are few active members and the associations meet only infrequently, so the constituency is relatively weak within the power structure of the party.

The provincial associations generally coordinate and plan strategy and activities for implementation at the constituency level. The provincial executive has the ultimate responsibility for all federal constituencies in the province. Sometimes regional organizations exist within the provincial structures. Provincial-level organization may be shared with provincial party counterparts.

The small, permanent national office varies from party to party, but it consists essentially of a small elite that conducts business on behalf of the party as a whole. It generally includes a president, vice president and other officers as well as several executive committees. The national offices of the traditional parties function as links between the provincial organizations and the elected members of Parliament. They organize conventions, by-elections and general elections.

Party Membership

Parties want members, so they impose few restrictions on who can join. The separation of federal and provincial organizations even allows individuals to join different parties at different levels. The typical local association of a major party has between roughly three hundred and five hundred members on the books in an average non-election year but this mushrooms by 60 or 70 percent before an election when members are mobilized to find a candidate and help in the ensuing campaign.[4] Normally, members seek candidates to run, but sometimes individuals who want to be candidates recruit members to vote for them. This circumstance tends to create "instant members" who join solely to help a certain candidate win the nomination. The NDP has been most adept at keeping membership numbers up between elections and also at keeping instant members out.[5]

Men are more numerous than women as members of political parties. Once they have joined, however, women are "as likely or almost as likely as their male counterparts to participate in party activities."[6] There are not large patterns of gender difference in either extent or form of basic partisan party activities such as attending riding association meetings or contributing funds. Women are not, however, equally represented in political parties themselves, their campaign offices or national conventions. Fewer women participate in federal and provincial politics than they do in municipal politics, perhaps because of family responsibilities and financial limitations.[7] Federal parties have created special funds and taken other measures to encourage female candidates, but it has not been enough to significantly increase female candidates and MPs.

Party Leaders

A party leader is much more than "first among equals" in the party. A **party leader** is the individual chosen by party members to fulfil the pre-eminent role of decision-maker, figurehead and spokesperson in both the parliamentary and extra-parliamentary branches of the party. The party leader with majority support in the House of Commons is, of course, the prime minister. (The role of the PM is discussed in Chapter 6.) The leader is the main focus of media attention for the party, an extremely important "ambassador" who projects the ideas and abilities of the party as a potential government. The position is prestigious, carrying considerable powers in the parliamentary system.

The **leader of Her Majesty's Loyal Opposition** is the leader of the party with the second-largest number of seats in Parliament. The individual in this role spearheads the offensive against the party in power. His or her functions are not governed by statute, but the role is officially recognized in the procedures of the House of Commons. This party leader has special status at official functions, in parliamentary ceremonies and even with foreign governments. He or she also enjoys a host of minor perks, such as a car allowance and an official residence. Within the parliamentary party, the Opposition leader appoints a "shadow Cabinet," which is a government-in-waiting, but his or her position is inferior to that of the prime minister, who heads the government and public service as well as a political party.

Party Financing

Parties need money for three main purposes: to support research and advisory services for the leader and elected MPs; to maintain a small, permanent staff between elections; and most importantly to fund election campaigns. Party caucuses receive money from the government for the first of these purposes according to a House of Commons formula. To get such funds, parties must have a minimum of twelve elected members in Parliament. It is difficult for parties to operate effectively without this funding.

To supplement these funds, parties seek money outside of Parliament. The *Election Expenses Act* (1974) had a profound influence on the fundraising patterns of political parties. The new fundraising rules established in the Act made the process more open, and parties could seek both corporate and individual donations. Above all, the Act recognized parties as legal entities, thereby rendering them publicly accountable. While they benefit from this recognition, it also means that parties can be prosecuted for transgressions against the Act.

The *Election Expenses Act* was amended in a major way in 2003 by the departing Chrétien government in order to make the funding process more transparent. The changes shifted the main financing of political parties from corporate and union donations to the taxpayers.

The parties now receive quarterly allowances from public funds, based on their performance in the previous general election. For example, in 2004, Ottawa assigned $22 million in public funds to the four major parties that qualified: the Liberals, Conservatives, Bloc and NDP. (The Conservatives got the amount assigned to the PC and Alliance vote in 2000.) Every registered party that gets at least two percent of the popular vote earns annual stipends calculated by multiplying $1.75 times the number of votes received. Parties also qualify if they do not get 2 percent of the popular vote but win at least five percent of the vote in ridings where they run candidates. On the basis of its results in the 2004 election, the Green party is now eligible for funding.

To receive these funds, parties have to produce detailed financial reports, including a statement on revenue and trust funds. Similarly, they are required to file detailed returns after each election. The new rules remove the influence of unions in the NDP. They also force the Liberals and Conservatives, who in the past relied heavily on corporate donations, to cultivate more individual donations. The Bloc never got many corporate donations, so it is doing vastly better under the new system. As well, the new system gives financial incentives for parties to run in every riding and get all the votes they can. Every vote counts.

Parties have other sources of funds, but they are severely limited. *Citizens* or *permanent residents* can give a registered political party up to $5000 each year; up to $5000 per contest to the leadership contestants of a registered party; up to $5000 to a candidate in an election who is not endorsed by a registered party. *Corporations and trade unions* that operate in Canada may not make contributions to leadership contestants or registered parties; they may give up to $1000 a year to the registered electoral district associations, candidates and nomination contestants of a registered party; up to $1000 to a candidate in an election who is not endorsed by a registered party. *Unincorporated associations* may not make contributions to leadership contestants or registered parties; they may give up to $1000 each year to a registered electoral district association, nomination contestant and candidate of a registered party (with certain restrictions).

To prevent wealthy individuals from "buying" their positions, the amount a candidate, nomination contestant or leadership contestant can contribute to his or her own campaign is limited to a total of $10 000.

The *Canada Elections Act* provides detailed rules for the administration of the electoral process and the raising and spending of campaign funds. There is a ceiling on how much both national parties and candidates can spend. Election financing is discussed in the next chapter.

PARTIES AT WORK

The two wings of federal parties, the parliamentary party and the extra-parliamentary party, meet regularly for conventions designed to keep the party in touch with its *grassroots*. These are normally signified as either policy conventions or leadership conventions. The trend in recent years has been to keep leadership and policy conventions separate because of the complexity of each type.

Policy Conventions

Roughly every two years, each party holds a convention to elect party officials, debate policy resolutions and constitutional amendments and raise morale. The policy resolutions have no formal authority and are not binding on the party leadership, but they do constitute important policy guidelines. The NDP, historically, has taken its policy resolutions more seriously than have the other parties, but since 1995, it has become almost indistinguishable from the other parties in this respect. In all parties, the debates give delegates the opportunity to air their views and communicate their policy concerns to the political wing; they also attract free publicity for the parties.

Party conventions in the traditional parties are large, widely representative gatherings of several thousand delegates, most of whom have already invested considerable time and energy as executive officers for the party or as members of women's or youth associations. The Liberal party sends an equal number of delegates from each constituency to its conventions; these delegates join senators, MPs and defeated candidates among others. A number of delegates-at-large from the provinces also attend, including people who are prominent in party affairs but are not eligible to become delegates in one of the other categories. They also allow *appointed* delegates-at-large and committee members to attend their national conventions, often in the face of vociferous objections that such appointments are elitist and undemocratic. Rules for the first convention of the new Conservative Party of Canada state that ridings will be equally represented and that categories of ex-officio delegates will be named.

As a social democratic party, the NDP emphasizes the importance of the individual member. The NDP's national conventions include broad representation from Parliament, constituencies, youth groups and affiliated organizations such as trade unions and farm groups. The number of delegates from any particular constituency is based on how many members it has. This rewards active associations but does not help the party make inroads into areas where it is weak.

Party conventions clearly are not designed to be representative of Canadian society as a whole but of that party in society.[8] Delegates are much better educated and economically better off than the general population. Conventions cannot, therefore, be defended as truly representative in any strict sense. Terms such as *democratic* and *representative* are merely part of the rhetoric used by parties and commentators to generate respect and approval for their party conventions.

Before a policy convention assembles, party associations are invited to send in suggestions for consideration by the convention. In theory, the resolutions presented to the delegates are debated and passed item by item. However, in fact, the resolutions committee often determines the success of resolutions.

Party platforms have contributions from both intra- and extra-parliamentary branches of the parties; they are generally what R.M. Dawson called "conspicuously unsatisfactory documents."[9] Of necessity, items must be vague enough to carry wide appeal — examples are social reform or improved education — and so end up reading rather like a list of New Year's resolutions. They must also appeal to regional interests such as Maritime rights or economic sectors such as wheat exporters. Party platforms are therefore deliberately vague, broadly based documents of compromise that can be used to unite the party nationally. As the three traditional parties have vied for the middle ground, their policy resolutions have often overlapped.

Even after the platform is drawn up and approved by the national convention, it is little more than a guide or, as Mackenzie King was fond of stating, a "chart and compass" for the party leader to interpret and follow as deemed opportune when steering the ship of state. The party constitutions give no official status to policy resolutions emanating from the national associations.

The Reform party, more than any of the traditional parties, emphasized grassroots input into policy-making. It is not yet clear whether the new Conservative party will be closer to Reform or the more traditional Progressive Conservative pattern of policy formation. A grave shortcoming of the pragmatic policy formulation procedures followed by modern Canadian parties is that parochial concerns often dominate at the expense of a national vision. This has discouraged creative thinking about long-term policy solutions to problems, so that parties have been called "political dinosaurs" — with great weight and presence but small brains.

Leadership Conventions and Leadership Reviews

Leadership conventions provide a democratic element to parties and give them a great deal of media attention. Party leadership selection has changed dramatically over the years from a closed, elite system to a very open, broadly based, democratic one.

Until 1919, leadership selection in Canada followed the British model. Members of the parliamentary caucus and the retiring leader selected the new leader, occasionally with the advice of the governor general, and then presented the new leader to the party. The Liberal party was the first national political party in Canada to select a leader with the active participation of its extra-parliamentary wing. Open, more US-style conventions were established, gradually becoming more lavish. Modern leadership conventions are similar to policy conventions in terms of basic organization and participation, and their general rules are common to the main parties, although details vary.

The appeal of the convention method is that it gives the impression, justified or not, that the party is "open," "democratic" and "representative" in making its decisions. A drawback is that it was not designed for parliamentary government but rather for a system with separate legislative and executive offices. It was adapted to Canada's unique federal, parliamentary needs but not without inevitable contradictions. For example, leadership candidates must support their party in Parliament at the same time as they appeal for delegate support — something very difficult to do when Cabinet solidarity is at stake. A legacy of bitter feelings often makes it difficult for the new leader to command the full support of the caucus.

Modern leadership conventions are called after a leader resigns or dies and sometimes even if he or she does not score sufficiently high on a **leadership review** vote. Rules about when a leadership review will be held differ from party to party. Currently, the Liberal constitution states that:

> a resolution calling for a leadership convention shall be placed auto-
> matically on the agenda of the convention next following a general
> election. If such a resolution is duly adopted by a secret ballot the
> National Executive shall call a leadership convention to take place
> within one year . . .

In practice, leadership review votes at Liberal conventions have never called for a leadership convention, but the procedure remains a significant reminder that the leader is responsible to the party. In 1992, the Liberals approved giving *all* party members a direct say in reviewing the leader's performance after each election, thereby ending the practice of choosing delegates to vote on the leader's performance at a national convention. To avoid a potential leadership review, Jean Chrétien resigned as leader in November 2003 when it became clear that Paul Martin would be able to defeat him because of his superior strength in the constituency delegate selection committees.

In the Progressive Conservative party, the first leadership review was initiated to assess John Diefenbaker's performance in 1967.[10] Reviews later became a regular feature of party conventions. Technically, a Tory leader needed to win only 50 percent of the leadership review vote to continue in office. In 1983, however, Joe Clark resigned as PC leader after he failed to secure more than 67 percent of the voting delegates' support. He then submitted himself as a leadership candidate to consolidate his party support. At the subsequent leadership convention, the party elected Brian Mulroney. The PC party amended its review procedure at the 1983 convention to reduce the opportunities for a leadership review vote. The new Conservatives have yet to ratify their new rules.

The NDP has no leadership review procedure as such but requires its leader to seek re-election automatically at its biennial national conventions. It opens nominations for the position of leader, but if there is no challenger, no vote is required. In practice, an incumbent has never been defeated.

In all of the parties, if the leadership review vote requires it or if the current leader resigns or dies, a leadership convention is held. Traditional leadership conventions are huge events. Delegates must be chosen and the manner in which this is done has important consequences for the leadership candidates.

Canadian leadership conventions have tended to adopt the festive atmosphere of Republican or Democratic conventions in the US, with flamboyant speeches, entertainment and full national television coverage. There are some important differences, however. Balloting at US conventions is by states rather than individuals, and the votes are announced openly, making the event quite ritualistic and predictable. The US primary system and open delegate selection process tend to produce a winner long before the convention. In Canada, the secret ballot can lend a degree of suspense that is missing from the American process. However, the Liberals' selection of Paul Martin in 2003 provided no suspense because of his overwhelming lead in the numbers of grassroots delegates.

Under new rules for the 2003 Liberal leadership convention, all Liberal party members in each riding had the opportunity to vote for their preferred candidate. Each riding then sent delegates, proportional to the support garnered by each candidate, to the national convention. The delegates were required to vote at the convention according to their mandate. Martin had over 90 percent of the delegate votes assured by September so, at the November 2003 convention, there was no surprise when Martin won more than 93 percent of the ballots. By the time of the convention, only one candidate opposed him, and she (Sheila Copps) had already conceded. Controversies over the delegate selection process took some gloss from the occasion, with accusations that Martin's forces had gained overwhelming control over the party machinery and used it to set membership rules that favoured the front-runner.[11] The convention had a note of bitterness. As one candidate noted:

> It's the worst convention I've ever seen. . . . Everybody's angry. This is supposed to be about coming together, family, unity, happy happy. I get here and the big headline is "PURGE!"[12]

In spite of the controversy, or perhaps because of it, party memberships increased to record highs, even in Western Canada; by the closing date in June, the Liberals had almost double the membership of all the other parties combined.[13]

When the new Conservative Party of Canada chose Stephen Harper as leader in March 2004, it was under new rules that will not necessarily be repeated for their next leadership vote. The rules featured a new point system in which:

- a vote was held in each riding;
- each riding was weighted equally;
- each riding was worth one hundred points (i.e., 100 percent);
- in each riding a preferential ballot (single transferable vote) was used — i.e., when party members ranked their choices in order of preference, if no candidate received more than 50 percent, then the same ballots were counted again. Candidates with the lowest number of first-place choices were dropped and those ballots went to the second choices;
- candidates were assigned points based on their percentage of the vote in the riding (e.g., a candidate winning 29 percent of the vote got twenty-nine points);
- to win, a candidate had to obtain a majority of points overall.

Stephen Harper won a majority on the first ballot (see Table 10.1). It was an interesting feature of the convention rules that all ridings were weighted equally. This meant that although neither the Alliance nor the PCs had held any seats, or much support, in Québec, that province's seventy-five constituencies each got one hundred points, just the same as constituencies in Alberta which had as many as 100 000 members. Therefore, although Québec members made up only about 4 percent of the party's 275 000 members, the province had 25 percent of the weight in the race. As the only bilingual candidate, this undoubtedly strengthened Harper's position.

Rather than have delegates at a convention choose the leader, Conservative party members voted for the leader in their constituencies, while in Toronto, the three leadership candidates made final presentations that were beamed to the ridings. The results were announced from Toronto. Belinda Stronach led in Atlantic Canada and Québec while Harper won in British Columbia, the Prairie provinces and Ontario.

At its leadership convention in 2003, the NDP also opened the vote to all party members. They devised a complex system that combined member and delegate votes. All party members were eligible to vote, ranking leadership candidates in order of preference. Unions and other interest groups were allotted 25 percent of the vote. Some members voted in advance, over the internet, and did not attend the convention. The result was a small turnout of about nine hundred and less hoopla than usual. The party used a preferential one-member, one-vote, ballot system for the first time. The winner needed 50 percent plus one on the first ballot. If no candidate received 50 percent plus one, there would be more rounds of voting with the last-place candidate eliminated. Jack Layton won 53 percent on the first ballot to replace Alexa McDonough.

The Bloc Québécois, too, has made its leadership selection more democratic. Leader Lucien Bouchard was acclaimed at a party congress in 1991. Five years later, his successor, Michel Gauthier, was elected by fewer than 160 Québeckers in one of the fastest, smallest and least publicized gatherings to elect an Opposition leader in the post-war era. However, Gilles Duceppe was elected in March 1997 by the entire party membership, using the format of mailed ballots plus a two-day convention.

Leadership campaign costs have escalated dramatically in recent years. In order to keep costs low and to discourage candidates from relying on large sums of money from a few donors who hope for future considerations, leadership contestant spending was strictly regulated under the *Canada Elections Act* by June 2003 legislation. The new rules limit individual contributions to leadership contestants to $5000. No corporation or other entity may contribute funds to a leadership contestant. This should counter the general

Table 10. 1 Leadership Convention Vote, Conservative Party of Canada, March 21, 2004

1st Ballot:	Tony Clement		Stephen Harper		Belinda Stronach	
	vote	%	vote	%	vote	%
	2887	(9.4%)	17 296	(56.2%)	10 613	(34.5%)

criticism that the convention process is too expensive and allows those with the money to walk away with the prize. It is unlikely that parties will abandon conventions because of the media exposure they provide. Nor will they risk returning to earlier models of parliamentary selections that were swift and inexpensive but smacked of undemocratic elitism.

INTEREST GROUPS IN CANADA

Many Canadians who want to influence public policy prefer to do so more directly than through party activity. An alternative is to join a group that is organized to influence governments in a specific policy area. Such groups are normally called *interest groups*, or more pejoratively, *pressure groups*. The context of government, whether it is in a majority or minority situation, helps determine the kind of action interest groups can take. Minority governments are by nature fragile and vulnerable and can more easily be coerced into acting in favour of groups in order to stay in office.

Some political scientists maintain that Canadian parties are "in decline," or at least "in transition," as part of a general decline in the role of Parliament.[14] It is argued that ideological differences between the parties have broken down and other organizations such as interest groups have taken their place. Interest groups have proliferated, the theory goes, because groups prefer to bypass politicians and go directly to more knowledgeable bureaucrats and influential ministers in order to influence policy formulation. In any case, interest groups are flourishing and increasingly sophisticated. They have even usurped some of the traditional functions of parties.

We can define an **interest group** as an "organized association, which engages in activity relative to governmental decisions."[15] Interest groups are important to the practice of democratic politics. They also play an important role in the theory of liberal democracy, which holds that the struggle between individual and group self-interest produces the public good. According to **pluralist theory**, one that most interest groups espouse, there are many centres of power in society and a state's public policy reflects the conflict, co-operation and compromise of many independent interest groups. Pluralist theory considers interest groups to be relatively active and the state relatively passive in generating public policy. It makes public interest synonymous with competitive self-interest.[16]

The Nature of Interest Groups

Some interest groups are relatively transient and issue-oriented while others are institutionalized with many general as well as specific interests.

There are four prime characteristics of interest groups:

1. they have a formal structure of organization;
2. they articulate and aggregate interests;
3. they act within the political system to influence policy outputs; and
4. they seek to influence power rather than exercise the responsibility of government themselves — i.e., they do not put candidates forward in elections.[17]

Like parties, interest groups perform several important functions in liberal democracies:

- they are a major source of communication and mediation between society and government;

- they are a means of articulating opinions;

- they provide a mechanism for political representation that supplements parties and the electoral process;

- they educate governments and keep them in touch with citizens, providing a valuable link between citizens and public policy;

- they keep the government in touch with shifts of opinion in society; and

- they disseminate information by passing on explanations of government policy to their members and to government officials.

Interest groups in Canada reflect a wide range of issues and concerns. The Directory of Associations in Canada lists several thousand organizations. Because of the federal political structure of the country, most major interest groups have federated organizations. Both federal and provincial governments, for example, regulate interests in the economic sphere.

While the majority of interest groups are privately funded, a number of them, such as the Canadian Labour Congress, the Consumers' Association of Canada and Pollution Probe, are partially financed by government. Funding began in the 1970s to help social groups, such as the National Poverty Organization, that could not achieve as high a degree of access to government as established groups with good political connections. Groups that receive government money are often criticized because they receive assistance directly through grants and/or contributions, or indirectly through tax breaks, even though they may not reflect the views of the public at large. In the February 1995 budget, finance minister Paul Martin announced that the government's approach to interest group funding would change:

> Some groups will continue to be funded. . . . For others in a position to secure financial support from outside government, we will move toward a system based on the provision of matching funds. For still other groups continued funding will not be possible due to our financial situation.[18]

Interest Groups and Lobbying

The political activity of interest groups is known as lobbying. **Lobbying** is activity aimed at securing favourable policy decisions or the appointment of specific government personnel. **Lobbyists** are individuals who are paid by interest groups to influence government legislation. Governments, too, hire lobbyists and periodically call on them for advice or research. Lobbyists are useful to governments because their information enables bureaucrats and politicians to develop policies that may gain approval and possibly votes. Lobbying is, in fact, the other side of the patronage coin. The government has many lucrative contracts to give out. Both lobbying and patronage involve the use of political leverage to seek advantage for an individual, group, company or project. Some interest groups lobby on their own behalf, sending local officials or chief executive officers to argue their cases; others employ experts such as professional lobbyists, public relations firms or highly paid tax lawyers to promote their interests.

Lobbying has acquired a bad reputation in many quarters. There is nothing wrong with lobbying — at least not in principle. People who make decisions about public policy should receive as much information from the various interested parties as possible. However, lobbying becomes worrisome when special interests use money, "entertainment," cash, gifts, donations to campaign funds and so on, to cross the line between persuading politicians or bureaucrats and bribing them.

To make lobbying open and fair, Parliament has established rules to regulate it. The *Lobbyist Registration Act* of 1989 confirmed the legitimacy of lobbying and set up a registry of lobbying consultants. However, although the term *lobbying* covers any effort to interact with government on matters of policy or procurement, federal restrictions only apply when such activities are undertaken for compensation. Only paid lobbyists have to register. For this reason in particular, the 1989 regulation was not stringent enough for many observers. One lobbyist even declared that the registration rules were a farce, estimating that, at the federal level alone, roughly 100 000 people "devote a significant portion of their time trying to convince government of the rightness of their position."[19]

In 1993, the Liberal party campaigned on reforming the lobbying business. The government passed bill 43, which made some relatively minor amendments to the *Lobbyist Registration Act* in June 1995. As amended, the Act continues to divide lobbyists into two tiers — "professional" or "consultant" lobbyists and "in-house corporate and organization" lobbyists.

Tier I consists of professional lobbyists — those who, for pay, provide certain lobbying services on behalf of a client. They must 1) file a new registration form for every lobbyist-client

Table 10.2 Examples of Consultant Lobbying Firms and Their Clients, 2004

Firm	Clients
Capital Hill Group	Lockheed Martin; Loews; Canadian Tire
CFN Consultants	Lockheed Martin; Microsoft
Earnscliffe Strategy Group	Petro-Canada; Microsoft; Labatt
Global Public Affairs Inc	BP Canada; Shell Canada
GPC International	Government of Hong Kong; Labatt
Hill & Knowlton Canada Ltd	Motorola; Dow Chemical; Alcan
Sussex Strategy Group	Molson; Ontario Dental Association; Bell Canada

Source: From Industry Canada Website of Lobbyist registrations, available at http://strategis.gc.ca/lobbyist

relationship within ten days; and 2) include in every registration their own name; the name and address of their firm; name of client; name of corporate owners or subsidiaries of the client; subject matter of the lobbying effort; the class of undertaking that the lobbying is intended to influence; and the techniques that will be used, including grassroots campaigning with letter-writing and similar instruments. They must also directly name each government department (not names of individuals) or other government institutions lobbied.

Tier II consists of two types of paid lobbyists "whose job involves a 'significant' amount of government lobbying for his or her employer." These lobbyists are required to register annually or semi-annually (depending on their degree of interaction with government) and must provide the same detailed information to the registrar as first-tier lobbyists — except that they do not report on any contingency fees (which is a new requirement for "consultant" lobbyists).

In June 1995, the functions of the registrar (who monitors the Registry of Lobbyists) were subsumed in the duties of the *ethics counsellor*. The ethics counsellor submits an annual report to Parliament about the workings of the *Lobbyist Registration Act* and works with interested parties to develop a code of conduct for lobbyists. The job of the ethics counsellor is to enforce the code after it has been approved by a parliamentary committee. The penalties for non-compliance are a maximum fine of $100 000 and/or a two-year prison sentence.

Relatively minor amendments to the *Lobbyist Registration Act* were passed in June 1995. As amended, the Act continued to divide lobbyists into two tiers. Tier I included "professional" or "consultant" lobbyists; and Tier II included two defined groups, those being in-house "corporate" and in-house "organization" lobbyists — employees of corporations or interest group organizations who do lobbying as a "significant part" of their duties. The amendment also required somewhat more detailed reporting. For example, lobbyists had to identify specifics about what they were lobbying for and what departments or governmental institutions they lobbied. Contingency fees also had to be disclosed as well as their source and any government funding of the client.

In spite of these regulations, several problems remain to this day:

- Only paid lobbyists have to register — others have *no obligation* to file or disclose information. This provides a gigantic loophole for the use of contingency fees. Essentially, lobbyists who do not receive payment until *after* contacting the office-holder or bureaucrat can avoid disclosing information because they have not been paid.

- The *definition* of Tier II lobbyists is weak. It only includes someone who devotes a "significant" part of his or her duties to lobbying. A lobbyist who does not want to register can simply maintain that lobbying is not a "significant" part of his or her duties.

- Not enough information is required, especially of Tier II lobbyists. Spending *disclosure* might relieve the negative image of lobbyists. As well, the subject categories given are too vague and can be used to mislead rivals or critics.

- Interest groups do not have to file any *information* about their objectives.

- *Enforcement* is inadequate. The ethics counsellor has no power to verify the information submitted by the lobbyists. The RCMP, which enforces the *Lobbyist Registration Act*, will launch an investigation only when a complaint is raised against an individual. The *Criminal Code*'s statute of limitations on summary offences limits the ability of the RCMP to obtain prosecutions under the Act to a period of six months. By the time a complaint is made, it may be too late to punish the perpetrator.

- *Non-compliance* is a problem. Many lobbyists are reportedly still refusing to register and are getting away with it. A bureaucrat or individual being lobbied is not required to ensure that the lobbyist is registered.

- There is a strong argument that *all* lobbyists should have the same requirements. The two-tier system creates a hierarchy of lobbyists, which can lead people to infer that some individuals have the potential to be worse transgressors of the policy process than others.

Furthermore, one of the main factors behind cynicism about interest groups is that governments spend more money because of lobbying. Governments make direct payments to some groups. They also allow corporations to treat lobbying as a business expense, and some types of interest groups are allowed to register as charities and receive tax credits for charitable donations. It can be argued that a more open system would eliminate the source of public discontent. Reformers maintain, therefore, that it is in the public interest that the lobbying registration procedure provide *access* and *transparency*. Public access should be equitable, not selective or privileged, and the public should have the opportunity to know who is attempting to influence the government. The public is given the impression that lobbying in Ottawa is controlled, when in fact it is not.

Targets of Interest Group Activity

In seeking access to the political system to further their particular cause, interest groups and lobbyists in democracies focus on one or more of three main target areas: *politicians*, the *bureaucracy* and *political parties*. It is important for interest groups to use the access points provided within the political system and establish a framework for mutual consultation. Once a pattern is established, it indicates that the group has obtained recognition as the representative for its particular interests. The Canadian Council of Chief Executives has achieved recognition as the lobby for business interests and was extraordinarily successful in campaigning for the FTA and NAFTA.

Groups target different access points depending on the type of group, its resources, the type of issues involved and the circumstances of the government — whether majority or minority. Most lobbyists establish friendly relationships with legislators, bureaucrats and media, or other group contacts, in order to present their cases in informal, friendly ways.

In Parliament, access to the policy process is available through individual MPs, via the committee system or caucus and of course the Cabinet. Successful access requires knowledge of the institutional and procedural structures of government and the legislative system — such as how a bill originates and what affects its passage. The early stages of a bill are particularly important for interest groups because Parliament passes laws but rarely originates them. Legislation and expenditures are generally approved by the executive as a package. By the time a particular package reaches Parliament, the government has publicly committed itself to the policies therein, and little can be done to change the details. Some lobbies, however, have been powerful enough to delay legislation or cause it to be altered.

CLOSE-UP   The Government vs. Lobbyists in the "Smoking Wars"

Most of the lobbying tactics and strategies described here have been, and continue to be, used by pro- and anti-tobacco legislation lobby groups. On one side are the tobacco companies; on the other are various health groups such as the Canadian Medical Association (CMA) and the Non-Smokers' Rights Association. The Canadian government in some ways is the umpire between the two factions.

The "war" began in earnest in 1987–1988 over the government's Bill C51 to ban tobacco advertising and promotion. Regulating the industry was not an easy decision for the government. The tobacco industry has many influential allies; some are directors of tobacco companies or on their boards, and other allies are in Parliament itself. Tobacco companies have been generous contributors to the coffers of political parties, and governments make huge sums of money from cigarette taxes.

However, the Liberal government was determined to ban tobacco advertisements. Health groups banded together to support the bill, while the tobacco manufacturers engaged lobbyist William Neville to prevent regulation of their industry. The campaign quickly went public with newspaper advertisements and a sophisticated direct-mail campaign by both sides.

The tobacco lobby appealed to the Supreme Court of Canada and in 1995, received a ruling in its favour. The Supreme Court found the 1988 *Tobacco Products Control Act* unconstitutional because Ottawa's nearly total advertising ban violated the industry's right to free speech. Companies were allowed to put their logos and trademarks back on their promotional items and to resume all forms of advertising.

The Supreme Court did preserve Parliament's right to legislate in the matter, however. It said that the federal government should pass a new law if it wanted to restrict tobacco advertising. In late 1996, the government tabled another bill on smoking. Bill C71 was designed to give the feds sweeping powers to regulate the content of tobacco products and to severely limit advertising — including where and in what form tobacco company logos could appear on advertisements for arts and sporting events.

The tobacco CEOs and their allies made the survival of the industry a national unity issue by arguing that since most of Canada's cigarettes are made in Québec, impeding the tobacco industry would badly hurt the depressed Montréal economy. The industry also appealed to Canadian nationalism. Tobacco companies for some time had sponsored sports teams and events such as car races and arts events such as the Vancouver International Film Festival. Many of these groups depended on tobacco sponsorship and several threatened to leave Canada if the government went ahead with its policy.

The *Tobacco Act* finally was passed in 1997 with regulations that included restrictions on how tobacco is manufactured, packaged, displayed and sold. Packages must display information about the product, its emissions and the health hazards associated with it. The Act banned tobacco ads in public places and inside stores but permitted them in print publications with a "primarily adult readership." Display of brand names at cultural or sports events was limited to 10 percent of available signage. It became more difficult for young people to buy cigarettes. An amendment to the Act allowed a five-year transitional period leading to a full ban on sponsorship promotions on October 1, 2003.

While the controls achieved have been significant, as of 2003, roughly 21 percent of Canadians 15 years of age and older still smoke.

The "front line" of the war now is over regulations to prohibit cigarette packaging that displays the terms "light" or "mild." Vigorous lobbying is still taking place. The tobacco lobby has already lasted over seventeen years and is certain to continue.

Which side are you on in this ongoing debate? Does the fact that smoking-related diseases kill nearly 45 000 Canadians a year justify tough government restrictions on the industry?

Cabinet is responsible for initiating and controlling legislation, so it is a natural target for interest-group activity. In the pre-parliamentary stages of a bill, the minister preparing a new policy is responsible for gathering information from interest groups. At the same time, government secrecy requires that the groups not be informed about the government's intentions regarding decisions or policy details.

Interest groups seek access to *individual* MPs more for their long-term political influence than because the groups need immediate assistance. Unless an MP has special information or interest, he or she can be of little direct help. Sometimes, however, an MP may take up the cause of an interest group — perhaps because it is politically expedient to do so, or because the group provides information for a well-informed question or speech in the House that would earn the MP credit and recognition within party caucus.

The committee system is an attractive access point for interest groups because the purpose of committees is to gather information. When legislation is before a House committee, all interests are invited to present briefs. It is not uncommon for interest groups to have representatives on legislative committees. Some interest groups prefer to lobby Senate committees rather than House committees. Senate committees tend to handle testimony from corporations less politically than do House committees.

The bureaucracy is a significant access point in the pre-parliamentary stages of a bill because it is concerned with policy in its earliest formation. Civil servants are required by their ministers to research and evaluate policy proposals for Cabinet, give advice on the public acceptability of these policies and even to help educate and inform the public about them. Another opportunity for pressure exists again during the drafting and amendment of a bill, but this is more difficult to achieve.

Interest groups also attempt to influence parties. Political parties provide government leaders and therefore party decisions may become government policy decisions. Some interest groups, particularly labour associations, openly collaborate with specific political parties, and even affiliate with them, providing both financial and political support for the party (as the Canadian Labour Congress is affiliated with the NDP). Sometimes, however, groups do not want to be identified with one particular party in case it might harm their cause. Parties also are often wary of affiliation with specific group interests, particularly if such a connection might alienate voters. They often prefer discreet collaboration and support.

Lobbying MPs is probably least effective when the policy is already before Parliament in the form of legislation. Once it has reached this stage, legislation is more apt to be blocked or delayed than changed. The most effective form of lobbying, therefore, is generally to target key bureaucrats and ministers while policy is in the gestation stage and before it is introduced in Parliament.

To be successful, groups must be flexible enough to approach and adapt to all available access points. Often, the key to lobbying success is in the timing. If lobbyists have failed at the pre-parliamentary phase, they can try again when legislation is before the House of Commons. To be successful, lobbyists must "throw out their line everywhere," especially during general elections.

During minority governments, the channels of access for interest groups shift somewhat. The diffuse structure of minority governments makes it difficult for those in power to develop coherent programs. They must continually bargain for support. Individual MPs and opposition parties become more significant access points for interest groups because their votes are vital to the government. David Kilgour in 2005, for example, bargained hard with the government to get significant funds for victims of the genocide in Darfur.

KEY TERMS

brokerage theory, p. 222
competitive party systems, p. 220
constituency, p. 230
extra-parliamentary wing, p. 230
interest group, p. 238
leader of Her Majesty's Loyal Opposition,
    p. 231
lobbying, p. 239
lobbyists, p. 239
multi-party systems, p. 220

one-party dominant systems, p. 222
one-party dominant thesis, p. 230
parliamentary wing, p. 231
party leader, p. 231
party system, p. 220
pluralist theory, p. 238
political parties, p. 220
Tier I, p. 240
Tier II, p. 241
two-party systems, p. 220

DISCUSSION QUESTIONS

1. How would you classify the Canadian party system?

2. Which of the two schools of thought concerning ideology in Canadian political parties do you think is most accurate? Substantiate your opinion.

3. What evidence is there to support the view that Canadian political parties have shifted further to the right toward conservative values?

4. Are lobbyists sufficiently well regulated?

WEBLINKS

Bloc Québécois (French only)

www.blocquebecois.org

Canadian Federation of Students

www.cfs-fcee.ca

Canadian Labour Congress

www.clc-ctc.ca

Conservative Party of Canada

www.conservative.ca

Liberal Party of Canada

www.liberal.ca

New Democratic Party of Canada

www.ndp.ca

11

Elections and Political Behaviour
The Contests and the Messengers

Learning Objectives

After reading this chapter, you should be able to

1. Trace the origins and development of the Canadian electoral system and the general historical pattern of votes in Canada.

2. Outline the basic rules concerning how elections are called, how numbers of seats and constituency boundaries are determined, who can run and who can vote and how elections are financed.

3. Explain the strengths and weaknesses of a single-member constituency voting system and compare it to the benefits and drawbacks of a proportional representation system.

4. Explain the advantages and drawbacks of referendums.

5. Identify short-term and long-term factors that have an impact on Canadian voting patterns, and discuss their implications in the 2004 election.

6. Describe the role of the media in the political system.

*E*lections are indispensable to democratic government. They link political authorities with the public and bring together political and state institutions. They are "championship" contests that bestow power and prestige on the winners. Elections enable voters to make individual political decisions which, taken together, determine the composition of the government.

Elections enable voters to elect fellow citizens to serve for a limited time in positions of political power. They also provide a peaceful way of resolving disputes. Above all, they provide for the orderly succession of government by the transfer of authority to new rulers. Competitive elections form the crucial difference between democratic and non-democratic states. Without elections, leaders generally emerge through heredity (as in a monarchy) or by force (as in a military government).

In democracies, public opinion and the media also provide a link between politicians and the people. Politicians depend on the media to communicate with the public. They do their best to control what the public will hear and see, but they cannot do this entirely *because the media are independent of the political process. Both politicians and journalists rely heavily on being able to gauge public opinion through opinion polls.*

In this chapter, we survey Canada's electoral history up to 2004 and the rules governing these tumultuous events that determine political winners and losers. We assess whether or not our electoral system is democratic and examine recent elections and their results. The role of the media in elections is discussed in the last sections of the chapter.

FEDERAL ELECTIONS IN CANADA

Voting is the main political activity of most Canadians. General elections are exciting, ritualized events that unite the public in a common cause. For the limited time of the electoral campaign, Canadians of all regions interact as they discuss the same issues and focus on the same task. They learn about issues of national concern, examine the qualities of potential leaders and, theoretically at least, raise their focus beyond local or regional concerns. Citizens who hold strong opinions about certain issues, or who are dissatisfied with a political party or leader, have the opportunity to express their points of view publicly.

When Canadians participate in elections, they legitimize the new government that is formed. When they express confidence in the system through their participation, they provide the new leaders with the legitimacy they need to generate support and acceptance for their policy decisions. In short, by participating they help to govern Canada. As we shall see, it is therefore a matter of concern that, although virtually all Canadians 18 years of age and over are eligible to vote, a great many do not.

Electoral History

In 2004, Canada held its thirty-eighth general election. If founding father and our first Prime Minister, Sir John A. Macdonald, had been alive, he would likely have been amazed to see how elections have changed. Over time, electoral law has become much more democratic. The basic structure of the Canadian system was imported from Britain. Competitive elections were established there during the eighteenth and nineteenth centuries, even though only a small number of males were allowed to vote. As British society changed over time, the **franchise** — the right to vote — was gradually extended.

At Confederation, Canada accepted the British concept of representative government. As in Britain, voting was restricted to a chosen few — only males were enfranchised, and they had to own property. In the first two elections after Confederation, people voted orally, which meant that they were open to intimidation and bribery. Different constituencies voted on different days, which allowed the government to manipulate public opinion by calling the election in safe areas first, hoping that they could create a bandwagon effect in their favour.

A great many reforms have been made since those early days. The property requirement was gradually eliminated. In 1917, the vote was extended to women who served in the war or who were related to men fighting overseas. At the same time, however, it was also denied to Canadian citizens who had come from "enemy alien" countries. At the end of the war in 1918, the right to vote was extended to all women, and two years later, in 1920, a uniform federal franchise was established. Restrictions on Canadians of Asian ancestry were removed by 1948, but religious conscientious objectors, mainly Mennonites, who had been disenfranchised as early as 1920, did not have their voting rights restored until 1955. Inuit people first received the vote in 1950 and Native people living on reserves were enfranchised in 1960. In 1970, voting age was lowered from 21 to 18, and in 1975, British subjects who were not Canadians lost their right to vote here. As we shall see, the franchise was extended again at the time of the 1993 general election.

Are Our Elections Democratic?

Many people believe that elections in Canada could be made still more just and democratic.[1] Little remains of fraudulent election irregularities from earlier times such as multiple voting (ballot stuffing), impersonating, bribing, intimidating and either excluding real names from (false enumeration) or adding fictitious names to (padding) voters' lists. However, there are many examples of situations that are questionable from a point of view of fairness.

In spite of rhetoric about "one person, one vote," individual votes are far from equal; some count much more than others. The system makes it possible for a political party that has won a high percentage of the total vote across the country to receive absolutely no seats in Parliament, while a party that has won only a small percentage of the popular vote, but has benefited from votes clustered in a particular area, might be over-represented. In addition, although we commonly talk about the government as expressing the will of the majority, it is usual for the Canadian government to have the electoral backing of much fewer than 50 percent of all voters. If only 60 percent of eligible voters vote, and fewer than 50 percent of them vote for the winning party, this means that the government is actually chosen by less than 30 percent of the electorate.

There is considerable discussion about changing Canada's electoral system in the hopes that it could be made fairer. Proponents of change in the provinces and at the federal level point to chronic misrepresentation of voter support in legislatures throughout the country. In the past several federal elections, the second and third parties have received considerably fewer seats than was warranted by their popular vote.

THE ELECTORAL SYSTEM AND ITS RULES

The term **electoral system** refers to the means by which votes cast for candidates are translated into legislative seats. No electoral system is neutral. Each has advantages and inherent biases. As we shall see later in the chapter, the basic rule of the Canadian system is that governments are formed on the basis of the number of MPs elected to the House of Commons, regardless of the overall percentage of votes their parties achieve.

In Canada's **single-member plurality electoral system,** one member or representative is elected from each constituency. This member does not need to gain an absolute majority of votes — just more than any other candidate.

The rules concerning the conduct of elections are set down in the *Canada Elections Act*, which was first passed in 1974 and has been amended many times over the years, most recently in 2003. **Elections Canada** is a special government agency that administers elections and is responsible solely to the House of Commons, not the government.

When Are Elections Called?

The Constitution stipulates that a House of Commons can sit for no more than five years after the date of the election of its members, except in wartime emergencies. Choice of the election date is normally the prerogative of the prime minister who, as a rule, allows plenty of leeway and chooses a day several months before the government's full term of office expires. In minority governments, the PM generally loses this advantage as the opposition parties manoeuvre to defeat the government and force an election. Some countries, such as the United States and New Zealand, have fixed electoral dates in order to eliminate the advantage that such a choice gives to incumbents. Ontario has recently introduced fixed provincial election dates for the same reason.

The election is always held on a Monday unless the Monday in question is a statutory holiday, in which case it is held the next day.

How Are Numbers of Seats and Constituency Boundaries Determined?

The number of MPs overall, and how many of them come from each province, may change from one election to another. This is because the Constitution provides that these numbers will be based on population as determined by the decennial census. The *Representation Act* (1985) was passed to achieve representation by population as closely as possible, while at the same time guaranteeing the smaller provinces a minimum number of MPs.

To achieve this dual objective, four steps are followed:

1. Two hundred and eighty-two (the number of MPs in 1985 when the rules were adopted), is retained as the base number: From this, one seat is allocated to the Northwest Territories, one to Yukon, and one to Nunavut, leaving 279 seats.

2. An electoral quotient is established by dividing the total population of the ten provinces by 279.

3. This electoral quotient is divided into the population of each province to obtain the number of seats to which each is entitled. (Remainders over 0.5 are rounded to the next whole number.)

4. If the provincial seat allocations result in any province having fewer seats than it has senators, then a "senatorial clause" in the Constitution guarantees that no province has fewer members in the House of Commons than it has in the Senate; and a "grandfather clause" guarantees that no province shall have fewer seats than it had in 1976, during the thirty-third Parliament.

These four steps establish the number of seats each province will have. The seats for NWT, Yukon and Nunavut are added to this total to determine the size of the House of Commons. Part 4 of the formula ensures a gradual increase in the size of the House of Commons as the overall population increases (see Figure 11.1).

The *Electoral Boundaries Readjustment Act* (1964) and its amendments require that all constituency boundaries be examined and readjusted, if necessary, after each decennial census. For this purpose, eleven federal boundary commissions are established after each full census. Each commission has three members; a judge (designated by the chief justice of the province) and two other residents of the province (appointed by the speaker of the House of Commons).

The 2001 Census figures (in conjunction with the above rules) increased the size of the House of Commons to 308, and increased the number of seats for Ontario by three, British Columbia by two and Alberta by two. The redistribution altered boundaries in all provinces, reflecting the shift of population away from the Atlantic provinces and from rural areas into big cities.

The *Electoral Boundaries Readjustment Act* brought the readjustment of constituency boundaries under the control of independent electoral boundaries commissions, ending the unfair practice known as gerrymandering. Before the Act, readjustments had been controlled by the House of Commons, and the majority party often engaged in **gerrymandering** — wherein a party sought to take advantage of its position in government by redrawing electoral boundaries in such a way as to enable it to win more seats in the future. Gerrymandering is no longer an accepted part of the political culture and is prohibited by law.

The number of voters in any constituency is not to vary by more than 25 percent above or below the electoral quotient (see Figure 11.1) except in "extraordinary circumstances." Each electoral boundaries commission presents its initial proposals to public hearings and within a year, must table a report in the House of Commons. There, within another thirty days, the standing committee on elections and privileges reviews the report, and MPs have an opportunity to lodge objections for the commissioners to review. Parliament, however, retains the final authority to amend the Act or to delay its implementation.

Figure 11.1 Formula for Calculating Representation in the House of Commons

282 seats	−	1 NWT	−	1 Yukon	−	1 Nunavut	=	279
population of provinces	+	279					=	electoral quotient
provincial population	+	electoral quotient					=	provincial seat allocation

*The calculation starts with the 282 seats that made up the House of Commons in 1985.

Who Can Run and Who Can Vote?

Virtually any elector can become a candidate (except persons convicted of certain crimes, mental patients and those holding certain public offices or appointments). All that is necessary is to file nomination papers, including the signatures of one hundred other electors, and deposit $1000 with a returning officer. However, since very few independent candidates win, most seek official party endorsement.

In light of the *Charter of Rights and Freedoms*, which states that every citizen of Canada has democratic rights "subject only to such reasonable limits prescribed by law as can be demonstrably justified in a free and democratic society," the government decided to amend the *Canada Elections Act*. In 1993, a bill was passed removing a few remaining electoral disqualifications for specific groups — including judges, persons who are "restrained of their liberty of movement or deprived of the management of their property by reason of mental disease" and inmates serving sentences of less than two years in a correctional institution. New mechanisms were also established to allow Canadian citizens to vote if they are absent from Canada at election time. The only persons still specifically prohibited from voting include the chief electoral officer (CEO), the assistant electoral officer, returning officers in each riding, inmates of penal institutions serving a sentence of more than two years and individuals disqualified by law for corrupt or illegal practices.

Who Pays for Elections?

Elections are very expensive. They are funded largely by taxpayers and political parties. Tax dollars pay for drawing up voters' lists and running the election. The tax system also allows taxpayers to obtain a deduction for contributions to political parties so that, in a sense, every taxpayer contributes to the democratic process because the money has to come from the public coffers. Political parties and individual candidates pay many election bills from donations and fundraising, but they also get substantial refunds from the government — in other words, from the taxpayer.

The rising cost of financing general election campaigns raises questions about the degree and fairness of political competitiveness. Does the expense hinder or exclude individuals, groups and parties from active involvement in the election process? The *Election Expenses Act* of 1974 represented an important attempt to address such questions. For the first time, federal candidates were required to give a detailed accounting of money received and spent. They were also compelled to observe spending limits, and candidates who received 15 percent of the votes were eligible for subsidies from government funds.

The *Election Expenses Act* requires parties to provide audited financial statements in order to expose fundraising practices and election expenses to public scrutiny. Six months after the end of the party's fiscal year, an audited return containing a detailed statement of the party's contributions and operating expenses must be sent to the chief electoral officer. Candidates are also required to file detailed, audited returns after each general or by-election. These are public documents and are thus available for scrutiny. In order to prevent outside interference in elections, a 1993 amendment to the *Canada Elections Act* prohibited contributions to a candidate from sources outside the country.[2]

The 2003 amendment to the *Election Expenses Act* made other changes. Every registered party is limited in the amount it can spend for an election. The formula for deciding how much it can spend is based on multiplying seventy cents by the number of names on the preliminary list of electors for electoral districts in which the registered party has endorsed a candidate, or by the number of names on the revised list of electors for those electoral districts, whichever is greater. There is also an inflation adjustment factor. A new allowable electoral expense for a registered party is the cost of election surveys or research during an election period. Spending limits also apply to candidates in an election campaign. The limits vary according to the number of electors in a constituency.[3]

Recently there have also been major changes in the funding of elections. Corporations and trade unions are banned from donating to parties and leadership candidates. Individuals may give up to $5000 a year to a registered party, its riding associations, nomination contestants and candidates. Contributors are named publicly if they donate more than $200 to a party or candidate, and parties and candidates have to disclose the addresses as well as the names of donors. Individuals making contributions up to $500 may claim a tax credit (the 2003 amendment also changed the *Income Tax Act* to allow higher income tax credits for political contributions by an individual). Each national party must file a detailed expenditure and revenue report within six months of the end of its fiscal year. Each also must submit to the Department of National Revenue an annual report of contributions received and income tax receipts issued.

If they comply with requirements concerning the filing of a tax return for election expenses, and if they spend at least 10 percent of an expense ceiling as determined by Elections Canada, registered parties are reimbursed 60 percent of their total national expenditures. They are also refunded for half the costs they incur in the purchase of permitted radio and television advertising time. Individual candidates, too, receive refunds from Elections Canada. Those who garner at least 15 percent of the valid votes cast in their electoral district are refunded their $1000 deposit and reimbursed by the receiver-general of Canada for 50 percent of their election expenses.

KEY ELECTORAL PARTICIPANTS: PLAYERS, REFEREES AND COACHES

Many individuals and groups play a role in general elections. Some, like candidates for election, are easily distinguishable as players. Others, like the media, seem to seek a dual role as both players and referees.

> *If you have good players on the ice, it's*
> *because you have a coach who knows the game.*
>
> Jean Chrétien

The Prime Minister and Cabinet

The prime minister decides when to call an election and advises the governor general on the dissolution of Parliament. *Dissolution*, as we have seen, is the formal ending of the life of a particular Parliament. Occasionally, when the government is defeated in a "vote of confidence" in the House of Commons, the prime minister loses this prerogative. In such a case, the prime minister may be forced to advise the governor general to dissolve Parliament before he or she would wish to do so. Once Parliament is dissolved, the members of Parliament are regular citizens once again and an election must be held.

Following dissolution, the government, through the governor general, formally instructs the chief electoral officer to issue writs of election to each constituency. A **writ** is a document commanding that an election be held, giving the date of the election, the date by which nominations must be received and the date by which results must be finalized. The Cabinet continues to govern until the new House of Commons is elected.

The Chief Electoral Officer and the Electoral Commissions

The **chief electoral officer (CEO)** is a permanent public employee appointed by the Cabinet to head Elections Canada (an agency that is responsible only to the House of Commons). CEOs hold office "on good behaviour," meaning that they may be dismissed before retirement age only by Parliament. This ensures that the CEO can be completely impartial in the administration of elections. The current CEO is Jean-Pierre Kingsley.

In preparation for an election call, the CEO informs the electoral commissions how many seats will be allotted to each province and provides electoral boundary maps.

Returning Officers, Candidates, Leaders, Parties and Voters

Returning officers have a significant role in activating the formal election machinery. They are officially appointed for each constituency by the CEO, although the appointments are normally the result of party patronage. It is common, however, for competent officers to retain their position even though the party in power changes.

Prospective candidates need not have the backing of a political party or even reside in the constituency they would like to represent. However, as we have said, it is extremely difficult to be elected without party endorsement, and candidates normally run in their home constituency. Local party organizations generally take the initiative in candidate recruitment by organizing delegate conventions. It is an opportunity to recruit new members and raise money.

The *Canada Elections Act* gives party leaders a veto over their party's candidates, but only in exceptional cases, do they interfere with local nominations. A statement signed by the party leader or a designated representative confirming the party's endorsement must be filed with a candidate's nomination papers. The ability to withhold endorsement is a significant sanction. During the thirty-fifth Parliament, Prime Minister Jean Chrétien threatened backbenchers who dissented from the party line on the gun control legislation and other issues that he might not endorse them for the next election.

All parties must be registered by the chief electoral officer. Recognized parties and their candidates receive partial compensation for electoral expenses. In turn, the parties assume certain legal responsibilities. Official agents of the parties and candidates keep track of and report all revenues and expenses incurred following the issuance of writs for an election.

Parties provide much of the organization for elections. When an election is called, the national headquarters of the largest parties become nerve centres of nationwide campaigns. Party advisors plan strategy, collect public opinion data, coordinate meetings and tours of party leaders, issue literature, arrange broadcasts, employ public relations firms, issue news releases and so on. Party advisors include media specialists, advertising personnel, public relations experts and public opinion pollsters. They have two focuses during an election campaign: the national campaign, where the aim is to elect the party; and 308 separate constituency campaigns, where the aim is to elect individual candidates.

Once a party candidate is selected in a given constituency, the party helps prepare for the campaign. A campaign committee is established and quickly broken down into subcommittees responsible for jobs such as fundraising, advertising, canvassing, etc. The candidate must hire a campaign manager and if one cannot be found locally, the party can usually assist. Party headquarters supplies literature, guidance, and most of all a recognizable label, which gives the candidate immediate recognition as well as association with a (hopefully popular) party leader. Party volunteers phone constituents, distribute literature, organize babysitting and coordinate rides to and from the polling booths on election day. Party leaders have the paramount role in the national campaign. They are the focus of intensive media attention, and their image impacts greatly on the election results.

ELECTORAL STAGES: FROM DISSOLUTION TO A NEW GOVERNMENT

Electoral Preparations and the Campaign

An election call initiates a frenetic scramble at the upper levels of each party, as each endeavours to ensure that the best possible selection of candidates is in place; that sufficient funds are at hand; that platforms and literature are ready; and that campaign organizers and strategists are appointed and prepared to begin directing the campaign.

At the constituency level, as soon as the election is announced, the returning officers appoint assistants at each poll from lists supplied by the incumbent party. These temporary positions include deputy returning officers who administer the polls and a poll clerk at each poll. The returning officer assigns voting venues for each poll, generally a public building such as a school.

When candidates are nominated, the returning officer has ballots printed, listing the candidates in alphabetical order and showing party affiliation. Candidates not representing a registered party are listed as independents unless they request to show no designation.

Elections Canada produces a permanent voters list (used for the first time in 2000). For those who have to be away from their constituency on polling day, including ordinary citizens, members of the armed forces and diplomatic personnel, the returning officer must arrange an advance poll and then forward the ballots to the chief electoral officer.

Campaigns are the visible part of elections. Compared to the Unites States where elections take well over a year, campaigns are very short. From the issuing of the writ to the closing of the polls, Canadian elections last a minimum of thirty-six days. During that time, voters are bombarded with party and candidate literature, advertising, debates and daily news reports about leaders. The authors of a comprehensive analysis of the data yielded by the 1988 National Election Study argue that campaigns do indeed matter. In that election, the major issue was Free Trade, and the study by Johnston et al. shows that opinion on this issue, as well as voting intentions, changed considerably during the campaign.[4]

At the national level, experts are carrying out and constantly monitoring and revising their overall campaign strategies. In what geographical areas does a party have a great chance of winning? Where is there little chance? What issues would it be most advantageous to stress? How should financial and other resources be allocated? Party campaign strategists must answer these and many other such questions.

At the constituency level, candidates are busy with speeches, door-to-door canvassing, coffee parties and media appearances as they attempt to retain traditional party supporters and attract as many undecided and opponent votes as possible. Analysis and targeting of the various voting groups in the constituency is essential.

The Vote

On election day, the balloting is overseen at each polling station by deputy returning officers and their clerks and each candidate is allowed two. The voter identifies himself or herself to the polling clerk, who has a list of eligible voters for that polling station and gives the voter an official, bilingual ballot.

Voters mark their ballot in a private booth and place it in the box. When the polling booth closes, the deputy returning officer, with the polling clerk and scrutineers, counts the ballots, seals them in the box and delivers them to the returning officer. An unofficial result is made public shortly after balloting is closed. The official count by the returning officer is not made until later, in some cases not for several days when the overseas vote is in. A recount is automatically requested by the returning officer if the difference between the first and second candidates is less than one-thousandth of the ballots cast. In the very rare event of a tie vote, the returning officer casts the deciding ballot.

THE NET WORTH OF A VOTE: DOES CANADA NEED A NEW ELECTORAL SYSTEM?

History shows that Canadians have long been preoccupied with achieving "rep by pop," a situation in which the size of the population of a given area is represented proportionally in the legislature. However, this quest for one vote for each person, with each vote counting the same, has not been achieved perfectly because of compromises in the field of redistribution and the impact of the single-member plurality system itself.

In an attempt to preserve electoral equality in terms of representation by population, the electoral boundaries commission in each province tries to ensure that the constituency boundaries follow the established boundaries of cities, towns and counties. Rural and northern constituencies are thinly populated, however, and to allocate them the same number of voters as in the cities or towns would make them geographically huge and unmanageable. As a result, these constituencies are generally larger with smaller populations than their urban counterparts, so that individual votes here count more than in a more densely populated area.

Similarly, as we have seen above, the electoral weight of sparsely populated provinces is protected by rules that distort the general rule of representation by population. An individual's vote in Prince Edward Island has considerably more weight than one in Ontario, for example. The rule that boundaries must be redrawn after every major census (every ten years) is meant to keep the value of votes relatively similar by adjusting for major population shifts. However, legislation is not always passed in time for the next general election after a census.

One of the big advantages of a single-member plurality system like Canada's is that it is simple to comprehend and to administer. The individual who gets the most votes in a given constituency simply wins that seat. On the whole, but not always, this type of electoral system tends to produce more stable, majoritarian governments than do other types. However, there are disadvantages associated with it. The most significant drawback is that party seat allocation in the House of Commons is not determined by percentage share of the popular vote. If the electorate votes in a similar fashion across the country, there is an arithmetic tendency to favour the two largest parties, with an additional "bonus" of seats for the larger one; and, conversely, a tendency to under-represent third or minor parties, especially those whose support is spread fairly evenly but thinly across the country. As a consequence, Canada's electoral system is often said to favour the development or maintenance of one dominant party. Of course, when there is a maldistribution of the votes across the regions, it may easily result in a multi-party system in this type of system.

According to French political scientist Maurice Duverger, there are two reasons why a single-member plurality system tends to reward the party that comes first with more seats than it deserves and the second and following parties with fewer seats.[5] First, an arithmetical consequence rewards the party that gets the largest share of the vote with more seats. The only exception to this general rule occurs when a minor party has its support strongly concentrated in a particular region. Second, according to Duverger, voters who might otherwise support a minor party tend to refrain from voting for it for fear of "wasting" their votes — casting votes that have no effect on the election of individual representatives or on the formation of a government. Thus, Duverger suggested that the association between the plurality electoral formula and the two-party system is close to being a "true sociological law."[6]

In 1993, the Liberals won 177 seats (60 percent) with only 41 percent of the vote. The Progressive Conservatives were reduced to two seats even though they had won 16 percent of the vote. It took roughly 31 320 votes to elect a Liberal but more than one million to elect a Conservative!

In 1997, the PC and Reform parties each won 19 percent of the vote but Reform got sixty seats, the Tories only twenty. The Bloc got forty-four seats with 11 percent of the national vote. Again in 2000, the BQ took thirty-eight seats with just 11 percent of the vote, while the PCs got only twelve seats from 12 percent of the vote (see Table 11.1). A party with a wide but scattered following, such as the Tories had in 1993, 1997 and 2000, is severely disadvantaged by the electoral system compared to a party with support totally concentrated geographically, like the Bloc Québécois.

The type of electoral system has an impact on the formation of governments. The plurality formula favours the development of a two-party or one dominant party system, resulting in relatively stable governments. Most of the time, these governments enjoy majority support in Parliament, although minority governments occasionally occur, especially when parties become strongly regionally based. This means that Cabinets are based on one party, and that fact promotes stable, responsible government. Voters know which party to hold responsible for laws and policies and can either vote for it or vote to "throw the rascals out" at the next electoral opportunity.

Some other countries have chosen to forego such a simple electoral process in order to achieve more voter equality. They place a high premium on the concept of equal "representation," in that their electoral systems are designed to ensure that all significant shades of public opinion are represented in Parliament. One such system is known as **proportional representation (PR)** — an electoral system that attempts to ensure that parties receive representation in Parliament in proportion to their respective shares of the popular vote.[7] There are many varieties of PR. One of the most frequently suggested electoral reforms in Canada is to change to some kind of a PR system.

However, the general problem with PR systems is that they tend to promote multiple parties, and multi-party systems may in turn give rise to extremist or narrow-interest parties because they can easily win enough votes across a whole country to gain some

Table 11.1 How Votes Translated into Seats in the 2004 Election, and How They Would Have Translated in a Pure PR Ssytem

	Popular Vote (%)	Seats Won under the Current Single-Member Plurality System	Seats That Would Have Been Won under Pure PR*
Liberal	36.7	135	113
Conservative	29.6	99	91
Bloc	12.4	54	38
NDP	15.7	19	48
Greens	4.3	0	13
Other	1.4	1	4

* PR Numbers do not add to 308 due to statistical rounding.

Source: Elections Canada. Election data available at http://enr.elections.ca/National_e.aspx

seats. Generally in PR systems, no party wins a majority of seats, so Cabinets are based on fragile coalitions. This promotes Cabinet instability and increases the possibility of governmental problems and constant elections. With a coalition Cabinet, voters do not know which party to hold responsible. Nor do they have an opportunity to vote for or against specific would-be coalitions.

To a large extent, *representation* and *governing* are competing and contradictory principles. Democracy requires an acceptance of *both* of these principles. Obviously, the people need to be represented in a democracy in some form or other. Equally, democracy requires a government that can produce coherent policies to be judged by the electorate. It may be impossible to have perfection in both areas at once. Even "perfect" representation of every group in society would have no benefit if it produced fractious, unstable governments based on ever-changing coalitions.

In the 2004 election, the Liberals obtained twenty-two seats more than they would have if the country had had a pure proportional system of representation. The Conservatives received eight seats more, and the Bloc sixteen seats more, than they would have deserved under PR rules. On the other hand, the NDP lost twenty-nine seats because of the current electoral system and seventeen members would have been elected to various other smaller parties if Canada had had pure proportional representation. In other words, a pure PR system would have given Canada an even more highly fractured party system than it possesses with the present electoral set-up.

The adoption of PR requires other specific political conditions in order to achieve stable government. Such conditions are rare. Stable governments elected by versions of PR do exist, but they require conditions such as a relatively small geographical area to administer and a form of coalition spirit found only in what are called *consociational democracies*.[8] The cultural and procedural consensus required to make governments effective in countries with PR has been well documented. The few European countries with PR and stable governments are the exception. New Zealand is often held up as a positive example of PR, but its recent history is a mixed bag, with its relatively new PR system having produced both stable and unstable governments.

Advocates who wish to reform the electoral system generally present electoral systems that combine the advantages and disadvantages of PR and the single-member constituency system.[9] In 2004, the Law Commission of Canada produced a report that called for a mixed-member proportional electoral system. Such a system provides dual forms of representation — some members are elected in single-member constituencies and others by a proportional representation system. Such mixed member systems are used in New Zealand, Germany and in regional elections in Scotland and Wales. Citizens can vote for the same party or split their tickets, that is, vote for a candidate of one party in the riding and yet choose a member of another party in the proportional representation system. The Law Commission recommended that two-thirds of the members of the House of Commons should be elected in constituencies using the first-past-the-post method, and the remaining one-third should be elected from provincial or territorial party lists. In addition, they said one list seat each should be allotted to the three territories.[10]

The system, as proposed, is unlikely to receive the support of federal parties — especially the Liberals. It would reduce the chances of majority governments being elected and threaten the integrity of the responsible Cabinet system. Canada does not possess many of the components of the few countries that have adopted PR successfully, so the trade-off of stable government for better representation could have severe repercussions that have not yet been adequately considered.

Another distortion in the value of an individual vote is caused by low voter turnout. The 2004 turnout was the lowest ever, 60.5 percent (down from 64.1 percent in 2000).[11] The fewer people who vote, the greater the likelihood of distortion between the kind of government the people want and what they actually get. For example, in 2000, because turnout was so low, only about 41 percent of the votes cast (or about 25 percent of registered voters) chose the Liberal party, but it was enough to give it a large majority.

In some countries, such as Australia, this argument convinced leaders to instigate compulsory voting. If everyone turned out to vote, it was argued, then whatever the result, the government's laws and decisions would thus carry more legitimacy and be binding on the whole community.

The argument against compulsory voting, of course, is that citizens should have the right *not* to vote. As well, election results could be determined by the votes of those with no knowledge or interest in the political issues at stake. In Australia, many electors who are forced to vote simply cast their ballot for the first name on the list — a so-called "donkey" vote.

BY-ELECTIONS

A **by-election** is an election held in a constituency to fill a legislative seat that has fallen vacant between general elections. Within six months of the date at which the speaker issues the notification warrant acknowledging the vacancy, the prime minister may name any date he or she chooses. By-elections may be held soon after a vacancy appears, a year or more later, or not at all if the writs for a general election are issued before the by-election takes place. The prime minister and his or her advisors are not anxious to call a by-election if they believe the result will be perceived as unfavourable, a hesitancy that is reinforced by the tendency of governments often to be defeated in many by-elections. Usually a by-election is called because an MP dies or resigns, but occasionally, an MP will be asked to resign in order to allow another individual to win a seat.

REFERENDUMS

A **referendum** is a means by which a policy question is submitted directly to the electorate for a decision rather than being decided exclusively by elected representatives. Around the world, some referendums are merely consultative, providing a kind of official public opinion poll on an issue in order to guide politicians. Others are binding in that the government must follow the majority decision the referendum provides. Still others are essentially instruments of ratification, the final seal of approval on a course of action adopted by a law-making institution; for example, where proposed constitutional amendments must be ratified by the electorate, as in Australia.

Most countries use referendums with extreme caution and only in specific circumstances because there are many problems associated with them. Arguments for and against can be summarized as follows:

Arguments for:

- they represent a form of direct democracy;
- widespread consultation increases the legitimacy of political decisions.

Arguments against:

- they detract from the sovereignty of Parliament, downgrading its importance as a sovereign law-making body;
- they can be extremely divisive because they divide the electorate into winners and losers, and this can have severe negative impacts when the division is along regional or ethnic lines;
- they require a Yes or No answer to sophisticated and complex questions and do not allow for any compromise solution;
- citizens are relatively uninformed to make decisions, especially on technical or legal matters;
- it is not feasible to consult citizens on every issue that might be regarded as fundamental;
- often they do not offer a meaningful choice but are merely symbolic.

Although there have been several referendums at the provincial level in Canada, only three have been held at the national level, all of which were of the consultative type. The first was held in 1898 when the federal government was contemplating the prohibition of alcohol. Although a small majority voted in favour of prohibition (51 percent), there was a very low turnout (44 percent) and Prime Minister Wilfrid Laurier did not believe that the level of support was strong enough to go ahead with the plan.

The second national referendum was called during the Conscription Crisis of 1942. Prime Minister Mackenzie King proceeded with conscription only after a referendum that asked the people whether the federal government could overturn its previous electoral pledge not to institute a draft. The referendum received the support of 65 percent of the voters. Québec, however, voted heavily against conscription (71 percent), thus exacerbating relations between English and French Canadians. King delayed conscription to reduce the potential impact of the issue (see Chapter 5).

The third and most recent referendum was on the Charlottetown Accord in 1992. In the end, 54.4 percent voted against the agreement and 44.6 percent for it, a result that represented a humiliating defeat for Prime Minister Brian Mulroney. It set the stage for his retirement and the massive defeat of the Progressive Conservative party in 1993.

ELECTORAL BEHAVIOUR: VOTING PATTERNS IN CANADA

Political scientists study the details of Canadian elections in order to analyze what motivates people to participate in them and why elections turn out as they do.

Voters and Non-Voters

In the 2004 election, barely more than 60 percent of registered voters bothered to cast their ballots. This was *despite* an $11 million campaign by Elections Canada to encourage voting; a tight race; stories of political scandal and warnings of a hidden agenda. Voter turnout has gradually slid to the low 60s from nearly 80 percent a couple of generations ago. Given that the voting list can miss up to about 10 percent of eligible voters, the actual percentage of eligible voters casting their ballots could be as low as the mid-50s.

Why Do Canadians Not Vote?

The drop in voter turnout is worrying to many, especially those who blame poor turnout on increased cynicism about elections,

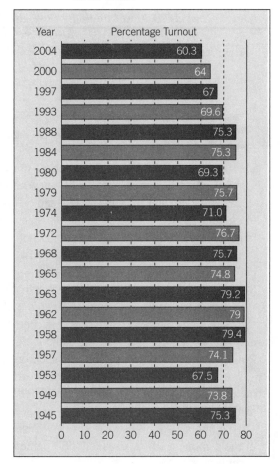

Figure 11.2 Voter Turnout, Federal Elections, 1945–2004

Year	Percentage Turnout
2004	60.3
2000	64
1997	67
1993	69.6
1988	75.3
1984	75.3
1980	69.3
1979	75.7
1974	71.0
1972	76.7
1968	75.7
1965	74.8
1963	79.2
1962	79
1958	79.4
1957	74.1
1953	67.5
1949	73.8
1945	75.3

Source: Elections Canada.

governments, politicians and elected officials. Many are particularly concerned with the lack of interest and participation among Canadian youth. To this end, proposals abound about how to reduce the democratic deficit and provide more incentive to participate.

Why is voter turnout so low? Did government waste and negative campaigning affect the public? Perhaps demographics played a role. The generations who grew up in the Depression found politics central to their lives. They paid more attention to politics and valued voting more. Many people today just don't care about electoral democracy. When asked why they do not vote, some say because they are bored by politics or their vote doesn't matter because we now live in a one-party state. Others feel the Charter means that judges now make policy and define the rights of citizens. Some prefer the excitement of working with an interest group. Still others blame the "negativity" of the media. Professor Anthony Sayers of Calgary attributes much of the apathy to a culture that is motivated more by self-interest than by sense of duty and community-mindedness.[12]

> *Only a very small group of men control the political system. The rest of us are low in the caste system. They try to make us feel as if we're important, but we are not.*
>
> *A non-voter, Toronto riding of York West*

CLOSE-UP   Why Do Young People Not Vote?*

Election studies indicate that much of the decline in voter turnout since the 1988 election has been because the new generation of voters is not turning out to cast a ballot. Just 25 percent of eligible 18–24 year olds participated in 2000, more than 35 percentage points lower than the average turnout. The decline has largely been confined to those who had not completed a university education.

In fact, it may be that a diminished sense of duty combined with ignorance was behind the dismal youth turnout.[2] In 2004, respondents to the National Election Study who were in their twenties indicated that they were relatively satisfied with the way democracy works in Canada: 63 percent of them said they were at least fairly satisfied. Many, however, were skeptical. One in two thought political parties hardly ever kept their promises. They indicated more disengagement than discontent. Only 20 percent were very angry about the sponsorship scandal.

Perhaps most revealing was evidence that these young people were badly informed. During the first ten days of the campaign, only 38 percent of the youth sampled in the National Election Survey knew that Paul Martin led the Liberals. The numbers were even worse for the Conservative, NDP and Bloc leaders. Even in the campaign's final days, only 60 percent could name Paul Martin as Liberal party leader.[3]

There were issues in the campaign that should have interested young people, but few paid enough attention to know about them. They said they considered health care to be the most important issue, but only 29 percent knew that the Liberals were promising to spend $4 billion to reduce waiting times for surgery. When asked which party would be best at dealing with their number one issue, 35 percent said they didn't know.[4]

Why do you think young people find Canadian politics boring?

The National Election Study, The Globe and Mail, August 4, 2004. Also see Anatomy of a Liberal Victory, Chapter 3.

Meaningful generalizations about political participation — why people vote or not — are difficult to make with precision. However, some studies have given some clues as to what motivates people to cast a ballot. One aggregate-level study of turnout levels concluded that the most important determinants of voter turnout are regional and socio-economic. The strongest predictive variables in the study were residential stability and economic affluence.[13] There is little doubt that socio-economic factors are significant in motivating political participation. The poor and uneducated are much less apt to vote than are individuals with higher income levels and college educations. The wealthy may feel they have more at stake in an election outcome, and more highly educated people are generally better informed and more interested in political issues. Workers at the lower end of the socio-economic spectrum tend to be preoccupied with factors of survival and have a low feeling of efficacy. Those at the other end of the spectrum are more apt to believe that they can further their own and society's interests by electing the right candidate.

Other factors undoubtedly are involved in voter participation. Voter turnout in Canada is highest in the middle-age range; the youngest and the oldest voters tend to abstain most. Men cast their vote slightly more often than women. On the other hand, studies have found no significant difference between ethnic groups in terms of whether or not they vote, and levels of participation have also been discovered to be roughly similar in the various regions across the country.

When Jerome Black examined Canadian voter turnout from a comparative perspective, analyzing voting in eighteen countries, he concluded that participation in Canada consistently ranks in the lower quartile of democratic nations.[14] In fact, voter turnout is always highest when it is compulsory. As mentioned, Australia has implemented compulsory voting and almost all citizens cast a ballot. Should Canada adopt compulsory voting and assign penalties for not voting?

Short- and Long-Term Factors

Factors that influence *how* Canadians vote can be grouped loosely into long-term and short-term factors. Long-term factors contribute to an individual's basic *party identification* with a political party. They include socio-economic indicators such as class, religion, gender and ethnicity, urban–rural distinctions and so on. Short-term factors arise from the specifics of election campaigns, including issues, leaders, candidates, debates, polls and media coverage.

Long-term factors begin early in life, as attitudes toward politics and political parties are acquired through socialization and social group factors. These factors influence one's political ideas, party identification and voting intentions to varying degrees. Long before an election campaign starts, some individuals may have acquired a degree of party identification. However, this is far from universal. A study of the 1988 federal election showed that 35 percent of the electorate had no party identification at all (larger than the 23 percent, on average, reported by previous studies).[15]

Short-term factors take effect during the campaign, making impacts on voters that confirm or change the effect of long-term factors.[16] Two short-term factors in particular have been significant in recent elections: leadership and issues. These, of course, change from one election to another. At the expense of long-term factors, changing technology, campaign strategies and the media, especially television, have increased the impact of short-term factors on voting in recent years.[17]

Of the long-term factors, region and ethnicity are the most significant — and in Canada, religion is closely tied to ethnicity. Class has rarely proven very significant.

Region: People in specific areas of the country have traditionally supported one party over others and shifted their allegiance only periodically, and in unusual circumstances. However, as a long-term factor, region has shown wide variations over time. Québec, for example, voted massively Liberal in the twentieth century from the days of Laurier until 1984. However, aberrations in this pattern occurred, first with the severe defeat of the Liberals by the Progressive Conservatives under Diefenbaker in 1958 and then again by Brian Mulroney's Tories in 1984 and 1988. From 1993 to 2004, it was the Bloc Québécois that defeated the Liberals in Québec.

The Prairie provinces and British Columbia voted heavily Progressive Conservative in federal elections from about 1957 to 1993 when they switched their support — largely to the new, populist Reform party, which became the Canadian Alliance. British Columbia, Saskatchewan and Manitoba also have a history of periodic support for the NDP. The Prairie provinces have a tradition of supporting protest parties. The region gave rise to the Progressives, the CCF/NDP and more recently Reform/Alliance. In 1997, the West as a whole gave Reform 60 seats out of 91. In 2000, it delivered 64 of 101 seats to the Alliance.

Regional voting patterns have not been consistent even in the Maritimes. Newfoundland voted strongly Liberal from 1949 to 1968 (while Joey Smallwood led the Liberal party in the province) but that support diminished, particularly while Robert Stanfield was leader of the Conservatives, until 1993, when Newfoundlanders once more gave the Liberals all of their seats. In 1993, the Liberals won thirty-one of the thirty-two seats in the Atlantic region. This was reduced to eleven in 1997, restored to nineteen in 2000 and twenty-two in 2004.

While Liberals have attracted a disproportionate number of urban voters, the Conservatives and Western protest parties traditionally received a higher degree of rural support. However, these associations may not be statistically meaningful. In Canada, the impact of community size on voting is likely to be associated with several other cleavages and voting influences, and so it is impossible to separate its impact from other variables. In any case, the Liberals have been the party most able to attract a variety of voters by cutting across urban–rural lines.

Ethnicity: The major ethnic distinction in Canadian voting behaviour is between French- and English-speaking Canadians. In recent years, French Canadians have awarded a high level of support to the separatist Bloc Québécois and to a lesser extent the Liberals. Until 1993, English-speaking Canadians were more evenly divided in their support for the Liberals and the Conservatives throughout the country. Post–Second World War immigrant voters have been more attracted to the Liberals. The ability of the Liberals to bridge the two founding ethnic groups and at the same time to appeal to immigrant voters has been the principal reason for its dominance of Canadian politics during most of the last hundred years.

The 1984 and 1988 elections shattered many traditional ethnic patterns of voter support for the Tories, as Québec and the West voted massively for Brian Mulroney and the Progressive Conservative party. With the rise of the Bloc Québécois in the 1990s, the pattern shifted again with the Tories and Liberals routed from francophone areas. In the 1997, 2000 and 2004 elections, Liberal support in Québec was restricted mainly to urban areas where the composition of the ridings was not largely francophone.

Class: In many countries, social class is an important determinant of voting behaviour; however, it has not proven to be so in Canada. Only a small proportion of working-class voters has consistently supported the NDP; the Liberal party has attracted support from all classes, as have the Conservatives.

Religion: Religion has consistently correlated strongly with voting behaviour in Canada. Roman Catholics show a strong tendency to vote Liberal regardless of their ethnicity, region or class. This held true even during the Free Trade campaign of 1988 when Protestants still tended to be Conservatives and Catholics Liberals, while the NDP had no religiously differentiated base. Canadians of "other" or "no" religion were the least partisan politically.[18] Richard Johnston found that Catholics are distributed unevenly across the country, and this allows them to control the electoral agenda where their numbers are relatively large. "Where Catholics are numerous, class or union/non-union differences are suppressed. . . . where Catholics are few, class differences, at least in NDP voting, can flourish."[19]

No simple logic is adequate to explain the impact of religious affiliation on voting preference. Religion is often confounded with linguistic and regional patterns. Since 1984, the Liberal French Catholic base in Québec has been greatly eroded because the rise of the nationalist Bloc Québécois split the Catholic vote. The 2000 election was the first time that the Liberals enjoyed a higher percentage of the vote than the Bloc in Québec since the BQ was formed, but the Grits could not maintain that lead in 2004.

HISTORICAL ANALYSIS OF ELECTORAL OUTCOMES

One of the most controversial topics in electoral studies is the role of **party identification** — the degree to which citizens identify with a particular party. It is thought by some that parental party identification is transmitted to children through the socialization process and that the resulting attachment has a long-term effect on voting behaviour, filtering the effects of short-term factors such as party leaders or campaign issues. While in the preceding analysis, we discussed essentially "group" phenomena such as region, class, religion and ethnic identity, the question of party identification directs us to the level of the individual voter.

Studies of electoral behaviour indicate that party identification is widespread in Canada but is relatively low in intensity.[20] In 1988, only 35 percent of the electorate did not identify with a party. This was similar to percentages of non-identifiers in the previous four elections.[21] Non-partisans are particularly susceptible to influence by issues, leaders and other short-term factors in the election campaign. Transient and newly eligible voters generally seem to favour the incumbent government. While there is a small, stable core of loyalists who remain set in their views, a significant number of identifiers shift from one party affiliation to another, crediting specific issues and the image of the leader with their shifting loyalty.

Party identification helps to explain the Liberals' success in recent elections. Over half of party identifiers in Canada and almost 30 percent of identifiers outside of Québec think of themselves as Liberals. This means that the other parties go into elections with serious handicaps because they do not have as large a base of supporters.[22]

In Canada, volatility of party identification is tending to increase over time, and this suggests the increasing possibility of large pendulum swings of political support. Michael Stevenson has found that unstable partisanship is at least partially related to ideology. His research indicates that in the 1977–88 period, "the largest bloc of unstable partisans was closest ideologically to the more left-wing stable New Democratic Party partisans, and shifted only between the New Democratic and Liberal Parties." He also found that the smaller bloc of unstable partisans, which moved to the Progressive Conservatives, "was ideologically closest to its more right-wing stable partisans."[23]

FEDERAL ELECTION RESULTS

Since Confederation, Canada has held thirty-eight general elections, which either the Liberals or the Conservatives have won. The Liberal party held power for most of the twentieth century (see Table 11.2). The longest continuous time it has been in opposition was when the Progressive Conservatives under Brian Mulroney governed from 1984 to 1993. The dramatic collapse of the PCs in the 1993 election left the Liberals with no strong, united challenger until 2004 with the formation of the Conservative Party of Canada.

As we noted in the discussion of the party system above, the 1993 federal election was a watershed for the country. It created a fundamental realignment of parties, from which the Liberals profited. Capturing 41 percent of the vote, the Liberals obtained 177 seats in the House of Commons, regained power and formed a strong majority government. After the election, it was the only party that could claim national status. The Bloc ran candidates only in Québec, and Reform avoided Québec altogether. The Tories were reduced to a historic low of two seats, even though they won 16 percent of the popular vote nationwide. The most important element in the Liberals' success during earlier years was the capture and maintenance of Québec. Today, it is the Liberals' control of Ontario along with a more restricted Québec base that makes it the predominant party in the country.

In 1997, the Liberals won a razor-thin majority with 155 seats, but like the four opposition parties, their representation was basically regional. Roughly two-thirds of the Liberal caucus was from Ontario. Reform replaced the Bloc in second place and therefore won recognition as the Official Opposition. In 2000, the Liberals regained a strong majority government. In 2004, they were restricted to a weak minority government largely because of voter support for the new Conservative party.

Table 11.2 General Election Results, 1945–2004

Election Year	Gov't Formed	Total Seats	PC Seats	PC % Votes	Lib Seats	Lib % Votes	Con Seats	Con % Votes	CCF/ NDP Seats	CCF/ NDP % Votes	Ref[2] Seats	Ref[2] % Votes	Bloc Seats	Bloc % Votes	Oth Seats	Oth % Votes
1945	Lib	245	67	27	125	41	–	–	28	16	–	–	–	–	24	16
1949	Lib	262	41	30	190	49	–	–	13	13	–	–	–	–	18	8
1953	Lib	265	51	31	170	49	–	–	23	11	–	–	–	–	21	9
1957	Con	265	112	39	105	41	–	–	25	11	–	–	–	–	23	9
1958	Con	265	208	54	48	34	–	–	8	9	–	–	–	–	1	3
1962	Con	265	116	37	100	37	–	–	19	14	–	–	–	–	31	12
1963	Lib	265	95	33	129	42	–	–	17	13	–	–	–	–	24	12
1965	Lib	265	97	32	131	40	–	–	21	18	–	–	–	–	16	10
1968	Lib	264	72	31	155	45	–	–	22	17	–	–	–	–	15	7
1972	Lib	264	107	35	109	38	–	–	31	18	–	–	–	–	16	9
1974	Lib	264	95	35	141	43	–	–	16	15	–	–	–	–	12	6
1979	Con	282	136	36	114	40	–	–	26	18	–	–	–	–	6	7
1980	Lib	282	103	33	147	44	–	–	32	20	–	–	–	–	0	3
1984	Con	282	211	50	40	28	–	–	30	19	–	–	–	–	1	–
1988	Con	295	169[1]	43	83	32	–	–	43	20	–	–	–	–	–	4
1993	Lib	295	2	16	177	41	–	–	9	7	52	19	54	13	1	4
1997	Lib	301	20	19	155	38	–	–	21	11	60	19	44	11	1	2
2000	Lib	301	12	12	172	40	–	–	13	9	66	26	38	11	–	2
2004	Lib	308	–	–	135	37	99	30	19	16	–	–	54	12	1	6

[1] 169 Conservatives were elected on November 21, 1988, but one died before being officially sworn in, leaving the seat technically vacant.

[2] Includes Alliance

Source: Elections Canada 2004 results available at http://enr.elections.ca/National_e.aspx

THE 2004 GENERAL ELECTION: OUTCOME AND ANALYSIS

In 2004, the Liberals dropped from a 172-seat majority government (out of 301 in total) in 2000 to a 135-seat minority status (out of 308). Their biggest loss of seats was in Ontario — twenty-five in total. In fact, they were twenty seats short of the number needed to control the House of Commons with a majority, with no obvious coalition to be formed. The NDP fell one seat short of holding the balance of power, so that the combined seat count of the Conservatives, Bloc and independent MP Chuck Cadman was 154, the same number exactly as the combined Liberal–NDP total. The Liberals were supported by only 36.7 percent of voters, their fourth-worst showing since Confederation. The Liberals picked up seats in BC, New Brunswick and Nova Scotia. Their big losses were in their strongholds of Ontario and Québec. They lost 10 percentage points of support in Québec, and their seat count there fell to twenty-one from thirty-six in 2000.

The Conservative party won ninety-nine seats across the country, sixty-eight of them in British Columbia, Alberta, Saskatchewan and Manitoba. Their total seat count of ninety-nine compared favourably with seventy-eight for the combined Alliance and PCs in 2000, but their percentage of the popular vote fell to 29.6 from the 37.7 combined vote of the Alliance and PCs in 2000. Many former PC supporters deserted them. In Ontario and the West combined, the Conservatives outpolled the Liberals 3.36 million votes to 3.3 million. In those five provinces, the Conservatives also won more seats than the Liberals — ninety-two to eighty-nine.

Entering the election, the NDP had more money than ever, a new leader and a vulnerable Liberal government, but it did not achieve the heights it had scaled from 1963 to 1988. The party gained in British Columbia and Ontario, but, with no seats in Saskatchewan, it got no representation in five of the ten provinces. The NDP and Conservatives both lost votes to the Liberals.

Women increased their representation in the House of Commons slightly, to a new high. Of 302 women candidates, 65 were elected — 2 more than in 2000 (34 Liberals, 12 Conservatives, 14 Bloc and 5 NDP). Women now make up 21.1 percent of the House — a 0.2 percent increase since 2000.

In spite of all the scandals, a grumpy electorate, leadership debates and volatile polls, the popular vote per party ended up almost where polls said it would when the writ was dropped. The potential for electoral trouble for the Liberals began well before Paul Martin took over as leader. His tactics to force Chrétien to resign had ostracized many supporters, alienated some local Liberal officials and volunteers and those who opposed his long run for the leadership.[24] Then, before Martin could call an election, Liberal disunity was fractured further by the sponsorship scandal.

Table 11.3 General Election Results, 2004

Party	Total	Nfld.	PEI	NS	NB	Qué.	Ont.	Man.	Sask.	Alta.	BC	Y	NWT	Nun
Lib	135	5	4	6	7	21	75	3	1	2	8	1	1	1
Bloc	54	–	–	–	–	54	–	–	–	–	–	–	–	–
NDP	19	–	–	2	1	–	7	4	5	–	5	1	–	–
Cons	99	2	–	3	2	–	24	7	13	26	22	–	–	–
Ind	1	–	–	–	–	–	–	–	–	1	–	–	–	–
Total	308	7	4	11	10	75	106	14	14	28	36	1	1	1

Source: Elections Canada and CBC. For detailed official results, consult Elections Canada at www.elections.ca.

Many voters simply did not like their options. As one commentator noted, it became a contest between fear and loathing, "fear of the Conservatives, loathing of the Liberals. Fear ultimately prevailed."[25] In the end, voters may have feared the consequences of turning the established party of government out of office. Certainly they were nervous about a major shift to the Conservatives or NDP.

The Conservatives campaigned well but lost in the end for many reasons: overconfidence after the debates; passivity when Liberals attacked with negative ads; failure to set the agenda; outspoken fringe conservatives; a gaffe-obsessed media; blunders like the cynical attempt to exploit the child pornography issue; and negative publicity from Ralph Klein in the last week when he mused about dramatic, unspecified changes to the health system.

The Conservatives won ninety-nine seats overall and had a possibility of doing much better. Twenty-five to thirty more seats were very close, half of them in Ontario. Positively stated, they gained several seats in Ontario and came close to taking more. They reduced the Liberals to a minority government. They restored competitive opposition — the first potential alternative government in eleven years. They made gains in the Prairies and Ontario compared to 2000. They wiped out the NDP in Saskatchewan, taking all but one seat there. In Ontario, where the Alliance had only two seats in 2000 and the PCs none, they won twenty-four. Despite these positive results, generally the Conservatives lacked high support among urban populations (except in Alberta and Saskatchewan) and also throughout Québec.

The theory behind the union of the Progressive Conservatives and the Canadian Alliance had been that uniting the right would enable them to be competitive with the Liberals, particularly in Ontario. However there had been no time to hold a policy convention and deal with uniting the fledgling party. In the end, however, there were not enough wholly disenchanted and right-leaning voters willing to back Harper's new Conservatives. Perhaps there is simply not a large enough constituency of right wing voters. Many who consider themselves as right-of-centre seem to be reasonably content with the Liberals. Red Tories may have voted for Liberals, helping to buoy their fortunes and future.

A COMPAS poll on voting day showed that one-quarter of voters in the survey made up their minds only twenty-four hours before the election, favouring Liberals over Conservatives by two to one. About two-fifths of voters made their decisions in the last week of the campaign. Conservatives, on the other hand, said their private polls showed the two parties in a tie right to the end. They said the discrepancy between the predicted and real results was explained by undecided voters who opted for the Liberals because they decided to stick with the familiar.

Regionally, voting patterns changed little outside of Québec.

In Ontario, in the early days of the campaign, Liberal premier Dalton McGuinty produced a May budget with a new health-care premium that infuriated many voters. McGuinty had assured them during the provincial election the previous fall that taxes would not rise under the Liberals. Ontario already was in a grumpy mood at the time the writ was dropped because of the scandal situation. A week later, when the provincial Liberals reneged on their promise and raised taxes, the mood became hostile.

In the 2000 federal election, twenty-six Ontario ridings in the so-called "blue belt" (consisting mainly of small-town and rural ridings between the Ottawa River across the north of Toronto to Georgian Bay and down to Lake Erie) had a combined PC–Alliance vote higher than the Liberal winning vote. In 2004, the newly united Conservatives won nineteen of the twenty-six seats in this area. The Liberals retained the remaining seven. This meant that the Conservatives had regained almost all of the most conservative ridings in Ontario, but Ontario has 106 ridings and the Conservatives got only twenty-four of them. Thirty-two percent of Ontarians voted for the Conservatives, down from the 38 percent that the PCs and Alliance combined won in 2000. This means that most of the urban areas voted Liberal, or occasionally, NDP.

Conservatives had hoped to make headway in the ethnically diverse Toronto suburbs, but they won none of the ridings there. They won only four of the twenty-two seats available in the greater Toronto region and they were not suburban. The Liberals held on to the suburban ridings partially because of the large ethnic and immigrant communities.

Are there more potential Conservative seats in Ontario? Perhaps. Roughly twenty-five to thirty seats were very close in the 2004 election. However, even with evidence of Liberal scandals, corruption, millions missing, waste, mismanagement, abandonment of the military, taxes, and health-care problems, Ontario voters did not rally to the new party.

In Atlantic Canada, only 30 percent voted for the new Conservative party, down from 42 percent who voted for them in 2000. The Liberals gained three seats, two in Nova Scotia and one in New Brunswick for a total of twenty-two. The NDP lost a seat in Nova Scotia (to end up with three in the region) and the Conservatives lost two, one in Nova Scotia and the other in New Brunswick (to end up with seven in the region). It appears that the Atlantic provinces feared that Harper did not accept the need for economic development and other programs to help their region.

In the West, the Liberals gained fourteen seats overall, the same as they had in 2000. They gained three in BC, stayed even in Alberta, lost one in Saskatchewan and lost two in Manitoba. British Columbia gave the Conservatives only 36 percent of the vote, considerably less than the 49 percent it gave the Canadian Alliance in 2000, and this translated into twenty-two seats, down from twenty-seven. Like the Liberals, the NDP picked up three seats more than in the 2000 election. Reform–Alliance votes may have gone to the NDP whose vote share nearly doubled. The Green party won over 6 percent of the popular vote in both BC and Alberta.

Alberta remained strongly Conservative with 61.6 percent of the vote and twenty-five of twenty-eight seats. The popular vote in Saskatchewan was divided, even though the Conservatives took all but one of the fourteen seats. The Conservatives got 41.8 percent of the popular vote, the NDP 23.4 and the Liberals 27.2. The NDP wound up with no seats, however. In Manitoba, the Conservatives picked up two seats for a total of seven, while the Liberals and NDP split the remaining seven seats three and four respectively. Following the election, westerners expressed anger that Ontario's Liberal strength had kept the party in power once again.

In Québec, the Liberals experienced their largest drop in voter support — they fell 10 percentage points. The Bloc Québécois was the biggest winner. Not only did it capture the vast majority of French speaking ridings, many of their majorities were very large, much more than 50 percent. It gained twenty seats, giving it a total of fifty-four and became the dominant party in Québec. This does not mean that the cause of separatism was successful. The Bloc did not make sovereignty an issue and avoided the topic whenever possible. The main issue discussed was the Liberal sponsorship scandal. Moreover, Jean Charest's Liberal provincial government was very unpopular. The sponsorship scandal may have had an impact here, however, the authors of the Canadian Election Study reported that their data did not support this. They found that the scandal did hurt the Liberals in Québec but no more than elsewhere. According to their data, Québeckers were less likely than residents of other provinces to believe there was a lot of corruption under the Chrétien government (69 percent versus 82 percent).[26] They also were less willing than other Canadians to believe that Martin would prevent such a scandal from happening again and were more likely than others to believe he knew about the scandal when he claimed he didn't.[27]

Perhaps more influential than the scandal was the fact that Québeckers viewed Gilles Duceppe as the clear winner of the French-language leadership debate. Some even thought he won the English language debate.[28] Polls supporting Mr. Duceppe climbed considerably after the debates, and support for the Bloc jumped about 10 percentage points.

The primary focus of the Bloc campaign was corruption. The party's slogan was *un parti propre au Québec* — a clean party for Québec. They ran a low-key, cautious campaign and Duceppe controlled his exposure to the public. The Bloc gained 9 percentage points of the vote share over the previous election.

The Conservatives got fewer votes in 2004 than in 2000 in every province, but their support was lowest in Québec, at least 20 points lower than in any other province. The Canadian Election Study found that Québeckers thought less of Harper (27 percent positive versus 36 percent) and also of the Conservative party (25 percent versus 38 percent).[29] Policy issues were also a problem for Conservatives in Québec. Québeckers are generally supportive of progressive social programs such as same-sex marriages, opposition to the death penalty and rehabilitation of young offenders. In some other areas, however, such as favouring the idea of private hospitals (which is a more right-wing issue), a majority of Québeckers were supportive of Conservative policies.

ELECTIONS AND THE MEDIA

Over time, the mass media have become a vitally important link between political institutions and private citizens, especially during elections. By media we mean communication media — radio, television, newspapers (both broadsheets and internet editions) and magazines. As intermediaries between governments and the population, media play a significant role in legitimizing government, making it more effective and preventing abuses of power. Most journalists take their role of exposing wrongdoing seriously. What they select and how they present it to the public have a great impact on public opinion. If unflattering pictures and reports concentrating on the negative characteristics of a person are all that voters hear, for example, their opinions will be coloured accordingly.

Television and newspapers in particular help to shape public opinion. Communications guru Marshall McLuhan noted decades ago that "the medium is the message," by which he meant that we should look beyond the content of the media to understand the effects various forms of media have on our lives and on our thinking. Mass media are crucial sources of political information, suggesting the topics citizens ought to think about and often what to think about the topics.

Media presentations are not neutral. They inform and persuade. They are extensive but not comprehensive. There is little depth of coverage and stories appear and disappear as if by magic. Reporters and their stories may be biased. Journalists today are commonly criticized for their tendency to report on events as a game that is largely about winning and losing. Reporting, it is said, is based on cynicism rather than skepticism, so that public figures and political events are discussed in negative terms. This magnifies the bad and ignores or underplays the good, casting doubt and even distorting events to suggest scandal, even where there is none. Journalists have learned that they get more personal rewards for outrageous opinions, and this creates an incentive to oversimplify and sensationalize.

All political news is delivered to the public through media intermediaries — journalists, editors, and producers — and they have their own biases and agendas. The biases may include cultural gender biases: "far from being neutral . . . the imagery and language of mediated politics is heavily gendered, supporting male as norm and regarding women politicians as novelties".[30] Other researchers have called the assessment of women party leaders by Canada's English-language national newspapers as following a gender-based double standard.[31] The biases of media owners can also be expected to be reflected in presentations. The more chain-owned newspapers there are instead of independents, for example, the more newspapers appear to be stamped from a giant corporate cookie-cutter, all taking the same point of view.

Political leaders and parties learn to use and manipulate the media to their advantage. Media exposure is vital, and experts are hired to assure that the message conveyed is the right one. Political leaders have learned standard "tricks" to get the media coverage they seek. Announcements are carefully timed for optimum exposure and generally delivered in a carefully prepared setting with a phalanx of cameras. Leaders are taught by specialists how to improve their television image. Other specialists concentrate on producing just the right "sound bites and news clips" for television news. Spin doctors, too, routinely make sure that the appropriate "interpretation" of events is disseminated to foster the appropriate attitudes and opinions in the public.

At election time, the media provide information that helps voters choose among parties. Television is the most powerful medium because of the vast number of voters who can be reached: about three out of every four Canadians obtain their political news from television. Parties have increasingly tailored their campaigns to achieve the maximum media coverage, attempting to ensure that every evening the desired "clip" will appear. The commercial needs of the media to attract the public encourages the oversimplification of election issues to the point that elections essentially become "horse races," or popularity contests among party leaders.

The law strictly governs media time for party advertising during election campaigns. According to the *Election Expenses Act*, all broadcasters are required to make several hours of prime-time spots available to registered political parties at a most-favoured advertising rate. The number of hours is divided among the parties according to a formula based on the number of seats held in the House, the number of candidates each party ran in the previous election and the percentage of the popular vote each party won. Free time is allocated on the same basis as paid advertising. No political advertising is allowed during the first four weeks of the campaign, the last two days before the election or on polling day itself.

The 2004 election demonstrated once again the key role of the media in modern Canadian elections. Operating alongside the traditional media, there was a remarkable flood of new electronic information, as innovative websites on the internet proliferated. Campaign strategists, as usual, tried to harness the media and employ it for their own purposes. Since paid ads and free-time broadcasts are strictly regulated, party strategists focused on the "earned media" of news broadcasts. Also, as usual, the media in turn focused public attention on leaders' personalities with much less emphasis on local candidates and extremely little discussion of the details of policy issues.

Initially, media coverage focused negatively on Paul Martin and the circumstances of the sponsorship scandals. Ten days into the campaign, the Liberals were "getting beaten up everywhere" but especially in the conservative *National Post.*[32] At that time, the Conservative party and leader Stephen Harper were receiving better press across the board. *The Globe and Mail, Vancouver Sun* and *La Presse* were seen as the most neutral. As the possibility of a minority government became more real, focus shifted to other parties. Then the spotlight turned on Harper when it appeared he might form the government.

Emotions ran high in editorials across the country. For example, a single editorial in *The Windsor Star* used all of the following negative words to attack the Liberals: *arrogant, complacent, undeniably corrupt, inertia, malaise, disconcerting lack of vision, desperately need . . . to cleanse . . . and rejuvenate, abysmal record, broken promises, mismanagement, corruption, waste, scandalous, corruption, contempt.* The paper vented rage on "Liberal income tax write-offs," "multi-million-dollar junkets," "billion-dollar boondoggles," "perversion of influence" and so on.[33]

As has become customary, there were two televised leadership debates, one in each official language. Polls showed that a majority of Canadians watched at least one of the national debates. This made the debates the most salient single vehicle for communicating political ideas in the campaign.

This was the first Canadian federal election in which the results were not initially blacked out across the country. Chief electoral officer Jean-Pierre Kingsley decided, following a BC court decision, to lift the traditional time zone blackout and allow results to be announced across the country as they trickled in. It made a long evening of coverage. The results started coming in by 8:00 p.m. EDT, first from Newfoundland and Labrador. By 10:05 p.m. EDT, the first predictions of a Liberal minority were announced. By 11:00 p.m. EDT, party leaders began to appear before the cameras heralding their successes.

KEY TERMS

by-election, p. 261
chief electoral officer (CEO), p. 255
Elections Canada, p. 251
electoral system, p. 250
franchise, p. 249
gerrymandering, p. 252

party identification, p. 267
proportional representation (PR), p. 259
referendum, p. 261
single-member plurality electoral system,
   p. 250
writ, p. 255

DISCUSSION QUESTIONS

1. In what respects could Canadian elections be made more democratic? Be sure to consider the method of determining who wins, the technique for counting votes, who runs for office, who is allowed to vote, who finances political parties and how electoral boundaries are drawn.

2. Given the low turnout in the 2004 general election, do you believe Canada should adopt compulsory voting? Why or why not?

3. Do you think that Canada should hold more referendums to allow more direct citizen input into decision-making? Why or why not?

4. The media are not elected, yet they have a great influence on what voters see, hear and think about during an election. Do politicians use the media, or do the media use politicians? Are voters manipulated in the process?

WEBLINKS

Elections Canada

www.elections.ca

Electoral Boundaries Readjustment Act

http://laws.justice.gc.ca/en/E-3

PlanetVote Canada

www.planetvote.net

Office of the Chief Electoral Officer

www.elections.ca/intro.asp?section=ceo&document=index&lang=e&textonly=false

12 Ethics in Canadian Government and Politics

Honesty and Corruption

Learning Objectives

After reading this chapter, you should be able to

1. Define *patronage* and *conflict of interest*.

2. Identify the rules in place to prevent misconduct by members of Parliament, senators and cabinet ministers.

3. Name some of the major allegations of ethical misconduct in the Chrétien government.

4. Critique the new ethical rules introduced by the Martin government.

We have seen that Canadians say they are skeptical about politicians and politics generally. Their confidence in the system of government has declined, and in recent elections, fewer of them are turning out to vote. Is the reputation of politics, politicians and our political institutions being destroyed by improperly regulated, selfish behaviour?

Almost every government in recent years has been plagued by scandals. Pierre Trudeau's outgoing patronage appointments in 1984 created a furor that largely cost John Turner a renewed mandate as prime minister. Scandalous behaviour in the Mulroney government eventually brought it down and also damaged Kim Campbell's chances of forming a government. Now, scandals of Jean Chrétien's government have undermined the government of his successor, Paul Martin. The political chicanery uncovered by the auditor general and exposed in the Gomery Inquiry in 2005 highlighted once again the issue of ethics in government.

When politicians engage in conflicts of interest, patronage, acceptance of inappropriate gifts and other forms of unethical conduct, they create situations in which officials may be beholden to private interests. The relationship between ministers, MPs, senators and the public is one in which politicians are in positions of public trust.[1]

Canadians expect a high degree of integrity from their public leaders. Laws, rules and regulations have been written to ensure the ethical conduct of politicians and public servants. These rules are far from uniform across the country, with some provinces having more stringent rules than Ottawa.[2] On the whole, these regulations have emerged haphazardly and as the result of scandals. However, until very recently, there has been little effort to write new, more coherent sets of guidelines or laws.

This chapter examines the main types of behaviour that create ethical problems for politicians and the rules that are in place to prevent them. We summarize the major cases of alleged government impropriety since 1995, and we provide a critical review of the ethics in the regime of Jean Chrétien's Liberal government and the initial steps for reform taken by Prime Minister Paul Martin's minority government. Throughout, we look for answers to important questions: Is skepticism and lack of trust in government deserved? Is the problem with the institutions, the individuals or the regulations governing them? How do our politicians treat the institutions of politics and government? Do they act ethically when they are in office or are they prone to misconduct? What rules are in place to prevent unethical behaviour? Why don't they work? What could be improved?

CONFLICT OF INTEREST

A **conflict of interest** is a situation in which a prime minister, cabinet minister, member of Parliament or public servant has knowledge of a private, personal economic interest sufficient to influence how he or she exercises public duties and responsibilities. Such conflict may or may not be illegal. Even if it is legal, it may create doubts or suspicions that the decisions or actions taken are not impartial.

Public attitudes have changed considerably over the years; activities which were considered acceptable a few decades ago now engender public condemnation. Until relatively recently, MPs would routinely run their private businesses even after becoming ministers. Conflict-of-interest queries were not raised unless ministerial decisions clearly and publicly produced private advantage for someone. In those years, politics was still a part-time, rather poorly paid occupation, and ministers and prime ministers frequently engaged openly in potentially conflicting activities. They sat on boards of directors, carried on legal practices and accepted private trust funds. It is even said that C.D. Howe, a respected Liberal minister, routinely checked his stock listings before going to Cabinet to make important economic decisions for the country.

After several mini-scandals in the 1950s, acceptance of such practices began to wane. Ministerial guidelines first emerged in 1964 when Prime Minister Pearson wrote to his ministers stressing the need to be ethical. In 1972, Prime Minister Trudeau went further and issued formal guidelines for cabinet ministers. Like Pearson, he chose to rely on guidelines rather than legislation to handle the problem.

Ordinary MPs and senators have never been subject to specific rules apart from the *Criminal Code*, the *Parliament of Canada Act*, and the Rules of the House and Senate, which prohibit specific forms of behaviour. Reformers have tried to make the rules more specific but to little avail. In 1973, Allan MacEachen tabled a Green Paper entitled *Members of Parliament and Conflict of Interest*, which called for legislation that would apply to all politicians. The Green Paper defined conflict of interest as a "situation in which a Member of Parliament has a personal or private pecuniary interest sufficient to influence, or appear to influence, the exercise of his public duties and responsibilities."[3] Opposition to legislation was severe in both houses and no legislation could be passed. On the first attempt to pass legislation based on the Green Paper, the Senate blocked the proposal; on the second attempt, Parliament was dissolved in 1979 before the bill reached second reading.

Cabinet members, however, continued to receive letters from the prime minister admonishing them to be ethical. Blind trusts became mandatory for all ministers, and for two years after leaving Cabinet, ex-ministers could not serve on boards of directors of corporations with which they had dealt as ministers; they could not act on behalf of such people or corporations, or act as lobbyists. For one year, ministers could not accept jobs from companies with which they had dealt, nor could they act as consultants for them. These guidelines were enforced throughout the Clark and Mulroney governments.

In 1984, the government set up a Task Force on Conflict of Interest (the Sharp-Starr Report), which concluded that there was a need to improve the regulations. It proposed appointing two ethics officers: a counsellor and a commissioner. The *commissioner* would function as a policeman responsible for seeking out and investigating potential conflicts of interest, whereas the **ethics counsellor** would inform ministers what the law and ethics code demanded of them so that they could obey it. No specific action was taken on the report.

In 1985, Prime Minister Mulroney introduced new conflict of interest guidelines for cabinet ministers and civil servants. Like the earlier version, it stopped short of full, mandatory disclosure in order to strike a balance between protecting the public interest and protecting the private affairs of ministers. The restrictions on business dealings of immediate family members were dropped. The new regulations did, however, make it clear that ministers could not hire their own immediate relatives (or other ministers' relatives) for government jobs.

Ambiguity and lack of enforcement provisions in Mulroney's code led to a major conflict-of-interest case. In 1986–1987, cabinet minister Sinclair Stevens was faced with a series of conflict allegations. Stevens had placed his assets in a blind trust — i.e., he did not sell them, but put them in the hands of someone else. However, the trust was considerably less than "blind." The Parker Commission, which investigated the case, concluded that Stevens had violated the conflict code fourteen times and that he "knew about and was involved with the York Centre companies and thus with trust assets because his wife and special assistant told him about the trust assets and because his wife participated in joint management of the assets with him."[4]

Mulroney introduced conflict-of-interest legislation in early 1988. Bill C114 attempted to force enough disclosure to keep the government leaders honest, yet not infringe unduly on their private lives. However, this bill died on the Order Paper when the 1988 general election was called. Various other attempts to legislate about conflict of interest have also failed. In the last days of the Mulroney government in 1993, another more stringent bill — bill C43 — was introduced but it, too, died on the Order Paper when the thirty-fourth Parliament was dissolved.

POLITICAL PATRONAGE

Political **patronage** in the broad sense refers to awarding contracts, employment and other material benefits to individuals or groups on the basis of partisan support rather than merit. Patronage is usually done carefully in order to avoid charges under the *Criminal Code*. It is generally claimed to be part of the normal democratic practice of rewarding followers, constituents, regional representatives and political friends for their support. However, patronage can include illegal practices such as vote buying, "treating" (paying for votes with liquor) and other forms of bribery.

Pork-barrelling, on the other hand, extends favours to whole regions or communities as an inducement for support. Like patronage, pork-barrelling usually breaks no laws but often raises serious questions about ethical conduct.

Several aspects of patronage raise problems. It plays to human weaknesses, encouraging unethical behaviour by individuals, institutions and groups in society. It also has an inflationary aspect: one reward creates a demand for more, and the demand always exceeds supply. Clearly, recent prime ministers have been unable to resolve the problem of dispensing patronage without compromising their public position. In fact, public cynicism and media investigations make all major forms of patronage suspect.

Some commentators regard patronage and pork-barrelling as essential parts of politics, providing the oil that makes the system run smoothly and the glue that keeps parties together and the political system stable. For others, patronage and pork-barrelling are corrupt, immoral activities that impede honest, efficient government services. All would agree, however, that patronage has been an enduring feature of the Canadian political system. It is in the shadowy world where interest-group behaviour, patronage and pork-barrelling meet, and where influence and favours result from secret negotiations, that corruption is generally found.

Government contracts are perhaps the most noticeable form of patronage. Most large contracts come under strict rules of tendering — but a few, especially smaller personal contracts, are let without tender and sometimes there are preferred suppliers. The auditor general, who reports to Parliament on government expenditures, has significantly reduced patronage and inefficiencies in the field of contracts. However, as the Gomery Inquiry showed, questionable practices continue, though for the most part in a more nuanced fashion than previously.

Patronage extends well beyond the scope of public relations for the government. Even inside the public service, the government has considerable patronage to hand out in the form of senior appointments. In all, there are over three thousand political appointments to be made by the prime minister and Cabinet in the federal government.

The history of patronage crosses party lines. In 1979, Prime Minister Joe Clark incurred the wrath of his party rank-and-file when he delayed too long and lost his chance to dispense rewards when his minority government was defeated. John Turner lost the 1984 election when he declared he had "no option" but to honour the "orgy" of appointments demanded by the departing Prime Minister, Pierre Trudeau. Brian Mulroney made a major issue out of patronage in his 1984 election campaign but then proceeded to fill patronage positions and award government business to party and personal friends. In 1993, the new Chrétien government promised to decrease patronage appointments, but by 2005, almost all government appointments continued to go to well-known Liberals.

GIFTS AND GAINS

There is a catch-all category of other misconduct by public officials. Maureen Mancuso calls this broad category "gifts and gains" — i.e., situations where public officials gain perquisites from holding public office.[5] If gifts or gains are large, such misdeeds are considered to be bribes and covered by the *Criminal Code*. However, a large number of relatively small tokens of esteem can also provide expectations of mutual obligation based on the money, perks or benefits offered and received.

Gifts to prime ministers are good examples,[6] but even here it is difficult to come to fair conclusions about what is a polite show of respect and what is inappropriate behaviour. Consider, for example, the fact that the minister of Indian and northern affairs generally gets more gifts of substantial value than the rest of the Cabinet put together.

THE CHRÉTIEN REGIME: LAWS, RULES AND INSTITUTIONS

Today the *Criminal Code*, the *Parliament of Canada Act*, Standing Orders of the House of Commons and Rules of the Senate continue to apply to any minister or ordinary member or senator involved in fraud, influence peddling or breach of trust. The *Criminal Code* makes certain practices such as bribery illegal; the *Parliament of Canada Act* forbids MPs from having government contracts; and the Standing Orders of House of Commons and Senate rules ban certain behaviour and require certain activities — such as the necessity to disclose a financial interest when speaking or voting in Parliament. However, much of the unethical conduct that has taken place has not been illegal or even against parliamentary rules. Most of the conflict of interest, patronage and gains have been about broad unethical behaviour that is not covered by the rules.

When he came to office in 1993, Jean Chrétien took a new approach to conflict of interest. He said he wanted to set up an "integrity regime," where he himself would be responsible for his ministers' actions. Arguing that this was what the Constitution required, he opted against passing laws or even regulations concerning ethics in his government. He hired former minister Mitchell Sharp as ethics advisor on integrity in government for one dollar a year, saying "integrity in government is not simply a matter of rules and regulations — it is also a matter of personal standards and conduct." Then, in June 1994, the prime minister unveiled yet another "ethics package" — a conflict-of-interest code for senior officials and lobbying rules.

Ministers, Parliamentary Secretaries and Senior Officials

The new code covers all members of Cabinet, parliamentary secretaries, members of the ministers' staffs and over twelve hundred senior officials in the federal public service. The wives and dependants of ministers are also covered, but they are not required to follow the rules of the code in regard to disclosure, etc.

The code demands in Section 3(1) that "public office holders shall act with honesty and uphold the highest ethical standards so that public confidence and trust in the integrity, objectivity and impartiality of government are conserved and enhanced." The code lists in Section 3(5) the principles and compliance measures to prevent "real, potential or apparent conflicts of interest."

Public employees are required to provide a report to the ethics counsellor, tabulating his or her assets, liabilities and outside activities. The counsellor reviews the list and tells the public official appointees what to do to be in accordance with the code. Ministers are prohibited from engaging in a profession, actively managing or operating a business or serving as a corporate director. Moreover, they cannot hold office in a union or professional association or act as a paid consultant.

Appointees' assets are also listed and monitored. Exempt assets such as homes, vacation properties, bank accounts, and fixed income investments as well as mutual funds are not further controlled. "Declarable" assets must be made public, but the office-holder may continue to handle them. They include ownership of family or local businesses, farms under commercial operation and rental properties. "Controllable" assets are those such as publicly traded securities, including shares in a stock market, which could be affected directly or indirectly by government action. Office-holders are required to divest themselves of all these types of controlled instruments.

Office-holders may use one of three strategies — they may sell the assets; put them in a "blind trust" (i.e., they cannot obtain information on the composition of their assets as they are managed at arm's length); or in certain cases, create a "blind management" agreement where, for example, one owns a private company that might do business with the government. In the latter case, the office-holder is prevented from making any decision on the management of his or her assets.

With Mitchell Sharp (who co-authored the Sharp-Starr report in 1984) acting as an advisor, only one other position, that of ethics counsellor, was formally created. In 1994, Howard Wilson became Prime Minister Chrétien's ethics counsellor. Wilson reported directly and only to Chrétien. It was his duty to uphold the code of conduct for public office-holders as well as to enforce the *Lobbyists Registration Act*. However, his most important responsibility was to probe the ethical conduct of cabinet ministers when requested to do so by the prime minister.

Jean Chrétien had Mitchell Sharp interview prospective cabinet ministers in order to identify anything in their records that might embarrass the new government. Sharp interviewed each prospective cabinet minister, asking them whether they and their spouses could live with conflict-of-interest guidelines and whether they had skeletons in their closet, tax arrears or personal problems.

Aside from the public code, the prime minister, with the advice of Wilson and Sharp, also declared that ministers may never communicate with government tribunals, except under very specific circumstances. The ethics counsellor summarized this rule as, "Ministers shall not intervene, or appear to intervene, on behalf of any person or entity, with federal quasi-judicial tribunals on any matter before them that requires a decision in their quasi-judicial capacity, unless otherwise authorized by law."[7] The rule did not restrict ordinary MPs in their dealings with administrative tribunals but did hold ministers to a higher standard of accountability. At issue was, and is, finding the right balance between ensuring ministers do not use their positions to unduly influence tribunals and giving them enough freedom to help their constituents.

CLOSE-UP   ## Conflict of Interest and Post-Employment Code for Public Office-Holders under Jean Chrétien

The major provisions for Cabinet members, secretaries of state, parliamentary secretaries, ministerial staffs and full-time governor-in-council positions were requirements to:

- disclose all assets and liabilities to the ethics counsellor including the assets and liabilities of spouses and dependent children;
- disclose all business interests and either sell or put into trust those interests whose value could be affected by government decisions or policy;
- disclose all significant outside activities during the previous two years including charity work and trusteeships;
- not retain or accept directorships or offices in a financial or commercial operation, hold a union or professional position, practice a profession, operate a business or serve as a paid consultant;
- for a period of one year (two years for cabinet ministers) after leaving office, not lobby their former department or work for any person or entity they dealt with in the year before they left their office.

ETHICS INVESTIGATIONS, 1994–2005

Well-publicized allegations against Liberal cabinet ministers since the code was put into effect include the following cases:[8]

- 1995: Michel Dupuy, Heritage Minister, wrote to the Canadian Radio-television and Telecommunications Corporation (CRTC) asking them to consider a constituent's application for a radio licence in Montréal. Despite the fact that the rules about ministers contacting quasi-judicial bodies were somewhat vague, Dupuis did break the prime minister's code. The PM defended Dupuy but later dropped him from Cabinet. The guidelines for ministers writing to tribunals were also tightened.

- 1995: When critics asked Prime Minister Chrétien to instruct the ethics counsellor to examine an alleged improper relationship between Liberal senator Pierre DeBane and Canada Post president George Clermont, the prime minister replied that it is not the government's duty to impose ethics standards on MPs and senators but up to Parliament.

- 1996: Defence Minister David Collenette was accused of interfering with a quasi-judicial body after he wrote to the Immigration Board on behalf of a constituent. Collenette clearly had violated the rules and had to leave. Wilson concluded that Collenette had broken the Cabinet rules. Collenette (a close personal friend of the prime minister) resigned but later returned to Cabinet in another portfolio.

- 1996: Former Immigration Minister Sergio Marchi was questioned for writing a letter to the Immigration Board. Marchi wrote about a board decision involving a killer who successfully appealed his deportation order. Wilson declared that the letter was not an attempt to intervene and did not violate any Cabinet guidelines.

- 1996: Youth Minister Ethel Blondin-Andrew was found to have used government credit cards to pay for her Hawaii vacation and a fur coat. She claimed that she paid the government back. Wilson concluded that there was no wrongdoing.

- 1998: Finance Minister Paul Martin was accused of a conflict of interest over changes to the *Income Tax Act* that benefited shipping companies. Opposition parties alleged that the changes could benefit Martin's company, Canada Steamship Lines Ltd., but Wilson said Martin was unaware of the changes because a junior minister had handled the issue in government and this cleared him of any conflict.

- 1998: Former Transport Minister Doug Young was accused of a conflict when, after being defeated in the previous election, he obtained a share in a toll-highway company that received federal funding when he was transport minister. Wilson found that there was no conflict.

- 1998: The Andy Scott Affair. Solicitor General Andy Scott's conversation about the Asia-Pacific Economic Co-operation conference inquiry was overheard on an airplane and subsequently reported in the media. Sharp admitted in one news article that he had discussed the solicitor general's conduct with the prime minister, but Wilson was not consulted. When Wilson was asked by a reporter whether the prime minister asked him to investigate Scott, Wilson replied, "No." However, Scott did resign from his Cabinet post in November 1998.

- 2000: Jane Stewart, Minister of Human Resources, was held responsible for the "job-creation scandal" in which grants and contribution programs such as the Canada Jobs Fund were shown to have been mismanaged for over $1 billion in annual programs. The department approved the majority of applications even though crucial information was missing and then failed to follow up on most of them. The auditor general concluded that there had been widespread deficiencies in the process, and this allegation launched a series of other allegations about political interference. The case raised the issue of whether a minister who provides benefits to his or her constituents is engaging in ethical misconduct or simply following democratic practices. Just what is ethical misconduct in such a case? Wilson maintained this did not come under the guidelines.

- 2000–2001: During the 2000 election campaign, Jean Chrétien was accused of phoning the head of the Business Development Bank of Canada on behalf of a constituent. Chrétien asked him to help secure a mortgage of $615 000 for the owner of the Auberge Grand-Mère, a hotel in the PM's hometown of Shawinigan. Wilson was asked to investigate and did so. He concluded that this action did not constitute ethical misconduct under the rules, as the prime minister was acting like any other MP in supporting members of his riding. However, the facts in this case are murky, and Chrétien's behaviour continued to be questioned. The so-called Shawinigate was one of the major causes of Chrétien's downfall as leader of the Liberal party and prime minister.

- 2002–2005: After the near success of the separatists in the 1995 Québec referendum on sovereignty, the federal Liberal government began a series of actions to strengthen support for Canada in Québec. They aimed to spread money throughout the province to show Ottawa's largesse in the competition with the separatists. In what became known in the press as AdScam, questionable decisions and sloppy administration allowed the auditor general, Sheila Fraser, to find that the sponsorship program was administered outside normal Treasury Board and Public Works guidelines. She concluded that over $100 000 had been misappropriated and given to a handful of Liberal advertising firms, and also concluded that the department "broke every rule in the book." The Crown corporations ViaRail, Canada Post, the Old Port of Montréal and the Business Development Bank (BDB) were all implicated.

Political fallout, an RCMP investigation, Commons committee hearings and a judicial inquiry (the Gomery Commission) followed to determine if there was any wrongdoing or criminal activity. Among the casualties was former Public Works Minister Alfonso Gagliano who, as former minister responsible for Québec, took much of the political blame and was recalled from his position as ambassador to Denmark. His officials in the Department of Public Works were also censured by the House committee, but they fought back. Chuck Guité, a former public servant who was given wide powers to distribute the funds in Québec denied any wrongdoing and said that in regard to Québec separatism he had to act. "When you're at war, you drop . . . the rules."[9] Among other events, Michel Vennat was fired as head of the BDB, André Ouellet was dismissed as head of Canada Post and Jean Pelletier was fired as head of ViaRail.

Dolighan. Liberal Stronghold. Reprinted with permission.

Perhaps the most damaging political fallout was for the new Prime Minister, Paul Martin. Martin had been minister of finance during AdScam and, just before the 2004 election, he was forced to declare he knew nothing about the scandal until it became public in 2002. However, the allegations of corruption helped to turn the public against Martin's Liberals and reduce the Liberals to a minority government. The Gomery Inquiry had not reported at the time of writing, but developments in the inquiry provided the opposition parties in Parliament with fodder to bring down the minority government. A judicial inquiry is not like a court; it has no provision for cross-examination of witnesses. Trial by inquiry can thus be a very one-sided exposure. It is not yet clear whether any criminal charges will be laid in the affair.

Evaluations of Ethics in the Chrétien Regime

There were four significant problem areas in the Chrétien code:

1. *Minimal Consultation with Opposition Leaders:* The Liberal campaign platform in 1993 stated that opposition leaders would participate in developing the ethical guidelines governing cabinet ministers. This was not done.

2. *Ad Hoc Nature of Rules:* The rules are not regularized in the form of regulations or laws approved by Parliament so that the next PM can change them at will.

3. *Independent Investigative Powers:* The ethics counsellor was responsible for investigating conflict-of-interest allegations against anyone in the government when the prime minister asked him to. Findings were reported directly to the prime minister. There was nothing to compel the ethics counsellor to investigate conflict-of-interest allegations raised in the media or by the House. He did not seek out and investigate possible conflicts of interest but merely advised those who asked him what the law was, so that they could obey it.

4. *Lack of Accountability and Openness:* The Liberals promised that the "Ethics Counsellor . . . would report directly to Parliament"; however, Wilson was not accountable to Parliament. He reported, personally and privately, to the prime minister.

Critics of the ethics counsellor raised an important issue: why should the ethics counsellor not report to Parliament as well? If the counsellor reported to Parliament, it was argued, the office would gain a degree of independence that traditional Cabinet appointees lack. Moreover, there was no provision for what would happen if the prime minister were in conflict of interest himself.

Just how effective the ethics counsellor and ethics advisor were in regulating levels of honesty in public life is somewhat difficult to assess as the officials carried out their activities in secret. Mitchell Sharp did, however, produce some notable results. Two potential ministers withdrew their names for Cabinet appointments in 1994 when they were told of the conditions in the prime minister's code. However, both MPs did join the Cabinet at a later date. No potential ministers were prevented from joining the Cabinet in later Chrétien governments.

Did these new offices and guidelines mean that the government and its ministers acted more ethically? The Liberal government and Ethics Counsellor's Office said, definitely yes; however, the opposition parties said, definitely no. The Liberal government and the ethics counsellor stressed what they called "integrity," while the opposition parties and some reformers put more emphasis on "compliance" and enforcement. The AdScam scandal illustrated the weakness of the code when the prime minister himself was potentially in a conflict situation.

Members of Parliament and Senate

A joint committee of the two houses in the thirty-sixth Parliament concluded that there should be a code for both senators and MPs, but a bill was not produced.

The *Criminal Code* and House and Senate rules continued to apply, but there were no general disclosure rules for MPs or senators. The few general rules were not codified or coherent and were often contradictory. Loopholes existed in many fields. Free foreign travel in the Chrétien regime was unregulated, although MPs (but not senators) had to declare trips. Fees for speaking and consulting did not require declaration, and relations with lobbyists were uncontrolled. In other words, there was no systematic transparency. Under the Standing Orders, MPs had to declare any private interests in any matter before the House, but there was no annual registry to summarize this material.[10]

CLOSE-UP	Conflict-of-Interest Rules for MPs and Senators

General Rules

- Under the *Criminal Code,* it is illegal for any cabinet minister, MP or senator to accept or solicit bribes or to accept a benefit for helping someone in a transaction with government (influence peddling).

Senators and MPs

- The *Parliament of Canada Act* declares that senators and MPs cannot be a party to any contract paid for with federal funds. Nor can they sell their services.
- Standing orders of the House of Commons prevent MPs from voting on any question in which they have a direct financial interest.
- Senate rules declare that senators cannot vote on any question or sit on a committee dealing with a matter in which they have a financial interest not generally held by members of the public.

The Martin Proposed Regime: Laws, Rules and Institutions

As part of Paul Martin's effort to differentiate his new December 2003 government from that of Jean Chrétien, he declared, "The core principles of the new government will be transparency, accountability, financial responsibility and ethical conduct." On taking office, Martin updated the conflict-of-interest and post-employment code for public office-holders and made a new ethics commissioner responsible for its administration. The code covers ministers, ministers of state, parliamentary secretaries, members of ministerial staff and all Order-in-Council appointees. He did not rescind Chrétien's old code but added more rules to reduce the possibility for the improper use of government aircraft; to require that all gifts worth more than $1000 be put into the government inventory; to require approval of the commissioner before accepting any gifts, hospitality or benefits; and public disclosure of liabilities. Martin said that as prime minister he would be required to make a public statement to the commissioner of his own compliance with the rules.

In 2004, Parliament passed new legislation to formally establish the position of the **ethics commissioner** and also a Senate ethics officer. The new, independent commissioner reports directly to the House of Commons (i.e., not the PM) and has the authority to review the actions of all members of Parliament, including cabinet ministers and the prime minister. Bernard Shapiro replaced Howard Wilson and was given new powers of investigation and independence.

As well, just before the 2004 election was called, new conflict of interest rules were added to the Standing Orders. Essentially, the 25th Report of the Standing Committee on Procedure and House Affairs was added to the Orders and made applicable to MPs at the beginning of the next Parliament. These rules require the disclosure of major assets, liabilities and income of MPs, their spouses and dependant children. The disclosure must be made to the Commissioner within sixty days of resumption of Parliament. In particular, all funds received from the government must be noted. This information will be kept confidential by the commissioner, but he or she will be required to prepare a public summary of the most important aspects of the disclosed materials.[11]

It remains to be seen if these new rules and officials will end conflict of interest in Canadian politics. Its long history makes one cautious in judgment.

KEY TERMS

conflict of interest, p. 278
ethics counsellor, p. 279
ethics commissioner, p. 288

patronage, p. 280
pork-barrelling, p. 280

DISCUSSION QUESTIONS

1. What are some of the possible major forms of misconduct in government?

2. What are some of the special ethical rules that apply to MPs today? To senators? To cabinet ministers? Are they adequate? Why or why not?

3. Is the Canadian government corrupt? Present information from this chapter and current issues to support your argument. Make reference to the final report of the Gomery Commission.

4. Devise an ethics code that you think would deal with any ethical problems you identified in the third question.

WEBLINKS

CBC News — The Role of the Ethics Commissioner

www.cbc.ca/news/background/cdngovernment/ethics.html

Transparency International Canada

www.transparency.ca

Sheldon Chumir Foundation for Ethics in Leadership

www.chumirethicsfoundation.ca

Gomery Commission

www.gomery.ca

Federal Sponsorship Scandal

www.cbc.ca/news/background/groupaction

Endnotes

CHAPTER 1

1. Michael B. Poliakoff, *Combat Sports in the Ancient World: Competition, Violence, and Culture* (New Haven, CT: Yale, 1987).

2. Max Weber, *The Theory of Social and Economic Organizations*, edited and translated by A. M. Henderson and Talcott Parsons (New York: Oxford, 1947), p. 154.

3. For a comparison of types of governments, see Robert J. Jackson and Doreen Jackson, *Introduction to Political Science: Comparative and World Politics* (Don Mills: Prentice Hall, 2003).

4. Definitions of politics vary widely. See in particular, Harold Lasswell, *Politics: Who Gets What, When and How* (New York: McGraw-Hill, 1965).

5. See Jean Bethke Elshtain, *Democracy on Trial* (New York: Basic Books, 1994), and Robert D. Putnam, *Making Democracy Work: Civic Traditions in Modern Italy* (Princeton, NJ: Princeton University Press, 1993).

CHAPTER 2

1. The official count was 30 007 094 million as of the 2001 Census.

2. See Ronald D. Lambert, James E. Curtis, Barry J. Kay and Steven D. Brown, "The Social Sources of Political Knowledge," *CJPS*, vol. 21, no. 2 (June 1988), pp. 359–374.

3. John Locke, *Two Treatises on Government*, Peter Lasleet, ed. (New York: New American Library, 1965).

4. Ibid., "Second Treatise," Chapter 4.

5. C.A.R. Crosland, *The Future of Socialism* (New York: Schocken, 1963), p. 67.

6. See Ronald D. Lambert et al. "The Sources of Political Knowledge," *CJPS*, vol. 21, no. 2 (June 1988), p. 373.

7. *Canada Year Book, 1999*, p. 243.

8. Economic Council of Canada, *Legacies: Twenty-Sixth Annual Review* (Ottawa: Supply and Services, 1989), p. 35.

9. Poverty Profile, National Council of Welfare, 1999.

10. In dollar terms, Statistics Canada defined this line according to family type and location; for example, as an annual income below $26 049 for a family of four in a city of one hundred thousand to five million people.

11. See, for example, James J. Teevan, ed., *Introduction to Sociology: A Canadian Focus*, 4th ed. (Scarborough: Prentice Hall, 1992), p. 78.

12. Dennis Olsen, "The State Elites," in Leo Panitch, ed., *The Canadian State* (Toronto: University of Toronto Press, 1977).

13. See Morley Gunderson, Andrew Sharpe and Steven Wald, "Youth Unemployment in Canada, 1976—1998," available at http://ideas.repec.org/a/cpp/issued/v26y2000is1p85-100.html. Accessed 2/28/2005.

14. Léon Dion, *Quebec: The Unfinished Revolution* (Montréal: McGill-Queen's University Press, 1976), p. 180.

15. These events are discussed in Chapters 3 and 5.

16. *Immigrants* are people who have been granted the right to live in Canada permanently by immigration authorities. Some are recent arrivals, others have lived in Canada for several years.

17. See Neil Bissoondath, *Selling Illusions: The Cult of Multiculturalism in Canada* (Toronto: Penguin Books, 1995).

18. See Jeffrey Reitz and Raymond Breton, *The Illusion of Difference: Realities of Ethnicity in Canada and the United States* (Toronto: C.D. Howe Institute, 1994).

19. David J. Elkins, "The Sense of Place," in David J. Elkins and Richard Simeon, eds., *Small Worlds: Provinces and Parties in Canadian Political Life* (Toronto: Methuen, 1980), pp. 1–30.

20. Jean Burnet, "The Policy of Multiculturalism within a Bilingual Framework: An Interpretation," in A. Wolfgang, ed., *The Education of Immigrant Students: Issues and Answers* (Toronto: Ontario Institute for Studies in Education, 1975).

21. 2001 Census.

22. See Jean Leonard Elliot and Augie Fleras, *Unequal Relations: An Introduction to Race and Ethnic Dynamics in Canada* (Scarborough: Prentice Hall, 1992).

23. From www.statcann.ca/Daily/English/030929/d030929a.htm. Accessed July 5, 2004.

24. *The Globe and Mail*, March 25, 2005.

25. *BNA Act* 91:24. For background, see J.R. Miller, *Skyscrapers Hide the Heavens: A History of Indian–White Relations in Canada* (Toronto: University of Toronto Press, 1989).

26. Statistics Canada figures reported in *The Globe and Mail*, November 30, 1994.

27. From a draft report by Health Canada and Indian and Northern Affairs in the *Ottawa Citizen*, May 3, 1995.

28. As recorded in documents sent to Québec premier Robert Bourassa, August 20, 1990.

29. *Calder v Attorney General of B.C.*, [1973] S.C.R. 313.

30. The government has stated that it will cede no more than 5 percent of the total BC land mass to settle all claims, and no privately owned land will be included. Most Crown land will also be protected. This figure was chosen because Indians make up about 5 percent of the BC population. *The Globe and Mail*, May 29, 1995.

31. Michael Whittington, "Aboriginal self-government in Canada" in Michael Whittington and Glen Williams, eds., *Canadian Politics in the 21st Century* (Scarborough: Nelson, 2000), p. 109. Also see John H. Hylton, *Aboriginal Self-Government in Canada: Current Trends and Issues*, (Saskatoon: Purich Publishing Ltd., 1999).

32. Ibid., p. 115. See also Gurston Dacks, "Implementing First Nations Self-Government in Yukon: Lessons for Canada," *CJPS*, 37:3 (Sept. 2004), pp. 671–694.

33. Ailsa Henderson identified nine distinct regional variant cultures in Canada, each with unique political attitudes and behaviours that cannot be explained by provincial boundaries. See Ailsa Henderson, "Regional Political Cultures in Canada," *CJPS*, 37:3 (September 2004), pp. 595–616.

34. Roger Gibbins, *Regionalism and Territorial Politics in Canada and the United States* (Toronto: Butterworths, 1982), p. 181.

35. David J. Elkins, "The Sense of Place," in *Small Worlds*, p. 23.

36. Robert J. Jackson and Doreen Jackson, *Politics in Canada*, 6th ed. (Don Mills: Prentice Hall, 2006), Chapter 15.

37. United Nations, *Human Development Report 2004* (New York: Oxford University Press, 2004).

38. Robert Reich, in *USA Today*, June 27, p. 2A.

CHAPTER 3

1. See Garth Stevenson, *Unfulfilled Union: Canadian Federalism and National Unity*, revised ed. (Toronto: Macmillan, 1982).

2. Letters Patent are instruments by which prerogative powers are delegated by the Queen on the advice of her Canadian cabinet to her representative, the governor general. See also Chapter 6.

3. See Peter J.T. O'Hearn, *Peace, Order and Good Government* (Toronto: Macmillan, 1964).

4. For opposing arguments about Québec's use of the notwithstanding clause in the Charter of Rights to defend its language bill, see Reg Whitaker, "The Overriding Right," and P.K. Kuruvilla, "Why Quebec was Wrong," in *Policy Options*, vol. 10, no. 4 (May 1989), pp. 3–6 and 7–8.

5. *Ontario Film and Video Appreciation Society vs Ontario Board of Censors* (1984) 45 O.R. (2d)80.

6. *Shaping Canada's Future Together* (Ottawa: Supply and Services, 1991).

7. For more detail, see Robert J. Jackson and Doreen Jackson, *Politics in Canada*, 5th ed. (Scarborough: Prentice Hall, 2000), pp. 176–182.

CHAPTER 4

1. William H. Riker, "Federalism," in Fred I. Greenstein and Nelson W. Polsby, eds., *Handbook of Political Science Vol. 5: Government Institutions and Processes* (Reading, Mass.: Addison and Wesley, 1975), p. 101.

2. Ronald Watts, *Comparing Federal Systems in the 1990s* (Kingston: Institute of Intergovernmental Relations, 1996), p. xi.

3. See Donald Creighton, *John A. Macdonald: The Young Politician* (Toronto: Macmillan, 1952); and *The Road to Confederation: The Emergence of Canada 1863–1867* (Toronto: Macmillan, 1964).

4. The Québec City Conference on Confederation was decisive. It convened on October 10, 1864 and lasted seventeen days. Delegates representing Upper and Lower Canada, New Brunswick, Nova Scotia, Prince Edward Island and Newfoundland worked out the terms of political and economic association. The final agreement was signed in Charlottetown.

5. P.B. Waite, *The Life and Times of Confederation, 1864–1867* (Toronto: University of Toronto Press, 1962).

6. The most recent case occurred in 1961 when the lieutenant-governor of Saskatchewan, Frank Bastedo, without first consulting with the federal government, reserved provincial legislation that he believed was of doubtful validity. The Department of Justice quickly decided that the bill was within provincial jurisdiction and assent was given. R. MacGregor Dawson, *Government of Canada*, 5th ed., revised by Norman Ward (Toronto: University of Toronto Press, 1970), pp. 213–217.

7. Garth Stevenson, "Federalism and Intergovernmental Relations," in M.S. Whittington and G. Williams, eds., *Canadian Politics in the 1980s*, 2nd ed. (Toronto: Methuen, 1984), p. 378.

8. See Alain C. Cairns, "The Judicial Committee and its Critics," *Canadian Journal of Political Science* (*CJPS*), vol. 4, no. 3 (September 1971), pp. 301–345.

9. See Donald Swainson, ed., *Oliver Mowat's Ontario* (Toronto: Macmillan, 1972), especially Bruce W. Hodgins, "Disagreement at the Commencement: Divergent Ontarian Views of Federalism, 1867–1871," pp. 52–68.

10. See D.V. Smiley, ed., *The Rowell–Sirois Report: An Abridgement of Book I of the Royal Commission Report on Dominion–Provincial Relations*, The Carleton Library No. 5 (Toronto: McClelland & Stewart, 1963).

11. D.V. Smiley, "An Outsider's Observations of Federal–Provincial Relations Among Consenting Adults," in R. Simeon, ed., *Confrontation and Collaboration—Intergovernmental Relations in Canada Today* (Toronto: The Institute of Public Administration of Canada, 1979), pp. 109–111.

12. J.C. Strick, *Canadian Public Finance*, 2nd ed. (Toronto: Holt, Rinehart and Winston, 1978), pp. 100–101.

13. David B. Perry, "The Federal–Provincial Fiscal Arrangement Introduced in 1977," *Canadian Tax Journal*, vol. XXV. no. 4 (July/August, 1977), pp. 429–440.

14. Tax points or tax transfers consist of a reduction in federal taxes and an equivalent increase in provincial taxes.

15. Government of Canada, *Budget Plan*, February 27, 1995, p. 51ff.

16. *Ottawa Citizen*, February 28, 1995.

17. Studies for the PQ government in Québec, however, showed that federal transfers and equalization payments to Québec did not boost the case for separation. In fact, with only 25 percent of the population, Québec received 30 percent of the transfers in 1994. *The Globe and Mail*, May 19, 1995.

18. *The Globe and Mail*, September 19, 2000.

19. See Gerard W. Boychuk, "The Federal Role in Health Care Reform: Legacy or Limbo," in G. Bruce Doern, ed., *How Ottawa Spends, 2003–2004*, pp.89–104 (Don Mills: Oxford, 2003).

20. See http://pm.ca/grfx/docs/QuebecENG.pdf.

CHAPTER 5

1. On the types of nationalism, see Anthony D. Smith, *Nationalism in the Twentieth Century* (Oxford: Martin Robertson, 1979). On the "new" nationalism, see Michael Ignatieff, *Blood and Belonging: Journeys into the New Nationalism* (Toronto: Viking, 1993).

2. Attributed to Albert Einstein in Martin Levin, "Nationalism: disease or plague," *The Globe and Mail*, June 15, 1995.

3. There are many interpretations of nationalism. See A.D. Smith, *Theories of Nationalism* (Oxford: Oxford University Press, 1994); A.D. Smith, *Ethnicity and Nationalism* (Leiden, the Netherlands: Brill, 1992); the classic by Hans Kohn, *The Idea of Nationalism: A Study of its Origins and Background* (New York: Macmillan, 1944); and Liah Greenfeld, *Five Roads to Modernity* (Cambridge, Mass.: Harvard University Press, 1992).

4. Governments cannot use the notwithstanding clause to exempt the application of these Charter guarantees. In early 1993, Parliament and the New Brunswick legislature passed a constitutional amendment guaranteeing equal status for New Brunswick's French- and English-language communities. See Chapters 3, "The Constitutional Framework," for a discussion of the notwithstanding clause; see also Chapter 4, "Contested Federalism."

5. See, for example, Kenneth McRoberts, "Making Canada Bilingual: Illusions and Delusions of Federal Language Policy," in David Shugarman and Reg Whitaker, eds., *Federalism and Political Community* (Peterborough, Ont.: Broadview Press, 1989).

6. See Léon Dion, *Québec: The Unfinished Revolution* (Montréal: McGill–Queen's University Press, 1976); Herbert Guindon, "The Modernization of Québec and the Legitimacy of the Canadian State," in D. Glenday, et.al., *Modernization and the Canadian State* (Toronto: Macmillan, 1978), pp. 212–246.

7. See Denis Smith, *Bleeding Hearts . . . Bleeding Country: Canada and the Québec Crisis* (Edmonton: Hurtig, 1971).

8. For Trudeau's position, see Pierre Elliott Trudeau, *Federalism and the French Canadians* (Toronto: Macmillan, 1968), pp. 207–209.

9. For a summary, see William Coleman, *The Independence Movement in Quebec 1945–1980* (Toronto: University of Toronto Press, 1984); and John Saywell, *The Rise of the Parti Québécois, 1967–1976* (Toronto: University of Toronto Press, 1977).

10. Parti Québécois, *La Souveraineté* (Montréal: Service de communications du Parti Québécois, 1990).

11. *The Globe and Mail*, May 4, 1995.

12. *The Globe and Mail*, October 31, 1995.

13. See the review article by Stéphane Dion, "The Dynamic of Secessions: Scenarios after a Pro-Separatist Vote in a Québec Referendum," *Canadian Journal of Political Science* (*CJPS*), vol. XXVII, no. 3 (Sept. 1995), pp. 533–551.

14. *The Globe and Mail*, December 20, 1994.

15. For a comparative study of peaceful secessions, see Robert A. Young, "How Do Peaceful Secessions Happen?" *Canadian Journal of Political Science* (*CJPS*), vol. XXVII, no. 4 (Dec. 1994), pp. 773–792.

16. Stephane Dion, "Tell the truth, Bernard," *The Globe and Mail*, March 15, 2001.

17. Riccardo Petrella, "Nationalist and Regionalist Movements in Western Europe," in C. Foster, ed., *Nations Without A State* (New York: Praeger, 1980), p. 10. Emphasis has been added.

18. On the concept of Western alienation, see Roger Gibbins, *Prairie Politics and Society* (Toronto: Butterworths, 1980); and Larry Pratt and Garth Stevenson, eds., *Western Separatism* (Edmonton: Hurtig, 1981).

19. Quoted in David Elton and Roger Gibbins, " Western Alienation and Political Culture," in R. Schultz et al., eds., *The Canadian Political Process*, 3rd ed. (Toronto: Holt, Rinehart and Winston, 1979), p. 8.

20. Gibbins, *Regionalism*, p. 181. See also J.F. Conway, *The West: The History of a Region in Confederation* (Toronto: Lorimer, 1983).

21. See note 18.

22. *The Economist*, July 17, 2004, p. 37.

23. Andrew Cohen, "Ten little men short of ideas," *The Globe and Mail*, July 15, 2003.

24. F.L. (Ted) Morton, "The firewall's looking good again," *The Globe and Mail*, July 2, 2004.

25. Quoted in *The Globe and Mail*, July 2, 2004.

26. Roger Gibbins and Loleen Berdahl, *Western Visions, Western Futures: Perspectives on the West in Canada* (Peterborough, Ont.: Broadview Press, 2003), p. 209.

CHAPTER 6

1. Richard Rose and Ezra N. Suleiman, eds., *Presidents and Prime Ministers* (Washington: AEIPR, 1980).

2. See Chapter 7, "Parliament."

3. This is based on area of residence in adult life.

4. Judy La Marsh, *Memoirs of a Bird in a Gilded Cage* (Toronto: McClelland and Stewart, 1969), p. 57.

5. For example, all provincial premiers were made privy councillors in 1967 to celebrate Canada's Centennial.

6. Malcolm Punnett, *The Prime Minister in Canadian Government and Politics* (Toronto: Macmillan, 1977), p. 56.

7. For comparison of the Chrétien and Martin governing styles, see "The Chrétien Legacy," *Policy Options* (November 2002), pp.6–43; and "Paul Martin's Legacy," *Policy Options* (October 2002), pp.6–18.

8. Denis Smith, "President and Parliament: The Transformation of Parliamentary Government in Canada," in Tom Hockin, ed., *Apex of Power*, pp. 308–325.

9. Walter Stewart, *Shrug: Trudeau in Power* (Toronto: New Press, 1971).

CHAPTER 7

1. In theory, the governor general retains some discretionary power in the matter of dissolution; see Chapter 3.

2. The prayer was altered in February 1994 to make it non-denominational by eliminating reference to Jesus Christ. It also deleted archaic references to the British Empire and the royal family.

3. Private Members Business Office, *A Practical Guide to Private Members' Business* (Ottawa: Clerk of the House of Commons, 1993), p. 7.

4. For processes and reform proposals, see Peter C. Dobell and John Reid, "A Larger Role for the House of Commons," *Parliamentary Government*, vol. 40 (1992).

5. See Robert J. Jackson and Doreen Jackson, *Politics in Canada*, 6th ed. (Don Mills: Prentice Hall, 2006), Chapter 9.

6. See Robert J. Jackson and Paul Conlin, "The Imperative of Party Discipline in the Canadian Political System," in Mark Charlton and Paul Basher, eds., *Contemporary Political Issues*, 2nd ed. (Scarborough: Nelson, 1994).

7. Sydney Sharpe and Don Braid, *Storming Babylon: Preston Manning and the Rise of the Reform Party* (Toronto: Key Porter, 1992).

8. *The Globe and Mail*, March 19, 1994.

9. See House of Commons, *Précis of Procedure*, 4th ed. (Ottawa: Clerk of the House of Commons, 1991), and rule updates from that period forward.

10. For example, in 1992–1993, Senate committees held 301 meetings to discuss legislation, estimates and special studies. In fact, most senators' time (62.7 percent) was spent during that period in special committees discussing key social issues and making recommendations for policy initiatives.

11. This happened, for example, in 1979 under Joe Clark, who had only two Progressive Conservative MPs elected in Québec — so he named three ministers from Québec provincial politics to the Senate to bolster francophone representation in the federal Cabinet.

12. See J.R. Robertson, "Rejection of Bills by the Canadian Senate," unpublished, Library of Parliament Research Paper, 1990; and J. Stilborn, "The Powers of the Senate: Theory and Practice," unpublished, Library of Parliament Research Paper, 1990.

13. Frank Kunz, *The Modern Senate of Canada* (Toronto: University of Toronto Press, 1965), p. 118.

CHAPTER 8

1. H.H. Gerth and C. Wright Mills, eds. and trans., *From Max Weber: Essays in Sociology* (New York: Oxford University Press, 1946), pp. 232–235.

2. For elaboration of the theories and models of policy-making, see Robert J. Jackson and Doreen Jackson, *Politics in Canada*, 5th ed. (Scarborough: Prentice Hall, 2000), Chapter 13.

3. Historically, in departments where the minister's official designation was secretary of State (as in secretary of state for foreign affairs), the senior public servant was known as the undersecretary of state rather than the deputy minister.

4. John Langford, "Crown Corporations as Instruments of Policy," in G.G. Doern and P. Aucoin, eds., *Public Policy in Canada; Organization, Process and Management* (Toronto; Macmillan, 1979), pp. 239–274.

5. Economic Council of Canada, *Interim Report: Responsible Regulation*, p. xi.

6. "Governmental" task forces should not be confused with the "Special Committees" of the House of Commons.

7. See Sharon Sutherland, "Responsible Government and Ministerial Responsibility," *CJPS*, vol. 24, no. 1 (March 1991), pp. 91–120.

8. Kenneth Kernaghan, "Power, Parliament and Public Servants in Canada: Ministerial Responsibility Re-examined," in H.D. Clarke et al., eds., *Parliament, Policy and Representation* (Toronto: Methuen, 1980), p. 128.

9. Unless otherwise acknowledged, figures relating to Public Service employees are drawn from the appropriate Annual Reports of the Public Service Commission and Statistics Canada or the Treasury Board secretariat, 1999 report on public service enlargement.

10. Adapted from Government of Canada, *Budget Plan 1999*.

11. On one occasion, in May 1995, the auditor general deviated from his role as a financial watchdog and issued a report criticizing public servants' ethics. After surveying senior officials in several departments, he concluded that too many employees had a limited understanding of public sector ethics. As an example, the auditor pointed to the fact that four percent would accept a free stay at a ski chalet if offered by one of his or her grant recipients, and eleven percent would hire a brother-in-law for an untendered contract. Auditor General, *Interim Report* (Ottawa: 1995).

12. Donald J. Savoie, "Who is auditing the Auditor-General?" *The Globe and Mail*, August 25, 1995.

13. D.C. Rowat, "The Right of Public Access to Official Documents," in O.P. Dwivedi, ed., *The Administrative State in Canada: Essays in Honour of J.E. Hodgetts* (Toronto: University of Toronto Press, 1982), pp. 185–186.

14. See D.C. Rowat, "Reflections on the Ombudsman Concept," Nova Scotia Ombudsman's *Annual Report*, Dec. 31, 1990, pp. 26–34. For a critique of the proposed *Ombudsman Act*, see K.A. Friedmann and A.G. Milne, "The Federal Ombudsman Legislation: A Critique of Bill C-43," *Canadian Public Policy*, vol. 6, no. 1 (winter 1980), pp. 63–77.

15. Paul Thomas, "Courts Can't be Saviours," *Policy Options*, vol. 5, no. 3 (May/June 1984), p. 27.

CHAPTER 9

1. "Governor-in-council" is the formal or legal name under which Cabinet makes decisions. For a full explanation, see Chapter 6, "The Executive."

2. Peter H. Russell, "The Jurisdiction of the Supreme Court of Canada: Present Policies and a Programme for Reform," *Osgoode Hall Law Journal* (1969), p. 29.

3. Peter H. Russell, *The Judiciary in Canada: The Third Branch of Government* (Toronto: McGraw-Hill Ryerson, 1987), p. 335.

4. In 1971, when the *Yukon Act* and the *Northwest Territories Act* were proclaimed, they included the right of territorial governments to assume responsibility for the administration of justice with the exception of criminal matters.

5. For an excellent summary, see Andrew D. Heard, "The Charter in the Supreme Court of Canada: The Importance of Which Judges Hear an Appeal," *CJPS*, vol. XXIV, no. 2 (June 1991), pp. 289–307.

6. Jacob S. Ziegel, "Merit Selection and Democratization of Appointments to the Supreme Court of Canada," *Choices: Courts and Legislatures*, vol. 5, no. 2 (June 1999), pp. 3–19.

7. Supreme Court Judge Gérard LaForest, quoted in *The Globe and Mail*, April 14, 1987.

8. Peter H. Russell, *The Judiciary in Canada*, p. 360. For a detailed study of Charter cases and the Constitution, see Rainer Knopff and F.L. Morton, *Charter Politics* (Scarborough: Nelson, 1992).

9. *R. v. Morgentaler* (1988) 1 S.C.R. 30.

10. Mr. Justice Lamer, quoted in *The Globe and Mail*, April 14, 1987.

11. Margaret Wente, "The unintended results of new obscenity law," *The Globe and Mail*, October 15, 1994.

12. R.I. Cheffins and P.A. Johnson, *The Revised Canadian Constitution: Politics as Law* (Toronto: McGraw-Hill Ryerson, 1986), p. 152.

13. *The Globe and Mail*, April 17, 1995.

14. *The Globe and Mail*, May 26, 1995.

15. Ibid.

16. *The Globe and Mail*, May 26, 1995.

17. Frederick Vaughan, "Judicial Politics in Canada: Patterns and Trends," *Choices: Courts and Legislatures*, vol. 5, no. 1 (June 1999), p. 15.

18. *Maclean's*, March 29, 1999.

19. Statistics are from *Juristat*, vol. 12, no. 20 (Ottawa: Canadian Centre for Justice Statistics, 1991).

20. T. D'Arcy Finn, "Independent Review Agencies and Accountability," *Optimum*, vol. 24, no. 2 (Autumn 1993), pp. 9–23; Geoffrey Weller, "Accountability in Canadian Intelligence Services," in *International Journal of Intelligence and Counter-Intelligence*, vol. 2 (1988), pp. 415–41.

21. "Is Canada's Spy Agency out of Control?" *The Globe and Mail*, September 10, 1994.

22. The only exception is in Newfoundland, where the province maintains jurisdiction by a special arrangement with the federal government.

23. For details, see http://pco-bcp.gc.ca/docs/Publications/NatSecurnat/natsecurnat_e.pdf

CHAPTER 10

1. The collapse of the party system and the reasons for it are discussed in R. Kenneth Carty, William Cross and Lisa Young, *Rebuilding Canadian Party Politcs* (Vancouver: UBC Press, 2000, Chapter 1). For information on the rise of third parties, see Eric Bélanger, "The Rise of Third Parties in the 1993 Canadian Federal Election: Pinard Revisited," *CJPS*, 37:3 (Sept 2004), pp.561–580.

2. Hugh Thorburn, "Interpretations of the Canadian Party System," in H.G. Thorburn, ed., *Party Politics in Canada*, 6th ed. (Scarborough: Prentice Hall, 1991).

3. Reform adopted a traditional shadow Cabinet system in which individual MPs were given responsibility for questioning and criticizing specific cabinet ministers. Before that period, Reform's organization had allowed no specialization and many areas of government activity were not adequately monitored. These changes complemented a more aggressive Question Period strategy.

4. Carty and Young, *Rebuilding Party Politics*, p. 158.

5. Ibid., p. 159.

6. Lisa Young and William Cross, "Women's Involvement in Canadian Political Parties, Manon Tremblay and Linda Trimble, eds., *Women and Electoral Politics in Canada* (Toronto: Oxford University Press, 2003), p. 99.

7. See Maillé, C., *Primed for Power: Women in Canadian Politics* (Ottawa: Canadian Advisory Council on the Status of Women, 1990).

8. See J. Lele, G.C. Perlin and H.G. Thorburn, "The National Party Convention," in Thorburn, 5th ed., *Party Politics in Canada*, pp. 89–97.

9. R.M. Dawson, *The Government of Canada*, 5th ed. (Toronto: University of Toronto Press, 1970), p. 504.

10. John Diefenbaker's leadership was in dispute following his defeat in the 1963 general election, and party president Dalton Camp seized the opportunity to argue for the need to "democratize" the party by assessing the leadership. After a bitter struggle, the Camp faction won and a leadership convention was called in 1967.

11. The main complaint was that members had to join on or before June 20 to qualify to vote for delegates to the November convention. By controlling most riding associations, the Martin people could sign up members faster because they had more forms and could slow down the ability of rivals to get the necessary forms. In three of the four largest provinces, Ontario, Alberta and British Columbia, access to membership forms was controlled entirely by Martin supporters.

12. "Liberal Red: Bad Blood," *Maclean's,* Nov. 24, 2003.

13. *Ottawa Citizen*, July 25, 2003, A5.

14. See John Meisel, "The Decline of Party in Canada," in H.G. Thorburn, ed., *Party Politics in Canada*, 5th ed. (Scarborough: Prentice Hall, 1984).

15. Robert H. Salisbury, "Interest Groups," in Fred I. Greenstein and Nelson W. Polsby, eds., *Handbook of Political Science*, vol. 4 (Reading, Mass.: Addison-Welsey, 1975), p. 175.

16. The pluralist perspective is discussed along with other theories and critiques of democracy in Robert J. Jackson and Doreen Jackson, *Comparative Government*, 2nd ed. (Scarborough: Prentice Hall, 1997), Chapters 5 and 16. The number of lobbyists is monitored by the Lobbyists Registration Branch. The numbers are updated regularly — see http://strategis.ic.gc.ca/lobbyist.

17. A. Paul Pross, "Pressure Groups: Adaptive Instruments of Political Communication," in A. Paul Pross, ed., *Pressure Group Behaviour in Canadian Politics* (Toronto: McGraw-Hill Ryerson, 1975).

18. *The Globe and Mail*, April 1, 1995.

19. *The Ottawa Citizen*, December 2, 1994.

CHAPTER 11

1. In 1989, a Royal Commission on Electoral Reform and Party Financing produced a report, issued in four volumes in late 1991, containing many recommendations for reforms. Some minor ideas were enacted by legislation in 1993, before the election, but others languished and remain as part of the ongoing debate on electoral reform.

2. Specifically, contributions are prohibited from an individual who is not a Canadian citizen or permanent resident in Canada; an association that does not carry on activities in Canada; a union that is not entitled to bargain collectively in Canada; and a foreign state or political party.

3. The limit is calculated at $2.07 for each of the first 15 000 electors, $1.04 for each of the next 10 000 electors and $0.52 for each elector over 25 000. The formula is subject to certain adjustments and an inflation adjustment factor.

4. Richard Johnston, André Blais, Henry E. Brady and Jean Crête, *Letting the People Decide* (Montréal: McGill–Queen's University Press, 1992), p. 160.

5. Maurice Duverger, *Political Parties*, translated by B. and R. North (London: Methuen, 1954), Book II, Chapter 1.

6. Ibid., p. 217.

7. For further information about kinds of electoral systems and the effects they have on electoral outcomes, see Robert J. Jackson and Doreen Jackson, *Comparative Government* (Scarborough: Prentice Hall, 1997).

8. A. Lijphart, *Democracies: Patterns of Majoritarian and Consensus Government* (New Haven, Conn.: Yale, 1984).

9. See, for example, Daniel Pellerin and Patrick Thomson, "Proportional Representation is Likely to Create more Problems than it would solve; the Single Transferable vote offers a Better Choice" *Policy Options*, October 2004, pp. 54–59.

10. Law Commission of Canada, *Voting Counts: Electoral Reform for Canada* (Ottawa: Minister of Public Works, 2004), p. 104.

11. In 2000, turnout was actually 64 percent, not the 61 percent that was initially registered by Elections Canada because of a methodological flaw.

12. *The Globe and Mail*, June 29, 2004, A9. See also Brenda O'Neill, "Generational Patterns in the Political Opinions and Behaviour of Canadians," *Policy Matters* vol. 2, no. 5 (October 2001).

13. Munroe Eagles, "Voting and Non-voting in Canadian Federal Elections: An Ecological Analysis," in Herman Bakvis, ed., *Voter Turnout in Canada, Royal Commission on Electoral Reform and Party Financing* (Toronto: Dundurn Press, 1991), p. 25.

14. Jerome Black, "Reforming the Context of the Voting Process in Canada: Lessons from Other Democracies," in Herman Bakvis, ed., *Voter Turnout in Canada*, pp. 61–82.

15. Richard Johnston, André Blais, Henry E., Brady and Jean Crête, *Letting the People Decide* (Montréal: McGill–Queen's University Press, 1992), pp. 82–84.

16. The Canadian national election surveys of 1988 and 1993 used a research design that was especially sensitive to short-term factors and was able to capture the aggregate movement of voters among the parties during the campaigns.

17. For an extensive review of the debates about the role of class, region and religion in Canadian voting, and of the concept of party identification, see Elisabeth Gidengil, "Canada Votes: A Quarter Century of Canadian National Election Studies," *Canadian Journal of Political Science (CJPS)* vol. 25, no. 2 (June 1992), 219–248.

18. Richard Johnston et al., *Letting the People Decide*, p. 86.

19. Richard Johnston, "The Geography of Class and Religion in Canadian Elections," in Joseph Wearing, ed., *The Ballot and Its Message: Voting in Canada* (Toronto: Copp Clark Pitman, 1991), p. 128.

20. See Lawrence LeDuc, "The Flexible Canadian Electorate," in H.R. Penniman, *Canada at the Polls, 1984* (Washington D.C.: American Enterprise Institute for Public Policy Research, 1995), pp. 40–41.

21. Party identification percentages for the main parties in 1988 were Conservative 29, Liberal 24, NDP 11. Johnston et al., *Letting the People Decide* (Montréal: McGill–Queen's University Press, 1992), pp. 82–84.

22. See Chapter 8 on partisan loyalties in André Blais, et al., *Anatomy of a Liberal Victory: Making Sense of the Vote in the 2000 Canadian Election* (Peterborough, Ont.: Broadview Press, 2002).

23. H. Michael Stevenson, "Ideology and Unstable Party Identification in Canada: Limited Rationality in a Brokerage Party System," *Canadian Journal of Political Science (CJPS)*, vol. 20, no. 4 (December 1987), p. 815.

24. Susan Delacourt, *Juggernaut: Paul Martin's Campaign for Chrétien's Crown* (Toronto: McClelland & Stewart, 2003).

25. Jeffrey Simpson, *The Globe and Mail*, June 30.

26. *The Globe and Mail*, July 21, 2004.

27. Ibid.

28. Ibid.

29. Ibid.

30. Annabelle Sreberny-Mohammadi and Karen Ross, "Women MPs and the Media: Representing the Body Politic," *Parliamentary Affairs* (49:1996), p. 112.

31. See Shannon Sampert and Linda Trimble, "'Wham, Bam, No Thank you Ma'am': Gender and the Game Frame in National Newspaper Coverage of Election 2000," in Manon Tremblay and Linda Trimble, eds., *Women and Electoral Politics in Canada*, (Don Mills: Oxford University Press, 2003), pp. 211–226.

32. The McGill Observatory on Media and Public Policy, independent tracking and evaluation of the campaign coverage of seven newspapers. Reported in *The Globe and Mail*, June 12, 2004, A2 and June 5, A11.

33. *The Windsor Star*, June 27, 2004.

CHAPTER 12

1. For a more detailed examination, see Robert J. Jackson, "Honesty and Corruption in Canadian Federal Government and Politics," in Jenny Fleming and Ian Holland, eds., *Motivating Ministers to Morality* (London: Ashgate, 2001).

2. For example, Ontario appointed an integrity commissioner in 1988 and has an *Integrity Act*. British Columbia appointed a conflict of interest commissioner in 1990.

3. Privy Council Office, Canada. *Members of Parliament and Conflict of Interest*, MacEachen Green Paper, (Ottawa: Information Canada, 1973).

4. Canada. Commission of Inquiry into the Facts and Allegations of Conflict of Interest Concerning the Honourable Sinclair M. Stevens, *Report* (Ottawa: Supply and Services, 1987).

5. Maureen Mancuso, et al., *A Question of Ethics: Canadians Speak Out* (Don Mills: Oxford University Press, 1998).

6. Ibid., p. 97.

7. Howard Wilson, "Principles Respecting Government Contacts with Judicial and Quasi-Judicial Bodies." Notes for Speech to the 15th Annual Administrative Law Seminar (Ottawa 1998); "Ethics and Government: the Canadian Case," in *Australia and Parliamentary Orthodoxy* (Canberra: Department of the Senate, 1999).

8. For greater detail on these cases and the ethic counsellor's action, see Robert J. Jackson, "Honesty and Corruption."

9. *The Globe and Mail*, April 3, 2004.

10. The UK Register of Members' Interests requires the detailing of private interests, holdings, investments, gifts received, trips taken and other sources of income. See Maureen Mancuso, *The Ethical World of British MPs* (Kingston: McGill–Queen's Press, 1995).

11. For details, see Report 25, Standing Committee on Procedure, April 27, 2003.

Further Reading

CHAPTER 2

Axworthy, Lloyd. *Navigating a New World: Canada's Global Future.* Toronto: Knopf Canada, 2003.

Bell, David V.J. *The Roots of Disunity: A Study of Canadian Political Culture.* Don Mills: Oxford University Press, 1992.

Berry, J.W., and J.A. Laponce. *Ethnicity and Culture in Canada.* Toronto: University of Toronto Press, 1994.

Bissoondath, Neil. *Selling Illusions: The Cult of Multiculturalism in Canada.* Toronto: Penguin Books, 1995.

Cairns, Alan C. *Aboriginal Peoples and the Canadian State.* Vancouver: UBC Press, 2000.

Flanagan, Tom. *First Nations? Second Thoughts.* McGill-Queen's University Press, 2000.

Gibbins, Roger and Loleen Berdahl. *Western Visions, Western Futures.* Peterborough, Ont.: Broadview Press, 2003.

Hamilton, Roberta. *Gendering the Vertical Mosaic.* Toronto: Copp Clark, 1996.

Joy, Richard J. *Canada's Official Languages.* Toronto: University of Toronto Press, 1992.

Kaplan, William, ed. *Belonging: The Meaning and Future of Canadian Citizenship.* Montréal; McGill–Queen's University Press, 1993.

Kymlicka, Will. *Multicultural Citizenship.* Oxford: Clarendon Press, 1995.

MacIvor, H. *Women and Politics in Canada.* Peterborough, Ont., Broadview, 1994.

Molot, M. ed. *Vanishing Borders.* Don Mills: Oxford University Press, 2000.

Ponting, J. Rick. *First Nations in Canada: Perspectives on Opportunity, Empowerment and Self Determination.* Toronto: McGraw-Hill Ryerson, 1997.

Riddell-Dixon, Elizabeth. *Canada and Beijing Conference on Women: Governmental Politics and NGO Participation.* Vancouver: UBC Press, 2001.

Roach, Ruth, Paula Bourne, Marjorie Cohen and Philinda Masters. *Canadian Women's Issues.* Toronto: James Lorimer, 1993.

Thomas, David M., ed. *Canada and the U.S.: Differences that Count,* 2nd ed. Toronto: Broadview Press, 2000.

Webber, Jeremy. *Reimagining Canada: Language, Culture, Community and the Canadian Constitution.* Montréal: McGill–Queen's University Press, 1994.

CHAPTER 3

See also the further reading in Chapter 9.

Ajzenstat, Janet, ed. *Canadian Constitutionalism: 1791–1991.* Ottawa: Canadian Study of Parliament Group, 1992.

Bakan, Joel, and David Schneiderman. *Social Justice and the Constitution.* Don Mills: Oxford University Press, 1992.

Behiels, Michael, ed. *The Meech Lake Primer: Conflicting Views of the 1987 Constitutional Accord.* Ottawa: University of Ottawa Press, 1989.

Cairns, A.C. *Charter Versus Federalism: The Dilemmas of Constitutional Reform.* Montréal: McGill–Queen's University Press, 1992.

Conklin, William. *Images of a Constitution.* Toronto: University of Toronto Press, 1993.

Cook, Curtis, ed. *Constitutional Predicament.* Montréal: McGill–Queen's Press, 1994.

Funston, Bernard, and Eugene Meehan. *Canada's Constitutional Law in a Nutshell,* 2nd ed. Toronto: Carswell, 1998.

Heard, Andrew. *Canadian Constitutional Conventions.* Don Mills: Oxford University Press, 1991.

Hogg, Peter. *Constitutional Law of Canada,* 3rd ed. Toronto: Carswell, 1992; Student Edition, 1999.

Jackson, Robert, and Doreen Jackson. *Stand Up for Canada: Leadership and the Canadian Crisis.* Scarborough: Prentice Hall, 1992.

Knopff, Rainer, and F.L. Morton. *Charter Politics.* Scarborough: Nelson, 1992.

Lazar, Harvey, ed. *The State of the Federation 1997: Non-Constitutional Renewal.* Kingston: Institute of Intergovernmental Relations, 1997.

Russell, Peter H. *Constitutional Odyssey.* Toronto: University of Toronto Press, 1993.

CHAPTER 4

Bakvis, Herman and Grace Skogstad, eds. *Canadian Federalism: Performance, Effectiveness and Legitimacy.* Don Mills: Oxford University Press, 2002).

Bercuson, David J., and Barry Cooper. *Deconfederation: Canada Without Québec.* Toronto: Key Porter, 1991.

Howlett, Michael, and David Laycock. *The Puzzles of Power.* Mississauga: Copp Clark Pittman, Ltd., 1994.

La Selva, Samuel. *The Moral Foundations of Canadian Federalism: Paradoxes, Achievements and Tragedies of Nationhood.* Montréal: McGill–Queen's University Press, 1997.

Rocher, Francois, and Miriam Smith, eds. *New Trends in Canadian Federalism.* Peterborough, Ont.: Broadview Press, 1995.

Stevenson, Garth. *Federalism in Canada.* Toronto: McClelland & Stewart, 1990.

———. *Unfulfilled Union, Canadian Federalism and National Unity,* 4th ed. Montréal: McGill Queen's University Press, 2004.

Watts, Ronald L. *Comparing Federal Systems in the 1990s.* Kingston: Institute of Intergovernmental Relations, 1996.

Westmacott, Martin, and Hugh Mellon, eds. *Challenges to Canadian Federalism.* Scarborough: Prentice Hall, 1998.

Young, Robert A., ed. *Stretching the Federation: The Art of State in Canada.* Montréal: McGill–Queen's University Press, 1999.

CHAPTER 5

Braid, Don, and Sydney Sharpe. *Breakup: Why the West Feels Left out of Canada.* Toronto: Key Porter Books, 1990.

Côté, Marcel, and David Johnson. *If Québec Goes: The Real Cost of Separation*. Toronto: Stoddart, 1994.

Freeman, Alan, and Patrick Grady. *Dividing the House: Planning for a Canada without Québec*. Toronto: HarperCollins, 1994.

Gibbins, Roger. *Conflict and Unity*, 3rd ed. Scarborough: Nelson, 1994.

Gibbins, Roger and Loleen Berdahl. *Western Visions, Western Futures: Perspectives on the West in Canada*. Peterborough, Ont.: Broadview Press, 2003.

Gibson, Gordon. *Plan B: The Future of the Rest of Canada*. Vancouver: Fraser Institute, 1994.

Johnston, Richard, et al. *The Challenge of Direct Democracy: The 1992 Canadian Referendum*. Montréal: McGill–Queen's University Press, 1996.

Lamont, Lansing. *Breakup: The Coming End of Canada and the Stakes for America*. New York: Norton, 1994.

Lemco, Jonathan. *Turmoil in the Peaceable Kingdom: The Quebec Sovereignty Movement and its Implications for Canada and the United States*. Toronto: University of Toronto Press, 1994.

McRoberts, Kenneth. *Misconceiving Canada: The Struggle for Unity*. Don Mills: Oxford University Press, 1997.

Monahan, Patrick J. *Cooler Heads Shall Prevail: Assessing the Costs and Consequences of Québec Separation*. Toronto: C.D. Howe Institute, 1994.

Saul, John Ralston. *Reflections of a Siamese Twin: Canada at the End of the Twentieth Century*. Toronto: Viking, 1997.

Tomblin, Stephen. *Ottawa and the Outer Provinces* (Halifax: Lorimer, 1995).

Young, Robert A. *The Secession of Québec and the Future of Canada*. Montréal: McGill–Queen's University Press, 1995.

CHAPTER 6

Bakvis, H. *Regional Ministers: Power and Influence in the Canadian Cabinet*. Toronto: University of Toronto Press, 1991.

Bliss, Michael. *Right Honourable Men: The Descent of Canadian Politics from Macdonald to Mulroney*. Toronto: HarperCollins, 1994.

Cameron, Stevie. *On the Take: Crime, Corruption and Greed in the Mulroney Years*. Toronto: Macfarlane, Walter and Ross, 1994.

Granastein, J.L. *Prime Ministers*. Toronto: HarperCollins, 1999.

Levine, Allan. *Scrum Wars: The Prime Minister and the Media*. Toronto: Dundurn Press, 1993.

Mancuso, Maureen, ed. *Leaders and Leadership in Canada*. Don Mills: Oxford University Press, 1994.

Matheson, William A. *The Prime Minister and the Cabinet*. Toronto: Methuen, 1976.

McCall, Christina, and Stephen Clarkson. *Trudeau and Our Times*, vol.2. Toronto: McClelland and Stewart, 1994.

Savoie, Donald J. *Governing from the Centre* (Toronto: University of Toronto Press, 1999).

CHAPTER 7

Docherty, David C. *Mr. Smith Goes to Ottawa: Life in the House of Commons*. Vancouver: UBC Press, 1997.

Franks, C.E.S. *The Parliament of Canada*. Toronto: University of Toronto Press, 1987.

Gunther, J., and C. Winn, eds. *House of Commons Reform*. Ottawa: Parliamentary Internship Programme, 1991.

Jackson, Robert J., and Michael M. Atkinson. *The Canadian Legislative System*, 2nd ed. Toronto: Macmillan, 1980.

Weaver, R. Kent, and Bert A. Rockman, eds. *Do Institutions Matter: Government Capabilities in the United States and Abroad*. Washington: The Brookings Institution, 1993.

CHAPTER 8

Adie, Robert F., and Paul G. Thomas. *Canadian Public Administration*, 2nd ed. Scarborough: Prentice Hall, 1987.

Doern, G. Bruce. *How Ottawa Spends, 2004–2005*. Montréal: McGill-Queen's University Press, 2004.

Dwivedi, O.P., and James Iain Gow. *From Bureaucracy to Public Management: The Administrative Culture of the Government of Canada*. Peterborough, Ont.: Broadview Press, 1999.

Hodgetts, J.E. *Public Management: Emblem of Reform of the Canadian Public Service*. Ottawa: Canadian Centre for Management Development, 1991.

Kernaghan, Kenneth, and John Langford. *The Responsible Public Servant*. Halifax: IRPP, 1990.

───── and David Siegal. *Public Administration in Canada: A Text*, 4th ed. Scarborough: Nelson, 1999.

McQuaig, Linda. *Shooting the Hippo: Death by Deficit and Other Canadian Myths*. Toronto: Viking, 1995.

Osbaldeston, Gordon F. *Organizing to Govern*, vols. I and II. Whitby, Ont.: McGraw-Hill Ryerson, 1992.

Pal, Leslie A. *How Ottawa Spends 2000–2001*. Don Mills: Oxford University Press, 2000.

Peters, B. Guy, and Donald J. Savoie, eds. *Taking Stock: Assessing Public Sector Reforms*. Montréal: McGill–Queen's University Press, 1998.

Savoie, Donald J. *Thatcher, Reagan and Mulroney: In Search of a New Bureaucracy*. Toronto: University of Toronto Press, 1994.

CHAPTER 9

Case, Roland. *Understanding Judicial Reasoning: Controversies, Concepts and Cases*. Toronto: Thompson Book, 1997.

Gall, Gerald L. *The Canadian Legal System*, 4th ed. Toronto: Carswell, 1995.

Government of Canada. *A Vision of the Future of Policing in Canada*. Ottawa: Solicitor General, 1990.

Greenawalt, Kent. *Fighting Words: Individuals, Communities and Liberties of Speech*. Princeton: Princeton University Press, 1995.

Hogg, Peter. *Constitutional Law of Canada*, 2nd ed. Toronto: Carswell, student edition, 1999.

Knopff, Rainer, and F.L. Morton. *Charter Politics*. Scarborough: Nelson, 1992.

Manfredi, Christopher P. *Judicial Power and the Charter: Canada and the Paradox of Liberal Constitutionalism*. Toronto: McClelland and Stewart, 1993.

McCormick, P. *Supreme at Last*. Toronto: Lorimer, 2000.

McCormick, P., and I. Greene. *Judges and Judging*. Toronto: Lorimer, 1990.

Millar, Perry S., and Carl Baar. *Judicial Administration in Canada*. Montréal: McGill–Queen's Press, 1981.

Morton, F.L. *Law, Politics and the Judicial Process in Canada*, 3rd ed. Calgary: University of Calgary Press, 2002.

Sawatsky, John. *Men in the Shadows: The RCMP Security Service*. Toronto: Doubleday, 1980.

Seagrave, Jayne. *Introduction to Policing in Canada*. Scarborough: Prentice Hall, 1997).

Sharpe, Rjobert J., Katherine Swinton and Ken Roach. *The Charter of Rights and Freedoms*, 2nd ed. Toronto: Irwin Law, 2003.

CHAPTER 10

Archer, Keith, and Alan Whitehorn. *Canadian Trade Unions and the New Democratic Party*. Kingston, Ont.: Industrial Relations Centre, 1993.

Azoulay, Dan. *Canadian Political Parties: Historical Readings*. Toronto: Irwin, 1999.

Bakvis, Herman, ed. *Canadian Political Parties: Leaders, Candidates and Organization, Royal Commission on Electoral Reform and Party Financing*, vol. 13. Toronto: Dundurn Press, 1991.

Campbell, Colin, and William Christian. *Parties, Leaders and Ideologies in Canada*. Whitby, Ont.: McGraw-Hill Ryerson, 1996.

Carty, K.R., ed. *Canadian Political Party Systems*. Peterborough, Ont.: Broadview Press, 1992.

Chenier, J.A., and Scott Duncan, eds. *The Federal Lobbyists, 1999*. Ottawa: ARC Publications, 1999.

Pross, Paul. *Group Politics and Public Policy*. Don Mills: Oxford University Press, 1986.

Reddick, Andrew. *The Duality of the Public Interest: Networks, Policy and People*. Ottawa: Ph.D. thesis, 2002.

Seidle, F. Leslie, ed. *Interest Groups and Elections in Canada*, vol. 2 of the Research Studies of the Royal Commission on Election Financing and Party Reform. Toronto: Dundurn Press, 1991.

Tanguay, A.B., and A.G. Gagnon, eds. *Canadian Parties in Transition*, 2nd ed. Scarborough: Nelson, 1996.

Thorburn, H.G. *Party Politics in Canada*, 7th ed. Scarborough: Prentice Hall, 1994).

CHAPTER 11

Archer, Keith. *Political Choices and Electoral Consequences*. Montréal: McGill–Queen's University Press, 1990.

Bakvis, Herman, ed. *Voter Turnout in Canada*, Royal Commission on Electoral Reform and Party Financing (RCERPF), vol. 15. Toronto: Dundurn Press 1991.

Blais, André et al. *Anatomy of a Liberal Victory: Making Sense of the Vote in the 2000 Canadian Election*. Peterborough, Ont.: Broadview Press, 2002.

Boyer, Patrick. *Direct Democracy in Canada: The History and Future of Referendums.* Toronto: Dundurn Press, 1992.

Brook, Tom. *Getting Elected in Canada.* Stratford: Mercury Press, 1991.

Cassidy, Michael, ed. *Democratic Rights and Electoral Reform in Canada*, Royal Commission on Electoral Reform and Party Financing (RCERPF), vol. 10. Toronto: Dundurn Press, 1991.

John C. Courtney, Peter MacKinnon, and David E. Smith, eds. *Drawing Boundaries: Legislatures, Courts, and Electoral Values.* Saskatoon: Fifth House Publishers, 1992.

Everitt, Joanna, and Brenda O'Neill, eds. *Citizen Politics: Research and Theory in Canadian Political Behaviour.* Don Mills: Oxford University Press, 2002.

Frizzell, Alan, and Jon H. Pammett. *The Canadian General Election of 1997.* Toronto: Dundurn Press, 1997.

Johnston, Richard, André Blais, Henry E. Brady, and Jean Crête. *Letting the People Decide: Dynamics of A Canadian Election.* Montréal: McGill–Queen's University Press, 1992.

Martin, Michèle. *Communication and Mass Media.* Scarborough: Prentice Hall, 1997.

Nevitte, Neil, et al. *Unsteady State: The 1997 Canadian Federal Election.* Don Mills: Oxford University Press, 2000.

Jon H. Pammett and Christopher Dornan, eds. *The Canadian General Election of 2000.* Toronto: Dundurn, 2001.

Taras, David. *The Newsmakers.* Scarborough: Nelson Canada, 1990.

Tremblay, Manon, and Linda Trimble, eds. *Women and Electoral Politics in Canada.* Don Mills: Oxford University Press, 2003.

Wearing, Joseph, ed. *The Ballot and Its Message.* Toronto: Copp Clark Pitman, 1991.

CHAPTER 12

Fife, Robert, and John Warren. *A Capital Scandal.* Toronto: Key Porter, 1991.

Greene, Ian, and David Shugarman. *Honest Politics.* Toronto: Lorimer, 1997.

Hoy, Claire. *Friends in High Places: Politics and Patronage in the Mulroney Government.* Toronto: Key Porter, 1987.

Hyde, Anthony. *Promises, Promises: Breaking Faith in Canadian Politics.* Toronto: Viking, 1997.

Kernaghan, Kenneth, ed. *Do Unto Others: Ethics in Government and Business.* Toronto: Institute of Public Administration of Canada, 1991.

Langford, John W., and Allan Tupper, eds. *Corruption, Character and Conduct: Essays on Canadian Government Ethics.* Don Mills: Oxford University Press, 1994, pp. 67–89.

Mancuso, Maureen, et al. *A Question of Ethics: Canadians Speak Out.* Don Mills: Oxford University Press, 1998.

McQueen, Rod. *Blind Trust.* Toronto: Macmillan, 1992.

Simpson, Jeffrey. *Spoils of Power.* Toronto: Collins, 1988.

Glossary

aboriginal rights — historic rights (mostly in the form of land claims) for various groups of Aboriginals, based on Native occupancy and use of North American land before Europeans arrived.

adjournment (recess) — a break period taken by the House of Commons within a session.

advisory bodies — federal organizations whose activities are closely related to the formulation of public policies. They include Royal Commissions, government and departmental task forces and advisory councils.

amendment formula — the procedure required to change a constitution.

assistant deputy minister (ADM) — one of two or more individuals who heads a branch or bureau and reports directly to the deputy minister (DM).

attitudes — orientations toward political objects that are more differentiated and fleeting than basic values, but which may be more immediate determinants of political behaviour.

auditor general — provides a critical appraisal of the effectiveness of both public spending and accounting practices — to Parliament, and in particular, to the Public Accounts Committee. The auditor general is directly responsible to Parliament (not the executive).

authoritarian political system — a system of government which imposes one dominant interest, that of the political elite, on all others.

authority — the government's power to amake binding decisions and issue obligatory commands.

backbenchers — MPs on the government side who are not ministers, or on the opposition side who are not designated party critics.

bicameral — refers to a legislature composed of two houses.

bills — legislation presented to the House of Commons that may be passed into law. There are two categories of bills: public and private.

block grant — a grant of one large sum of money from the federal government to the provinces to be spent in certain policy fields.

brokerage theory — maintains that the two oldest parties in Canada have no central ideological interests, but rather act as brokers of ideas, selecting those that have the widest appeal and the best likelihood of attracting electoral support.

budget — a document primarily concerned with setting out where the revenue will come from to carry out the government's program.

budget debate — the four-day (not necessarily consecutive) debate that follows the presentation of the budget.

bureaucracy — refers to a specific form of government organization based on the premise that it should be structured to provide as much efficiency as possible and that this is best achieved by setting up a hierarchically structured decision-making process which minimizes arbitrary decision-making.

by-election — an election held in a constituency to fill a legislative seat which has fallen vacant between general elections.

Cabinet and ministry — the Cabinet is a body of the most powerful ministers appointed by the prime minister, which acts in the name of the Privy Council. The ministry is composed of all ministers who are appointed by the PM; it consists of both full ministers of the Crown and ministers of state.

Canada Assistance Program (CAP) — a program by which the federal government helps to finance welfare and other provincial social services.

Canada Health and Social Transfer (CHST) — a lock grant system that took effect in 1996–1997; formed from the Established Program Financing and the Canada Assistance Program.

Canadian Bill of Rights — a piece of legislation passed in 1960 that listed fundamental freedoms but was never entrenched in the Constitution.

Canadian Security Intelligence Service (CSIS) — an intelligence-gathering institution. Its operations, headed by a director, are governed by the 1984 *Canadian Security Intelligence Act.*

Charlottetown Accord — an August 1992 agreement in principle on what changes needed to be made to the Constitution; rejected in a countrywide referendum.

chief electoral officer (CEO) — a permanent public employee appointed by the Cabinet under the authority of the *Canadian Election Act* to head Elections Canada.

citizen — an individual who is a formal member of a state, and therefore eligible to enjoy specified rights and privileges.

civil law — regulates relations between or among private individuals and corporations. It is concerned mainly with disputes over property and commercial contracts. Following laws based on provincial authority in the fields of "property and civil rights," judges and juries render decisions about the amount of damages and payments.

Clarity Act — from a government bill of 1999 that sets out the rules by which the government and Parliament of Canada would react to any future separatist referendum. It concludes that the government will not enter into any negotiations over separation with a province unless the House of Commons determines that 1) the referendum question is "clear" and 2) a "clear" expression of will has been obtained by a "clear" majority of the population.

class — refers to a rank or order in society determined by such characteristics as education, occupation and income.

clerk of the House — an official responsible for ensuring that relevant documents are printed and circulated and advising the speaker of the House on the parliamentary business of the day.

clerk of the Privy Council — the top position in the Privy Council

Office (PCO).

closure — a measure to terminate debate in the House.

coalition government — a government formed from more than one party.

code — a legislative law that is brought together in a single body to provide a relatively complete set of rules in one or more fields of law.

collective ministerial responsibility — an ethical standard for the federal Cabinet; as a group, cabinet ministers are supposed to be held accountable to Parliament for their government's actions.

collective rights — entitlements or duties owed to certain groups by the state.

committee of the whole — a committee of the House in which all MPs sit in the chamber in one large committee chaired by the deputy speaker or the deputy chair of committees.

common law — the precise form of customary law that developed in twelfth century Britain as a body of established rules based on the principle of *stare decisis*.

Communications Security Establishment (CSE) — established in 1949 as part of the National Research Council to intercept the communications of clandestine organizations.

compact theory of Confederation — the notion of "two founding nations" which provides French Canadians a collective claim to equality rather than simple minority status within Canada.

competitive party system — allows parties to compete for, and have access to, legislative power.

concurrent powers — power shared between the Parliament of Canada and the provincial legislatures.

conditional grants — funds given by the federal government to provincial governments on the condition that they be spent in a certain way.

confederation — a form of political organization that loosely unites strong provincial units under a weak central government.

conflict of interest — a situation in which a prime minister, cabinet minister, member of Parliament or public servant has knowledge of a private, personal economic interest sufficient to influence how he or she exercises public duties and responsibilities.

constituency — a geographical area which provides the locus of the grassroots organization of political parties; also known as a *riding*.

constitution — a body of fundamental rules, written and unwritten, under which government operates.

constitutional law — a body of fundamental rules in a constitution, written and unwritten, that influence the making of other laws.

constitutional monarchy — a form of government in which the head of state is the Queen, but the constitution shapes the arrangements of political power.

constitutionalism — a system in which everyone, including the government, is subject to the rules of the constitution.

convention — a custom or practice that, while not necessarily a legal necessity, is nevertheless based on accepted reasons and practices.

Corrections Canada — government officials responsible for inmates in federal prisons and for parolees.

criminal law — pits individuals charged with criminal offences against the state. Unlike civil law, criminal law comes under federal authority in Canada.

Crown — refers to the composite symbol of the institutions of the state. The Crown assumes a variety of duties and responsibilities; for example, it may be involved in court proceedings.

Crown agencies — include a wide variety of non-departmental organizations, including Crown corporations, regulatory agencies, administrative tribunals and some advisory bodies.

Crown corporation — a semi-autonomous agency of government organized under the corporate form to perform a task or group of related tasks in the national interest.

customary law — results from the evolution of norms which affect the way individuals and groups are expected to act toward one another.

debt — the accumulation of deficits over the years.

declaratory power — allows the federal government to assume jurisdiction over any "work" considered to be for the benefit of Canada as a whole (e.g., uranium exploration).

deficit — the amount by which government spending exceeds revenues in one year.

democratic political system — is a system of government which reconciles competing interests through competitive elections.

Department of Finance — one of four central coordinating agencies of the executive, it analyzes taxation policy and the impact of government activity on the economy.

Department of Public Safety and Emergency Preparedness — an organization set up by the federal government in 2003 to monitor national security, crisis management, emergency preparedness, border functions, corrections, policing and crime prevention.

deputy minister (DM) — the administrative and managerial head of each department or ministry — its senior public servant.

direct taxation — refers to taxes which are collected directly by the government, such as individual income tax, corporate income tax and succession duties.

disallowance — the power to disallow provincial legislation even though the subject matter of the legislation is assigned to the provinces by the *BNA Act*.

dissolution — the end of a particular Parliament, which occurs at the request of a prime minister who seeks a new mandate or whose government has been defeated in the House of Commons.

distinct society — a term that the Charlottetown Accord called to be added to the Constitution to describe Québec; "Quebec constitutes within Canada a distinct society, which includes a French-speaking majority, a unique culture and a civil law tradition."

doctrine of parliamentary supremacy — a basic premise of British parliamentary democracy. In Canada, it means that, subject to the Constitution, all eleven legislatures have the authority, in theory, to repeal or modify any principle set out in common law.

Elections Canada — a special government agency that administers elections and is responsible solely to the House of Commons.

electoral system — refers to the means by which votes cast for candidates are translated into legislative seats.

entrenchment — means to embody provisions in a constitution so that they are protected and can be changed only by formal amendment procedures.

equalization payments — unconditional transfer payments to the provinces from the federal government calculated according to the ability of each province to raise revenue.

Established Program Financing (EPF) — a federal block grant program that is essentially conditional in nature.

estimates — the government's spending proposals for the next fiscal year.

ethics commissioner — a new (as of 2004), independent commissioner who reports directly to the House of Commons (i.e., not the prime minister) and has the authority to review the actions of all members of Parliament, including cabinet ministers and the prime minister. A Senate ethics officer position was also created in 2004.

ethics counsellor — a position formally created in 1994 by the federal Liberals, ten years after the governing Tories commissioned the Task Force on Conflict of Interest (or Sharp-Starr Report); the ethics counsellor's mandate was to uphold the code of conduct for public office-holders as well as to enforce the *Lobbyists Registration Act*. However, the counsellor's most important responsibility was to probe the ethical conduct of cabinet ministers when requested to do so by the prime minister. This became problematic when it became understood that the ethics counsellor reported directly to the PM.

ethnicity — primarily a subjective term used to describe groups of people who share customs, language, dialect and/or cultural heritage, and sometimes distinct physical or racial characteristics.

ethnic origin — refers to the ethnic or cultural group(s) to which an individual's ancestors belonged; it pertains to the ancestral roots or origins of the population, and not to place of birth, citizenship or nationality.

executive — a broad term that refers to the institutions, personnel and behaviour of governmental power. In modern times, executives are the organizational centres of political systems.

expenditure process — brings together the estimated spending requirements of all government departments and agencies for the next fiscal year.

Expenditure Review — a subcommittee mandated to see that government expenditures are related to government priorities.

extra-parliamentary wing — a wing of traditional parties comprised of the national executive, standing committees and permanent national office as well as provincial associations and local constituency organizations.

Federal Court of Canada — established by Parliament in 1971 to settle claims by or against the federal government on matters relating to Maritime law, copyright, patent and trademark law, and federal taxation statutes, and to undertake a supervisory role related to the decisions of tribunals and inferior bodies established by federal law.

federal system — a system in which legal powers are divided between a central government and regional governments in such a way that each level of government has some kind of activities on which it makes final decisions.

federation — a form of political organization in which the activities of government are divided between regional governments and a central government in such a way that each level of government has activities on which it makes final decisions.

"flexible" constitution — a constitution that can be amended easily and adapted to changing circumstances.

franchise — the right to vote.

gerrymandering — when a party seeks to take advantage of its position in government to redraw electoral boundaries in such a way as to enable it to win more seats.

government — consists of the authoritative structures of the political system.

government bills — bills introduced by the Cabinet as government policy.

government department — an administrative unit of government which is headed by a cabinet minister and largely responsible for the administration of a range of programs serving the public.

governor general — the representative of the monarch in Canada, appointed by Her Majesty on the recommendation of the Canadian prime minister and Cabinet.

governor-in-council — the formal executive authority of the governor general applied upon the advice and consultation of the Cabinet is referred to as a decision of the governor-in-council.

gross domestic product (GDP) — the market value of all final goods and services produced in a specific period.

House leader — an MP designated by the leader of each party in the House of Commons as manager of party conduct in the House.

ideology — an explicit doctrinal structure which provides a particular diagnosis of the ills of society, plus an accompanying "action program" for implementing prescribed solutions for them.

indirect taxation — refers to taxes that are collected by other persons or institutions and passed along to the government (e.g., sales tax).

individual rights — refers to individual claims against the state.

individual ministerial responsibility — refers to the personal responsibility of each minister in Cabinet. As heads of departments, ministers receive confidential advice from pubic servants, make important decisions, and then are held accountable for those decisions in Parliament and in the country.

interest group — an organized association which engages in activity which is related to governmental decisions.

joint standing committee — committee composed of members of both the House of Commons and the Senate.

Judicial Committee of the Privy Council (JCPC) — the superior court of the United Kingdom which, until 1949 when the Supreme Court of Canada was established, was the court of final appeal in Canada.

law — consists of a special body of rules originating with government and backed up by the threat of state coercion.

leader of Her Majesty's Loyal Opposition — the leader of the party with the second largest number of seats in the House of Commons.

leadership review — a vote held at a party convention that acts as an appraisal of the incumbent party leader; if he or she does not score sufficiently high on a vote, then a leadership convention will likely be held.

legislative committees — committees that may be set up to receive bills for examination after they have passed second reading.

legislative (statute) law — law created by governmental bodies to supplement customary or common law.

legislature — the branch of government which makes or amends laws.

legitimacy — when citizens accept that a government should, or has the right to, make decisions for them.

Letters Patent — the prerogative instruments defining the office of the governor general which the monarch makes applicable to each governor general through his or her commission of appointment.

lieutenant-governor — appointed by the governor-in-council on the advice of the prime minister to represent the monarch in each province.

lobbying — activity aimed at securing favourable policy decisions or the appointment of specific government personnel.

lobbyists — individuals who are paid by interest groups to influence government legislation.

majority government — a government based on the support of only one party in the House of Commons.

majority principle — system of government in which policy decisions are made by a majority of the people or elected body.

Meech Lake Accord — an April 1987 agreement, made between the federal Progressive Conservative government and the ten provinces, for a constitutional amendment.

ministerial responsibility — refers to the personal responsibility of each minister. As heads of departments, ministers receive confidential advice from public servants, make important decisions, and are held accountable for those decisions in Parliament and the country.

minister of public safety and emergency preparedness — cabinet minister responsible for the Correctional Service of Canada and the National Parole Board (as well as CSIS, the RCMP and other areas).

ministers of state — like full cabinet ministers, ministers of state are sworn to the Privy Council and bound by the rules of collective responsibility, but are only allowed to attend meetings of Cabinet on request, and their salary and staff allotments are lower than those of full cabinet ministers.

ministry — larger than Cabinet, the group composed of all ministers who are appointed by the prime minister. It consists of both full ministers of the Crown and ministers of state.

minority government — a government in which the governing party has less than a majority of the members of Parliament.

monarch — currently Queen Elizabeth II, the monarch is the personal embodiment of the Crown.

money bills — government bills for raising or spending money.

multiculturalism — a policy which assumes that ethnic customs and cultures should be valued, preserved and shared within the context of citizenship and economic and political integration.

multi-party systems — systems in which popular support is divided among several parties, so that the largest party must generally form a coalition with one or more other parties to form a government.

nation — a politically conscious and mobilized group of people, often with a sense of territory, which may aspire to greater autonomy, or even statehood.

nationalism — the collective action of a politically conscious ethnic group (or nation) in pursuit of increased territorial autonomy or sovereignty.

notwithstanding clause — a clause in the Constitution which allows Parliament or a provincial legislature to override most Charter provisions by a simple declaration to that effect when passing legislation.

official bilingualism — as outlined in the *Official Languages Act*, it means that Canadians have the right to communicate with the federal government in the official language of their choice.

ombudsman — an independent officer who is responsible to Parliament for the investigation of citizens' complaints against the bureaucracy.

one-party dominant systems — electoral party systems in which a single party regularly wins almost

311

every election, even though opposition parties function freely.

one-party dominant thesis — a general theory about Canadian parties which holds that since Canadian government has been dominated by one party — the Liberal party, since 1896 — the Liberals are the "natural" governing party.

Ontario Provincial Police (OPP) — Ontario's province-wide police force.

Opposition Days (Supply Days) — days on which opposition motions can be debated (there are twenty per session).

Oral Question Period — a forty-five-minute period held in Parliament five days a week which provides a forum for the opposition parties to try to embarrass the government, criticize its policies and force discussion on selected issues.

order paper — the schedule pending parliamentary business.

orders-in-council — decisions rendered by Cabinet under the auspices of the Privy Council that carry legal force.

Orders of the Day — The procedure under which the House of Commons deals with the public business placed before it. Orders guide the speaker and other members and direct the officers of the House to pursue particular courses of action.

parliamentary government — a British model of government with two houses — an elected lower house, the House of Commons, and an appointed upper house, the Senate — and a representative of the Queen.

parliamentary press gallery — a formal organization in Ottawa to which print and broadcast media assign journalists to cover the activities of the legislature and government.

parliamentary privilege — a House of Commons rule which enables MPs to express themselves freely and without intimidation.

parliamentary secretaries — MPs who aid ministers in their duties, but have no statutory authority.

parliamentary wing — one wing of traditional parties, comprised of the party leader and caucus.

party caucus — a group formed by each party in Parliament. Every Wednesday morning when Parliament is in session, all members of the House of Commons (and any senators who wish to attend) meet in their respective party groups.

party identification — the degree to which citizens identify with a particular party.

party leader — the individual chosen by party members to fulfil the pre-eminent role as decision-maker, figurehead and spokesperson in both the parliamentary and extra-parliamentary branches of the party. The party leader with the majority support in the House of Commons is the prime minister.

party system — the series of relationships among parties in a political system.

patriation — bringing a constitutional document to its home country.

patronage — in the broadest sense, concerns the awarding of contracts, employment and other material benefits to individuals or groups on the basis of partisan support rather than strictly on merit.

Plan A — a plan by the federal government after the 1995 Québec referendum to sell a majority of Québeckers on the success of Canada and the benefits of staying in the federal union.

Plan B — a plan by the federal government after the 1995 Québec referendum to clarify rational, logical terms for secession — without using harsh federal threats about the risks of partition.

pluralist theory — a theory of interest group activity which holds that there are many centres of power in society, and public policy in a state reflects the conflict, co-operation and compromise of mainly independent interest groups.

policy — a broadly based pattern of government action.

political culture — the broad pat-terns of values, beliefs and attitudes in a society toward political objects.

political customs — the conventional and accepted practices which are part of the political system.

political executive — the wing of government comprising the ministry and Cabinet and headed by the prime minister.

political institutions — institutions that structure democratic expression within states and relate more closely to citizen behaviour, such as parties, interest groups, elections and the media.

political parties — organizations which are designed to secure the power of the state for their leaders.

political patronage — refers to awarding contracts, employment and other material benefits to individuals or groups on the basis of partisan support rather than merit.

politics — the activity that impinges upon the making of binding decisions about who gets what, when and how.

pork-barrelling — an abuse of power, whereby a member of Parliament extends political favours to whole regions or communities as an inducement for support.

prerogative authority — powers of a monarch (or his or her representatives) that have not been bypassed by constitutional or state law.

Prime Minister's Office (PMO) — one of the four central agencies assisting Cabinet, the upper echelons of which are personal appointees of the prime minister.

private bills — bills that confer special power or rights upon specific individuals, groups or corporations, rather than upon society as a whole.

private members' bills — bills sponsored by individual MPs.

Privy Council Office (PCO) — the main public service organization supporting the Cabinet and prime minister.

procedural rights — rights of citizens to gain access to certain processes such as a fair trial. They are devices to protect individuals from arbitrary action by governments.

proclamation — involves proclaiming, publishing or declaring under the Great Seal a statute that thereby becomes law.

proportional representation (PR) — an electoral system which attempts to ensure that parties receive representation in Parliament in proportion to their respective shares of the popular vote.

prorogation — closing a session of Parliament. Formally, this is done by the governor general upon the advice of the prime minister.

public bills — such bills seek to change the law concerning the public as a whole. There are two kinds of public bills: government bills and private members' bills. The vast majority are government bills.

public opinion — the sum of individual opinions on a given topic.

public opinion polls — studies of the aggregate of individuals' opinions on specific topics.

public servants (bureaucrats) — tenured state officials involved in advising government ministers and implementing policies.

public service — the collective term in Canada for the personnel employed in the administrative arm of government.

Queen's Privy Council for Canada — established at Confederation in the Constitution to assist and advise the governor general. Today, the body is largely ceremonial and members are nominated for life by the prime minister.

Question Period — see **Oral Question Period.**

Quiet Revolution — a period in Québec in the 1960s, during which a new, confident French-Canadian elite led an assault on Ottawa's "paternalism."

racial discrimination — the imposition of handicaps, barriers and different treatment on individuals because of their race.

recall — a device to promote public participation whereby constituents can recall an MP if he or she does not vote as instructed.

referendum — a means by which a policy question can be submitted directly to the electorate for a decision rather than being decided exclusively by elected representatives.

regionalism — refers to territorial tensions brought about by certain groups that demand a change in the political, economic and cultural relations between regions and central powers within the existing state.

regulation — the imposition of constraints, backed by government authority, that are intended to modify economic behaviour of individuals in the private sector significantly.

representative democracy — a democracy in which elected officials make decisions with the force of law because they have achieved legitimacy through some form of election.

republic — system of government in which the government of the state is carried out by the people or their elected representatives; there is no monarch.

reservation — the constitutional ability of lieutenant-governors to reserve provincial legislation for federal approval.

residual clause — a clause in the Constitution which allows the federal government to intervene in any matter not specifically assigned to the provinces.

responsible government — the prime minister and Cabinet are accountable to Parliament and may govern only so long as they retain the "confidence" of the majority of the House of Commons.

revenue process — concerns the means by which funds are to be raised — by taxation and other measures.

rights — legal entitlements owed to individuals or groups, as duties by others, or by the government.

"rigid" constitution — a constitution that is difficult to amend.

royal assent — when the governor general, sitting in the Senate chambers before the assembled members of both Houses, puts the final seal of approval on a bill.

Royal Canadian Mounted Police (RCMP) — the police force responsible for enforcing all federal statutes; it is also under contract to many provinces and municipalities, and also polices the territories.

Royal Commissions — are widely employed as sources of public policy advice to the executive. They are generally set up by the government to investigate an area of critical public concern and to recommend a suitable course of action.

Royal Newfoundland Constabulary — the Newfoundland and Labrador police force that shares policing responsibilities on the island with the RCMP.

rule of law — a guarantee that the state's actions will be governed by law, with fairness, and without malice. No individual should be above the law, and no one ought to be exempt from it.

Section 91 — a section of the Constitution that specifies the areas belonging exclusively to the federal government. It also contains a residual clause.

Section 92 — a section of the Constitution that delineates sixteen specific areas of provincial jurisdiction, including direct taxation, hospitals, prisons, property and civil rights.

Security Intelligence Review Committee — a committee that monitors the activities of the Canadian Security Intelligence Service (CSIS).

self-determination — a shared belief that people ought to have the right to establish their collective identity in the form of a sovereign state.

session — working period when Parliament is open for business.

shared-cost programs — so-called "50-cent dollar" programs in which the federal government pays 50 percent of costs.

single-member plurality electoral system — commonly referred to as first-past-the-post, a system by which the candidate who receives the most votes, a plurality in each constituency, wins that constituency.

solicitor-general of Canada — the minister responsible for the Correctional Service of Canada and the National Parole Board.

sovereign state — a state that wields authority and power in that it is capable of maintaining order within its territory, is able to tax its citizens, and is also recognized by the international community as having the right to run its own affairs free from external interference.

sovereignty — a form of government in which final authority rests in the national government, which is free from outside interference by other states or governments.

sovereignty-association — political independence, but with economic association.

speaker of the House of Commons — an official of the House who is officially an impartial arbiter elected by the whole House.

speaker of the Senate — appointed by the governor general on the recommendation of the prime minister for the term of Parliament. The duties of this position are similar to those of the speaker of the House of Commons.

Speech from the Throne — delivered by the governor general, outlines the government's proposed legislative program for the forthcoming session.

spending power — refers to the federal government's blanket authority to spend money for any purpose in any field, even if it has no legal jurisdiction over the area.

standing committee — a committee that is relatively permanent for the life of a Parliament.

Standing Orders — contains the rules of the House of Commons that are of a general nature and more or less permanent.

stare decisis — the principle of following precedents set down in earlier court cases, a principle which binds lower courts to follow decisions of higher level courts.

state — the political unit of an entire territory; it comprises a territory, population and a government. It is also an abstraction that incorporates many institutions and rules.

state institutions — institutions that are related closely to the Constitution and federalism; they include the executive, legislature, bureaucracy, courts, police and prisons.

statute law — consists of the authoritative rules set by the Parliament of Canada or the legislative assemblies of the provinces.

substantive rights — fundamental rights as defined in a constitution.

supply (appropriation) bills — bills that authorize the spending of money by the government.

Supreme Court of Canada — Canada's highest court for civil, criminal and constitutional cases.

Sûreté du Québec (SQ) — Québec's province-wide police force.

surplus — money that is left over after a government's bills for that year are paid.

Tier I — level of lobbyists, as defined under the *Lobbyist Registration Act*, who, for pay, provide certain lobbying services on behalf of a client.

Tier II — level of lobbyists, as defined under the *Lobbyist Registration Act*, "whose job involves a 'significant' amount of government lobbying for his or her employer."

time allocation — a device to limit debate in the House.

Treasury Board — a central coordinating agency that is constitutionally a committee of the Privy Council.

Treasury Board secretariat (TBS) — an administrative unit of government with a highly qualified staff to assist the six Cabinet members of the Treasury Board.

"Triple E" Senate — a proposal that the Senate be elected, effective and equal in its representation of all provinces.

two-party systems — systems in which two major parties dominate and others have only minor political strength.

ultra vires — a legislative act that is beyond a legislature's jurisdiction on the basis of Canada's federal division of powers.

unconditional grants — money from the federal government that the provinces can spend in any way they wish since they were not designated for any specific policy field.

unilateral declaration of independence (UDI) — a potential declaration of independence by Québec.

unitary system — form of government in which the power and authority to govern is centralized in one government.

unwritten constitution — a constitution that consists mainly of custom, convention, or statutes and is not written down in one comprehensive document.

values — shared beliefs that provide standards of judgment about what is right, important, and desirable in society. They are deeply held convictions.

veto — the power to block legislation or to block a constitutional amendment.

visible minorities — defined in the *Employment Equity Act* as "persons other than Aboriginal peoples, who are non-Caucasian in race or non-white in colour."

ways and means committee — a committee of the whole; it considers the resolutions that contain the proposals of the minister of finance.

ways and means motions — motions that introduce bills to authorize the raising of money by taxation.

whip — an MP assigned by each party leader to help maintain party cohesion.

writ — a document commanding that an election be held, giving the date of the election, the date by which nominations must be received and the date by which results must be finalized.

written constitution — the fundamental state law set down in one or more documents.

Index